The State of the Nations: Constraints on Development in Independent Africa

Published under the Auspicies of the
African Studies Center and the
Committee on Political Change
University of California, Los Angeles

The State of the Nations:
Constraints on
Development in
Independent Africa

Edited by
Michael F. Lofchie, 1936-

University of California Press
Berkeley, Los Angeles, London 1971

University of California Press
Berkeley and Los Angeles, California

University of California Press, Ltd.
London, England

Contributors

JONATHAN BARKER received his B.A. degree from Harvard University and his Ph.D. from the University of California, Berkeley. He is an Assistant Professor in the Department of Political Economy at the University of Toronto and is currently on leave teaching in the Department of Political Science at the University of Dar es Salaam. Professor Barker served as Guest Editor for the Winter, 1970 issue of the *Canadian Journal of African Studies* to which he contributed an article entitled "Local-Central Relations: A Perspective on the Politics of Development in Africa."

HENRY BIENEN is Associate Professor and Vice-Chairman in the Department of Politics and Faculty Associate of the Center of International Studies at Princeton University. He received his A.B. from Cornell University and his Ph.D. from the University of Chicago. Professor Bienen has also taught at the University of Chicago, Makerere University, and University College, Nairobi. He is the author of *Tanzania: Party Transformation and Economic Development*; *Violence and Social Change*; and editor and coauthor of *The Military Intervenes: Case Studies in Political Development*. He has contributed to many journals and is an editor of *World Politics*.

BARBARA CALLAWAY received her Ph.D. from Boston University and is an Associate Professor of Political Science at California State College, Los Angeles. Professor Callaway has done field research in Nigeria and Ghana and is affiliated with the Institute of African Studies at the University of Ibadan and with the University of Ghana. Her previous articles on African politics have appeared in the *Legon Observer*, *Africa Report*, and the *Canadian Journal of African Studies*. Professor Callaway is currently editing a volume on Ghanaian local politics.

EMILY CARD received her B.A. degree at Tulane University and is currently completing a doctoral dissertation on Ghanaian politics at Columbia University. Ms. Card is a Lecturer in Comparative Cultures at the University of California, Irvine, where she teaches courses in African politics and women's studies. Previous work on Ghana by Ms. Card has appeared in *Africa Report*.

MARTIN R. DOORNBOS, Senior Lecturer in Political Science at the

Institute of Social Studies, The Hague, was educated in Amsterdam and at the University of California, Berkeley. He has been affiliated with Makerere University and Syracuse University on visiting terms. His research and publications are mainly concerned with issues of political modernization affecting regional social and political structures and include an article on protest movements in western Uganda which appeared in *Protest and Power in Black Africa* (1970). He is Editor of *Development and Change*.

RUPERT EMERSON is Professor Emeritus of Government at Harvard University and has served as Visiting Professor at Yale, and at both the Berkeley and Los Angeles campuses of the University of California. A past president of the Far Eastern Association and the African Studies Association, his principal spheres of interest have been colonialism, the rise of nationalism, and the development of the new states. He is the author of *Malaysia, From Empire to Nation* and *Africa and United States Policy*.

MICHAEL F. LOFCHIE received his B.A. degree from Harvard University and his Ph.D. from the University of California, Berkeley. He is Associate Professor of Political Science and Assistant Director of the African Studies Center at the University of California, Los Angeles, and is the author of *Zanzibar: Background to Revolution*.

R. CRANFORD PRATT is Professor of Political Science at the University of Toronto where he is also Chairman of the International Studies Programme. Professor Pratt was the first Principal of the University College, Dar es Salaam, and has since returned to Tanzania on several occasions for assignments within the Office of the President. His previous articles on Tanzania have included "The Administration of Economic Planning in a Newly Independent State: The Tanzanian Experience 1963–1966" which appeared in the March 1967 issue of *The Journal of Commonwealth Political Studies*.

RICHARD E. STRYKER received his Ph.D. from the University of California, Los Angeles. He is Assistant Professor of Political Science at the University of Indiana. Professor Stryker was the recipient of a Foreign Area Fellowship during the period 1965 to 1967 when he did field research in the Ivory Coast. The title of his dissertation is *Center and Locality: Linkage and Political Change in the Ivory Coast*.

IMMANUEL WALLERSTEIN, of the Department of Sociology, Columbia University, is currently a Fellow at the Center for Advanced Study in the Behavioral Sciences. He is the author of *Africa: The Politics of Unity*; *Africa: The Politics of Independence*; and of numerous other writings on Africa and more generally on social change.

CLAUDE E. WELCH, Jr., received his B.A. degree from Harvard University and his D.Phil. from Oxford University. He is Associate Professor of Political Science at the State University of New York at Buffalo. His principal publications are *Dream of Unity: Pan-Africanism and Political Unification in West Africa* (1966); *Political Modernization* (1967); and *Soldier and State in Africa* (1970).

M. CRAWFORD YOUNG received his B.A. from the University of Michigan and his Ph.D. from Harvard University. He is Professor of Political Science at the University of Wisconsin where he has been a member of the faculty since 1963. Professor Young is the author of *Politics in the Congo* (1965) and, in collaboration with Charles Anderson and Fred von der Mehden, *Issues of Political Development* (1968). He has written numerous articles on Congolese, Uganda, and African politics. Professor Young served as Chairman of the African Studies Program at the University of Wisconsin from 1964 to 1968.

Contents

PART I: GENERAL PERSPECTIVES ON CONSTRAINT

PREFACE TO PART I   3

Chapter 1   Political Constraints on African
            Development   Michael F. Lochie   9

Chapter 2   The Range of Choice: Con-
            straints on the Policies of Gov-
            ernments of Contemporary
            African Independent States Immanuel Wallerstein 19

PART II: THE PARAMETERS OF POLITICAL CHOICE

PREFACE TO PART II   37

Chapter 3   The Paradox of Development:
            Reflections on a Study of Local-
            Central Political Relations in
            Senegal   Jonathan S. Barker   47

Chapter 4   Political Constraints on Eco-   Barbara Callaway
            nomic Development in Ghana   and Emily Card   65

Chapter 5   The Cabinet and Presidential
            Leadership in Tanzania: 1960-
            1966   R. Cranford Pratt   93

Chapter 6   A Local Perspective on Devel-
            opmental Strategy in the Ivory
            Coast   Richard E. Stryker 119

Chapter 7   Agricultural Policy in Uganda:
            Capability and Choice   M. Crawford Young   141

Chapter 8   Ranching and Scheming: A   Martin R. Doornbos
            Case Study of the Ankole   and Michael F. Lochie 165
            Ranching Scheme

PART III:
THE POLITICAL CONTEXT OF FUTURE DEVELOPMENT

PREFACE TO PART III   191

Chapter 9   Political Parties and Political
             Machines in Africa   Henry Bienen   195

Chapter 10   Cincinnatus in Africa: The
             Possibility of Military With-
             drawal from Politics   Claude E. Welch, Jr. 215

Chapter 11   The Prospects for Democracy
             in Africa   Rupert Emerson   239

CONCLUSION

             Observations on Social and In-
             stitutional Change in Indepen-
             dent Africa   Michael F. Lofchie   261

BIBLIOGRAPHY   287

INDEX   295

Part I General Perspectives on Constraint

Preface to Part I

"Development" is one of the most over-used terms in the lexicon of social science. It first came into widespread use after World War II in the scholarly effort to establish a common intellectual frame of reference for a large number of countries that were, for a variety of reasons, relatively new subjects of systematic political analysis, and which appeared to share a common set of socioeconomic characteristics such as colonial background, low per capita income, heavy dependence upon agriculture, and low levels of popular access to government-operated social services. The term also had considerable utility as a loose all-encompassing rubric referring broadly to the politics of Africa, Asia, Latin America, and the Middle East and as a notion intended to convey the sense that these nations had more in common with one another, at least for purposes of analysis, than they did with the countries of Europe and North America (excluding Mexico). It became widespread and accepted practice to refer to such nations as "the developing areas" and to speak broadly of the "development process."

Vast difficulties have arisen, however, in the attempt to transform this loose term of reference into an analytically clear and precise concept. In *Aspects of Political Development* Lucian Pye identifies at least ten distinguishable common usages for the term.[1] These range in sense from the creation of democratic political institutions to the use of political means for the creation of a stable and orderly society. Since there is practically no aspect of the political process in these particular world areas to which the term "development" has not been applied, it has lost much of its claim to analytical cogency. In some cases the term has been used as little more than a catch-all description of the political history of one or more countries. At best, the notion of development has become so diffuse that it must be redefined afresh by each scholar who wishes to use it, a situation that adds further to the lack of any agreed-upon scholarly meaning.

[1] Lucian Pye, *Aspects of Political Development* (Boston and Toronto, 1966), pp. 33–48.

Lack of conceptual clarity, however, is only one reason for the dwindling status of the term "development." Another, perhaps more compelling, is that over the past decade the term has seemed to bear very little descriptive relationship to objective events and processes in a large number of countries in nonindustrial areas of the world. Numerous societies have experienced a succession of military coups, a high incidence of political violence, recurrences of corruption and disorder, and frequent governmental recourse to coercive means to maintain stability. These problems do not coincide even remotely with the somewhat progressive or positive implications of the notion of development. Political conditions in many nonindustrial societies are so poor that Samuel Huntington and S. N. Eisenstadt have suggested the introduction of such terms as "decay" and "breakdown" as all-encompassing descriptions of the political process.[2] The polarity of attitudes inherent in these terms suggests something of the enormous diversity of political patterns to be found in Africa, Asia, Latin America, and the Middle East.

Independent African nations exhibit within themselves fully as wide a range of phenomena as are to be found throughout these continents: stable single and multiparty systems as well as unstable ones, more or less assertive efforts to achieve a socialist organization of economy and society, engulfment in civil chaos, and a variety of forms of rule that include personalistic, elitist, and military as well as democratic control. Any attempt to generalize about so diverse an array of political phenomena is an extremely hazardous undertaking. All-encompassing notions such as "decay" and "breakdown" with an implicit across-the-board prognosis of disruption, disunity, and instability seem as inappropriate as "development" and "modernization" with an equally broad suggestion of responsible government and visible social progress. The following essays do not discard the notion of development but treat it somewhat differently by employing the notion of constraint. This idea may be defined quite simply as an impediment to development. Given the developmental objectives of African states, what are the obstacles that stand in the way of these objectives being achieved? Constraint is a working concept. Its purpose is less to produce a new conceptual formulation than to help illuminate the concrete processes and problems of African development.

The vantage point of the authors in this volume is primarily political but their understanding of African development encompasses the political, social, and economic spheres. In broad terms this understanding may be spelled out as follows: In the political sphere it means the growth of repre-

[2] See Samuel P. Huntington, "Political Development and Political Decay," *World Politics*, XVII (Jan. 1965), 386–430; and S. N. Eisenstadt, "Breakdowns of Modernization," *Economic Development and Cultural Change*," XII (July 1964), 345–367.

sentative civil authority responsive to the diverse human interests of plural-istic societies; in the social sphere it represents reduction or elimination of inequalities and a widening of popular access to government services for health, education, and welfare; and in the economic sphere it includes steady improvement of the material conditions of life, agricultural diversifi-cation, the promotion of an industrial capacity, and a generally heightened level of self-sufficiency. The constraints that impede achievement of these objectives are varied and many, of course, are not political. Geographical factors, for example, are supremely relevant in accounting for the avail-ability of mineral, land, and other resources, or in explaining the extent to which national boundaries promote or retard development processes. The principal justification for emphasizing political rather than other constraints is the extent to which political will and political action can stimulate de-velopment in spite of other, countervailing obstacles.

Michael F. Lofchie's essay, "Political Constraints on African Develop-ment," attempts to assess the prospects of constitutionalism in Africa in the light of an emergent socioeconomic transformation from a rural-agrarian society to a more urbanized and commercial pattern. His principal argument is that industrialization in the West occurred in such a way as to create a number of favorable prospects for constitutionalism, while in Africa the opposite is the case. Basically, the political environment of Western society during early industrialization was such as to insulate fledgling state institutions from the social misery generated by an incipient industrial process. A widening of the political franchise and a change of political values from laissez-faire to welfare liberalism did not occur until the industrialization process was well advanced and many of its more harsh social consequences had been ameliorated. In Africa the process of indus-trial revolution is not an abbreviated version of the historical pattern experienced earlier by Western society. It is an altogether different one and the differences largely account for many of the political difficulties being experienced by African nations today.

Two such difficulties may be singled out for special attention. In West-ern society the political burden on state institutions was lightened consider-ably by the fact that the basic dynamism for economic transformation was supplied by an autonomous entrepreneurial class outside the state. Although the state frequently played an important facilitative role, for example in creating a protective climate for infant industries, the stimulation of eco-nomic growth was not a governmental function. In Africa, where autono-mous economic elites are largely lacking, the generation of economic growth is a state function. This means that embryonic political institutions have a twofold task to perform. They must be concerned both with eco-nomic growth and with alleviation of the human hardships created by economic change. Issues of priority between the two which were of relatively minor political importance during early Western industrialization are, from the very beginning, of major importance in Africa. Secondly, African nations do not benefit from a fairly gradual transition from labor-intensive to automated industrial systems. Technological gradualism was of major importance in the West in helping to absorb culturally disparate peoples into a common socioeconomic environment and in helping to reduce the cleavage between industrialized and nonindustrialized sectors of the society. African nations do not have the advantage of technological gradualism. Their industrialization begins under conditions of high automation and the social problems created by this fact are immense.

Immanuel Wallerstein's essay, "The Range of Choice," articulates a set of themes which reappear in the essays that follow in Part II. In identifying the obstacles to the achievement of national goals, Wallerstein argues that African nations have been plagued by two overwhelming difficulties. Their capacity to use the state to achieve developmental objectives is continually frustrated by weaknesses and fragility in their state machinery. This is true both of conciliar organs of government such as political parties and legislatures and of the bureaucracy as well. Developmental capacity is also limited by a perennial shortage of state revenue and by a growing gap between revenue and expenditure which has created larger and larger budgetary deficits. Wallerstein observes that "as long as the state machinery remains fragile, and the state's revenue so uncertain, there will be a chronic gap between promise and reality and hence chronic instability." This generalization applies, in Wallerstein's view, regardless of the ideology or mode of organization an African state has chosen.

Two basic patterns of sociopolitical organization are characterized by Wallerstein, the "conservative" and the "radical." The "conservative" states are distinguished by their maintenance of an open economy allowing for private investment from both external and internal sources and by their continuing close ties with Western powers. The "radical" states are distinguished by their attempt to achieve closed economies and to insulate themselves from the international capital economy, as well as by their emphasis on state rather than private economic enterprise. Both types of state have encountered serious difficulties in development. The former have experienced a growing socioeconomic cleavage between elite and mass with increasing disaffection of younger, more radical elements in the society, while the latter have found it necessary to impose policies of austerity which have provoked resentment within affected elements of the society, particularly the military. In some cases the "radical" states have relaxed their economic policies somewhat in order to increase revenue. Due, however, to revenue shortages and the weakness of state machinery, neither of these patterns can be said to have been successful in development and both face continuing problems of political instability. Although the alternative modes of internal organization by "conservative" and "radical" styles do in some sense represent choices, the problems of each are so great that it is impossible to assess at this stage which, if either, will produce more meaningful developmental change.

Michael F. Lofchie

Chapter 1 Political Constraints on African Development

Michael F. Lofchie

Political studies of Africa have undergone a discernible shift in mood since their inception. When political scientists began to study Africa in significant numbers, in the mid to late 1950s, there was on the whole an attitude of optimism and buoyancy. African nationalist movements enlisted the sympathy and imagination of scholars who believed that alien rule had completely failed to legitimize itself on social and economic—not to speak of moral—grounds and that substantial and rapid progress would occur once colonialism was removed. The dialog among scholars reflected this spirit. Such topics as the conditions under which parliamentary forms of government would become institutionalized in Africa, what modifications African states might introduce in these forms of government, or whether one-party dominance was consistent with democratic values seemed to predominate. The implicit premise of much of this analysis was that the survival of civil institutions per se could be taken for granted and that these institutions would benefit from the enthusiastic and popular support that had been aroused during the nationalist period.

The postindependence politics of some African states has been such as to invite a reassessment of this assumption. A series of military coups, recurrent patterns of civil strife, and seemingly insoluble economic difficulties, together with major problems of political breakdown in Africa's two largest independent states (Nigeria and Congo-Kinshasa), have altered the frame of reference of political analysis. The early theoretical debate about the conditions for institutionalized parliamentarism and the variant forms such parliamentarism might take has been replaced by a more somber dialog over whether such terms as "decay" and "breakdown" do not deserve equal prominence with "development" and "modernization" as all-encompassing descriptions of the political process in new nations. Among some, optimism has given way to a sense of gloom about the prospects of viable representative government in Africa. In the words of one scholar of developing countries, "the future of Africa is the past of Latin America." In this perspective, the best outlook seems to be one of stable military or civil dictatorship; at worst, the possibility that even dictatorial regimes would not possess sufficient power to prevent recurring bloodshed and violence.

The extent of theoretical disagreement represented by these positions suggests that it may be useful to consider the transformation of modern Africa in broad historical perspective, for the belief that rapid progress would follow the elimination of colonial rule depended in large measure upon a view of African politics which saw colonialism as the overwhelming obstacle to progress and development of the continent. Few today would feel it necessary to question the oppressive consequences of colonial subordination on Africa, or debate the fact that it stifled African initiative and creativity in a wide range of areas of human endeavor—political, economic, and cultural—for nearly a century. The important issue is not whether colonialism was a suppressive phenomenon but whether there might not well have been other, more consequential political factors at work whose operation has been concealed or badly obscured by the enormous salience and visibility of European colonial dominance.

In an essay contrasting social patterns of industrialization in the West with those in African and other new nations, Lloyd Fallers suggests that the fact of the West's having been first to industrialize creates a far greater handicap to new nations than the consequences of colonial rule. In his words:

The advantage of initiative gained by Western people in being first may well have been of greater magnitude than the social and cultural peculiarities that made them first. There is doubtless something in the claim of non-Western nationalists who say that, while Western colonial enterprise may have contributed in initiative to over-all economic development, it also inhibited the development of indigenous entrepreneurship simply by getting "in the way" quite apart from colonial policies favoring nationals of the metropolitan powers.[1]

If correct, the implications of this position are staggering.

Colonialism was, after all, a "movable" fact of history, something against which political will could be exerted and about which a great deal could be done. African nationalism has, at the very least, eliminated explicit European control from all but the southern areas of the African continent. Even if one subscribes to the concept of neocolonialism, the patterns most

---

[1] Lloyd Fallers, "Equality, Modernity and Democracy in New States," in Clifford Geertz, ed., *Old Societies and New States* (New York, 1963), p. 186.

frequently ascribed to this relationship are susceptible to political change. One social pattern often identified with a lingering colonial legacy is a scarcity of indigenous managerial, technical, and entrepreneurial elites with a corresponding dependence upon expatriate European personnel to perform these functions. However great such dependence, a solution exists in the capacity of a new nation to educate such elites. This may be extremely difficult given the scarcity of resources for education, the numerous competing demands upon available funds, and political pressures which help entrench the expatriate caste, but with time it can be accomplished.

A second pattern often viewed as neocolonial is the tendency for African economies to be geared heavily toward the export of unprocessed primary products, a situation that demands the import, at disadvantageous terms of trade, of manufactured and processed goods. It would be naive to underestimate the importance of such a dependence for Africa. It has enormous meaning, not only in making the poorer nations indebted customers of the rich for the foreseeable future, but, insofar as economic weakness is also political weakness, it also means that the capacity of African nations to negotiate their way out of this dependence is severely hampered. Nevertheless, the absolute extent of such dependence is indeterminate and solutions exist which are currently being attempted. There is some flexibility in international terms of trade. In this respect, the significance of the recent United Nations Conference on Trade and Development (UNCTAD) may well be less in its failure to provide the developing areas with generalized preferential tariffs than in the fact that this issue was seriously raised and considered. Moreover, the opportunity, with independence, to create local processing and manufacturing industries is considerable and there are already impressive strides in this direction.

A more subtle and elusive issue stemming out of the concept of neocolonialism is the extent to which transformation from rural-agrarian social patterns to those based on an urban-commercial pattern will give rise to social structures comparable to those of the West, with considerable economic discrepancies between buyers and sellers of labor. Industrialization in most Western nations has had an enormous impact in social patterns which reflect great inequalities between have and have-not. It is reasonable to ask whether the same consequences may be anticipated in Africa and other developing areas. A major historical difference between African and Western development bears on this question. Social egalitarianism became a salient value in Western society only toward the end of the industrial revolution, at a point when the social consequences of industrialization were already in being. Even now, political action to realize this value is hampered by the presence of countervailing values of the earlier period such as free enterprise and economic individualism. In independent African societies the norm of social equality already has great social currency and may be expected to play some role throughout the process of industrialization.

The point in the process of industrialization at which the norm of social equality becomes a pronounced political value is only one of a series of differences in the timing of industrialization between Africa and the West. Lloyd Fallers's observation about the importance of the fact of the West's having been first to industrialize becomes relevant here. It raises the question: Has this fact imposed on Africa a pattern of consequences which, while less easily discernible than those of colonialism, are more irreversible? The fact of the West's having been first to industrialize is an unchangeable aspect of history. No amount of political will can affect this fact. Are the consequences of Africa's status as a latecomer equally unsusceptible of change in the sense of their being situations about which realistic political choices do not exist? This question poses major theoretical issues. What were some of the advantages which the West might be said to have gained as a result of the timing of its industrialization? More importantly, exactly what consequences does Africa suffer as a result of being a latecomer and how do these affect the political processes of its independent states?

The process of industrialization produced a fairly common set of results in all countries that have experienced it. The early stages of transformation from a rural-agrarian economy with a high admixture of local subsistence activity to one based predominantly upon urban commerce and industry on a national scale seems to be accompanied almost everywhere by enormous human misery and suffering. The constellation of human conditions associated with early industrialization includes massive urban overcrowding, extreme material deprivation, and a number of psychic disorders associated with dislocation from a known and familiar environment to one characterized by great impersonality. In addition, there are often a number of social problems associated with these conditions such as high rates of thievery, prostitution, alcoholism, and other forms of anomic behavior. This syndrome of deprivation characterized Western societies, many of which have not yet fully used their economic resources to overcome it, and it is increasingly to be observed in many of Africa's largest and most rapidly growing cities.

One important difference between the timing of the industrial revolution in Western society and that currently underway in Africa is that in the West early industrialization occurred before the introduction of full democratic practices into the political process. In England, for example, the industrial revolution was well underway during the seventeenth and eighteenth centuries. Indeed, the enclosure movements which marked the beginnings of Britain's economic transformation began during the late sixteenth century. Voting rights, however, were not extended to the working classes until the nineteenth century and even then only gradually. A similar pattern has existed in the United States. Here, too, lower social classes were not extended the right to vote until fairly late in the process of industrialization. It is pertinent to note, for example, that the American constitution was not a highly participant document: that the President and Senate were to be indirectly elected and that suffrage was left to the states where property, educational, and other restrictions were common. Moreover, the urban working classes were composed of a heavy admixture of recent immigrants for whom citizenship, residence requirements, and language constituted major barriers to enfranchised participation. The political process of enfranchisement was not given a major boost until the latter half of the nineteenth century, and even now is strikingly incomplete particularly for lower socioeconomic strata. The political significance of the late enfranchisement of the lower classes in these societies has been enormous and bears directly on the emergence of representative government. It has meant that precisely those elements and strata which suffered most during early industrial change were not in a political position, at least in terms of voting rights, to exercise influence upon government. For all practical purposes, the political process did not have to take the working classes into account until the industrial revolution was sufficiently underway for their material situation to improve considerably.

Independent African nations face a completely different set of circumstances. In every case, these nations came to independence with constitutional provisions ensuring at least the formal right of full participation and, in most, the recent experience of mass nationalism had created an environment highly conducive to widespread and intense popular involvement in the political process. Thus African nations must cope with highly participant societies during the most difficult stage of socioeconomic transformation in terms of human misery and dislocation and at a time when the industrial revolution has not proceeded far enough to make resources available with which to undertake the ameliorative policies which a politically participant citizenry demands. In addition, African states enter the process of change at a time when the already industrialized nations of the world have attained great affluence, at least at the upper social levels, and represent a "model" or a standard against which African performance will be judged.

The evolution of political culture is also a factor which fundamentally distinguishes Western and African historical experience and which is closely related to the enfranchisement of the working or lower classes. During the early period of the industrial revolution, the prevailing politico-economic values of Western society were either mercantilist or laissez-faire.

In either case, they were not values which stressed the obligation of government to participate in society on behalf of socially deprived elements. Indeed, during the period of laissez-faire, the prevailing notion was that human satisfaction could be maximized only if the state remained completely outside society. This meant that any groups in the society which wished to make demands upon government for action to alleviate social suffering had to confront political cultures which were hostile to such activity. Liberalism or welfare socialism, like universal suffrage, did not emerge in the West until relatively late in the industrial era, at a time when industrial growth had proceeded to a point where substantial resources were available to the state with which to undertake social welfare policies. The fact that such resources have been available to Western governments at a time in their history when prevailing political values call upon them to initiate welfare activities has been an extremely important factor in helping to reinforce state legitimacy and authority.

As in the case of universal suffrage, African states possess an ethic of state welfare at a comparatively very early stage of industrial transformation vis-à-vis the West. Very few African governments do not profess some form of African socialism. As a result, state institutions which are in any case fragile because of their newness must contend with the demands of a participant citizenry whose requests for welfare measures to relieve the hardships of the poor are buttressed by prevailing political values that stress the obligation of the state to do so. Moreover, political institutions must cope with these demands at a time when industrialization has barely begun, when economic resources for alleviating poverty are practically nonexistent. In this perspective, the gap between expectation and performance which confounds and stymies African leaders who seek to base their regimes upon popular consent is the historical consequence of the timing of the industrial revolution. While it may be possible in some cases to place some responsibility for political breakdown on the failures or inadequacies of political leadership, the overwhelmingly important fact is the historical pattern of the timing of industrialization. It confronts African leadership with a political setting that in most cases would doom even the most herculean efforts to futility.

The evolution of political culture has an additional important relationship to the institutionalization of parliamentary government in Western society. Such value systems as mercantilism or laissez-faire operated effectively to remove such issues as social inequality, poverty, class relations, and the role of government in respect to these problems as issues from the legislative arena. In addition, since the dynamism for industrialization was supplied by autonomous nongovernmental political elites, the state did not need to function as an entrepreneurial force. Since class relations and state entrepreneurship were not legislative issues during the early period of industrialization, political structures were left to cope with a relatively manageable set of problems revolving around the management and administration of society. Parliamentary state structures thus benefited from fairly long periods of comparatively manageable political problems consisting largely of the maintenance of minimum state services such as schools, judiciary, police, and roads. This furnished the equivalent of a political "breaking in" period during which institutional procedures and rules of the game could be consolidated through practice and use. Later, when political culture changed and social welfare concepts introduced more difficult problems into the parliamentary arena, settled and agreed-upon institutional practices were available with which to cope with them. It is indicative of the extreme importance of such an institutional breaking in period that when the political system of the United States was compelled to confront two intensely controversial issues in the mid-nineteenth century, slavery and the tariff, the federal system broke down in an extended episode of internecine violence.

African political systems do not enjoy the advantage of an extended breaking in period during which institutional practices may harden and solidify. The presence of social welfare concepts in the political culture introduces the most difficult set political issues into the political process from the very moment independence is achieved. Moreover, since African societies do not often include autonomous economic elites of sufficient magnitude to stimulate industrialization, the state is compelled to function as an entrepreneurial force. Not only are state institutions forced to deal with issues of human deprivation and social inequality from the very beginning, but they must also be put to use as an entrepreneurial mechanism for development. This introduces one sort of issue into African politics that, in effect, never had to be dealt with during the early period of Western parliamentary experience; namely, how the state should divide its attention and resources between its entrepreneurial and welfare roles. Against the background of this differentiation in the timing patterns of industrialization, political culture, and parliamentarism between Africa and the West, it is not surprising that the scholarly optimism of the terminal colonial period was shortlived.

The timing of technological change has also introduced enormous differences in the experience of industrialization between Western nations and African states. It is fairly obvious that the West went through a lengthy and very gradual process of technological evolution from simple labor-intensive patterns to the complex highly automated industrial technology of the twentieth century. At the very least, this meant that there was a great deal of time for society to absorb technological innovations. Gradualism in

technological change had profoundly important sociopolitical consequences and advantages for the West. It made the process of urban absorption of rural immigrants far simpler, for example. Since work was
relatively simple, even unskilled immigrants from agricultural areas could
find employment in the urban setting. More importantly, the labor-intensive aspect of early industry meant that there was no shortage of jobs available. The social and material deprivations of the lower classes during early
industrialization in the West were considerable. But they did not include
unemployment. Indeed, such widespread practices as female and child
labor and extraordinarily long working days probably meant that there
were far more jobs than people. No matter how bad conditions became,
some forms of employment, ensuring, therefore, some level of income, were
almost always available.

The widespread availability of simple employment was especially important in American history. One major problem that the United States
has shared in common with the new nations of Africa has been the need to
absorb into the cities vast numbers of culturally and ethnically differentiated immigrant elements. Here, however, the problem was vastly simpli-
fied by the fact that these immigrants could nearly always find jobs at
which they were able to work. Either in the mines, on railroads, or in high-
way construction, some form of employment opportunity was available
on a widespread basis. Such employment furnished an ideal vehicle for
cultural absorption and assimilation into the society.

The widespread availability of simple employment was also important
in determining the nature of political demands. Since employment was
available, the emergence of a welfarist political culture did not, at least for
a considerable period of time, stimulate demands for the creation of employment opportunity. Rather, early demands upon the state took the form
of requests for regulation of the conditions of employment; for example,
shortening of the working day and elimination of child and female labor.
It is intrinsically far simpler for a political system to regulate the conditions
of work and employment than it is to create employment opportunity
where none exists. As a regulatory matter, curtailment of abuses involves
police and judicial surveillance more than anything else. Creation of employment involves a whole range of highly sensitive issues including training, industrial location, state versus private industry, and economic versus
noneconomic goals. The Western state confronted demands which, for
some time, were principally regulatory in character. It was fairly simple
to accede to these demands on simple humanitarian grounds and, once
having acceded to them, to enforce the social changes they implied. As in
the case of its ability to divert economic resources toward actual welfare

policies later in its history, the Western state's capacity to meet and enforce demands of a regulatory kind during the late nineteenth and early twentieth centuries had an important side benefit in helping to buttress and enhance the legitimacy of parliamentary institutional structures.

From all these perspectives, the timing of technological transformation has saddled African nations with the worst of all possible worlds. Africa begins the process of industrial revolution during an era of high technological complexity and automation. African states do not industrialize with the plants and machinery of the eighteenth and nineteenth centuries. They do so with those of the twentieth. Although new factories and industries are established, they have only minimal effect in generating additional employment. In fact, a number of African states experienced a decline in the level of industrial employment shortly after independence. Although there is an enormous task of absorbing unskilled and culturally diverse rural immigrant elements into the cities and into a new national identity, industrial employment does not constitute a viable mechanism for doing so. Indeed, the situation is precisely the opposite. Technologically sophisticated industries tend to create jobs only for a small, well-educated, and highly trained social stratum. Those who manage to obtain employment under these conditions are immediately propelled into high social status as an elite managerial and technological class. Those who do not qualify confront the bitter reality of technological unemployment. Unlike Western cities where unemployment did not constitute a major issue during early industrial change, African cities are in many cases becoming increasingly divided between the narrow technological elite at the top and a vast mass of unemployed and unemployable new rural immigrants at the bottom. The demands made upon African states are thus immeasurably more difficult to resolve. Whereas the Western state confronted demands of a regulatory sort, African states confront demands for the creation of employment and for a narrowing of the social gap between elite and mass.

Entering the industrial era in a period of high technological complexity creates an additional set of problems for Africa never confronted in the Western experience. In the West gradualism in the absorption of technology made it possible for technological innovations to be evenly diffused between the city and the countryside. Indeed, here, the industrial revolution was as much one affecting agriculture and the rural areas as it was one affecting industrial production in the cities. The highly mechanized aspect of modern technology makes it practically impossible for African countries to introduce technological innovations into the process of agricultural production in the rural areas. Not only is there an enormous and visible gap in the cities between the technological elite and the unemployed mass, but there is a vast and widening gap between the cities as scenes of automated twentieth-century life and the rural areas which remain tied to the production methods of the past. Since the gap between city and countryside is in many cases one which has ethnic and tribal components, the consequence of spacial unevenness in the diffusion of technology is to exacerbate these patterns of cleavage as well.

The fact is that in all these fundamental political matters Africans do not possess realistic political choices. African states cannot choose to suspend universal suffrage and modern social values temporarily while they undergo the most difficult period of socioeconomic transformation. No realistic choice between a welfarist ethic and the laissez-faire theory of the role of the state exists. Nor could an African government realistically choose to import an eighteenth-century technology or to undergo the entire process of gradual technological evolution that occurred in the West. While it would be far simpler for African states to cope with demands of a regulatory sort rather than demands for employment creation, there is no choice to be made between these. They confront the latter, not the former. The same is true with respect to the role of the state as an entrepreneurial force. While it might be far simpler and more politically expedient for the African state to function only in a managerial and welfare capacity, and to allow autonomous economic elite elements to stimulate economic growth, this is not an alternative susceptible of political decision making. These dilemmas represent a sort of overriding existential environment within which modern African politics occur. They constitute a set of fundamental constraints on African development.

Chapter 2 The Range of Choice: Constraints on the Policies of Governments of Contemporary African Independent States

Immanuel Wallerstein

The question to be discussed herein is the range of choice available to *governments* in contemporary African states. Governments at all times and places act within constraints. It will be argued that the range of such constraints for this set of governments is relatively narrow, the consequence of the low level of national integration. It should be underlined, however, that simply because a government is constrained, it does not necessarily follow that other actors (social groups within or outside the country, governments other than those under consideration, international agencies) are as narrowly constrained in their actions within the national arena.

THE COMPROMISE OF DECOLONIZATION

To permit us to deal with the whole set of governments simultaneously, it is necessary to review the common base points of these states.

They almost all came to independence approximately at the same time, the modal year being 1960. Virtually all these states passed through a similar scenario of political development. They were colonized in the late nineteenth century (although in some cases a small portion of the territory had a longer colonial history). The nationalist movement arose in the years after the Second World War. The leadership of the nationalist movement was drawn from urban middle-class, educated, or partially educated, elements who obtained some support for their movement from rural peasants as well as semiurbanized working-class groups. These nationalist movements tended in most cases to obtain widespread support, but in no case did they unify the entire population behind them before independence. In some cases their terminology and ideology were somewhat radical,[1] but on the whole the unifying theme was simply the antagonism to alien rule, whose illegitimacy was argued in terms of the liberal norms of the nineteenth and twentieth centuries.

The process of decolonization could be seen as involving basically a political compromise between the colonial powers and the middle-class leadership of the nationalist movements. The former turned over the political machinery to the latter, in return for which the latter implicitly promised to hold in check the radical tendencies of lower-class protest and to leave basically intact the overall economic links with the former (even if the interests of certain Europeans, particularly settlers, were damaged by such a transfer of power).

Since independence, and the drive toward it, came more or less within a narrow period of time throughout the continent, each national development occurred within the context of the same world situation. The basic given of this situation was an active competition for the favor of the Third World between the U.S.A. and the U.S.S.R. This competition served as very strong pressure on the colonial powers to make the compromise described above.

The major aspirations of various elements at the time of these political compromises were, as one would expect, sharply disparate. For the urban middle-class elements, independence represented the opportunity to play an autonomous (if you will, entrepreneurial) role in their economies, the loss of which opportunity had been one of the major consequences of the establishment of colonial rule. They saw the control of the political machinery as a path not only to social status but to capital accumulation.[2] The lower-class elements saw independence as providing the two levers of entry into the modern world: education and money employment. The

---

[1] See T. Hodgkin, "A Note on the Language of African Nationalism," in K. Kirkwood, ed., *African Papers, Number One* (London, 1961), pp. 22–40.

[2] No doubt there was a minority, a small one, who added specific radical political objectives: liberation of southern Africa, African unity, rapid national economic development. But even this minority, for the most part, did not consider these objectives incompatible with the more widely accepted group aspirations. Ukpabi Asika analyzes the ambivalent political objectives of this group quite well: "The Nigerian middle-class is characteristically a white-collar middle class. . . . Much of the impetus for their activity comes from their desire to transform themselves from a mere governing class

colonial powers saw independence as the political change least likely to bring about dislocation of existing political and economic relationships. The U.S.A. saw independence as the political change least likely to promote the expansion of Soviet influence. The U.S.S.R. saw it as the change most likely to permit an opening of contact.

THE DILEMMAS OF THE GOVERNMENTS

The governments of these states, once independent, were all confronted with two basic problems. One was the fragility of the state machinery. The second was the acute uncertainty of state revenue. The combination of these two problems resulted in a large and politically visible gap between governmental promises and politicoeconomic realities, which then posed further dilemmas for the governments. Let us review the manner in which each of these problems presents itself as a matter for governmental decision.

THE FRAGILITY OF THE STATE MACHINERY

The fragility of the state machinery was clear. The government was new and hence had neither experience nor the benefit of the accretion of loyalties through historical time. This was true both for the political cadres and the bureaucracy. The former had not the legitimacy of continuity from colonial rule, since they had come to power in opposition to and denigration of previous authority. They may have acquired a certain legitimacy from the nationalist struggle, but this was limited and applied in any case only to the first postindependence governments.

The bureaucracy (which includes the army and police) was small as a proportion of the population in comparison to more established and economically developed societies. This was so even though the costs of the bureaucracy were high as a percentage of the national budget. The expansion of the bureaucracy was hampered by lack both of funds and of personnel. A small bureaucracy meant that the capabilities of administration and hence of the effectiveness of central governmental decision were limited. In addition the smallness of the bureaucracy (as well as its largeness

---

to a ruling class. . . . Frightened and dazzled by the scale and power of the alien-capitalists, they are forced to espouse socialism; but frightened, no less, by the precariousness of their status, they seek to use their control of state power to consolidate and reinforce their position, to promote the growth of their class as indigenous capitalists. . . . Whatever the designation, the formulation of post-colonial ideology, African socialism, always includes these two elements: socialism, nationalisation of foreign enterprise and aids to Nigerian businessmen, i.e., the promotion of indigenous capitalism." —"The Uses of Literacy: Notes Towards a Definition of the Nigerian Intellectual," *Nigerian Opinion*, III, 1 (Jan. 1967), 154.

in budgetary terms) meant that it was relatively easy to reflect common consciousness of this class-stratum in the political arena.

In almost every instance there was some difference in the social base of the corps of nationalist politicians and the higher levels of the bureaucracy, and there was evident rivalry for control of the state machinery. The higher levels of the bureaucracy tended to have relatively more education than the politicians, whose claim to power was based on their ability to mobilize local support which meant by and large ethnically based support.

In the local arenas these same politicians had to face the competition for political support of those persons whose claim to authority rested on the "traditional" political systems, as these had evolved during the colonial era, and the consequent control of land. Let us for the sake of brevity call the latter "chiefs."

The most important given of the political arena was the crucial political importance of control of the central state machinery, despite its fragility or perhaps because of it. The central government was the only institution that controlled sufficient funds to make an important impact on the private and differential accumulation of consumption income and investment capital. Furthermore, this being so, politics turned out to be very largely a zero-sum game. Either you were in power or you were out (very likely in exile or in jail).

In this situation the politicians who controlled the initial postindependence governments tried three things to reinforce their control of the state machinery. First, at the local level, they tried to come to terms, in most instances, with the chiefs. They saw this as a process of absorbing an essentially weak group who could be better controlled if they were within the state and party machinery.

Secondly, they tried to establish controls over the national bureaucracy in two somewhat different ways. One might be called politization which meant surveillance of bureaucrats by loyal (party) elements and intrusion of some of these elements into key bureaucratic posts. The other was the exclusion of such bureaucrats from some key posts by the use of foreign (usually European) personnel. The latter was usually justified by a variant of the slogan of President Senghor of Senegal: "pas d'africanisation au rabais!" ("No cut-rate Africanization!")

Thirdly, they sought to eliminate rival party structures which could organize opposition, whatever its base. This was the almost ubiquitous and now well studied attempt to create one-party states by the absorption of other political groupings. The parties were organized as coalitions of political men with political bases (usually regional, sometimes functional) in which the basis of accord was logrolling in the distribution of governmental jobs and services.

The Uncertainty of State Revenue

African governments have operated on a very uncertain financial base. On the one hand there has been a steady internal political pressure to expand governmental expenditure, and very considerably, over what had been spent in the colonial era. On the other hand, governmental revenue from taxation has not been able to keep pace with increased expenditure despite an expanded tax base and greatly increased production, in large part because of a steady decline of the world terms of trade for underdeveloped countries.[3] The difference has been made up by various kinds of external assistance, which have also been declining. Table 1 gives an overall picture for a group of African countries.

Table 1 indicates a continuing and for the most part increasing deficit in the balance between internal expenditure and internal annual revenue since independence. The only seeming exceptions, Zambia and Ghana, actually reinforce the argument. Zambia showed a sudden increase in balance from 1963 to 1964, which lasted to 1967 and then showed a negative balance again. The increase is accounted for by a renegotiation of arrangements with the mining companies at the time of independence, which was abetted by certain fortuitous legalities. Ghana showed a sudden decrease in the negative balance in 1966 because of the severe austerity installed by the regime which has ousted Nkrumah. It could not keep it up and in two years returned to a gap as high as Nkrumah's regime ever showed.

The explanation behind these facts is relatively straightforward. Expenditures went up because of direct and simultaneous pressure on government from all segments of the political arena. Mass pressure (that is, pressure by uneducated or low-educated persons both in the rural and urban areas) was for very expensive items, listed in approximate descending order of priority: educational expansion, expansion of wage-earning opportunities, welfare, and infrastructure. All four were part of the package of promises of the nationalist movement. The government was expected to assume primary, often exclusive, responsibility for providing all four. Governments felt obliged to respond to these demands with a noticeable increase over parallel expenditures by the colonial governments (whose expenditures in their last years in office, it must be recalled, were appreciably higher already than expenditures, say, in 1945).

The educated urban middle class made similarly expensive demands. They wanted the development of expensive university facilities and overseas scholarships. They wanted salary levels for the bureaucracy and the

[3] The Ivory Coast—a country that reputedly has been doing very well economically since independence—lost over $200 million in earnings because of deterioration of the terms of trade between 1961 and 1966. Between 1959 and 1965, Senegal has had a 37% deterioration of terms of trade. See *Le Marche Ivoirien*, no. 13 (Feb. 1968), pp. 5–6.

TABLE 1
Trends in State Financial Balances*

	59	60	61	62	63	64	65	66	67	68
Ethiopia in Eth. $ Million										
Expenditures	187.3	211.3		243.2	290.1	364.4	390.1	470.2	479.6	
Receipts	160.1	168.5		210.3	216.7	272.1	295.8	327.1	357.1	
Balance	−27.2	−42.8		−33.1	−73.4	−92.3	−94.3	−143.1	−122.5	
Ghana in Million Cedis										
Expenditures			272.8	390.9	322.0	384.9	443.4			
Receipts			200.0	233.4	203.0	294.2	340.8			
Balance			−72.8	−157.5	−119.0	−90.7	−102.6			
Ghana in Million New Cedis										
Expenditures				253.0	268.6	365.2	368.6	269.0	318.3	398.9
Receipts				157.0	169.6	254.2	284.1	230.8	254.0	297.9
Balance				−96.0	−99.0	−101.0	−84.5	−38.2	−64.3	−101.0
Kenya in £ Million										
Expenditures			50.26	51.52	56.74	66.95	72.08	72.23		
Receipts			38.05	40.60	44.58	48.05	50.77	52.95		
Balance			−12.21	−10.92	−12.16	−18.90	−21.31	−19.28		
Malagasy Rep. in Billion Malagasy Fr.										
Expenditures						43.8	46.8	49.6		
Receipts						33.1	34.7	36.9		
Balance						−10.7	−12.1	−12.7		
Malawi in £ Million										
Expenditures			11.07	10.11	13.49	18.68	20.36	23.85		
Receipts			8.83	9.36	12.54	9.33	9.65	11.27		
Balance			−2.24	−0.75	−0.95	−9.35	−10.71	−12.58		

TABLE 1 (continued)

	59	60	61	62	63	64	65	66	67	68
Nigeria in £ Million										
Expenditures	108.03	133.39	154.25	161.29	163.48					
Receipts	87.93	95.95	118.51	128.40	135.30					
Balance	−20.11	−37.44	−35.74	−32.89	−28.18					
Rwanda in Million Rwanda Fr.										
Expenditures					549	716	932	1,424		
Receipts					342	546	619	1,112		
Balance					−207	−170	−313	−312		
Sierra Leone in Million Leones										
Expenditures		29.29	33.07	32.07	35.34	39.57				
Receipts		30.09	28.42	26.06	32.61	33.79				
Balance		+0.80	−4.65	−6.01	−2.73	−5.78				
Sudan in £ Million										
Expenditures	56.50			75.52	90.42	99.74	86.32	100.44		
Receipts	41.98			60.34	74.18	78.05	73.85	78.54		
Balance	−14.52			−15.18	−16.24	−21.69	−12.47	−21.90		
Tanzania in £ Million										
Expenditures					29.61	35.09	42.85	57.60		
Receipts					25.03	28.26	33.83	35.73		
Balance					−4.58	−6.85	−9.02	−21.87		
Togo in CFA Billion										
Expenditures			3.46	3.85	4.23	5.21	5.71	6.26		
Receipts			3.38	3.51	3.85	4.12	4.71	4.95		
Balance			−0.08	−0.34	−0.38	−1.09	−1.00	−1.31		

TABLE 1 (continued)

	59	60	61	62	63	64	65	66	67	68
Uganda in £ Million										
Expenditures		24.19		29.93	32.00	35.44	47.39	59.76		
Receipts		21.24		23.97	31.06	35.16	42.60	44.23		
Balance		−2.95		−5.96	−0.94	−0.28	−4.79	−17.42		
UAR in £ Million										
Expenditures	308.31		582.20		791.76	889.13	1,184.4	1,205.3		
Receipts	277.59		370.88		464.84	501.00	567.9	625.8		
Balance	−30.72		−211.32		−326.92	−388.13	−616.5	−579.5		
Zambia in £ Million										
Expenditures		27.9	27.2	27.7	30.0	47.9	81.4			
Receipts		23.5	23.5	23.7	23.2	61.2	97.4			
Balance		−4.4	−3.7	−4.0	−6.8	+13.3	+16.0			
Zambia in Million Kwacha										
Expenditures						116.6	175.0	236.4	406.0	391.5
Receipts						151.0	209.4	265.0	404.8	296.9
Balance						+34.4	+34.4	+28.6	−1.8	−94.6

*The figures for Ghana (first set), Kenya, Malawi, Nigeria, Sudan, Tanzania, Togo, Uganda, UAR, and Zambia (first set), are taken from the *U.N. Statistical Yearbook, 1966.* In the case of Nigeria, the figures are for the combined Federal and regional budgets. In the case of the UAR, the item "expenditures" includes a separately listed "Development Budget." The figures for the Malagasy Republic, Rwanda, and Sierra Leone are adapted from *International Financial Statistics*, XXI, 2 (Feb. 1968). The figures for Ethiopia, Ghana (second set), and Zambia (second set) are adapted from *International Financial Statistics*, XXII, 12 (Dec. 1969).

political cadres to be measured on an international scale, and expected many prerequisites such as financing of personal automobiles, international travel, expense accounts. It was they too who called for what Western observers often called "prestige projects"; jetliners that would compete on the international travel market, infrastructure that anticipated usage by many years, etc. External capitalist enterprises also expected considerable government assistance, such as subsidized facilities for foreign personnel and guarantees of risk to the companies (which one government civil servant has called "the individualization of profit, but the socialization of losses").

All of these expenditures have been compounded by the ubiquitous "corruption" which is thought by most observers to amount to a very high percentage of government costs, either by virtue of embezzled funds, kickbacks, or loss of revenue. It is difficult in the nature of the case to give precise figures.[4]

The difficulties in increasing internal revenue to match the needed increased expenditure are equally straightforward. There are three main barriers to obtaining more money. One is the ease of evasion of taxes due to the smallness of the bureaucracy, the abundance of frontiers, and the high percentage of illicit personal income. The second is the relative political cohesiveness of one of the easiest groups to tax: urban wage earners. For all their reputed political servility, African trade unions have played their major function in postindependence African states as a syndicate *in extremis* against the government revenue demands. The third is the relative seller's market of foreign investors who have demanded very favorable taxation and repatriation terms for the use of either their money or their management skills. The only relative exception to this has been in those countries like Zambia, Libya, Algeria, and to a certain extent the Congo and Nigeria, where rich and profitable mineral deposits altered, somewhat in favor of the African governments, the market relationship with external capital.

The gap in the national budgets has been met basically from two sources. One was the accumulated cash balances of the country which, however, have been used up over time (as, for example, in Ghana). The second has been external aid whether in the form of direct budgetary assistance, external and extrabudgetary personnel, development loans, or suppliers' credits. But in time the loans have come due and the direct grants have declined.

---

[4] See Colin Leys, "What is the Problem About Corruption?" *Journal of Modern African Studies*, III, 2 (1965), 215–230.

THE GAP BETWEEN PROMISE AND REALITY: ATTEMPTED SOLUTIONS

There have been two main ways in which African governments have responded to these dilemmas. Neither has been very successful in the sense of assuring either governmental stability or solvency. The two together probably exhaust what has been the effective range of choice for these governments.

THE CONSERVATIVE PATH

The essential feature of the conservative path has been the maintenance of a relatively open economy.[5] Internationally this has meant maintaining a currency within a world economic zone (such as the franc or pound), maintaining few import restrictions, low tariffs, and largely free transfer of capital. Internally it has meant the opportunity for local people to invest privately in commercial and agricultural enterprises. Politically it has meant, in the international arena, relatively close ties with one or another Western power and low commitment to Pan-African revolutionary activities. Internally it has generally meant repression of leftist agitation by intellectuals but otherwise little that would distinguish the government policy from that of a more radical regime. It has also meant the extensive use of European personnel in the bureaucracy.

The initial difficulties for such regimes have come about, as we have already indicated, as a result of the continuing and growing deficit in the government's budget. This was the result of a declining price on the world market for the cash-earning export commodities, to such a degree that despite increased production of the commodity, the net national income has remained roughly the same in the years since independence. This was even true for the states that received through their former metropolitan country a subsidized purchase price.

This was aggravated by the fact that much of the money earned was spent on luxury import items both for African urban middle-class groups and resident Europeans, so that it was not invested in ways that would expand employment possibilities. In addition, the free transfer of capital led to a steady drain of capital.

The earlier expansion of the educational system at the primary and secondary level during the last days of colonial rule plus its further acceleration after independence created what must be viewed as a glut on the market. This is the now celebrated problem of the "unemployed school

---

[5] The clearest account of the economic and political consequences of an open economy in an underdeveloped country, and one to which I am indebted, is D. Seers, "The Stages of Economic Development of a Primary Producer in the Middle of the Twentieth Century," *Economic Bulletin of Ghana*, VII, 4 (1963), 57–69.

leaver." [6] The job market was incapable in the system of the open economy of keeping pace with the expansion of graduates. Governments found it very difficult, nonetheless, to cut back on the production of these graduates (as the reaction to the reintroduction of fees in Eastern Nigeria demonstrated).

The close links with Western governments that this policy implied led to a spiraling disaffection among highly educated younger cadres for several reasons. It tended to make the governments adopt policies against their *weltanschauung*. The political leadership was furthermore reluctant to Africanize the bureaucracy totally because of its suspicions concerning the potential political role of this group. This reluctance to eliminate European personnel was reinforced in many cases by the fact that their salaries were not met out of the local budget, so that Africanization would have been all the more expensive. Thus many of the university graduates could not find adequate jobs in their government, despite the presumed shortage of trained personnel, and this led to still further hostility to the government by these graduates.

The various means by which Western governments met the governmental deficits have declined over the years for many reasons: the Soviet-American détente, the growing isolationism in Europe (Cartiérisme), the decline of the radical African states (which we shall describe shortly). Furthermore, despite their pro-Western foreign policy, and considerable concessions for foreign investors, the rate of external investment in the economy fell far below expectations in most cases (except for mineral economies).

In this tight situation for employment—both at the level of the primary-school leaver and at the level of the university graduate—there was a resurgence in these states of "tribalism." [7] That is to say, men fell back on the surest solidarity as a way of securing themselves against being left out in a situation of increasing scarcity. Such "tribalism" often moved in the direction of "secessionism" or "localism," in which slightly advantaged areas sought to retain their local appropriations of wealth or underadvantaged areas placed claims against the central government to reallocate investments, jobs, and welfare payments. At the national political level, this turmoil was reflected in maneuvering for political power by various

---

[6] There is now a considerable literature on this theme. See one of the earliest and best of them: A. Callaway, "Unemployment Among African School Leavers," *Journal of Modern African Studies*, I, 3 (1963), 351–371. For a detailed description of the life pattern of an unemployed school leaver, see P. C. Gutkind, "The Energy of Despair: Social Organization of the Unemployed in Two African Cities: Lagos and Nairobi (2nd part)," *Civilisations*, XVII, 4 (1967), 380–402.

[7] A similar point of view is argued in J. O'Connell, "The Inevitability of Instability," *Journal of Modern African Studies*, V, 2 (1967), 181–191. O'Connell says: "Tribalism can be seen as the competitive struggle for modernisation between the elite members of different ethnic groups" (p. 185).

semiconspiratorial methods which in turn led to repression and constant reshuffling of cabinets and regional commissioners as well as to party crises.

Such repression led to Fronde-like coalitions between local notables and the local peasantry, whose discontent had continued to simmer and in some cases led to extensive disorders (as in the western region of Nigeria in 1964–65 and Buganda in 1966).

In the towns the rapid accumulation of capital by the political cadres and some of the senior civil servants, as well as the high standard of living of the resident Europeans, led to an ever sharper gap in life-style. In the presence of luxury consumption which they did not share, the majority of the civil service and other wage earners, urged on by their parasitic cousins, the unemployed school leavers, became increasingly restive and therefore increasingly demanding of higher wages and increased governmental expenditure, precisely at a moment when the government began to feel the financial pinch of declining world prices and declining Western financial assistance.

It needed then only a small spark to set into motion the first coup. If the job squeeze led to acute ethnic rivalry and eventually conflict, government action to contain such rivalry usually led to an accumulation of enemies to the regime. When enough such had been accumulated, as in Nigeria, there was a coup. Or if the government, facing financial crisis, sought to limit expenditure or cut back on civil service salaries, there might be a crisis and a coup (as in Togo and Dahomey in 1963). Or if the government sought to contain the growing expression of political discontent by forced unity moves which would have the effect of limiting political outlets, there might be a coup (as in Congo-Brazzaville in 1963 and Sierra Leone in 1967). The fact that such a conservative regime was a one-party regime availed little because of the decline in the meaningfulness of the party structure.[8]

The postcoup regime, being faced with the same dilemmas, found it difficult to do better than the precoup regime, and was even more prone to further coups because of the illegitimacy of its own route to power. The fact that Dahomey has had the all-African record of coups is not unconnected with the acuteness of Dahomey's budgetary gap.

THE RADICAL PATH

The "radicals," the militant Pan-Africanists, the "socialists" saw all this coming. They saw that the system of the open economy could lead only to chronic instability and, at best, "growth without development." They therefore advocated an alternative set of policies which they have tried to implement, more or less, in the so-called radical states, such as Guinea, Mali

---

[8] I have analyzed this process in detail in "The Decline of the Party in Single-Party African States," in J. La Palombara and M. Weiner, eds., *Political Parties and Political Development* (Princeton, 1966), pp. 201–214.

(under Modibo Keita), Ghana (under Nkrumah), Congo-Brazzaville
(since 1963), Tanzania, Algeria, and the UAR. They have attempted, at
least at certain times, to move toward closure of the economy (and to some
extent of the polity and culture as well).

Internationally this changed policy has meant establishing control over
the currency by breaking with the old world economic zone in which it
had participated, or at least establishing strict currency controls. It has
meant import controls, limitations on currency transfers, and the introduction of protective tariffs. Internally it has meant limiting the role of the
indigenous nascent commercial bourgeoisie, although it has *not* meant exclusion of large-scale *foreign* private investment (Valco in Ghana, Fria in
Guinea, foreign oil interests in Algeria). Politically it has meant, in the
international arena, anti-Western neutralism and universal diplomatic ties
as well as a high degree of support for liberation movements in southern
Africa and radical opposition parties in more conservative African independent states. It has also meant a one-party regime combined with
preventive detention acts. European technicians have been used in the
bureaucracy but they have tended to be of more diverse national and political backgrounds than in the other states.

The problem of the budgetary gap has been, if anything, more severe
for these states, since their ideological posture has led them to even greater
internal expenditures (especially in the field of job creation).

The radical governments first sought to increase revenue through various
taxation mechanisms. This hit, in consecutive order, cash-crop farmers,
the urban middle class (especially the civil service), and the urban wage
earners. As each group was taxed and it protested, it met with political
repression.

These governments often sought to reduce certain kinds of governmental
expenditure by an ideology of austerity which hit most severely the senior
political cadres of the regimes and was therefore extremely difficult to
enforce. The governments also usually tried to tackle the problem indirectly, by restricting luxury imports. Such a move had the advantage of
enabling the governments to pursue their objective of local industrial development, which also made possible job creation. Another advantage was
aid to the country's balance-of-payments difficulties. The result of this
tactic was indeed an increase of local production. The reduction of luxury
imports also meant, however, in the eyes of the purchaser, higher prices for
inferior goods, adding to the discontent of the urban middle classes. The
steady inflation affected food prices as well, thus spreading discontent to
the petty traders and urban laborers.

This discontent was shared by foreign personnel in the country who
faced a steady reduction in life-style because of the import policy and
diminishing cash benefits (because of austerity). This was compounded by

increasing restrictions on currency transfer. Since capital accumulation is one of the principal motives for foreigners to seek employment in contemporary Africa, this led to a steady withdrawal of such cadres. At the same time, because these withdrawals were sometimes premature and precipitate, there was occasionally a sharp decline in efficiency and the rate of production.

Both the move toward economic closure and the international diplomatic stance of these countries led increasingly to strained relations with Western countries and hence to various kinds of economic retaliation. Foreign, nonmining investment dried up and intergovernmental assistance declined rapidly (including assistance from the World Bank). For a while, the radical countries sought foreign assistance from the U.S.S.R. and Eastern European countries, as well as China. But with the growing U.S.–Soviet détente and various kinds of political disillusionments, this alternate source became less liberal.

The radical governments, it is true, were able, far better than the conservative ones, to contain two problems (which are perhaps really only one). Because of their systematic, and, from the point of view of classical economics, "noneconomic," emphasis on job creation, and because of their lesser use of foreign technical personnel (for all the reasons adduced above), there was relatively less unemployment in these countries, both of primary-school leavers and of university graduates. This meant in turn that there was less of a resurgence of "tribalism," especially since these states were ideologically very strongly committed to the creation of a unitary society.

Despite this fact, the accumulating discontent of so many groups, combined with a deteriorating short-run economic situation, led the radical states to a crisis. The single parties, though stronger here than in the conservative states, were affected by the same kind of atrophy of effectiveness. In Ghana, when the cash reserves were exhausted, the army, which found itself under increasing economic pressure and political surveillance, took over and ended the whole attempt at closure. The same thing occurred in Mali. In other states (such as Guinea, Algeria, and for a while, Congo-Brazzaville), faced with similar crises, the regimes relaxed many of the measures they had instituted, moving closer to the reality of the conservative states. Whether they will be able to remain in an intermediate position for long is doubtful. Most probably, they will either convert themselves into conservative states and be faced with the problems outlined previously, or return to a radical path and eventually be overthrown. In short, the radical alternative failed because African independent states have at present too small an economic reserve and base to sustain the long period of siege involved in serious economic closure.

CONCLUSION

The range of choice for contemporary African governments is thus very small indeed. Governments are weak but their control is of key importance to the African middle classes. As one commentator has expressed it recently: "The alliance of the traditional elite with the administrative and professional classes provides the basis for the formation of a new ruling class. The state being the principal employer, access to political power gives this class possession of the means of production." [9] The other side of the coin, however, has been stated by a Nigerian analyst: "Because the governing middle class is characteristically non-entrepreneurial it lacks the organic interest which motivated the class-type European middle-class to promote an internal national market and economy, and hence to establish nationalism, in the form of mercantilism." [10]

Actually, as we have argued, some groups have the mercantilist vision but lack the strength to carry it out against opposing forces. And the majority of the middle-class cadres do not lack the vision of mercantilism, but simply see far larger short-run profits in an alliance with Western economies. They are using the state machinery and the outside links to transform themselves into a commercial bourgeoisie, but one which has a weak political and economic base.

As long as the state machinery remains fragile and the state's revenue so uncertain, there will be a chronic gap between promise and reality, and hence chronic instability. Over the next twenty years, this chronic instability will probably move in one of two directions. There could be a gradual reduction of the promise, and hence of expectations, and therefore to some extent of instability. This is the path of right-wing repression à la Salazar. Or the social conditions could change within some of the larger states—my candidates remain Nigeria, the Congo-Kinshasa, and a post-civil war South Africa—to permit a serious "nationalist" revolution, based on closure, which would transform the economy. This would basically involve an alliance between certain urban elements and a radicalized peasantry. This would also of course depend on a change in the world system such that the group attempting such a revolution would have more room to maneuver.

Until that time, however, the options are very few for a government that wishes to stay in power. As individuals and as a collective body, they must bend with the wind. And they are doing so.

[9] Marie-Hélène Le Divelec, "Les 'Nouvelles' Classes Sociales en Milieu Urbain: Le Cas du Sénègal et Celui du Nigéria du Nord," *Civilizations*, XVII, 3 (1967, 253.
[10] Ukpabi Asika, "The Uses of Literacy," *Nigerian Opinion*, III, 1 (Jan. 1967), 154.

Part II   The Parameters of Political Choice

Part II. The Politics of Personal Choice

Preface to Part II

One of the principal purposes of this volume is to dramatize the great complexity of the development process. This point is important to reenforce for it is far too easy to assume that the problem can be reduced to one of limited economic resources. In a sense, of course, this is true. If resources were not scarce, there would be no problem of development, in Africa or elsewhere. Limited resources, however, only begin to define the problem and acquiring resources with which to undertake programs neglected during the colonial period is only the beginning of a process of developmental change. The scarcity of resources has its major impact in politicizing the problem of development. It necessitates the establishment of priorities and compels choices between desirable but alternative policies. The benefits and costs of different development policies are extremely difficult to establish with any degree of certainty, however, and African governments confront a major dilemma of unknown consequences.

Immanuel Wallerstein's distinction between "conservative path" and "radical path" states is helpful in illustrating the extent of this dilemma. The conservative path, with an emphasis upon the role of foreign and private capital in generating economic growth, would appear at first glance to have a fairly clear set of benefits and costs. On the one hand, conservative path states seem to feature a relatively rapid rate of economic growth as measured by indices of gross output. Their principal urban centers are often the scene of considerable dynamism in the formation of new industries and in the spread of industrial support services such as banking, insurance, and transportation. Moreover, such states are able to provide considerable opportunity for Africans with technical, managerial, and administrative skills. On the other hand, conservative path states exhibit a growing cleavage between social classes, and the inequalities which accompany industrialization pose a major threat to political stability. The clearest example of a conservative path state discussed in this volume is the Ivory Coast.

Radical path states appear initially to reverse these patterns. Emphasis on state management of industrial enterprise helps avoid a bifurcation of society into possessors and nonpossessors of capital. A determination to create cooperatives in the rural areas expresses the objective of eliminating economic discrepancies between producers and traders and, to the extent to which cooperatives are successful, this goal can be achieved. At the same time, however, radical states have been considerably less successful in generating raw economic growth. The most well known example of a radical experiment considered in this volume is Ghana during the period of Kwame Nkrumah's leadership.

As clear as these patterns of benefit and cost may appear to be, the picture is somewhat misleading. The existence of such widely differing development strategies as the radical and conservative paths does not mean, for example, that African states may choose freely between the two. Economic and social patterns built up over many decades of colonial rule are not susceptible of easy alteration and choices of development policy necessarily reflect some degree of accommodation to historical realities. In regions where colonial rule led to the growth of a strong and fairly diversified private economy, there is a strong incentive to continue to rely upon this economy as a source of income and employment. Moreover, such economies are often supported by a variety of international and domestic pressures. In countries where colonialism was not accompanied by the growth of a large private economic structure, there is frequently little alternative to development through state enterprise. Oftentimes, this situation reflects a fairly low level of attractive opportunity for private investment. No state is rigidly locked into one pattern or the other and flexibility can be attained through the exercise of political will; but the parameters of choice are limited by a variety of external, domestic, and historical constraints.

Even if the circumstances of history were such that African governments could choose freely between the two paths, the number of imponderables and unknowns would be immense. The suggestion that almost any form of development strategy involves some trade off between social equality and economic growth is useful in identifying certain of these unknowns. There is, for example, no yardstick other than its own political values by which a government can give weight to these two alternatives. It is sometimes argued in defense of the conservative path that once a certain amount of economic growth has occurred, it will be possible to use the wealth created to solve the social problems of the society. This argument raises a host of further questions. May it not be equally possible that rapid industrialization generates social problems in excess of the government's capacity to introduce reform? To what extent is it possible, once having accepted inequality as the price of growth, to alter public policy in a more equalitarian direction?

It is at least arguable that economic conservatism implies a future of such considerable social inequality that there will be a heightened need to employ political coercion to maintain order. Privileged social classes are not well known for their willingness to surrender their status under pressure for equalitarian reforms. The history of political efforts to bring about a redistribution of wealth from proprietary, managerial, and technical strata in society to urban workers and rural farmers does not suggest that inequalities once in being can be easily resolved. Regimes that commit themselves to a policy of economic conservatism are often closely tied to the more privileged and powerful strata in society and for this reason, too, find it increasingly difficult to extricate themselves from this policy. Weak and fragile as African governments are, successful revolutions that have changed the social basis of political power from privileged to underprivileged elements in the society have been extremely rare.

A comparable set of unresolved questions confronts the radical path states. How real is the social equality obtained through state management of enterprise? Are the economic and social discrepancies between industrial management and industrial workers appreciably less under public than private ownership? A similar question can be asked of the difference between cooperative managers and peasant producers. To a large extent, the success of the radical path states depends upon the feasibility of achieving closure, a degree of economic autonomy and self-sufficiency adequate to permit participation in the international economy on a purely discretionary basis. The prospects of achieving and maintaining such closure are poor. Both radical and conservative states confront the problem of destabilizing feedback from international sources. In the more conservative states there is frequently an alter image of political radicalism connoting great success in eliminating human hardship and misery. In radical states there is sometimes to be found an alter image of economic conservatism connoting better living conditions and greater individual opportunity. In this respect, the radical and conservative paths become a source of constraint upon one another.

The purpose of the following case studies is to provide concrete illustration of these general patterns of constraint on African development. As Martin Doornbos and Michael Lofchie comment in their analysis of the Ankole Ranching Scheme, the exact value of case studies is a matter of some disagreement among social scientists. Some argue that case studies are a source of verifiable theoretical hypotheses on the basis of which an empirically rooted social science can be gradually constructed. Others view case studies more modestly as sources of detailed information which can later be synthesized by scholars with more general or comparative interests. Here the intention is to use case studies to exemplify some of the constraints inherent in the process of African development. The contributions in this section have in common that they deal with governments experiencing profoundly difficult dilemmas in their efforts to build politically unified, socially progressive, and economically viable societies.

Jonathan S. Barker's essay, "The Paradox of Development," illustrates the manner and extent to which the social pluralism of Senegalese society places narrow limits on the government's freedom to pursue developmental policies. The present political system of Senegal depends for its stability upon the support of certain groups and strata in the society, most particularly those which are in a position to exercise a high measure of political influence. This in itself does not distinguish the government of Senegal from most governments in the world. What is different is the extent to which the Senegalese conception of development, however broadly construed, implies an obligation to pursue policies intended to benefit all groups in society, particularly the less privileged. Barker suggests that the tension between a commitment to universalistic policies, on the one hand, and dependence upon particular social strata for support, on the other, confronts the government with a virtually insoluble predicament. To the extent that the government attempts to pursue developmental policies that have universal social objectives, it runs the risk of alienating its principal power base and thus of weakening its capacity to generate further change. In Barker's terms, "at the moment when it most needs widespread and deep support, the government finds that its policies undermine support rather than stimulate it." If, however, the government seeks to consolidate a more secure power base by continuing its appeal to dominant social groups, it must to some extent forego its commitment to widespread social change.

Ironically, certain of the arguments for authoritarian forms of rule in Africa take their theoretical point of departure by alluding precisely to the sort of dilemma in which the government of Senegal finds itself; namely, that any government which seeks to produce far-reaching transformation in society will experience difficulty in maintaining popular support. Barker's essay focuses attention on the still unresolved question of whether the concept of democratic planning does not involve a contradiction in terms. There are two principal democratic arguments against systematic long-range planning: first, that such planning involves decisions which, once taken, cannot be challenged for the duration of the plan; second, that systematic planning is of a piece and that in order to be successful it cannot be modified to accommodate the needs of particular groups in society. The contemporary political experience of Senegal would appear to indicate that under conditions of popularly elected government the political process is far more likely to be characterized by bargaining and compromise than by systematically planned change.

Independent Africa's best-known attempt at thoroughgoing transformation of inherited social and economic patterns occurred in Ghana during the presidency of Kwame Nkrumah. The Convention People's Party (CPP) had an array of radical objectives including reclamation of control over the economy through nationalization, human mobilization, and the promotion of a wholly new set of political attitudes among the population. Nkrumah's ultimate objective was the creation of a socialist society in which class discrepancies would be minimized and in which economic growth through industrialization would benefit all segments of society. A military coup in early 1966 signaled the failure of this experiment. The reasons for this failure are significant in indicating some of the difficulties which may be expected to confront other attempts at transformative change.

One of the principal reasons for the failure of Ghanaian socialism lay in the organizational deterioration of the government's major instrument for development, the CPP. In their article on "Political and Economic Constraints on Development in Ghana," Barbara Callaway and Emily Card suggest that by the end of the Nkrumah period the CPP had lapsed from a highly unified nationalist movement possessing considerable organizational esprit to a congeries of diverse factions engaged in bickering and conflict. Organizational weakness hampered the strategy of transformation in a number of ways; one of the most consequential of these ways was that it limited the capacity of the regime to sustain a high degree of political mobilization. There can be little doubt that Nkrumah harbored few illusions about the possibility of pursuing transformative programs under democratic conditions or that he saw the intimate connection between radical social objectives and the need for a governmental capacity to engage in coercion. Callaway and Card list a series of laws designed to stifle opposition including a Preventive Detention Act, an Offences Against the State Act, and a Sedition Bill. The paradoxical aspect of the situation was that although implementation of these laws would have required a considerable coercive capacity, the organizational weakness of the CPP represented a serious dilution of any such capacity.

The organizational weakness of the CPP compelled Nkrumah to depend primarily upon the state bureaucracy for the implementation of Ghanaian socialism. In terms of educational level and experience, the Ghanaian bureaucracy represented an impressive concentration of managerial, technical, and administrative skills. The difficulty for development lay in the fact that large numbers of civil servants were profoundly unsympathetic to the programs Nkrumah espoused. Three factors largely account for this opposition. The Ghanaian civil service had been largely educated and recruited during the colonial period and the elitist traditions of the colonial state continued to be a strong influence. Moreover, as a privileged class enjoying a highly differentiated position in society, many administrators felt economically threatened by the equalitarian aspects of the radical program. Finally, large numbers of civil servants had strong family and personal ties to some of the more affluent commercial and agricultural groups in the society and this reenforced their lack of sympathy for socialist programs. Since skilled civil servants were in short supply, Nkrumah was left with little alternative but to attempt to implement a radical program with an administrative establishment deeply hostile to it.

An additional constraint on Ghanaian development arose from the fact that in Ghana, as elsewhere in independent Africa, it was extremely difficult to make an unequivocal choice between radical path and conservative path policies. The strength of the private economy and the prospect of substantial foreign private investment, for example in the Volta River Project, were a strong incentive to continue to rely somewhat upon a private enterprise system. Nkrumah himself foresaw a period of mixed economic practices during which rapid economic growth would occur before the implementation of a full socialist program. This attitude led to a major contradiction in Ghanaian society. Dependence upon a residual private economy necessitated tolerance for the persistence of a large privileged stratum in the society, one which included both local and expatriate businessmen, entrepreneurs, and technicians. At the same time, incipient socialist programming was accompanied by the imposition of austerity measures upon urban workers and peasant farmers as a prelude to internal capital formation. The result of these contradictory policies was that the subordinate classes in the society who were intended to benefit from socialism and upon whose support the socialist strategy depended were confronted with a visible and growing gap between themselves and the more well-to-do elements. These groups, like those who felt threatened by socialism, became alienated from the regime and did not respond to its defense when the coup occurred.

Tanzania's postindependence political experience has been substantially different from that of Ghana, presenting a model of stable social democracy. In an era when many dominant single parties in Africa seem prone toward institutional atrophy, Tanzania's governing party, the Tanganyika African National Union (TANU), has been able not only to maintain a high degree of organizational dynamism but to improvise creatively in the formation of new structures of party and state. Underlying these efforts has been a strong determination to provide for widespread popular participation in the political process. The TANU government appears to enjoy overwhelming popular confidence among virtually all major social groups and in virtually all regions of the country. In a vast nation, poor in resources and infrastructure even by African standards, TANU has established itself as an effective vehicle of political unification.

One of the themes of R. Cranford Pratt's article, "Cabinet and Presidential Leadership in Tanzania, 1960–1966," is an inquiry into whether the Tanzanian political system has paid some sort of a price for this degree of unity and whether that price might, at some point, have become a source of systemic constraint. Partly as a legacy of the intense solidarity of the nationalist period, Pratt argues, the members of the Tanzanian cabinet continue to place a high value on the maintenance of unity and collegiality among themselves. Among the arguments Pratt advances is the view that this resulted, for a time, in a sort of "politics of accommodation" which allowed considerable freedom of action for individual government figures. Potentially serious or damaging conflicts were avoided but only at the price of a political style which sustained a substantial level of personal capriciousness and unpredictability, especially in the relations between the ministers and the bureaucracies over which they presided. A related aspect of the "politics of accommodation" was the tendency for major controversial issues which might not be susceptible of harmonious relations within the cabinet to be decided upon by the president himself. The overall impression is of a system in which the norm of unity was so strong that, during the period 1960–1966, it resulted in a substantial aggrandizement of personal power by the president and in the subordination of technical, economic, and bureaucratic values. This phase of Tanzanian politics declined markedly after 1966 when the leadership of TANU committed itself explicitly to a socialist program. Pratt concludes that more recent years have seen far greater unity of purpose and action than was the case in the period following independence.

Developmental planning and implementation are among the major activities of virtually every independent African government. The widening gap between rich nations and poor, growing popular expectations of social and economic progress, and the absence or relative recency of autonomous entrepreneurial elites are three of the principal forces which make developmental planning primarily a state responsibility. Broadly speaking, African nations have a choice between two alternative strategies of development: reliance upon foreign aid and capital or internal generation of development resources partly through human mobilization. Although these strategies are not mutually exclusive, and indeed most African states practice an admixture of the two, the distinction is an important one. The difference between countries that encourage and rely heavily upon foreign capital and those that seek to generate growth through internal resources appears to correspond roughly to the distinction between those countries that have high indices of economic output and those that do not.

Richard E. Stryker's article, "A Local Perspective on Developmental Strategy in the Ivory Coast," treats an African country that has deeply committed itself to a strategy of Western capital investment. The dominant theme of Stryker's analysis is that Western investment, while it has led to high indices of economic growth, has done so at the cost of creating serious socioeconomic imbalances in Ivorian society. This is principally because investment has been most attracted to areas of the country which are already overadvantaged, the southern region and the national capital, Abidjan. The south, which was already possessed of an abundant economic infrastructure, has thus enjoyed booming economic conditions while the north has developed more slowly. Despite the government's attempt to employ administrative mechanisms to bring about more rapid changes in the north, the gap between these two areas of the country continues to grow. There is not, in Stryker's view, an immediate threat to stability, "but the problems arising from these disequilibria are increasingly cumulative and the capability of the regime to deal with them will be correspondingly challenged." The inequality between north and south is, at the very least, a potential stimulus of immense popular unrest.

A large and growing socioeconomic gap between city and countryside, at the heart of Stryker's analysis of politics in the Ivory Coast, is a common affliction of many African states. One response has been the attempt to induce more rapid development in the rural areas and in the agricultural sector of the economy as a means of reducing the imbalance between city and countryside. In all these respects, Uganda and the Ivory Coast have much in common. Throughout the colonial and early postcolonial periods, commercial and industrial development has been heavily concentrated in the southern area of the country and especially in the largest cities. In both societies, this north–south imbalance has characterized agriculture as well. Due largely to geographical factors such as access to markets and the developmental activities of the colonial authorities, southern agriculture has been the scene of more far-reaching change than that in the north, especially in the introduction of new technology and the development of cash crops for an export market.

The government of Uganda has recently begun to attempt to induce agricultural development on a wide scale in the more northerly sections of the country as part of a broad effort to reduce the economic inequalities between north and south. M. Crawford Young's analysis of Uganda's efforts in this direction illuminates a number of difficult situations which may be expected to affect any country engaged in induced agricultural change. The first of these is a squeeze between the rapidly increasing cost of scientific and technical inputs on the one hand and, on the other, shrinking world market prices for primary agricultural commodities. A second problem or set of problems revolves around the gap between expectations and realistically attainable performance. In Young's view the transformation from colonial to independent status, with the attendant emergence of mass politics, heightened popular expectations beyond the limits of realism.

Unrealized expectations have already created a serious problem of faith in government in many areas. Their presence creates an extraordinarily difficult dilemma in the planning of agricultural policy. In order to heighten farmer and peasant participation in agricultural developmental programs, the government must encourage growing expectations, for unless the rural population can expect some gain from its added efforts, popular cooperation with the new programs is not likely to be forthcoming. Heightened expectations, however, could easily go beyond the point where the agricultural system could live up to them, a situation which would do further damage to confidence in governmental authority.

Developmental planning in Africa has cultural and social as well as economic objectives. It is concerned with the promotion of new ways of life and work, with the formation of new sets of attitudes and values, and with the creation of new social arrangements and institutions. Among the social objectives of developmental planning given prominent attention by African governments is the promotion of social equalitarianism. There is a widespread desire to furnish social opportunities to elements of the population which were formerly denied them and, as well, a determination to minimize political and economic inequalities. The equalitarian dimension of developmental planning is the principal focus of the Doornbos–Lofchie study of "The Ankole Ranching Scheme." As the authors explain, the project was intended to be a joint effort by the governments of Uganda and the United States to introduce commercial cattle ranching into the Ankole region of southwestern Uganda. Perhaps more importantly, it was also an attempt to stimulate equalitarian social change in a society which had in the past exhibited persistent social inequality.

Traditional Ankole society may be viewed as having been divided into two ethnic social strata: a pastoral elite, known as Bahima, who were also a governing class, and a peasant mass, known as Bairu, whose political position was generally a subordinate one. In recent years these political and class distinctions have begun to break down. The Bairu, who at one time were legally prevented from owning cattle, have not only taken up this occupation in larger and larger numbers but have also begun to gain a number of influential positions in the Ankole political system. The Bahima continued to retain a disproportionate number of both political and economic elite positions in society; but under the influence of public education, the introduction of merit criteria, and competitive electoral politics, the social system of Ankole had already evolved considerably in an equalitarian direction when the ranching scheme was initiated. The scheme was designed to help continue this process of change, and the method by which this was to be accomplished was through the selection of ranchers on an open competitive basis.

The general theme of "ranching and scheming" is the project's failure to achieve its equalitarian objective, and its subject is the interplay of international and domestic political forces which enabled high-ranking Bahima politicians and other Bahima influentials to gain possession of a majority of the first group of ranches.

Uganda society has gone through a constitutional revolution since the period when the ranching scheme was a subject of intense conflict.* Elected Kingdom governments have been constitutionally abolished and their functions taken over by the central government's district administration. The purport of this study, then, is not its treatment of modern Uganda politics, but rather its ability to illustrate, by example, the manner in which national and international objectives can be stymied at the level of local implementation.

Michael F. Lofchie

*On 25 January 1971 the Uganda army seized power in a successful coup d'etat which overthrew the government of President Milton Obote. At the present time (May 1971) the new government has dissolved the National Assembly and is ruling by decree. The military authorities have announced an intention to restore civilian government but the exact timing of this restoration is unclear. A longer discussion of this coup occurs in the conclusion.

Chapter 3 The Paradox of Development: Reflections on a Study of Local-Central Political Relations in Senegal

Jonathan S. Barker

This paper [1] directs attention to two subjects which attract relatively little attention in contemporary political science but which appear to be of great interest for understanding politics in Africa and in other parts of the Third World: the consequences of government policies and local-central political relations. Modern political analysis has concentrated on questions of how power is organized and how structures and policies originate. Both Marxian and liberal-democratic theories pose questions about the social determinants of policies, the one in terms of economic substructures and the class struggle, the other in terms of representation of individuals, interests, or groups.

Our custom of seeing politics as a resultant of social forces and the problem of politics as how to organize government to adequately reflect and control these forces leaves us in some ways ill-equipped to handle the problems of the politics of development. An emphasis on development policy promises to cast light on the problem of political instability in developing countries. Our procedure is to show that common assumptions about developing societies lead to a logical paradox: the government that promotes development destroys itself. Then we shall see that theorists who seek development in stability through a charismatic leader, a mobilizing organiza-

[1] Much of the research in which these reflections have their origin was financed by a Foreign Area Training Fellowship from the Joint Committee of the American Council of Learned Societies and the Social Science Research Council, but the reflections are entirely my own.

tion, a colonial regime, or a neocolonial government all share a common desire to escape the paradox by finding sources of government support outside the society. Finally, we shall examine two critiques of the formulation of the paradox, one taking a revolutionary the other a pluralist viewpoint. The argument is illustrated with material from Senegal.

THE PARADOX OF DEVELOPMENT

A government, we all know, in order to be effective and durable requires the support of its population. Some support can be enforced through coercion, but the most effective support derives from value consensus or legitimacy. If most people think it is proper to obey the government's directives, have confidence in its leaders, and are proud of its accomplishments, then the government is likely to be strong and capable of decisive action. It is also commonly supposed that a government which is able to satisfy a considerable portion of the demands placed upon it from the population is likely to retain a high degree of support. If demands are not met, then the affection people have for their government and the confidence they place in it will decline. What determines the pattern of demands? The usual answer, I think, is the social structure of the country—the configuration of interest groups, social stratification, political parties, and regional interests. In general, the pattern of demands reflects the existing social balance of forces, and therefore the pattern of policy that is most productive of support is one which substantially preserves the existing social balance, with suitable adjustment for newly emerging interests and for long-term social changes such as population growth.

But notice what happens to the correspondence of demands and policy if we postulate a government that takes as its objective the planned transformation of the social structure. The model of the desired society may bear very little resemblance to the existing society. The planners advise as to the most efficient series of steps for the movement from the present condition to the desired one. The pattern of policy is determined by the priorities of the plan. There is every reason to believe that the policy so designed will *not* correspond to the pattern of demands arising from the existing society. In fact, the policies may well spell the systematic contravention of important sets of demands. If this is true, support is likely to drop. At the moment when it most needs widespread and deep support the government finds that its policies undermine support rather than stimulate it. If this chain of reasoning is correct, the government which systematically pursues development contributes to its own instability and reduces its capacity to take the kind of strong consistent action development requires.

If the paradox is valid, it reflects a real dilemma facing governments committed to development policies. They are obliged to choose between a set of actions which favors development and a completely different set which favors support for the government and political stability. If the paradox of development is spurious, it reflects only the inadequacy of our conceptualization of the relations between government and society (or between the political system and its environment).

IMPLICATIONS OF THE PARADOX

The paradox of development is not original with me. David Apter, for example, has written: "Modernization itself helps to create those conflicts that political leaders must solve in order to pursue modernization." [2] Thus to pursue modernization is to create conflicts which render the pursuit of modernization difficult. John Stuart Mill in considering the social and cultural preconditions to representative government notes that uncivilized people are not capable of supporting governments which could start them on the road of progress through representative institutions. "A representative assembly drawn from among themselves would simply reflect their own turbulent insubordination." [3] Both Apter and Mill place their best hopes in a system of government which attracts support otherwise than by the fulfillment of demands whose pattern is conditioned by the existing social structure. The same kind of argument is made by the proponents of one-party regimes who distinguish between progressive and national elements which merit representation and backward and tribal elements which deserve to be repressed. The alternatives proposed include the mobilization system, charismatic leadership, and despotism. In the mobilization system support is organized and legitimacy created outside the existing social structure.[4] The possibility of a mobilization regime seems to be proportional to the degree of social strain and stress which makes people available for mobilization. Charismatic authority is the psychological analogue of the mobilization system. Desire and hope are loosened from their previous psychological organization by cultural strain and become available for attachment to an extraordinary leader. Charisma creates a basis for support outside the traditional value commitments of the society.[5] Mill is dimly aware of the significance of charisma. He despairs of a backward people finding it possible to create from within itself a progressive government. The best hope he says is an absolute ruler "deriving his power

[2] David Apter, *The Politics of Modernization* (Chicago, 1965), p. 433.

[3] John Stuart Mill, *Utilitarianism, Liberty and Representative Government* (New York, 1951), p. 296.

[4] Apter, p. 262.

[5] Max Weber, *Economy and Society* (New York, 1968), Vol I, p. 245; Vol II, p. 1115.

either from religion or military powers; very often from foreign arms." [6] Better still is benevolent rule by a more civilized people. Mill, too, perceives the need of finding support for a progressive government outside the backward people it governs.

Surprisingly enough, the reasoning of those who ask that rich developed countries support more or less authoritarian regimes in places deemed to be as yet incapable of democracy is similar to that of Apter and Mill. Authoritarian measures at home plus financial and moral support from abroad can protect a government from the reaction of its own people to policies that are a necessary but painful prelude to economic development and political liberalization. So runs the argument.[7]

In brief the arguments for benevolent despotism, charismatic leadership, colonial authoritarianism, and neocolonial support for authoritarianism bear a formal similarity to one another. In each case, the government is taken to be an agent of development or improvement and it is recognized that it cannot hope to retain the support of the society it seeks to transform. Therefore, some source of support which lies outside the given social structure is sought. Two general cases are made: one for a source of support which becomes available because of the malfunctions of the given society (mobilization, charisma) and one for a source of support outside the country in question (colonialism and neocolonialism).

A Case in Point: Senegal

Is this paradox a straw paradox? Do the governments of developing countries really face the dilemma of choosing between a policy of concerted and coordinated development that tends to undermine their authority and strength and one of piecemeal reaction to effective demands? Let me begin to answer these questions with reference to the case of one underdeveloped country: Senegal. My approach will be to characterize the government's sources of support and to ask what its reaction has been and is likely to be to major elements in the government's development program. For the purposes of this analysis I will restrict my attention to the peanut-growing region of Senegal. This region is composed of the administrative regions of Thies, Diourbel, and Sine-Saloum. Students of the nationalist movement and national politics in Senegal agree that this is the political center of gravity of the country. Overt opposition is virtually absent in this area. It is appropriate to test the hypothesized paradox of development in a region where support for the government is strong when development policies begin to be carried out so that the effects of the policies on support can be assessed.

[6] Mill, p. 265.

[7] Cf. Charles Wolf, *United States Policy and the Third World* (Boston and Toronto, 1967), pp. 23–45.

The peanut-growing region has a certain ecological unity given by its rainfall and temperature, the quality of the soil, and its relative accessibility to international transportation routes. These facts have made it suitable for the cultivation of peanuts, an activity which has given the region considerable economic unity. Another unifying feature is Islam which is professed by some 90 percent of the inhabitants. Finally, there is a culture complex common to the three major ethnic groups of the region, the Wolof, the Toucouleur, and the Serer. Its most prominent features are small agricultural villages, the existence of despised endogamous descent groups with recognized functions (usually artisanal) and statuses in the larger society, and a tradition of centralized kingdoms in which certain aristocratic descent groups played a prominent role. Islam and colonial rule have not destroyed the identity of the aristocratic and despised groups. They have added new elements of stratification, however, in the families of the great Islamic teacher-leaders (called *marabouts* in French and *serigne* in Wolof), the class of semibureaucratic chiefs often appointed from aristocratic families, and new occupational groups such as carpenters and mechanics. Giving meaning to the whole are beliefs derived from Islam and from pre-Islamic animist traditions. I cannot pretend to do justice to this very important aspect of society. All I can do is to mention the existence of some important types or models of relations of authority prevalent in the culture: Islamic teacher and disciple (*talibé*), father and son, patron and dependent.

Until 1946 popular politics as it is ordinarily conceived was confined to the three coastal cities which the French had early designated as communes. At the war's end the dominant party was a branch of the Section Française de l'Internationale Ouvrière (SFIO), the French socialist party. In Senegal the SFIO was headed by Lamine Gueye. The decade following 1946 saw the progressive enlargement of the Senegalese electorate and the gradual shift of the center of gravity of electoral support from the cities to the rural areas. When Lamine Gueye chose Leopold Senghor to run for the new seat of deputy to the French Chamber of Deputies from a rural constituency, he did not realize that he was placing his partner atop a wave which would carry him to political preeminence in Senegal. By 1956, under conditions of universal suffrage, Senghor, with a core of support in the peanut region, was clearly dominant. He could afford to bring *laministes* and other opposition groups into his party. Where did he garner his support? Ruth Schachter Morgenthau describes the tactics of Senghor's Bloc Democratique Sénégalais (BDS) after it broke with the SFIO in 1948 in the following terms: [8]

The leaders of the BDS entered into a series of negotiations with the major

8 *Political Parties in French-Speaking West Africa* (London, 1964), p. 147.

ethnic and interest groups. Perhaps the most important of these were Muslim, since at least four-fifths of the population of Senegal was Muslim. The centre of gravity of the Muslim groups, as indeed of the Senegalese economy, is the rich and densely populated Sine-Saloum area. . . .

Over the generations, through intermarriage and conversion to Islam, almost a single social category concentrating rural religious and secular power and wealth had emerged out of the maraboutic, trading and traditionally chiefly families. They have a remarkable circuit of communication, and their *talibés* or student-clients send contributions from trading, or give labour and grow peanuts. These important families were concentrated in the Sine-Saloum where . . . no party could hope to win in elections without either beating or joining them. The BDS tried to join them.

Morgenthau also cites the following tactics: [9] (1) the promise of cooperatives to capitalize on resentment against urban-based traders, (2) the maintenance of traditional chiefs, (3) higher pensions for veterans, and (4) the choice of locally supported native son candidates. After the success of the BDS in the 1952 elections it consolidated its position by arranging easy loans for traditional and Muslim leaders and by giving candidates elected to the territorial council positions on the locally influential *sociétés de prévoyance*.

My own research in Birkelane arrondissement in Sine-Saloum generally corroborates this picture. The strength of the colonial administration had rested upon the coercive power of the French *commandant de cercle* and *chef de subdivision* and upon the personal network of the *chef de canton*, an African trained as a bureaucrat but usually chosen from a chiefly family. The *chef de canton's* ability to gain support was reinforced by his influence with the *société de prévoyance* which provided seed peanuts to villagers at planting time for repayment plus 25 percent interest during the harvest. The administrative-*société* network was paralleled by and interacted with a commercial network which purchased peanuts for export to France and imported manufactured goods and rice for sale to the peanut producers. Controlled at the top by a handful of French trading companies, the network was represented in the rural trading centers by French, Lebanese, and African traders who sold goods on credit to villagers and then collected the debt plus 50 or 100 percent interest when the villagers sold their peanuts to the same trader. The peasant-producer often became a kind of client to his patron-trader who would help the peasant with personal problems and intervene on his behalf with the colonial administration.

The BDS confirmed its dominance in the 1956 elections and with the *loi cadre* reforms gained some control over policy in Senegal through its majority in the territorial assembly. It sought to gain the support of groups

[9] *Political Parties in French-Speaking West Africa*, pp. 147–153.

that remained outside its orbit: urban youth groups, trade unions, university graduates, *laministes*. It changed its name in a series of fusions to become the Union Progressiste Sénégalaise in 1958. Since then the younger educated urban radicals have been in and out of the party, but the support of the religious, chiefly, and commercial notables of the peanut region has never been seriously questioned. In Birkelane in 1968 the local party section had substantially the same leadership it had had in 1951–52 when it was organized.

Broadly speaking, it is possible to say that the pattern of political support represented by the UPS in the peanut-growing region accurately reflects the pattern of social stratification. The persons in the upper strata who are dominant in terms of prestige, wealth, and religious reputation have key positions in the political network that supports the government of Senghor. Testing the hypothesized paradox, the question is whether or not the government's development policies threaten this network of support. The answer, justified below, is that they appear to do so in principle but that practical experience has had ambiguous results.

In principle the UPS stands in favor of socialism in the rural sector of the economy. Such a reform would obviously challenge the interests and positions of traders and landholders. In practice two policies have had that effect, but it has been mitigated in several ways. The major step taken in the direction of socializing the rural economy was the creation of marketing cooperatives beginning in 1959. At the same time an Agricultural Marketing Board was created to handle placement abroad of the peanut crop and to control some importation. The credit was to be arranged by a new Senegalese Development Bank with substantial government participation. By 1965, 60 percent of the peanut crop was marketed through cooperatives and the credit circuit in which peasants had been enmeshed was largely broken. In 1967 private buying was forbidden. Major trading companies withdrew their operations to the large cities. Not only was the peanut trade removed from private hands, but a portion of rural expenditure was shifted out of the ordinary trading circuit. Fertilizer and simple farm implements were sold to peasants on credit through cooperatives. In Sine-Saloum in 1960, during the drive to organize cooperatives, there was concerted opposition to them. In Birkelane one of the three top leaders of the local UPS section is said to have campaigned actively against the cooperatives, which were being organized by a youthful government administrative agent. What probably prevented the opposition from being stronger (and especially strong within the party) was the fact that the first traders to be driven out of business were the French and Lebanese because of the competition of the cooperatives and because they felt threatened by the Africanization of the government and the socialist policies it espoused.

Some claimed discriminatory allocation of licenses and inequitable enforcement of price control legislation. The bigger African traders did not suffer very much and many of them were able to increase their turnover as the French and Lebanese left. Such was the case with the trader-politicians in Birkelane. The government waited until 1967 to eliminate private peanut buyers, but they were still needed as sources of credit by producers, who in 1968 often in effect sold their peanuts at a low price to the old traders, who in turn sold them to the cooperatives. Some traders became officers in the cooperatives. The government has not yet followed up pilot experiments in the establishment of consumer cooperatives which would strike at the interests of the remaining traders.

A second important aim of the rural development plan is to rationalize agriculture by encouraging crop diversification and by replacing extensive agriculture with its fixed inputs and techniques with intensive agriculture in which the input of all the various factors of production is calculated to maximize return on the investment. These changes require fundamental changes in habits and attitudes that have grown up over generations of making a living on the land. The government has concluded that it is necessary to change the pattern of land control so as to give more influence to technical experts and to motivate self-help. There is little detailed public knowledge of patterns of land control. In Birkelane the typical pattern was for the founding families of a village to control all or most of the land. Latecomers and their descendants were obliged to ask the founders and their descendants for the use of the land. Villagers usually claim that there is little economic benefit from being a landholder, but this may be because land until very recently has been plentiful in the area. Nonetheless, the fact that some families must ask for land and that others must be asked reinforces a prestige hierarchy. Furthermore, in order to forestall claims of ownership on the part of land borrowers, the lenders often shift their borrowers from field to field, thus thwarting any incentive to long-term improvement of particular fields. In order to end these practices and more abusive ones where land is scarcer, the government nationalized the land and gave security of tenure to the person actually cultivating it at the moment of promulgation of the law. Eventually some control over land use is to be vested in locally elected councils. This law had only begun to be enforced in 1965, but it carries with it a threat to the economic power of large-scale landholders including many religious leaders. Just as importantly, it promises to undermine one of the most important symbolic marks of prestige and influence in villages. Finally, the change in attitude and practice which the agricultural agents hope to realize is likely to spell the end of the inordinate influence of marabouts. Many government administrators hope that the villagers' relationship with government development agents will grow in confidence and become one of positive value to the villagers and that an attitude of rational calculation of economic return will weaken the spiritual dependence of peasants upon a religious master.

We conclude, then, that in principle, but only marginally as yet in practice, development policies threaten to undermine the support which the peanut region has accorded Senghor's party and government. The government appears to be caught between its need for support and its desire to implement its development policies, a circumstance that may explain the uncertainty surrounding the yet unimplemented policies. The dilemma is compounded by the fact that the conditions of political stability are not constant. Two of the fundamental parameters of the political economy of Senegal are in the process of change and shifts are coming about within the structure of the society. The changing parameters are the size of the population and the price of peanuts. Births exceed deaths at a rate which will double the population in twenty or thirty years. The price of peanuts is dropping as France withdraws its subsidy. Within Senegal, as in many undeveloped countries, urbanization, the production of unemployed or inadequately employed youths, the improvement of mass communications and transportation, and the growth of the government bureaucracy continue apace. A political strategy of maximizing short-run stability will only delay the day of reckoning.

CRITIQUE OF THE PARADOX (OR PARADOX LOST)

There are two directions from which the paradox of development can be criticized. One, the revolutionary critique, accepts the paradox but asserts that it does not go far enough. The second, which might be called the pluralist critique, holds that the paradox is founded upon mistaken assumptions about the structural or psychological characteristics of developing societies. We will consider these in turn.

THE REVOLUTIONARY CRITIQUE

The paradox as we have stated it points up the problem of political stability under conditions of development. Not all political theorists have been as concerned about political stability as most contemporary political scientists. For Marx political stability was of no intrinsic value at all. Yet he recognized the existence of the paradox of development as a part of the larger historical dialectic. In his generalizing moods, however, he added a crucial condition to the paradox. In promoting development a government is not only sealing its own doom; it is creating the social-economic foundation for a new political order. As the structural basis for the old regime is eroded the foundation for the new regime is brought into being. The revolution is very rapid and the problem of organizing support in a transitional period hardly arises. In this perspective the political revolution is simply a matter of placing a government atop a different but organized class.

In the Senegalese case, for example, it might be thought that unplanned social changes would automatically produce the social basis for a more radically oriented government. Lower peanut prices and population growth would produce a rural proletariat which, led by the dissatisfied educated class, would take power from the obsolete elites.

The classic argument against this is of course that of Lenin in *What is To Be Done?* There he argues that a revolutionary situation does not of itself create support for a revolutionary government. It is precisely under conditions of dissatisfaction and confusion that the revolutionary movement most requires organization and mobilization under the direction of a trained vanguard. If Lenin is right for other times and climes, then the revolutionary situation does not render the establishment of an autonomous political force unnecessary. Rather it intensifies the need of revolutionaries for autonomous organization. In Senegal the eventual growth of a rural proletariat is conceivable. Rural development within the existing framework might well favor the relatively large-scale cultivators who are in a position to take advantage of technological opportunities while the small cultivators with little or no control over land would lead a relatively more deprived existence. However, a number of factors would tend to prevent this group from achieving any kind of revolutionary consciousness. Even where villagers learn to connect their economic situation with government policy, the obstacles to rural political organization remain great. Peanut growers are dependent upon the government and the party for peanut seed. Islam provides an institutionalized escape for the discouraged. Rural, urban, and ethnic discontent do not spontaneously unite. Yet, as we shall see later, the eventual organization of a rural proletarian movement cannot be entirely ruled out.

In another vein the consideration of the Marxian argument raises an intriguing question. Might it be possible for a government while deriving its support from the existing social structure to prepare and organize a new basis of support which would not be used until it was strong enough to give the strength necessary to move forward with its development plans? We will come back to the question in considering another critique of the paradox of development.

THE PLURALIST CRITIQUE

The paradox of development, as I have stated it, makes three important assumptions. The pluralist critique calls them all into question. The first assumption is that the central government is the principal agent for development. The second assumption is that underdeveloped societies are unitary in the sense that some general changes, such as those identified by the parsonian pattern variables or by Mill's barbarism and civilization, affect all spheres of society. The third assumption is that demands placed upon the government reflect the general character of society and that failure to meet them will result in withdrawal of support from the government and that policies contrary to the interests the demands represent will stimulate political opposition.

I will take as a variant of the pluralist critique Bienen's model of the party machine in his essay in this volume.[10] In order to see the machine system as a critique of the paradox of development, it is necessary to go beyond what Bienen has written, for he does not pursue the question of the appropriateness of the machine system for handling the development process. He draws attention to the descriptive failings of the mobilization model rather than to its theoretical rationale. Here I will present the case for the machine system as a kind of regime capable of guiding and surviving the process of development. Then I shall ask whether the machine model fits Senegal.

If the major agents of development lie outside government, the paradox of development collapses. If a capitalist entrepreneurial system is the agent of change, then it is sufficient to have a political system that is capable of adjusting to the social changes originating in the economic sector. The pluralist argument at issue does not go this far. It agrees that the government is one of the principal agents of development but maintains that governmental stimulation and management of development can and should be decentralized. Local initiative should be encouraged. This means that the role of the central government is more reactive and less directive. Stability is achieved by a continuing process of communications and adjustments between government and society and within the decentralized structure of the government.

If society is fundamentally pluralistic, being divided into distinct cultural groups and definite interest groups, then it becomes difficult to speak of a general relation between society and government. Instead there is a series of quite separate relationships which must be separately conceived. A policy that wins support in one cultural or economic region may arouse opposition in another. Policies can be tailored to particular localities or particular interests. In fact one of the central functions of the political machine becomes the balancing and coordination of ethnic and interest group claims. With good management or clever manipulation the machine

---

[10] Henry Bienen, "Political Parties and Political Machines in Africa" (in this volume).

can risk opposition from established elites in other localities. Perhaps it can even prepare for local "revolutions" by encouraging the organization of new elites, new structures of authority, and new political arenas parallel to the existing ones. At the propitious moment the government would encourage the replacement of the local old guard. Then, the new basis of support solidified, the government could press ahead with development in another locality.

The preparation and encouragement of local "revolutions" is a combination of two strategies. One is the strategy of localized development, which depends upon the relative separateness and uniqueness of particular local communities for its success. If local communities are not relatively separate, then the consequences of the policies will spread horizontally through the society and local elites over a wide area are likely to withdraw support, thereby weakening the government. The second strategy is that of the creation of alternative political networks, which depends upon a discontinuity of the content of political allocations across time and between the center and the locality. This requires some explanation.

The central government, we assume, wishes to promote development. To this end it allocates investment in appropriate activities. It tries to change skills and behavior in accordance with some plan. Local communities we assume to remain preoccupied with traditional local issues. In Senegal these include the application of customs concerning the distribution of land, the resolution of conflicts, and the allocation of offices and honors. According to the machine model, political support from local communities is maintained by patronage, the provision of a channel of social mobility, the distribution of material rewards, and the prestige of position (Bienen, in this volume). These sources of support are relatively insulated from policy issues. Development allocations have little effect upon the support structures. The same machine can carry out either policies of development or policies of "decay."

The fact that local political institutions are not directly affected by development policies means that a choice must be made in the implementation of these policies about what institutions shall implement them. Should the existing networks and arenas be given the task, say, of carrying out land reform and engaging in cooperative methods of agriculture or should new ones be formed? Because the new tasks require new technical skills and new kinds of consultation, the tendency is to create new organizations. In Senegal these are cooperatives, technical administrative services, the Rural Animation Service, and local development committees. It may be possible to develop new authorities, arenas, and networks which will not immediately challenge the existing local elites because they will not be dealing in the same political commodities. Once they are established a base will exist for combating locally the old elites. When the local party has been taken over by the new groups, the local political subsystem will handle the same political values as the central government. The discontinuity between local and central politics will be reduced.

In short the pluralist critique of the paradox of development argues that there is no single source of development policies in the government, that there is no single pattern of response to development initiatives, and that the responses that do occur need not be translated into politically effective forces which undermine the political system. From the pluralist perspective the problem of development is no longer one of finding a place to stand while transforming a social order. It is a problem of adequate motivation and manipulative skill on the part of local and central leaders capable of initiatives.

Machine Politics in Senegal

William Foltz has given an analysis of politics in Senegal which is consistent with the machine model.[11] It has two principal aspects. The first is an analysis of Senegalese political culture as a modified version of traditional politics in which the principal motivation was the achievement of a position of social honor. Money, according to this interpretation, is not an end in itself but a means for demonstrating one's generosity and worthiness and for attracting a following. Politicians do not amass private fortunes; they conspicuously distribute their income. This kind of motivation does not encourage sound business practices and business is not a major channel of mobility. The traditional road to honor was military prowess and it was destroyed by French colonial peace. Left is politics, and a great deal of Senegalese politics seems to be motivated by the search for honor.

The second aspect of Foltz's analysis is structural. Around each position of honor and authority in the dominant party there form political fractions or *clans* in local parlance. A *clan* is made up of a leader and his dependent-supporters. It can be based on any combination of personal, religious, kinship, interest-group, and ethnic links. The followers tie their fortunes to the success of their leader. Because of the association of authority with personal honor, all opposition to persons in authority is a personal challenge and implies replacement of the person in authority. Therefore, all opposition is factional. Around almost every position of authority in the party are to be found manifest or latent factions. When a political crisis occurs, such as the conflict of December 1962 between the president of the republic and the prime minister, factions break out throughout the party.

11 William Foltz, "Social Structure and Political Behavior in Senegalese Elites," a paper read at the American Political Science Association meeting, Chicago, 1964.

The party in Senegal in this perspective is a pyramid of factions, each led by an entrepreneur of honor. Factions at each level of party organization seek alliances with factions above and below in order to maximize their chances of gaining the honor and patronage of office. Factional fights occur before elections and each year when party cards are sold. They tend to spread downward as potential factions at lower levels ally themselves with the challengers at the higher level in order to benefit should the challenger dislodge the incumbent at the higher level. According to Foltz, one of the rules of the game is that any faction can ally with any other. Another is that losers can attempt a comeback. Such a system spreads the spoils of office, allows widespread political participation, and softens the blows of political defeat.

From the point of view of development, the factional system of Senegal insulates the central government from the effects of its policies and gives it a great deal of flexibility in its search for support. It can always exploit local conflicts in order to gain favor for its policies and projects. On the other hand, the central authorities are obliged to bargain with important leaders of interests and regional machines concerning the actions to be undertaken in their bailiwicks. It becomes very difficult to say whether or when the objective of development has been sacrificed to stable political support.

Foltz's version of the machine model obliges us to revise our earlier assessment of the consequences of development in Senegal based on the analysis of social stratification in the peanut-growing region. The network of factions, it appears, can be led to support policies that threaten the interests of local elites as long as the losses of the local elites are adequately softened by their retention of political offices that give them honor and prestige. However, it is uncertain how far the factional system will enable the government to go in restructuring rural society. Presumably at some point the threat to the interests of local elites would move them into the opposition despite patronage and honor offered by the party. In order to gain some idea of where this point is we must reintroduce the question of the relation of the political system to its social environment, a subject the proponents of the machine model tend to ignore.

PARADOX REGAINED

The paradox of development is perceived by persons with either a theoretical or an ideological interest in the transformation of society. The paradox is encountered when it is asked how a society can get from here to there under political steam. Mobilization, charismatic leadership, colonial and neocolonial systems have been proposed as answers to the query.

The machine model is presented as an answer to a different question, the descriptive question. What model best summarizes the way party governments in Africa actually look? We have seen that there appears to be some validity to both the paradox of development and to the machine model in the case of Senegal. In this final section I propose to clarify the relation of the paradox of development to the machine model. I will conclude that the pluralist critique does reveal ways of dealing with the paradox of development, but that the paradox remains a useful way of stating an important dilemma faced by developing countries.

TIME AND PROCESS

The paradox of development is encountered when one thinks of the transformation of a society over time. The starting point is two different static pictures of society and its government separated by a period of time. The distortion involved in this kind of thinking is comparable to the distortion Carl Friedrich discovers in Max Weber's ideal types of legitimacy.[12] It ignores the fact that legitimation, or in our case the manufacture of support, is a continuous process. The machine model which replies to the descriptive question of how support is maintained comes closer to treating the question of process. As the time of observation is reduced, the degree of social and political change is also reduced. The transformation problem becomes an adaptation problem, but as the process of transformation speeds up, the difference between adaptation and transformation decreases. In the following paragraphs I intend to accept the machine model as an adequate description of the support-generating process in Senegal. The question is how far it can adapt to the exigencies of development.

We have seen that party machines can adapt to a changed social context most readily when the stress generated in different localities is not cumulative, which is the case under conditions of local pluralism, and when existing positions of authority do not come under direct challenge. I suggested that two strategies (localized development and the creation of alternative local political structures) would enhance the adaptivity of the political machine. How far can such adaptation be carried? Let me suggest some propositions which seem reasonable in the light of my research in Senegal.

1. If change is slow enough to allow role change to coincide with replacement of persons in authority, then gradual change and adaptation can be carried very far. The faster the change, the less adaptive is the machine system.

[12] Carl Friedrich, "Some Observations on Weber's Analysis of Bureaucracy," in Robert K. Merton et al., eds., *Reader in Bureaucracy* (New York, 1952), pp. 27–32.

2. Patronage, material rewards, honor, and influence are not universal solvents of commitment. Some positions of authority involve commitments that cannot be bought. In Senegal, Muslim religious authorities can be brought to accept change, but they will fight to maintain the essence of their spiritual hold on their followers, a hold which rests on belief in Islam and in the efficacy of certain marabouts as mediators between Allah and the faithful. (A great deal depends upon how they define the essence of their position.)

Likewise, there are commitments to style and custom which resist sudden change. Only gradually can the style of local political consultation which favors the elites of commerce, religion, and tradition be altered. In villages, for example, the young and the newcomers have relatively weak voices. It is probably easier to create new public arenas with new rules of behavior than to alter the rules in the old arenas.

3. Broad attacks upon the economic position of local elites would provoke strong resistance. Any rigorous nationalization of local commerce and land would probably provoke a united front of opposition from most local elites. On the other hand, adaptation might be possible if the process were stretched out over a couple of generations of local leadership.

These propositions neglect a matter of great importance: Can a machine government put development policies into effect? If the local branches of the machine are strong and protective of their interests, then the central government may not be able to implement development plans. In Senegal the party could not be the major instrument for the application of policy for this very reason, but the administration which is highly centralized seems capable of responding rather well to policy directives. Of course, the opposition of the local political networks to certain policy decisions, their resistance to the application of certain government policies, and their withdrawal of support in response to the implementation of certain policies are really three stages of the same reaction. For the purpose of this discussion we assume the existence of a central government like that of Senegal which claims planned development as one of its objectives.

EXTRA-SOCIETAL SUPPORT

If the preceding argument is correct, it is possible for the machine-style regime to adapt to considerable change, especially if the change is relatively slow. However, the paradox still appears to operate if change is very rapid and if certain key local commitments are transgressed. There is another sense in which the paradox continues to operate. The machine regime would appear to have a relatively low extractive capacity. Because of its need to satisfy local demands and to distribute favors it cannot easily mobilize resources for redistribution according to plans. The modernizing capacity of regimes then is likely to depend in part upon external support. Foreign aid and investment can supply resources for the pursuit of development. The machine regime which plans development requires foreign assistance. It tends toward neocolonial dependence with whatever social structural consequences that implies.[13]

The machine regime may find it possible also to incorporate mobilization in a limited way. In Senegal the Animation Service has some of the functions of a mobilizing party and some of its leaders see it as an instrument for the restructuring of rural society. It hopes to help form a new peasant elite in which progressive policies of rural development will find support. The youth section of the machine party may absorb and try to organize the youthful energy which no longer finds a home in the existing social structure. The problem for the machine is how to keep the youth wing relatively content without giving it much authority. Perhaps this can be done by investing the youths' energies in localized development schemes.

THE PARADOX AND THE POWER STRUCTURE

Even in the pluralistic model the paradox retains validity with respect to the consequences development has for the organization of the political network connecting center and localities. In Senegal factional conflicts in local party sections and subsections tend to be idiosyncratic. They reflect some peculiar local mixture of religious, kinship, and personal conflict. Thus the factional battles in a number of localities have little cumulative effect on higher levels. Discontent is not translated into withdrawal of support for the government. Development policies will change all that. The local population will learn that central policies affect local interests and that they affect the interests of different groups differentially. In Senegal the landless and those without access to private sources of credit should benefit relative to the landed and those having access to private credit. Furthermore, policies of improving transportation and of organizing cooperatives improve the communications among the less organized segment of the population. There should be a tendency for local factions to form around issues of development. When that happens the central government will no longer be insulated from the effects of its policies. A machine regime which is a successful agent of development tends to destroy the conditions of its own existence even if inadvertently.

[13] See Giovanni Arrighi and John Saul, "Socialism and Economic Development," *Journal of Modern African Studies*, VI, 2 (Aug. 1968), 141–170.

Chapter 4 Political Constraints on Economic Development in Ghana

Barbara Callaway
and Emily Card

INTRODUCTION

Because the colonial situation in Ghana created a condition of economic dependence which continues to ensnare the new state, political constraints on the country's economic development can be understood only in the context of the colonial past. Despite political independence, the Ghanaian economy is characterized by continuing, although modified relationships in the colonial model. Kwame Nkrumah, Ghana's first President, denounced neocolonialism and advocated socialism in order to liberate the country's economy from foreign domination. In actuality, however, Nkrumah's policies were directed primarily at consolidating the power of the Convention People's Party (CPP) until such time as he could establish a strong and independent Ghana; and as the CPP struggled with its internal opposition, preserving party power even became an end in itself.

Ghana in 1957 fit the economic model of a colony well: 95 percent of her exports were raw materials and 80 percent of her imports were manufactured goods.[1] A central dilemma in Ghanaian development was how to free the country's economy from foreign domination and break trade relationships that favored the developed countries while at the same time build a strong economic base. The Nkrumah government felt that it needed investment capital to spur economic growth even after independence and the rising level of public expectations concomitant with independence

[1] Walter Birmingham and E. N. Omaboe, *The Structure of Ghana: The Economy* (Evanston, 1966), pp. 334–336.

heightened this need. Investors from abroad did not need to fear possible nationalization because, despite Nkrumah's sometimes flamboyant denunciations of imperialism and his avowedly socialistic statements, his actual policies were clearly pragmatic and conciliatory. His attempt to achieve economic independence while relying upon foreign capital illustrates one of the constraints on political and economic development in Third World nations. The ultimate goal was a socialist economy not dominated by external forces, but during a preceding transition period Nkrumah was forced to accept the idea of a mixed economy.

While these contradictions in Nkrumah's version of socialism facilitated his rise to power, they also, as they became more clearly visible, contributed fundamentally to his fall and to the decline of his party. The CPP, once thought to be one of the more highly organized political parties in Africa, was dissolved by a decree read over the radio; and its dissolution failed to produce even an outcry from the party cadres. It is important to ask how much of the failure of the CPP and its program was due to mistaken tactics or objective errors of judgment, how much to unexpected and unfavorable turns of fate, and how much to an incorrect assessment of neocolonialism and the nature of international capital. In Ghana it is necessary to distinguish between personality and policy, between tactics and ideology, and between economic reality and social necessity.

Part of the CPP's failure can be understood in terms of the party's origins and history as an electoral organization. From 1951, when Nkrumah became Leader of Government Business, to 1957, when Ghana became the first Black African nation to gain its political independence, Nkrumah shared power with the British. During this period, the dyarchy, Nkrumah was dependent upon British supervised elections for the legitimization of his power and that of his party, the CPP. Instead of coming to power through a revolutionary colonial struggle, the CPP successfully fought a series of general elections. Indeed, concern with electoral politics rather than revolutionary action characterized the dyarchy years during which Nkrumah and the Ghanaian public accepted the British definition of the political context. Parliamentary politics was viewed as the legitimate arena of conflict, and the struggle within this context meant that attention was focused upon the CPP's electoral power rather than its capacity to mobilize the population for far-reaching social change. The British made it clear that upon the achievement of independence there was to be a single winner and that in order to be regarded as the legitimate heirs to colonial rule it was necessary to demonstrate not just the usual parliamentary majority but decisive electoral superiority. Indeed, as late as 1956, only one year before independence, the British insisted upon a general election on the grounds that a previous one, held only two years before, had not produced a clear mandate for the party.

Nkrumah's choice was difficult: without the cooperation of the British he could not have come to power unless he was willing to resort to a prolonged armed struggle. He won the electoral struggles but this partially prevented him from constructing an organizational instrument which he could use to initiate fundamental social change. From Nkrumah's point of view, the other options were limited. Organizing for revolutionary struggle in the face of British opposition was extremely difficult. If potential support for armed elimination of the British from Ghana existed, the British undercut it through their strategy of supporting the major nationalist demands. As long as no real struggle occurred, independence meant only shared power, rather than a complete break in British influence, especially in the economic sphere.

Nkrumah's stated goal consisted of economic independence with state control and planning of development; yet the base on which he had to implement this aim, the CPP, was not organized to carry out a policy of economic transformation. Like many nationalist leaders of the Third World nations, Nkrumah viewed a single unified party as the central organization for national development. He hoped that the party-state would unify the nation and create the basis for significant economic change. However, in its struggles with the opposition and in its own internal upheavals, the party lost the capacity for moral and political leadership. After independence, Nkrumah failed to develop the sort of party which would have been necessary to mount an effective national challenge to continued foreign economic domination. Before examining further the economic constraints on political development in Ghana, it is necessary to analyze more fully the failure of the CPP.

THE RISE AND DECLINE OF THE CPP

Upon gaining independence in 1957, Nkrumah embarked upon a program to consolidate the political gains of independence through attempts to strengthen the organizational and legal powers of his Convention People's Party. From 1961 until the assassination attempts of early 1964 and the legal institutionalization of the single-party state, the party attempted to make simultaneous major thrusts toward the development of the economy and mobilization of the population. This dual effort involved establishing new institutional frameworks of political control while expanding state control of the economy. Bureaucracies multiplied, the number of ministries almost tripled, and nearly a hundred specialized agencies were created. Many of these expanded bureaucracies were linked to the CPP as quasi-party/state organizations. Both party and state suffered as the pace of development began to strain staff capacities.

From the beginning the aims of the CPP had centered around the goals of decolonization and expansion of the economy. Yet, even during the years of the nationalist struggle, the CPP had made important compromises with the colonial administration. These compromises meant that, far from stimulating an effective grass-roots movement that could be used to mobilize the masses, the party's appeal was limited to anticolonial nationalism, which lost its galvanizing effect once independence was obtained.[2] Tribal and regional cleavages in the society began to take precedence over the demands of the national regime. The traditional north opposed the leadership of the Westernized south. In the cities, the Moslem Zongos (residential areas) opposed the Christian-led CPP. Tribal groups such as the Ewe, Fanti, Ashanti, Brong, and Ga viewed their needs in tribal rather than class terms. The differing religions, tribes, and regions had potential dissidents on one issue or another. These divisions were in part the consequence of the structure of the CPP which based itself on a wide appeal that contained within it all the cleavages of Ghanaian society. One alternative, a class-based party, was not feasible at that moment in Ghana's history. Given the small size of the urban working class as a potential base for such a party, a major struggle would have been necessary to overcome the tribal cleavages dividing the main class in Ghanaian society, the rural farmers.

The first demands for independence had come from middle-class, educated professionals, who viewed themselves as the logical heirs to colonial rule. Trained and socialized by the colonial regime, their vision of an independent Ghana was one in which they would play the same paternalistic role as the colonial administrators before them, instituting a black "indirect rule" over their less-educated brothers. While the middle-class professionals would control national and international affairs with the continued close cooperation of the British, the chiefs would continue in their role of authority (also instituted by the British). Although the legitimacy of the traditional institution of chieftaincy had been undermined by the imposition of the white man's authority above the chief, the power of individual chiefs had been strengthened by the presence of the colonial regime, which protected them from traditional checks on their power as long as they were its supporters. Thus the chiefs' interests were perceived as being linked to the preservation of the status quo, as were the professional and middle-class intellectuals' interests. Hence, as Nkrumah's new nationalist CPP arose to challenge the professional classes for leadership of the nationalist struggle, an alliance was formed between the professionals and the traditional elite.

Nkrumah, by contrast, cast his appeal to the emerging classes of the new urban environment; and, very importantly, he also thought of the

[2] Frantz Fanon in *The Wretched of the Earth* (New York, 1963) describes this process in general terms.

struggle for independence in mass terms. Not only did he appeal to the "young men," unemployed urban youths and school leavers, but he saw the struggle in terms of creating a nationwide base of voters. The professionals, on the other hand, had always thought only in terms of casting an appeal to a limited class of educated persons.[3] The emergence of the CPP meant that the nationalist struggle was cast in a new light; and the reaction was a fragmenting of the older nationalist party, the United Gold Coast Convention (UGCC), and the later development of essentially regional opposition parties.

This regionally based opposition was formed from a shifting coalition of the same professional and traditional interests which had split from the CPP during the early nationalist struggle. From the first national election in 1951 until the republican election of 1960, regional opposition along several dimensions developed. In the Trans-Volta Togo area the Ewe people demanded independence and then amalgamation with the Ewe in French Togoland; the CPP, on the other hand, wanted to incorporate both British and French Togoland into Ghana.[4] The more tradition-bound Moslem north distrusted Nkrumah's emphasis on a unitary form of government and his development of a radical ideology. The main opposition, however, centered in the cocoa-growing Ashanti areas. The Ashanti demanded a federal rather than a unitary form of government after independence. This opposition had its economic base in cocoa, Ghana's main export crop, 46 percent of which came from the Ashanti region in 1951-52. Cocoa farmers and chiefs in the region could unite over a shared common interest—the price paid to them for their cocoa. The cocoa growers opposed the Cocoa Marketing Board which purchased cocoa from them at a price set below prevailing world market prices. Their resentment also reflected Nkrumah's failure to implement his 1954 campaign promise to pay cocoa farmers £5 per load for their cocoa.[5] In addition, cocoa growers resented the drain of resources from the cocoa-growing regions to the center, where much of the capital obtained from their cocoa went into projects directly under CPP control. With a federal state, it was felt that the cocoa farmers could retain more of the cocoa profits in the region; and such a federal state would provide a base of opposition to the CPP.

Nkrumah's political opposition among the Ashanti professionals recognized the potential advantage of regionally based power for them, and in 1954 they linked with Ashanti cocoa interests to form the opposition National Liberation Movement (NLM) under the leadership of K. A. Busia. The NLM could draw on other interests in common for its basis of support

[3] See David Apter, *Ghana in Transition* (Princeton, 1962), pp. 209–210.
[4] Scott Thompson, *Ghana's Foreign Policy, 1957–1966* (Princeton, 1969), pp. 81–87.
[5] Dennis Austin, *Politics in Ghana: 1945–1960* (London, 1962), p. 278.

in Ashanti society. Not only was the Asantehene the biggest landowner in Ashanti cocoa, but the NLM was also able to draw upon a network of economic relationships which chiefs had built up under British superintendence in the prewar era. Many chiefs had utilized their new wealth to provide superior education for their children during the colonial era; by the end of the Second World War, therefore, a sizable segment of the most highly educated members of the "new elite" had kinship ties with the traditional elite. Both Busia and J. B. Danquah, head of the UGCC, had themselves renounced chieftaincy stools. Given their common economic, political, and social interests, it is not surprising that the chiefs were able to form an alliance with the professional groups in order to oppose Nkrumah and the CPP.[6]

In combating the NLM opposition, the CPP played upon the same regionalism on which the opposition itself was based. In 1956, for example, Nkrumah managed to split the NLM vote when he proposed the creation of a separate region for the Brong, which was an Akan but not an Ashanti group. In the 1956 election the CPP used this issue of Brong separatism to divide the NLM vote in the Brong area of the Ashanti region and thereby managed to deprive Busia's party of much of the Brong vote.

Another element in Nkrumah's strategy was the attempt to inhibit the development of a strong Ghanaian capitalist class which would be a threat to him. Although in the early years the influence of the CPP right wing was so strong as to force Nkrumah to give lip service to the idea of a highly mixed economy, he seemed to feel that it would be safer to coexist with a foreign capitalist class than to face a strongly based incipient national bourgeoisie. Nkrumah needed the right wing for support against the organized opposition centering around regional, ethnic, and occupational groups outside the CPP; he therefore promised Ghanaian businessmen significant government aid.[7] In the same way, although the party's avowed aim was state control of the economy, small-scale Ghanaian private enterprise was not discouraged in official party statements, because Nkrumah needed the support of the urban-based small businessmen, artisans, and shopkeepers in the cities. Nkrumah's dependence upon the middle class meant that programs had to be tailored to fit middle-class interests rather than the interests of the masses whom a true "socialist" regime would be expected to serve.

[6] For an elaboration of this theme see La Rey Denzer, *The National Congress of British West Africa* (unpublished M.A. thesis, University of Ghana, 1965, and David Kimble, *A Political History of Ghana, 1850–1928* (London, 1963). Both studies show that a majority of the founding members of the Aborigines Rights Protection Society (an anticolonial organization formed in 1898) and the National Congress of British West Africa, formed in 1920, were related to traditional rulers. It is maintained here that this interrelationship continues to the present day.

[7] *Parliamentary Debates*, XI (Accra, 18 July 1958).

By the middle of 1960 the opposition parties, independent cooperatives, labor unions, anti-CPP chiefs, and Moslem leaders who had formed the effective opposition had been eliminated or tamed; and the way was clear for Nkrumah to turn temporarily against the right wing of the CPP.[8] The party swing to the left was not to last, however, for the basis for radical political action had not been developed, and Nkrumah found that by mid-1962 he needed the confidence of long-standing personal supporters such as Kojo Botsio and Krobo Edusei to provide the support that could not come from the left, which had no political base.

During the brief period in which the opposition from outside the CPP was able to play an obstructionist role (1957-58), the CPP began to experience internal difficulties of its own. Although the CPP had gained control of the national government, it was becoming clear to one section of the CPP leadership that political mobilization for economic development could never occur in the context of a two-party system, particularly when the opposition, finding itself increasingly powerless, "hastened all the more anxiously to sponsor every outbreak of discontent with CPP rule." [9] While publicly keeping the parliamentary ideal as their model, inner-party councils tentatively began to move toward the creation of a single-party state.[10] One of the first signs of the CPP's new stance was a series of bills providing the regime with wide powers which could be exercised against the opposition. In July 1958, the CPP passed the Preventive Detention Act which provided for imprisonment up to five years without trial. Members of the opposition were soon occupying Accra jails under the provisions of this act and other legislative measures.[11]

Once the electoral opposition had been removed, the party had to combat twin tendencies toward mass apathy and individual aggrandizement by party members. Some single-party regimes have managed to combat these tendencies by transforming themselves into mass mobilization organiza-

[8] Dennis Austin, *Politics in Ghana: 1945-1960*, pp. 402-408.

[9] Austin, p. 311.

[10] See Emily Card, "Voluntary Associations and the Party Auxiliaries in Ghana," a paper presented to the African Studies Association, Los Angeles, 1968.

[11] Other acts included the Investigation of Crime Act which broadened the Attorney General's authority to compel any subject to supply information where crimes against the state are involved; an Offences Against the State Act which gave judges the authority to sentence persons up to fifteen years for making false statements about Ghana; a Sedition Bill which provided imprisonment for up to fifteen years of persons found guilty of intentionally exhorting the overthrow of the government by illegal means or inciting contempt of the government or judical branch; a Criminal Procedures Act which provided for special courts to enact the death penalty for political crimes without trial by jury; and an Emergency Powers Act which gave the president the right to declare a state of emergency by legislative instrument with the approval of the cabinet. In 1962 the attempts on Nkrumah's life resulted in the issuance of emergency regulations which among other things provided for the suspension of habeas corpus. For details of this legislation see Geoffrey Bing, *Reap the Whirlwind* (London, 1968).

tions; for example, in Cuba it appears that the party functions fairly effectively as a local link in the state apparatus.[12] For a variety of reasons, the gap between the CPP's ideal as a mass party and its reality was not overcome.

After 1964, when the CPP became Ghana's only constitutional party and Nkrumah became the lifetime chairman of the party, the ambiguity became more apparent. The "cult of personality" was encouraged, and the CPP became increasingly a political machine.[13] The party's ideology continued to be directed at mobilizing the people for the tasks of national development, but in actuality its dynamics led individuals to vie for positions of influence and power within the party's local branches and various auxiliaries. At the local level in Ghana, then, politics centered more in the party's trade unions, youth associations, marketing associations, and cooperatives than among rival claimants to power from among the local population. Local quarrels and divisions were manipulated to the party's advantage wherever they might occur. Eventually, corrupt party functionaries competing with each other for power in order to manipulate party resources led to popular alienation from the party. This alienation was evidenced by a lack of meaningful public participation in the polity and thus presented a contradiction to the party's own ideology at a time when major social reforms were in theory being attempted. Thus the CPP was a mass party only in the sense that it had a large membership base and could mobilize people for rallies and demonstrations. It failed, however, to bring a large number of politically conscious, committed, and dedicated people into the political arena as active participants. The party lacked both the necessary internal dynamics to prevent stagnation and the organizational capacity to sustain its legal monopoly of power.

The CPP also faced enormous leadership problems which grew out of its attempts to incorporate highly educated professionals into the government (which meant that in the party-state they would hold high party positions) while expanding the party machinery to provide positions for a host of second-echelon leaders. The expansion of the party provided outlets for the political ambitions of numerous party functionaries at the lower levels and provided a means of releasing tensions for leadership roles at the national level. For example, the United Ghana Farmers' Cooperative Council employed over 3,000 regional, district, and marketing officers, secretaries, and receivers, many of whom were political functionaries.[14] However, many of these functionaries were ill-equipped to run the party effectively, and corruption and inefficiency were rampant.

[12] See Lee Lockwood, *Castro's Cuba, Cuba's Fidel* (New York, 1967).

[13] Henry Bretton, *The Rise and Fall of Kwame Nkrumah* (New York, 1968).

[14] *Report of the Commission of Enquiry into the Local Purchasing of Cocoa* (Accra, 1967), p. 137.

After the 1960 elections, the local constituency organizations were no longer needed as electoral machines, since Ghana had become a de facto single-party state. The party branch had never become effectively instituted as the channel for grievances, and many participation needs were still being met by the traditional institutions on the local level.[15] The office of the district commissioner rather than the party secretariat was becoming the center of local operations. In order to revitalize the party as well as implement a new style of social and political life in Ghana, the party placed increasing emphasis on functional wings within the party which took precedence over constituency organizations. These new organizations, which theoretically would link the individual to the party-state, cut across more traditional local ethnic and religious groupings. The most important of these organizations were the Trades Union Congress (TUC), the United Ghana Farmers' Council Co-operatives (UGFCC), the National Council of Ghanaian Women (NCGW), the Ghana Young Pioneers (GYP), and the National Association of Socialist Students' Organizations (NASSO). In these organizations Nkrumah's philosophy, which spelled out the transformation of Ghana into an African socialist society, received much emphasis. The organizations, however, were fraught with the same difficulties the party itself faced, and the CPP became a party with an increasingly frightened and isolated leader presiding over a stagnating political machine, most of whose officials were dazzled by their own successes.

By remaining open to all comers and attempting to draw into itself all factions in Ghanaian society, the party failed to develop a revolutionary consciousness and cohesiveness. The open party meant that as Nkrumah took steps to try to implement "socialist" goals, he met with resistance not only from the civil service, university, judiciary, police, and traditional leaders, but even from officials within the party who were more interested in preserving their own positions of power than in achieving revolutionary goals.

The party's goal of economic and social transformation of the society could have been accomplished through creating a new national sense of purpose. The lack of a real struggle during the preindependence period and the early compromises with the British precluded the nationalist party from transforming itself into a party of revolutionary social change. Its problems were many: lack of dedicated cadres to carry out the ambitious vision of Nkrumah, lack of committed leadership, reliance on local influence networks to carry out national goals, and a decline of Nkrumah's own moral leadership.[16] (In the early days Nkrumah had provided the

[15] See Barbara Callaway, "Local Politics in Ho and Aba," *Canadian Journal of African Studies*, Winter 1970.
[16] In contrast stands the importance of Julius Nyerere's position of moral leadership

model of asceticism for the nation, sleeping as he did in modest quarters in Accra. In the final days Ghana was noted for its palatial presidential residences.) Despite the Dawn speech in April 1961 denouncing corruption, and similar continuing attacks in the press, it was evident that the party was a vast patronage machine; and corruption in high places was a common theme in the "rumor-mongering" in Accra. More important than inefficiency and organizational weakness was the loss of moral reputation by the party: the "Cipipi," once a source of national pride, became a national joke.

ECONOMICS: THE ACCOMPLISHMENTS

In spite of its apparent prosperity, large reserves ($800 million), impressive civil service, and relatively advanced infrastructure, Ghana in 1957 was still very much an underdeveloped, preindustrial, dependent economy which primarily exported raw materials and imported the bulk of its manufactured goods. The economic adviser to the Ghana government during the 1950s, Arthur Lewis, prepared a development plan which stressed economic pragmatism. During the first few years of its independence, Ghana essentially followed this plan, thus reinforcing its status as a neocolonial country.

Ghanaians rather optimistically assumed that after independence Africanization of the administration would mean the end of colonialism and all that it implied. By 1960 the Ghanaian leadership began to perceive that as long as political independence coexisted with economic dependence Ghana could not achieve the nationalists' ultimate objective of self-sustaining economic growth and true political independence. Thus in 1964 the CPP's program for Work and Happiness was translated into the Seven Year Development Plan[17] which set the goal of socializing the Ghanaian economy by giving the state the major role to play in development. Both the development and technical programs of the government and the political activities of the party were geared to achieving this socialistic goal.

Export of cocoa was controlled through the Cocoa Marketing Board. This buying-and-selling export monopoly had been established (along with similar commodity marketing boards in other West African countries) by the British Labour government in 1948 to buy cocoa at less than the world price from competing local producers and resell it on the world market for profit. The surplus price, then deposited in London banks, was held as a sterling balance credited to Ghana's account. During the postwar

---

in Tanzania. See Henry Bienen, *Tanzania* (Princeton, 1967), for a discussion of the role Nyerere's leadership played in the 1964 coup attempt in Tanzania.

[17] *The Seven Year Development Plan, 1963/64–1969/70* (Accra, 1964).

period a general rise in the world price of cocoa ensued, which meant that the prices paid to indigenous producers were generally below prevailing world prices. Cocoa farmers generally received 51 percent of Ghana's cocoa proceeds. The rest were held as low-interest earning reserves credited to Ghana's account. In this way cocoa and other primary products from Africa financed a significant portion of Britain's recovery after the war. It is often assumed that Britain played a major role in the economic advancement of Ghana, "but capital outflow on government account from Britain into Ghana has been of minor importance in her economic advancement. It is rather that Ghana has made substantial investment in Britain through the holding there of most all her foreign reserves." [18] In this way, after independence, Ghana continued to act as a source of foreign exchange for the British just as if it were a colony.

This procedure prevented the growth of a Ghanaian capitalist class centered around the buying and selling of cocoa. What did develop was a class of small businessmen, small contractors, small wholesalers, and small-scale cocoa brokers who aspired to become full-fledged capitalists. This class was frustrated by both the colonial system and by the socialism of the CPP. For example, many wanted loans to help finance African economic enterprises, but foreign banks were not in Ghana to lend money to the potential competitors of the firms they served. In addition, the CPP government became increasingly anticapitalist after 1961. A portion of this commercial group formed part of the right wing of the CPP and provided much of the internal basis for discontent with the policies of the Nkrumah government.

Nkrumah's vision of a socialist Ghana with a diversified and industrial economy, financed to a large extent by direct foreign private investment,[19] was frustrated both by the conservativism of his right wing and the radicalism of his left wing. Nkrumah seemed unable to find a coherent and viable middle ground. Government policy was directed toward securing the necessary private investment to sponsor the government's development plans. The right wing, on one side, felt that government economic policy should directly benefit them and their own private business interests. This group included such crucial advisers as the minister of Finance, K. A. Gbedemah; the director of the Industrial Development Corporation, E.

[18] E. N. Omaboe, "An Introductory Survey," in Birmingham and Omaboe, p. 31.
[19] Kwame Nkrumah, *Building a Socialist State* (Accra, 1963); *Africa Must Unite* London, 1963); and *Blueprint of Our Goal* (Accra, 1964). A similar but much expanded analysis of Nkrumah's economic policies is found in John D. Esseks's "Economic Decolonization in a New African State." Ph.D. dissertation, Harvard University, 1967. This article also benefits from discussions led by Mr. Esseks at the African Studies Association Conference in Los Angeles, October 1968.

Ayeh-Kumi; the editor of the *Guinea Press,* W. Baidoe-Ansah; the CPP Finance Committee chairman, C. C. K. Baah; and the minister of Trade, P. K. K. Quaidoo. Pushing on the left were Nkrumah's personal ideological sympathies and the Marxist-oriented left wing of the party. But Nkrumah was limited in the support he could give the left wing ideologues by his desire to use the technical skill and keep the support of the professionals on the right. The success of the program depended on converting the skilled administrators, intellectuals, and professionals of the right to the government's policy of mobilizing the population for development while imposing constraints on consumpton and consolidating the CPP political power base. Such a task is a complicated one even under the best of conditions, and in the 1960s the Ghana government did not have the best of conditions for carrying out its program.

The "right" did not identify the nationalist struggle with a social struggle. Their goal was to replace foreign influence with African predominance in all fields, but their model remained that of the colonial power. Therefore, they did not want to "Africanize" too quickly because they did not wanted to hinder the smooth functioning of the economy benefiting them. To a certain extent these goals were congruent with those of the left which also want to Africanize; but the model of the left was not the model of the colonial state. Therefore, the solidification of the CPP power base on the left in 1961 destroyed or weakened the allegiance of the intellectuals, civil servants, professionals, and chiefs.

The Seven Year Development Plan sought the use of foreign private capital to finance national development. Both expatriate firms and the Ghanaian government, Nkrumah thought, had an immediate interest in industrializing the Ghanaian economy in order to increase the market for manufactured products and to open up new areas of investment.[20] But Nkrumah knew that his ultimate goal was not that of the foreign powers. In his vision, Ghana was to serve as the center of a gradually industrializing continent. For this reason, his Pan-African policy was intimately tied up with his plans for Ghana's internal economic development.[21] Moreover, because the ultimate aim was socialism, the trade unions were to serve as a means of educating the labor force to the responsibilities of a socialist working class. The unions were not to be concerned with the same issues as their colonial prototypes, but were to play an active part in the general mobilization scheme of the CPP. Labor union leaders were to attend ideological training classes at Winneba and were to provide much of the leader-

[20] At least one economic report written for Western investors supports this contention. See *The Ghana Report,* G. H. Wittman, Inc., International Economic Consultants (New York, 1959).

[21] Thompson, pp. 207, 211, 349, and Roger Genoud, *Nationalism and Economic Development in Ghana* (New York, 1969), pp. 71–72.

ship for the transformation of the Ghanaian working force into socialist workers. Both labor leaders and civil servants were asked to change their orientations in order to restructure and rationalize the Ghanaian economy. Nkrumah felt that socialism in Ghana was necessary in order to gain control over the economy from the foreign firms. The absence of large accumulations of private capital in Ghanaian hands meant that only the state or foreign sources of capital could promote the basic services and industries which are prerequisites of an intensive agricultural and diversified industrial economy. This program of socialism, it was felt, had no internal enemies except those created by colonialism itself. It was the responsibility of the party, then, to attack these vestiges of colonialism and reeducate the population in order to create a socialist mentality.[22] The CPP program did have, however, external enemies in the forces of imperialism and neo-colonialism, which manipulated the economy through their entrenchment in commerce and their control of banking and industry. In order to free the economy from this external domination, the state had to develop an effective program of development in which the major means of production, distribution, and exchange would be brought under state control and ownership.

The government recognized five sectors of the economy which were to work side by side simultaneously during this transition period from a colonial dependent economy to a socialist independent economy. The five sectors initially included state enterprises, enterprises owned by foreign private interests, enterprises jointly owned, cooperatives, and small-scale Ghanaian private enterprise. The ultimate goal was a socialist economy liberated from control by external forces, but for a transitional period the economy was to be mixed. Domestic private enterprise was to be restricted to small-scale businesses, but this assurance was thought necessary, as mentioned earlier, in order not to alienate the small businessmen, artisans, and shopkeepers who formed the core of the CPP's political support in the cities.

The state was to perform essentially the same functions in Ghana as did private entrepreneurs in capitalist countries. The objective was not simply "Africanization" of personnel, but an actual restructuring of the inherited economic forms in which effective control would be gradually acquired through competition by the state against residual private enterprise. A mixed economy would exist for twenty or so years during which time the Ghana government would acquire control over the economy through effective competition with the foreign firms. How successful was this policy?

In 1957 when Ghana became politically independent, all major com-

<hr>

[22] For a development of these arguments, see Bob Fitch and Mary Oppenheimer, *Ghana: End of an Illusion* (New York, 1967), pp. 108–109, and Genoud, pp. 60–70.

mercial sectors of the economy were dominated by expatriates. For example, the seven gold mines, the four diamond quarries, and the one manganese and bauxite mine were foreign-owned.[23] Ten thousand square miles of timber lands were held under 99-year leases by American and European companies.[24] And, finally, 100 percent of the shipping and insurance business was in foreign hands.[25] Also, foreign companies acted as middlemen in the purchase of 67.6 percent of Ghana's cocoa.[26] These foreign firms dominated all important sectors of the economy in a laissez-faire atmosphere in which prices and wages were not controlled, 50 percent of incomes could be repatriated, and few import licenses were required.[27]

For the first five years of Nkrumah's government, 1957-1961, the policy appeared to be one of gradualism, coexistence, and restraint. No direct efforts were made to eliminate foreign influence. During this period of "coexistence" only the Ghana Commercial Bank, founded in 1953, provided serious competition for foreign business enterprises. CPP-affiliated ventures were launched during this time in insurance, shipping, lumber, construction, and cocoa purchasing, but foreign competition to these enterprises was not restricted. At the end of 1961 two state monopolies were established after a relatively long period of experimentation. The Timber Marketing Board was first given a monopoly over the buying of a single type of log from October 1960 to May 1961.[28] It was only after the board had illustrated its efficiency in this sector that it was given a monopoly over the buying of all timber in log form. By the same token, the United Ghana Farmers' Council became the largest purchaser for the Cocoa Marketing Board (buying 28.3 percent of the crop in 1961) before being given a monopoly over the whole crop.[29] As a result of these actions nine cocoa and sixteen foreign-owned timber companies were forced out of business.

The exception to this general policy of restraint was the requirement that all government departments switch their accounts from private firms to the Ghana Commercial Bank, the Ghana National Construction Company, or the National Development Corporation.[30]

During this time local businessmen and small entrepreneurs appeared

---

23 *Report of the Mines Department* (Accra, 1962), Appendix A.

24 *Report of the Commission of Enquiry into Concessions* (Accra, 1961).

25 *Report of the Chairman of the Committee on Aid to Ghanaian Business* (Accra, 1960).

26 *Local Purchasing of Cocoa*, p. 159.

27 *The Ghana Report*, p. 146.

28 *Report of the Commission of Enquiry into the Timber Marketing Board* (Accra, 1968), p. 28.

29 *Local Purchasing of Cocoa* . . . , p. 159.

30 For details on these arrangements, see *Commission to Enquire into the Affairs of NADECO Limited* (Accra, 1966).

optimistic about the economy and about their role in it. But there was pressure from the more militant elements in the party to immediately nationalize the economy through CPP-affiliated cooperative enterprises. Gbedemah, in the Ministry of Finance, and other senior civil servants, however, argued for restraint, stressing that the skilled manpower of the foreign investors was essential for effective economic growth.[31]

The major international pressure for a more pragmatic economic policy during this period, apparently, was the need for massive financing of the Volta River Project. The project would be the key to the future economic development of the country, since electric power was necessary if industrialization was to occur. The project was to consist of a hydroelectric dam at Akasombo on the Volta River and the building of an aluminum smelter and processing plant at Tema in conjunction with the dam. In order to make this particular dream a reality, Nkrumah felt he needed to consolidate his domestic political base as quickly as possible without frightening potential investors in the Volta project. Accordingly, Nkrumah felt that deference to the West and playing the role of a compromising pragmatist was a necessary price to pay to assure the success of this program.[32] Thus the major constraint on Nkrumah and the CPP left wing during this period was not Gbedemah and the right wing as much as it was Lord Jackson, the British economist, who was the director of the Volta River Project. Thompson argues that Lord Jackson was given something of a veto on anything which might compromise financial support for the project. Nkrumah wanted this project safely negotiated and safely inaugurated before adopting more openly radical economic policies.[33]

The second five years of the Nkrumah regime, 1961–1966, saw much growth in the state sector of the economy. The first really significant change in direction came in 1961 when alternate sources of industrial capital were tapped for the financing of the economic development plan. Prior to 1961 Nkrumah had assumed that his only source of foreign capital to finance projects in Ghana was the West. But, after the middle of 1961, six Eastern bloc countries (the Soviet Union, Czechoslovakia, Poland, Hungary, East Germany, and Yugoslavia) offered to help equip state factories through loans which were repayable over a twelve-year period at 3 percent interest.[34]

By this time, too, Nkrumah felt that the Volta financing was assured and that his political position was secure enough that he could afford

---

31 In 1960 48% of the skilled workers employed by the foreign firms in Ghana were non-Ghanaians. *1960 Population Census of Ghana* (Accra, 1964), vol. IV, 36 and 212.
32 Thompson, pp. 26–27.
33 Thompson, pp. 31 and 94.
34 *The Budget, 1965* (Accra, 1965), pt. II, pp. 41–42, and Thompson, pp. 362–364.

to ignore his right wing.[35] Accordingly, Gbedemah and Quaidoo were removed from office and other high party officials were warned to become practicing socialists or forfeit their positions.[36] In October 1960 Nkrumah announced that henceforth all industrial undertakings were to be funded by foreign capital or foreign enterprises in partnership with the Ghana government. The Ghanaian private sector was to be phased out.[37] Phasing out of Ghanaian private enterprise while allowing for foreign investment to continue is illustrative of Nkrumah's desire to inhibit the development of a national bourgeoisie in Ghana.

Shortly after this, in February 1962, the Kaiser Aluminum and Reynolds Metal Company officially agreed to raise $128 million for the Volta River Project's smelter plant. The United States, Great Britain, and the World Bank pledged another $98 million for the dam and the hydroelectric station on the Volta river.

Once the Volta project was secured and the government was no longer dependent on foreign capital resources, the CPP's economic policies were limited in effect only by the lack of skilled manpower with which to staff state concerns. This lack resulted in a lowering of standards and quality of service. Two exceptions to this general state of affairs were the Ghana National Trading Company (GNTC) and the State Insurance Corporation (SIC). The GNTC was established in November 1961 and inherited the staff of a well-established private firm which agreed to sell out and merge with the GNTC (Leventis). The SIC, established in February 1962, also bought out two private firms and took over their experienced staff (the Ghana Insurance Company and the Ghana General Insurance Company). This arrangement thus maintained the economic ties which permitted Britain to use Ghana as a source of investment and a place to find employment for her skilled manpower. Also, after 1962, East European countries made personnel available on secondment to Ghana state enterprises.

In the fields of importing, banking, insurance, construction, and shipping, the government hoped, then, to nationalize by gradually squeezing out its competition. By 1966 the State Insurance Corporation conducted 50 percent of all insurance business in Ghana,[38] the Ghana Commercial Bank held 63.6 percent of total deposits held by commercial banks in Ghana,[39] and the Black Star Line (established with the help of Israeli capital in 1957) carried 17 percent of Ghana's sea commerce.[40] In addition the

[35] Genoud, p. 110.
[36] Kwame Nkrumah, *Dawn Broadcast* (Accra, April 1961).
[37] *Ghana Times*, Accra (10 Oct. 1960).
[38] *The Budget Statement, 1966* (Accra, 1966), p. 3.
[39] *Economic Survey, 1965* (Accra, 1966), p. 135.
[40] Ibid., p. 90.

Ghana National Construction Company (GNCC) employed 70 percent of those in construction work.[41] Eighty percent of the work done by the GNCC was on state projects, but the GNTC, the Black Star Line, the SIC, and the Ghana Commercial Bank all conducted a considerable private business in addition to all the state work assigned them.

The United Ghana Farmers' Co-operative Council had successfully monopolized internal cocoa purchasing by 1962. Also, between 1961 and 1966 the government had established fifteen manufacturing enterprises and begun construction on twenty-six others. These enterprises were producing 27 percent of Ghana's manufacturing output by 1965.[42] By the beginning of 1966, before he was overthrown, Nkrumah had succeeded in impressive nationalization of significant sectors of the Ghanaian economy. In cocoa purchasing, commercial banking, insurance, mining, importing, manufacturing, and overseas shipping, the CPP's policies appeared to be working successfully.

A shift in emphasis in government expenditures after 1958–59 indicates Nkrumah's increasing commitment to industrialization rather than agricultural development as the path to development. In the late 1950s transportation and communication accounted for by far the greatest part of the total government development expenditures, about 40 percent of the total per year. A difficulty here was that while infrastructural development was essential for future industrialization, it was not capital-producing investment and added to the growth of a very large internal debt for projects which were not revenue producing. In the years 1962–1965 there was a further shift in emphasis and a sharp increase in direct government investment in agriculture, fisheries, and industrial projects while imports were significantly decreased. Most of these projects were financed through the issuing of stocks and bonds, national development bonds, Cocoa Marketing Board bonds, and treasury bills.

During the ten-year period, 1955–1965, Class I roads increased 46 percent and Class II roads increased 60 percent.[43] Ghana had doubled its production of electricity before the opening of the Volta dam. The dam itself created the largest inland lake in the world. This lake was to become the center of a modern Ghanaian fishing industry and provide water for irrigation of extensive agricultural projects on the Accra plains. Tema Harbour, built at a cost of £27 million, is the largest artificial harbor in Africa.

In the field of education, also, the Nkrumah legacy was on the surface impressive. In 1964, 1.4 million students, or 18 percent of the population, were in school. The enrollment in primary schools increased 200 percent

[41] Ibid., p. 92.
[42] *Economic Survey*, 1966 (Accra, 1967, p. 63.
[43] Genoud, pp. 109–110.

during the Nkrumah years; that of middle schools increased 140 percent; secondary schools increased their enrollment figures by 440 percent; and, most significantly of all, university enrollment increased 480 percent. However, rather than emphasize learning for development, this schooling by and large remained of the traditional British variety. Ironically, rather than use the educational system to "create socialists," this task was left to an increasingly demoralized political party while the educational system continued to produce a potential elite not in tune with the goals of the government.

POLITICS AND ECONOMICS: THE COSTS

If the main advantage of the CPP program was to gain significant control of its own economy, the disadvantage was to be found in the dislocations of goods and services, the reductions in the volume and/or quality of goods and in the services produced, a decline in the general growth rate of the country, and massive political discontent.

Nkrumah had hoped that state enterprises would be able to compete effectively with the private sector. But every sector of the economy into which the state entered was marked by a significant decline. For example, state printing firms averaged only one-half the productivity of private firms; public electricity firms were much less efficient and much more expensive than were private ones; and in construction and lumber the public firms had the lowest rate of productivity in the industry.[44] Between 1961 and 1965 gold production dropped 19 percent. A large part of this loss, however, is explained by the fact that the Nkrumah government bought out several exhausted and depleted British mines in 1963 and worked them at a considerable loss in order to save the jobs of some 10,000 unskilled workers.[45] During the same time period timber earnings were down some 44 percent, but this was due in part to a decline in the world market price,[46] There was also a serious shortage of consumer and producer goods during these years in spite of rationing and detailed import licensing which had been introduced to fight inflation and the depletion of foreign exchange reserves. Because of rising expectations the government attempted to keep consumption high while carrying out its development policies. It was not able to demand sacrifices in consumption of consumer goods partly because the party found itself unable to initiate significant social change.

Other factors contributing to the decline of the regime were the effects

[44] Tony Killick, "Labour: Industrial Labour Productivity in Ghana," in Walter Birmingham, I. Neustadt, and E. N. Omaboe, eds., *A Study of Contemporary Ghana*, (Evanston, 1966), p. 170.

[45] Tony Killick, "Mining," in Birmingham et al., pp. 257–262.

[46] *Economic Survey*, 1963 (Accra, 1964), p. 46.

of a lack of clear priorities, cumbersome administrative procedures, and general inefficiency and corruption which permeated the state enterprises.[46a]

The growth rate of the economy between 1961 and 1965 of 3 percent per annum was poor. By 1965 the real growth rate had declined to 0 percent.[46b] The investments from private foreign capital that Nkrumah had envisioned were not forthcoming. Historically, the principal foreign investment in Ghana (as elsewhere) has been that of the commercial firms whose main business was the importation of British manufactured goods for retail sale in Ghana. Much of the foreign "manufacturing" in Ghana consisted of these firms lowering the cost (and hence raising the profits) of imported commodities through processing, assembling, or packaging in Ghana. Eighty-five percent of Ghana's manufacturing falls into this category.[47] Special import privileges for this class of goods made it very profitable for the foreign firms to engage in this type of processing while inhibiting the development of an integrated manufacturing sector in Ghana.[48]

Despite considerable inducements and concessions on the part of the government in order to insure profits for investors, new capital was not forthcoming and there was a net outflow of private capital during these five years.[49] Tax relief was provided for foreign investors for as long as it took to recover the initial investment. But the only firms interested were the big merchants already firmly established. In part this was also due to the radicalization of the Ghanaian press after 1961 and its domination by the left wing of the party. The attacks on potential overseas investors in the Ghanaian press insured that these investors would be even more hesitant about investing in Ghana.

State outlays in manufacturing did not compensate for the decline in activity in the private sector. The result was that many factories were idle due to a lack of materials, materials which had to be imported using scarce foreign exchange. Such importations, while necessary for Ghana's "manufacturing," would also continue the dependency relationship out of which the economy was trying to break. In 1965 only two of fifteen state manufacturing endeavors were making a profit.[50] At the end of 1965 thirty-five of sixty-four state factories had been financed with foreign credits which

---

[46a] *Report of the Commission of Enquiry into Trade Malpractices in Ghana* (Accra, 1966).

[46b] *Economic Survey, 1966* (Accra, 1967) p. 57.

[47] See Jean M. Due, "Agricultural Development in the Ivory Coast and Ghana," *Journal of Modern African Studies*, vol. 7, no. 4 (Dec. 1969), pp. 637–60.

[48] See Fitch and Oppenheimer, p. 89, and Genoud, p. 136.

[49] Fitch and Oppenheimer, p. 93.

[50] *The Budget, 1965*, pt. IV, p. 45.

had to be paid either in scarce hard currency or in export surpluses to East European countries.[51]

The final calamity for Nkrumah's strategy for the Ghanaian economy came with the decline in the world price of cocoa. Between 1958 and 1964 world consumption of cocoa increased at an average annual rate of 5.7 percent while production rose by 7.8 percent. As a result the world price of cocoa dropped steadily from 39 cents per pound to 22 cents. Over the same period cocoa production in Ghana increased by 12.6 percent annually, thus raising its share of world production from 26 to 35 percent. The final breakdown in prices occurred in 1964–65 when world production increased by more than 25 percent; Ghana accounted for half of the increase. By July 1965, just six months before Nkrumah fell, the world price of cocoa was 12 cents a pound, almost half the average of the preceding year.[52] Cocoa, which accounted for an average of 64 percent of Ghana's foreign exchange earnings, appeared to offer no hope as a basis for capital formation. Production increases could barely keep up with world price declines. In 1965 the drop was so drastic that Ghana's foreign exchange reserves came close to extinction.[53]

Even in the case of gold, Ghana was not in a position to benefit from price stability. Gold price controls eliminated Ghana's effective competition. Such is the case in many developing countries with rare gems or precious metals. Income is tightly controlled by international corporations which can use their access to world markets as sources of political leverage within the producing countries. The position of the gold-producing companies is so strong that they can hold down local wages while maintaining their profits. This is particularly significant because gold miners compose 32 percent of the skilled work force in Ghana and 15 percent of the workers employed in the private sector. In this sector real wages have not risen since 1938. Low wages prevent or retard the growth of demands for consumer goods and this affects the growth of the manufacturing sectors.[54]

An increasing balance of payments deficit, dwindling reserves, and the failure to attract foreign investment or to find alternatives for it had grave repercussions for the Nkrumah regime. In 1961 the budget deficit was £35 million or 12 percent of the national product.[55] By 1965 the deficit was $135 million, or 40 percent of government revenue. Greatly increased demands for imported nondurable goods and the rising costs of invisibles such as shipping costs and freight insurance greatly strained the economy. Ghana found that in the 1960s it had to use the $800 million reserve accu-

[51] *The Budget, 1965*, pt. II, pp. 40–42.
[52] Tony Killick, "External Trade," in Birmingham et al., pp. 345–348.
[53] *The Ghana Report*, pp. 44–47.
[54] Tony Killick, "Mining," in Birmingham et al., pp. 131 and 264.
[55] Fitch and Oppenheimer, p. 91.

mulated in the 1950s to meet a skyrocketing balance of payments deficit
rather than for investment in capital-producing projects.

After 1961 (and prior to 1966) foreign capital poured in to the amount
of £168 million. But £157 million of this amount was in the form of "suppliers credits" (or contractor financing) with the bulk of repayments concentrated within 4 to 6 years.[56] This form of financing, in which the
contractor arranges the financing, is a major source of exploitation in
African countries. Such financing is not usually accompanied by centralized planning in the host country. It results in the sale of inferior or obsolete goods and services to African countries. In this way Ghana bought
obsolete West German textile equipment for which parts were unavail-
able, tractors from the Soviet Union which could not be serviced in Ghana,
and a £5 million submarine chaser from Great Britain. In 1966 Ghana owed
Drevici, the West German financier, £60 million in credits.[57]

In 1965 the interest and principal due on Ghana's foreign debts reached
$128 million.[58] Thus, by the end of 1965, the attempt to free Ghana's
economy from foreign domination through cooperation with foreign investors (private and government) ironically had the result of placing the
country even more at the mercy of its creditors, which potentially would
have meant more influence for foreign capital than ever before in Ghana's
history. This is particularly true in view of the fact that most debts of
private capital in Ghana were *guaranteed* by governments.

Nkrumah's policies, in combination with economic circumstances beyond his control (given the context within which he decided to operate),
contributed to an erosion of political support. Bad working conditions,
low wages, and high unemployment all helped to explain in part the failure
of the CPP's political and economic programs. Political support for the
party was further eroded when the indirect taxes on coffee, tea, tobacco,
cloth, vegetables, and fish increased some 50–100 percent in 1961. Also, in
1961, a 5 percent compulsory savings tax was placed on all incomes in
excess of £150 per year.[59] The timing could not have been worse for this
tax which was imposed during a period of falling real wages, rising prices,
and increasing unemployment. The response of the government to mounting labor unrest at its policies was to launch an ideological campaign in
which labor was to play a leading role.[60] By March of 1964 local food
prices had increased 400 percent from the 1961 level and the average rise

[56] *West Africa* (9 Oct. 1965), p. 1123.
[57] See *Legion Observer*, Accra, 1969–70, and Douglass A. Scott, "External Debt-
Management in a Developing Country," in Tom J. Farer, ed., *Financing African Development* (Cambridge, Mass., 1965), p. 55.
[58] *The Budget, 1965*, pt. II, pp. 41–43.
[59] Fitch and Oppenheimer, p. 102.
[60] John Tettegah, *Towards Nkrumahism* (Accra, 1962).

in prices across the board was 17 percent.[61] Thus, by 1966, Ghana was on the verge of bankruptcy in spite of Nkrumah's alleged assertion that he had never heard of a country being liquidated. Ghana may not have been liquidated, but after the coup it was placed in a type of receivership out of which the new regime has yet to climb.

The political costs of this program were enormous. The Cocoa Purchasing Company was riddled with corruption, speculation, bribery, and outright intimidation which alienated nearly 300,000 cocoa farmers from the regime.[62] The Ghana National Trading Company was resented by the 5,000 Ghanaian wholesalers who were virtually forced out of business and the hundreds of thousands of petty retailers who could not get access to imported commodities without paying bribes to the various GNTC agents. The Ghana National Construction Company preempted virtually all private contractors in Ghana and here, too, a significant segment of the population was alienated from the regime.

In addition to these difficulties, the government was dependent on civil servants, whose sympathies toward radical programs were at best indeterminate, to carry out the program of a highly ideological political party. The civil servants were "British-trained" and their commitment to the CPP was questionable. In the financial sphere the government found itself dependent on foreign capital to carry out a radical program and in the administrative sphere dependent on competent, but "nonpolitical," civil servants rather than on committed socialist administrators. For these reasons the CPP failed both politically in its aim of stimulating participation and mobilization and administratively in its program of socializing the economy. The whole purpose of the mobilization efforts of the CPP was to educate the people to the sacrifices they had to make for development. The party was to furnish the communications link that could transmit the desires and problems of the population into party actions. The lack of support for Nkrumah, then, was due to questionable economic policies and a nonrevolutionary, unsuccessful attempt at political mobilization.

There was also a frustrating dichotomy in the development of the country's economy. The more earnest the government's program of economic

---

[61] *West Africa* (19 Feb. 1966).

[62] *Local Purchasing of Cocoa* and the *Commission of Enquiry into the Cocoa Purchasing Company, Ltd.* (Jibowu Commission) (Accra, 1966). "Farmers often referred to opulence of UGFCC secretaries and other officers who earned £180 per year and owned Mercedes, Peugots, transport trucks and supported numerous wives. In Ashanti £G 500–1000 was required before agreeing to establish societies in villages" (p. 20). Cocoa smuggling was a reaction to the general disillusionment with the party personnel at this level. In 1965 fully 1/5 of Ghana's cocoa crop was smuggled out of the country. Officials at all levels were corrupt. Party funds were used to pay personal debts and such an open display of dishonesty created public cynicism. (*The Convention People's Party: Report of a Special Audit Investigation*, Accra, 1967.)

development became after independence, the more it had to postpone day-to-day economic benefits. At a time when the party was demanding austerity and patience on the part of the public, party and government officials were becoming openly corrupt and living far above the level of the average Ghanaian. The party had created a new elite of its own which became quickly accustomed to recently acquired consumption standards.[63]

Another contradiction was that Nkrumah hoped to derive maximum benefit from the continued development of a private, mostly foreign, sector of the economy. This policy required that the private sector be allowed to function in its normal capitalistic fashion, that is, that profits be repatriated and employees of the foreign firms be allowed to continue to live at their accustomed comfortable level. This concession to the neo-colonial situation, however, alienated both the lower classes and the right-wing Ghanaian businessmen who could not compete. In addition to this alienation of the more "modern" elements in Ghanaian society, the CPP also succeeded in bypassing and thus frustrating the more traditional elements. The chiefs found their power further eroded by a party that considered them willing tools of colonialism. In their frustration with local-level functionaries of the party, however, the people began turning more and more to their traditional leaders for guidelines on the redress of wrongs at the local level. Thus there was an upsurge of the influence of traditional leaders in local affairs.[64]

When these problems are added to those of the lack of skilled and dedicated manpower, the scarcity of investment capital, and the conflict between the local businessmen and the left-wing socialists of the CPP, it is evident that the policies of the CPP were not destined for success. Thus, while the state did regain control of the economy in the significant areas of banking, insurance, construction, and importing, and while an impressive infrastructure was laid and a pool of manpower created, the cost in terms of the dissipation of political support, the misuse of resources, and the reinforcement of a basically neocolonial position was exorbitantly high.

CONCLUSIONS

One of the most impressive accomplishments of the Nkrumah regime

[63] As Krobo Edusie, Nkrumah's minister of Communications and Transport, whose wife gained notoriety in attempting to import a solid gold bed into Ghana, once remarked, "Socialism doesn't mean that if you've made a lot of money, you can't keep it." Quoted in Fitch and Oppenheimer, p. 112.

[64] The new 1969 constitution recognizes the continuing importance of traditional leaders by providing that 2/3 of district councils under the new regime will be traditional members and that each of the nine regions will have a Regional House of Chiefs. Thus, there is a reemergence and solidification of the interests represented by the intellectuals and chiefs.

was the enormous growth in the infrastructural apparatus of Ghana. But this growth also had its built-in contradictions, since it required a corresponding growth in the administration and larger recurrent budget expenditures. There was a growing and inefficient and often incompetent administration contributing to an increasing deficit in budget financing. The tasks this administration was asked to perform were beyond its administrative capacity, which resulted in increasing inefficiency as the demands on the system became greater.

After 1961 the falling prices of cocoa and the rising demands for consumer goods presented hard choices for the Ghana government. This increase in demands was met by an attempt at austerity, an increase in forced savings, and a decrease in the availability of goods. At the same time, Nkrumah failed to develop a mass-based party to absorb the political and economic dislocations resulting from the government's policies.

Ghana's predicament typifies a paradox within many African states. Just as the demands for development and its implications in terms of goods and services increased, the world market for primary products, which are 95 percent of Ghana's exports, began to sag. Once this occurred the options open to the developing economy narrowed and Ghana became a victim of cycles outside its control. The Nkrumah government opted for tighter economic and political controls, but the intensity of the strain on the economy and the nature of the opposition to Nkrumah undermined the possibility of success. At a time when the economy was being closed, political options were also being closed off as the party became suppressive to an increasing number of Ghanaians. Nkrumah's government had further created false hopes by offering an alternative that promised social progress which it could not deliver, a problem faced by other African "socialist" governments.

An attempt to gain control of the economy and to give the impetus for planning and direction to the government could only be successful to a limited extent, because the very nature of the economy was one of dependence. Ghana depended on the demands of the world market for its earnings and on foreign investment for capital. The economy was fragile at best and its vulnerability seemed to increase as the economy was brought under control. Ironically, as the public sector of the economy was expanded by the central government it became more dependent on reserves and debtor financing to carry out its program, thus becoming more vulnerable to outside pressure. Most of Ghana's loans were guaranteed by the country of the supplier's origin, thereby putting political pressure on Ghana to remain within the "gentlemanly" rules of the Western political game at tremendous cost to herself.

Fluctuations in the world price of cocoa, the dependence on external credit, the necessity to support imports with dropping cocoa prices, and drastic changes in the balance of payments led to internal shortages, rising consumer prices, and massive unemployment. The policy options available to the government to meet these problems were slight in comparison to the nature and size of the problems. Given the magnitude and nature of world economic forces, would a program aimed at the growth of socialism before development eventually have collapsed regardless of the leadership and the effectiveness of the political program? Are underdeveloped countries and Third World nations doomed to their situations as long as their economies are dependent on outside forces? Considering how limited were his options, how successful was Nkrumah in gaining control of his economy?

After 1962 in Ghana the government found it necessary to introduce increased austerity programs at the same time that it was trying to continue with its ambitious development programs in the face of the deterioration of export prices. The lack of dedication to these measures by scores of party and government personnel, the rise in socioeconomic tensions, and the general bankruptcy of the regime handicapped Nkrumah and the CPP before the benefits of their programs were evident and when the costs were highest. The success of the program depended on the ability to invest large sums in development projects without restricting consumption. These resources were not available and the price in political terms was high. The CPP was eroded from within while proving unable to meet the challenges from without.

The intellectuals, in alliance with the chiefs, the civil service, and the army and police [65] form a formidable core of alienation for any regime, but more particularly for one caught in economic forces of a neocolonialist nature. In addition to alienating the right in Ghanaian terms, the party also was eroding its support on the left. The trade unions were held in check and were not allowed to express their discontent, and the party's "socialists" had to be content with their control of the press and the ideological propaganda machine of the party, and with positions in the second echelon of leadership.

Until the end Nkrumah depended on a close circle of foreign advisors and personal friends to keep the system functioning at the top. In order to control the party, power increasingly became fragmented and each element counterchecked another element. Pragmatic politicians such as Krobo Edusei, Kojo Botsio, and Henry Boateng kept the "socialist boys" at a distance while they occupied top positions in the party and in the government. As the difficulties increased, Nkrumah's personal power also

[65] Two books which explain in detail the disillusionment of the army and police with the Nkrumah government are Brigadier A. A. Afrifa, *The Ghana Coup* (London, 1968), and Major General A. K. Ocran, *A Myth is Broken* (London, 1968).

increased.[66] This increase in personal power was the antithesis of the socialism Nkrumah promised. He was not able to break colonial ties as the economy remained essentially capitalist in form. State factories and corporations were run at a loss and state economic planning was ineffective. With rising unemployment, rising prices, and scarcities of essential items, disillusionment with the whole economic and political apparatus characterized Ghana.

As the CPP lost its social base, no one group had a vested interest in the survival of the regime. This situation in part explains how such an extensive and highly organized party as the CPP could be dissolved by a simple proclamation over the radio on the morning of 24 February 1966. The press, which had been the main vehicle of the "cult of personality," became overnight dedicated to the destruction of the "myth of Kwame Nkrumah."

Another contradiction in the CPP policies and program was that the attempt to create a socialist state resulted in a deepening division between the urban and rural classes in Ghana. Undue emphasis on industrialization tends to widen the gap between the incomes of the rural and urban population, and the urban population becomes a relatively privileged one. Thus many socialist states have begun to recognize the need for an agricultural development base. Tanzania has, since President Julius Nyerere's Arusha Declaration, moved in this direction. The gulf between higher civil servants and party personnel, the managers of the state corporations, and the professionals and technicians in Ghana on the one hand, and the great mass of workers and petty traders, farmers, and fishermen on the other, widened after independence. The unpopular austerity policies were introduced at a time when the "conspicuous consumption" of numerous party and government personnel was evident for all to see.[67] What was called socialism in Ghana appeared to widen rather than lessen the gulf between the rich and the poor.

Nkrumah correctly perceived that Ghana's economy was weak and dependent in spite of its apparent wealth at independence, and that the foreign firms which dominated the economy were only small branches of much larger international organizations.[68] He hoped to gain control of Ghana's economy and break the neocolonial ties by building up the infrastructure in preparation for industrialization.[69] Socialism in Nkrumah's terms meant

[66] For an informative detailing of this development, see Bretton, *The Rise and Fall of Kwame Nkrumah.*

[67] For a documentation of the various manifestations of this "conspicuous consumption," see the numerous commissions of enquiry reports of the National Liberation Council, particularly the Jiagge, Sowah, and Manyo-Plange reports.

[68] Kwame Nkrumah, *Neo-Colonialism, the Last Stage of Capitalism* (London, 1965).

[69] Genoud, pp. 218–226.

freedom from foreign economic exploitation and the reconstruction of the society in order to increase social justice and equality. Nonetheless, Nkrumah's strategy of decolonization failed in spite of what appears to be a correct analysis of the nature of the problem, the formulation of a strategy to deal with it, and reasonably effective implementation. Why?

Several aspects of the answer to this question are suggested in this paper. The political failure is evident. The launching of an ideological campaign to answer real grievances while the party became more corrupt and while economic tensions increased was a serious tactical mistake, for it increased cynicism and alienation in every major section of the population. The great bureaucratization of the party at the top and the failure to secure the support or participation of the people at the bottom was a great mistake. As the economic difficulties increased, it was more imperative than ever that avenues of expression remain open. The decision to accelerate the development program in spite of the falling price of cocoa and dwindling reserves created more tensions than the regime could handle.

Ghana's experience was an attempt to decolonize and claim its colonial economy. Decolonization of significant sectors of the economy was understood in Ghana as being a prerequisite for development. This development was to lead to the creation of a modern socialized and industrial state.

CPP pragmatism, which defined itself as socialism, presented a set of techniques and institutions which enabled the government to think it could make rapid economic progress and achieve economic independence in spite of its colonial heritage and continued neocolonial relationships. The theme that foreign investment could still play a creative role in a socialist economy proved questionable.[70] In theory each sector had its role to play, the rule being that the rate of growth in the state sector should always exceed that of the private sector. But there would be no nationalization of foreign capital in Ghana.[71] Ghanaian capitalists would be regulated, not eliminated. Most of the CPP leaders thought that socialism did not require sweeping changes in the social relations of production. They thought that state ownership of the major means of production would lead to socialism, that the state sector would gradually overcome the private sector, and that foreign private capital would let itself be used to build a socialist state. The CPP, however, lacked the mass base and the degree of economic control necessary to establish the dominance of the state sector. After 1961 Ghana's reserves were exhausted, and so its program depended entirely on the inflow of foreign capital on a scale without precedent.[72]

The very nature of the options chosen by the state led it to reinforce

[70] *The Work and Happiness Program* (Accra, 1957), paras. 105–106.
[71] *Economic Bulletin of Ghana*, vol. IX, no. 1, 14.
[72] Tony Killick, "External Trade," in Birmingham et al., p. 359.

colonial patterns. Developments continued to center around the cities and along the coasts; trade continued to be determined by the nature of the world market; and Ghana continued to be dependent on outside forces for the capital for its internal development. The dilemma and contradiction in Ghana very quickly focused on the inability of the regime, professing to be socialist, to attract foreign capital, not the danger that too much foreign capital would dominate the economy internally. Ghana wanted to reduce its dependent status when it was most in need of external assistance. Its "socialist" strategy, which relied on financing from the West, was its own contradiction.

Fitch and Oppenheimer advance the argument that Ghana's attempt to break with the colonial past economically was too little and too late.[73] Other Western economists have argued that there was too much socialist bloc help and too much state interference in the economy. We maintain that Nkrumah lost his opportunity partly because, despite his ideological commitment to socialism, he did not have a vanguard party on which he could rely if he wished to nationalize the economy. Ghana's long dyarchy, 1951–1957, tempered Nkrumah, who basically followed a restrained policy both internally and internationally. He could have chosen the "conservative path" of development as did Houphouet-Boigny of the Ivory Coast; he could have envisioned development schemes based on diversification and growth of the agricultural base (Tanzania); or he could have opted for the "radical path" and become a committed member of the socialist camp. As the first independent African state and one of the few with real immediate development potential, Ghana was in a position to bargain for socialist cooperation, especially from the Soviet Union, which might possibly have put Ghana in a position similar to that of Cuba. Cuba, with a population about the size of Ghana's, has received a price from the Soviet Union for its primary export, sugar, which provides a basis for economic development. In 1968 Cuba received $365 million over the world price from the Soviet Union for its sugar.[74]

In the early 1960s, given the cold war situation and the relative concern with Africa's possible shift to communism, Nkrumah might have managed to make Ghana an African showplace by truly breaking with the West and courting the East.[75] Instead, few new economic directions were really established. Ghana remains a neocolonial state, more closely bound than before to its creditors.

[73] Fitch and Oppenheimer, p. 84.
[74] Lockwood, p. 92.
[75] Genoud, pp. 135–140.

Chapter 5 The Cabinet and Presidential Leadership in Tanzania: 1960-1966

R. Cranford Pratt

This essay seeks to clarify the position of the cabinet in Tanzania during the period 1960 to 1966, to trace the changes in the use made of the cabinet by President Nyerere, to note how these changes have affected the relationship of the cabinet to other major political and governmental institutions, and to offer an explanation for these developments.

On 1 July 1959 five elected members of Tanganyika's Legislative Council became the first elected members of the Council of Ministers. In September 1960 the British conceded responsible government in Tanganyika. On 1 May 1961 the Tanganyikans won full internal self-government and on 9 December 1961 Tanganyika became fully independent. During this brief period of thirty months the British installed in Tanganyika a system of government which was very much a copy of the Westminster model.

Nyerere and his colleagues thus came to power within a governmental system in which the central decision-making institution was the cabinet. By May 1961 all of the members of the cabinet were members of parliament and almost all of these members were elected rather than nominated members; each cabinet minister was individually responsible to parliament for the administration and for the detailed policies of his ministry; the members of the cabinet were collectively responsible to parliament and to the country for the major policies of the government.

Nyerere did not object to these institutions. Prior to 1962 he worked hard to assure the acceptance by his colleagues of the conventions on which their effective operation depended. For example, he agreed that the independence constitution should include articles entrenching the autonomous position of the Public Service Commission, the Judicial Service

Commission, and the Police Service Commission. Nyerere acquired for himself, first as chief minister and then as prime minister,[1] only a very limited portfolio of responsibilities, relying on his leadership within the cabinet to achieve the influence he wished to have on government policies. His first circular as chief minister, in October 1960, expounded in near-classical terms the need to keep the civil service out of politics and the politician out of the bureaucracy. He wrote: "Political parties, and therefore members of the Legislative Council, can certainly play their part in ensuring a good public reception of Government's policies. But I repeat that the responsibility for carrying out Government policies lies with the civil service." [2]

The lack of a well thought out alternative system and a strong desire not to complicate the constitutional negotiations with Britain are the major part of any explanation of this early acceptance of the Westminster model. But these factors are not in themselves sufficient; they do not explain the vigorous efforts made to assure that the inherited system worked according to its inner logic. Although the cabinet system was a British legacy, it met several immediate and obvious requirements in Tanganyika and was accepted by Nyerere and his colleagues as an appropriate institution through which to exercise governmental power.

The cabinet system provided an effective way to bestow high office upon comparatively inexperienced nationalist leaders without directly inserting them into senior positions within the bureaucracy. Thus there could be incontrovertible evidence of African control without that control being too disruptive to the administrative structure. The cabinet system was also a particularly appropriate way to bring the senior civil service into effective relationship with the political leaders. In few political settings is this more valuable than in a country in which the political leaders have had very little government experience and in which the senior civil servants are almost all expatriates. Moreover, a cabinet of ministers was compatible with Nyerere's unpretentious style of leadership. Nyerere was neither an insecure leader who dared not share power nor a self-important man who would not. A cabinet therefore seemed, and indeed was, an appropriate institution through which to involve his senior colleagues in major policy decisions.

There is one final important factor. Nyerere was certainly the unquestioned leader of the Tanganyika African National Union. The speed with which independence was won further increased his prestige and his popu-

---

[1] The title of prime minister was used after the achievement of internal self-government in May 1961.

[2] *Chief Minister's Circular No. 1 of 1960*. Government Printer, Dar es Salaam (1960), p. 3. This circular is reprinted in *Journal of African Administration*, vol. XIII, no. 2 (April 1961), pp. 108–111.

larity. However, he was not the sole leader in TANU. His colleagues included men of real political importance. Some of them were important because of their popularity within the party. Others were the accepted political leaders of a major tribe, a religious community, or an important cooperative or trade union. These men were united by their commitment to nationalism and to the early achievement of independence. However, they had made little effort in the 1950s to develop alternative policies which they would seek to introduce once they came to power. Indeed they had deliberately avoided the discussion of these policies lest they uncover disagreements which would lessen the unity of their effort to achieve independence.[3]

There were thus other leaders in the party who were important individuals politically and whose agreement on policy matters could not always be assumed. As the whole burden of political leadership did not rest solely on Nyerere himself, some institution was needed to secure the active participation of his colleagues in the making of policy and in its implementation. The cabinet was accepted as an institution particularly suited for this purpose. After Nyerere's resignation as prime minister in January 1962,[4] the cabinet system was even more appropriate. Without Nyerere, any system in Tanganyika other than one in which power and responsibility were shared by those who were his most senior colleagues would surely have produced grave political tensions and dissatisfaction.

Within the first thirteen months of independence there were two major developments each of which might have been expected to have a major impact upon the decision-making machinery of government. On 9 December 1962, only one year after achieving independence, Tanganyika became a republic under an executive president. Under the republican constitution the president was given very extensive powers in his own right. Second, by that date, one-party dominance, rather than interparty competition, had become an accepted and, indeed, an expected feature of the political system. Neither of these developments had the immediate consequences for the operation of the cabinet which might have been expected. The introduction of an executive presidency did not mean that the cabinet was transformed into a team of executive subordinates whose members were the appointed agents of the president and responsible solely to him. Single-party dominance did not lead to a decision to replace the cabinet by the National Executive Committee of the Tanganyika African National

---

[3] Nyerere makes this point in his Introduction to K. Stahl, *Tanganyika: Sails Against the Wilderness* (The Hague, 1962).

[4] Nyerere resigned the post of prime minister in January 1962, only six weeks after independence, in order to spend his full time as president of TANU. He returned to government office in December 1962 as the first president of the republic.

Union (TANU) or its Central Committee as the main initiator of government policies. These facts need first to be established.

THE CABINET AND THE INTRODUCTION
OF THE PRESIDENTIAL SYSTEM

In December 1962 the constitution of Tanganyika was radically altered.
The Republic of Tanganyika Act, which came into effect on 9 December
1962, vested the executive power of the republic in the president. The
legal powers given to him were very extensive. From that date, the ministers, whom he alone appointed, exercised executive responsibilities only
insofar as the president had delegated such powers to them. Moreover,
when they met together as a cabinet, their powers were merely advisory
to the president and could be exercised only "on such matters as may be
referred to it under any general or specific directions of the President." [5]
The president, too, had ultimate authority over the civil service and appointed the members of the judiciary.[6] To make his position absolutely
clear, the constitution adds that "except as may be otherwise provided by
law, in the exercise of his functions, the President shall act at his own
discretion and shall not be obliged to follow advice tendered by any other
person." [7]

This introduction of an executive presidency was a consequence of the
introduction of the republic. It was not the result of any desire by Nyerere
to secure a major concentration of authority in his own hands. Despite the
legal provisions of the constitution, Nyerere's first presidential circular
after the election in December 1962 was devoted entirely to a detailed
exposition of how cabinet business should be conducted, its purpose being
to increase the cabinet's efficiency as "the principal instrument of policy." [8]

The new constitution did not immediately result in any significant
downgrading of the importance of the cabinet ministers. The major departments of government continued to be included in the individual
portfolios of ministers. Nyerere was not interested in keeping important
portfolios under his direct responsibility. Important responsibilities have
from time to time been transferred from a ministry to the Office of the
President. Responsibility for the Africanization of the civil service, for
example, was moved in 1961 from the Treasury to the Office of the Prime
Minister, so that the Africanization program could have the authority of
the president immediately and directly behind it. For similar reasons, the

[5] Republic of Tanganyika Act, Constituent Assembly Act, no. 1 (1962), sect. 15.
[6] One of the few specific constitutional limitations to the powers of the president,
however, restricted his authority to dismiss judges.
[7] Republic of Tanganyika Act (1962), op. cit., sect. 3 (3).
[8] *Presidential Circular No. 1*, The Cabinet (Dec. 1962), p. 3.

Directorate of Planning was located in the Office of the President during the period from April 1964 to October 1965. On other occasions the president has hesitated, for political reasons, to give an important ministry to a powerful colleague who was expecting it and he has therefore brought this portfolio for a period into his own office. Thus, at different times, Foreign Affairs and Defence, Local Government, and Regional Administration have been directly under the president. Nyerere, however, shed most of these specific responsibilities as soon as he felt he could. In December 1962 the vice-president took charge of the civil service. A separate Ministry for Economic Affairs and Development Planning was established in October 1965. Foreign Affairs and Defence became a separate ministry in March 1963. Local Government, after a few months as a presidential responsibility, became a regular ministerial portfolio again in October 1965. There has not been any major trend toward a concentration of administrative responsibilities in the Office of the President in recent years.

Even when there have been important portfolios within his office, Nyerere normally assigned these responsibilities to a minister of state whom he appointed to his office. Thus, for example, after the introduction of the Five Year Plan, when the Directorate of Planning was located in the Office of the President, three ministers of state, Nsilo Swai, Amir Jamal, and A. M. Babu, were responsible for the work of the Directorate. The appointment of these ministers of state and their involvement with specific responsibilities which were formally assigned to the president meant that neither the president nor his principal secretary was much more involved with the administration of these matters than they were in the case of government activities falling within the portfolios of other ministers.

Final evidence of Nyerere's lack of interest in becoming an executive president in any directly operational sense is the fact that he allowed the Office of the President to be extraordinarily understaffed throughout the whole of the period under review. Nyerere never had a strong and substantial team of senior civil servants in his own immediate office. The Office of the President has been headed by a permanent secretary who has always been one of the ablest and most experienced African civil servants.[9] This senior civil servant has never had an adequate staff. The office normally included a principal assistant secretary who was clerk to the cabinet but who has had few other major responsibilities, and an assistant secretary who was primarily concerned with the management of the office and State House. The staff of the office has also included an invaluable personal assistant to the president, a press secretary, and a small subordinate staff. What has been missing is a small team of senior adminitsrators who

[9] It is interesting and revealing, however, to note that for a seven-month period in 1963 Nyerere and his office managed to get along without any principal secretary.

could collect and analyze the information the president might want, who could recommend upon issues of special interest to him, and who could directly administer any activity which he might wish to have under more direct control for a period. At the civil service level, Nyerere has had to depend very largely on the officials of other ministries for advice, for information, and for the implementation of his ideas. This failure to build a strong office of the president cannot be explained solely in terms of the scarcity of experienced officers. The conclusion is inescapable. Nyerere wanted to undermine neither the position of his ministers nor the role of the cabinet. The introduction of the republic and of the executive presidency thus did little to lessen the importance of the cabinet within the machinery of government.

ONE-PARTY DOMINANCE AND THE CABINET, 1960–1966

When Nyerere first came to power he decided that the position of the cabinet as the coordinating center of government and the primary initiator of government policies was compatible with a political system in which one party, TANU, had overwhelming support. This fact needs elaboration. TANU occupied a unique place in the political processes of Tanganyika and in the mythology of Tanganyikan nationalism. It was much more than a party. It was a national movement which spoke for virtually the whole of the African population of Tanganyika and for many non-African citizens as well.

Nevertheless, after the achievement of responsible government in 1960, the central institutions of TANU played only a minimal and sporadic role as initiators of policy and as a forum for the careful and detailed consideration of policies. When TANU came to power no one suggested that it ought to be reorganized and greatly strengthened so that it could become a powerful agent for the formation and direction of government policy. TANU leaders accepted that government policies were made within the machinery of government. Nyerere made this absolutely clear. In his Independence Day message to the party on 9 December 1961 he said: "It is the job of the government to work out an overall plan and to charter the direction in which we move." [10] He held to this view during the eleven months in 1962 which followed his resignation as prime minister. Nyerere made no attempt at this time to widen the definition of the role of the party, nor to reorganize or greatly strengthen its structure. He did not seek to equip the party either with the political machinery or the senior bureaucracy which would permit it actively to create policies and to

[10] Quoted in Julius Nyerere, *Freedom and Unity* (London: Oxford University Press, 1966), p. 140.

supervise their execution. Even during this period when he was outside the government and in charge of the party, Nyerere did not use the machinery of the party to exert any authority or influence upon the government. When there were policy matters which he wished to influence, he acted through the prime minister and through other ministers. On occasion, indeed, he attended cabinet meetings so as to be able to contribute directly to the discussion of policy. Nyerere accepted, in other words, that government policy was and should be made within the machinery of government.

Theoretically there was a clear alternative to this. The Central Committee of the party, its National Executive Committee, and its Annual Conference could conceivably have become very important elements in the policy-making process. The party bureaucracy could have been reinforced to the point where it would have been an important source of background memoranda and expert advice on policy matters. Well served by this bureaucracy, the Central Committee could have acted as a policy initiator. The National Executive Committee could, in turn, have organized itself to review the policy proposals which it received from the Central Committee and to prepare additional policy proposals. Both the National Executive Committee and the Annual Conference could have "legislated" on these proposals and presented them to the government as decisions binding upon it. It is crucial to realize that actual practice after 1960 bore no resemblance to this hypothetical development.

It is hard to exaggerate the disorganization and administrative incompetence of the central offices of the party. By 1965 the central office was receiving no regular payments of fees from party branches and was heavily dependent upon a government subsidy. There had been no approved estimates for two years. There were no staff records. There were no established salary scales, let alone any regular reporting to the center from the branches. The central office had no bureaucratic capacity and nothing in consequence was really expected of it.[11]

None of the three central institutions of the party, the Central Committee, the National Executive Committee, or the Annual Conference, threatened the cabinet as the main policy-deciding body. The Central Committee of TANU, despite a name which suggested it might be at the very center of power in Tanzania, was an oddly constituted and most casually run committee. It was not designed to be a major initiator of policy. It met informally on Saturday mornings and for years was little more than a housekeeping committee of the party.

The National Conference and the National Executive Committee are

---

[11] In that year Nyerere set in motion a determined effort to correct these gross inefficiencies. He did this in what was perhaps the only way feasible: he seconded to the party a number of able civil servants.

each major representative bodies.[12] The National Conference, because of its size and because it met only annually, could hardly have been other than a ratifying body. The National Executive Committee in contrast could possibly have played an important role in policy making, for it was of a more manageable size and met quarterly. But the N.E.C. was not organized to that purpose. It had no well-structured committee system; the party had no bureaucracy to advise it; most ministers were not members of the N.E.C., and only occasionally did the N.E.C. call before it a minister or a principal secretary whom it wished to question. These were not particular weaknesses of the N.E.C. The N.E.C., like the National Conference, was intended primarily to be representative of party opinion.[13] They were both well designed for this purpose. They represented not only the rank and file of the party but also the locally elected officials and the politically appointed area and regional commissioners. They were thus representative forums at which the party leadership sought the support of these crucial local cadres and learned at first hand of their preoccupations and their worries.

These institutions were important. Without them the government would have found it much more difficult to keep in effective communication with the people. The formal structures of government, including parliament, were still insecurely established as the national institutions through which Tanganyika took its legally binding collective decisions. Important further legitimacy for government measures could therefore be gained from TANU endorsement.

The party conference and the N.E.C. played a further important political role. They helped to clarify the political parameters within which the president and cabinet had to operate. There were few other ways for the government to inform itself of popular reactions to its proposals. Parliamentary discussion was none too vigorous and members were very cautious with any criticism they might wish to make of government policies. The newspapers were either controlled by the party or were extremely timid. The trade union movement had been brought increasingly under tighter government control. Within both the civil service and the party bureaucracy the upward flow of information on popular reactions to government policies was sporadic and inadequate.

---

[12] The National Conference includes all members of parliament, all regional and district chairmen of TANU, and all area commissioners. Regional commissioners are members of the National Conference in consequence of their being appointed members of parliament. The National Executive Committee includes seventeen elected members, one from each region, along with the regional chairmen of TANU and the regional commissioners.

[13] "TANU has a vital role to play. It is an organization of the people. Through it the people can and must express their desires and their worries to the Government.

Under Nyerere's guidance, TANU avoided a tendency that is easily discerned in many other African states: its representative bodies did not turn into well-staged rallies.[14] The Annual Conference and the National Executive Committee continued to be lively and independent-minded. The educational, legitimizing, and representational functions which they fulfilled were important. However, Nyerere did not at all attempt to develop any of the institutions of the party into creative instruments of policy formation. There did not emerge within the party either the institutions or the procedures to undermine the central position of the cabinet.

There is a further important aspect to this decision of Nyerere not to develop policy-making institutions within the party. It relates to the view that was taken of the party, particularly after the decision in January 1963, to introduce a one-party system in Tanganyika. TANU continued to be an open national movement in which all Africans of goodwill could comfortably be accommodated. The party had always been open to anyone willing to accept the statement of TANU's beliefs, aims, and objectives as they appear in the party's constitution. The decision to entrench the single-party system into the constitution did not change this. The Report of the Presidential Commission on the Establishment of a Democratic One-Party State argued in forthright terms that very few Tanganyikans need be excluded from membership in TANU:

The principles of TANU as set out in article 2 of the TANU constitution do not contain any narrow ideological formulations which might change with time and circumstances. They are a broad statement of political faith. We believe they carry the support of Tanganyika and must strike a responsive cord in men of good will in every civilized country in the world. A party based on these principles and requiring adherence to them as a condition of membership would be open to all but an insignificant minority of our citizens and would, I believe, be a truly national movement.[15]

This was an exaggeration, possibly even a deliberate one. There were elitist and oligarchic strands within TANU which were unsympathetic to any genuine democratization of the party. Nevertheless, the position which the commission took on this issue reflected the dominant attitude toward party membership at that time. It has, at least until recently, been Nyerere's view as well. In 1962 he secured N.E.C. support for a recommendation that all former TANU members who had been expelled from the party should be permitted to rejoin. He argued in his Inaugural Address in De-

---

Through it the Government can and must explain to the people what it is doing and why." From Nyerere's speech to TANU on 9 Dec. 1961, ibid., p. 100.

[14] By 1967 the National Conference had begun to move in this direction.

[15] *Report of the Presidential Commission on the Establishment of a Democratic One-Party State.* Dar es Salaam (1965), p. 16.

cember 1962: "It would be absurd to claim that TANU is a united national movement . . . if what one really meant was that TANU was a united movement led by an educated minority who were using that unity in order to rule the rest of the people." [16] Three years later in his speech to the National Assembly recommending acceptance of the report of this commission he reaffirmed his belief that TANU was and should remain a mass popular movement.

Actual practice relating to party membership in the period covered by this essay demonstrates that the party was assumed to be an open, mass party. Many efforts were made to enlist as many citizens as possible into the party. No ideological tests have ever been applied. The pledge which was required of every new member made no reference to the socialist principles of the party. It was much more a pledge by the new member to lead an exemplary life and to dedicate himself to the welfare of his fellow Tanganyikans than a statement of an acceptance of any political creed. Expulsions had been few and the party had been willing to accept back into its fold even such errant members as Chief Fundikira and Z. Mtemvu, once leader of the Tanganyika African Congress.

This view of the nature of the party was entirely compatible with actual practice. Policy formation was left to the government, with the party continuing to be a national forum at which policies were explained and ratified and at which the leaders gained a more sensitive insight into the aspirations and the concerns of the important middle ranks of the party and of ordinary citizens. By 1967 there was to emerge in some circles the view that the party had a special vanguard role to act on the people's behalf. Such a view of the party would lead inevitably to an effort to make the formation of major policies a party function, with the role of the government being merely to implement the decisions taken by the party. In the period under consideration such elitist views of the party were politically insignificant. There were no serious ideological obstacles to the continued reliance upon the ministries and the cabinet as the primary instruments of policy making.

THE OPERATION OF THE CABINET SYSTEM AFTER 1962

Neither the presidential system nor the one-party state directly undermined the role of the cabinet. Moreover, it was clearly the president's intention that the cabinet should remain the principal instrument of policy within the government. Nevertheless, it proved extremely difficult for the cabinet to operate in that capacity with any real efficiency. No grand design led to a decline in the position of the cabinet. The initial decline, which

[16] Julius Nyerere, *Freedom and Unity*, p. 180.

was real, was due to a number of secondary factors whose influence was cumulative. These factors were: the style of decision making to which TANU leaders had been accustomed; the range of opinions represented within the cabinet; the tensions which existed between politicians and the senior civil service; and the severely inadequate staffing of the Office of the President.

An effective cabinet system requires an ability and willingness among cabinet ministers to deal with many matters by written communication. It requires also the acceptance of major delegations of responsibility to colleagues and to committees. This style and manner of decision making is more easily accepted in a literate culture with long experience in the operation of sophisticated bureaucratic structures. By contrast, the Tanganyika National African Union was still very loosely organized. Within it decisions tended to emerge from informal face-to-face discussions. Many TANU leaders, including Nyerere, continued to prefer or at least to gravitate back to this style of decision making. Some government decisions continued, therefore, to be taken by the president on the basis of informal discussion and without reference to the carefully established procedures which the president himself had established.

There is a further example of the importance of the style and manner of the decision making which ministers were used to. Ministers tended not to accept as binding, decisions which had been taken either by committees of the cabinet or by the full cabinet but at a pace which precluded a full and relaxed discussion. A major illustration of this was the failure of many cabinet ministers to accept the major policy implications that were embodied in the First Five Year Development Plan. The preliminary discussion of this plan within the Economic Commission of the cabinet had been too hurried; the pressure applied to accept the plan had been too great; the details had been too difficult to comprehend; and as a result of these factors few ministers felt deeply committed to it. In consequence, within very few months, several ministers pressed for, and won, major, costly decisions which benefited their ministry but which ran counter to the details of the plan.[17]

Progress was made in 1962 and 1963 to tighten the operation of the cabinet. Some of these advances were undermined, in the short run at least, by two consequences of the union with Zanzibar in April 1964.[18] This

[17] See R. C. Pratt, "The Administration of Economic Planning in Newly Independent States. The Tanzanian Experience, 1963-66," *The Journal of Commonwealth Political Studies*, vol. 6, no. 1 (March 1967).

[18] In April 1964, following the Zanzibar revolution of January 1964, Tanganyika and Zanzibar were formally united into the United Republic of Tanganyika and Zanzibar. The name of the United Republic was later changed to the United Republic of Tanzania.

union brought into the cabinet several Zanzibar ministers, particularly the First Vice-President of the Union, Sheikh Abeid Karume, who were completely inexperienced in acting within a well-structured governmental system. They were, nevertheless, important men and care had to be taken to assure that they were not frustrated by the comparatively sophisticated system that was operating on the mainland. The cabinet could not too often take its decisions at a rate that precluded their participation nor could it carry on its discussions at a level of detail and sophistication which might leave the vice-president and possibly one or several of his colleagues entirely uninvolved.

Because several of the Zanzibar ministers spoke English only haltingly, Swahili replaced English as the working language of the cabinet after April 1964. In the judgment of several cabinet ministers this also added significantly to the difficulty of running efficient cabinet meetings. English had been the language of government in Dar es Salaam. Its more complete vocabulary facilitated clear decisions. It was as if the use of English made acceptable a more bureaucratic and more structured style of decision making. Swahili, in contrast, was the language of political life. Its associations were with an expansive style of exposition which was often imprecise and led to less clear decisions.

The second factor that complicated the operation of the cabinet and made it less effective was a consequence of the fact that TANU continued to be an open party. It takes great political skill to hold in a single party men of very widely ranging opinions and differing temperaments. During the whole of this period Nyerere had assiduously practiced what Dr. Carol Fisher first called "the politics of accommodation." [19] He always took great care not to drive into open opposition colleagues whom he might have been expected to drop, either because they proved themselves incompetent or because they were quite clearly committed to policies that were deeply contrary to his own.

The extent of Nyerere's toleration was shown when he failed to dismiss Kambona as his minister of External Affairs in 1964, after Kambona had given publicity to some crudely forged documents and, on their basis, had accused the United States of planning the overthrow of Nyerere. The great importance Nyerere attached to the politics of accommodation explains his acquiescence in Kambona's many arbitrary assertions of power. Nyerere attached greater importance at that time to holding within the party the leaders of several possibly divergent movements than he attached either to a more united pursuit of the policies of his government or to a more loyal and honest acceptance of cabinet decisions and governmental

[19] See R. C. Pratt, "The Administration of Economic Planning," *The Journal of Commonwealth Political Studies*, vol. 6, no. 1 (March 1967), pp. 54–56.

procedures. Whatever the wisdom of this concern to maintain the unity of the party, the persistent reluctance to discipline members who ignored the most obvious rules necessary to the smooth running of a cabinet must have increased tensions within the cabinet and lessened its efficiency.

The third factor that complicated the operation of the cabinet was the poor relationship which existed during the first years of independence between some ministers and the senior civil service. Appropriate though the cabinet system was for Tanganyika in the early 1960s, it was difficult to establish even a working approximation of that complex relationship between minister and senior civil servant which the system required. In the first year and a half after September 1960, the most obvious complication was that the senior civil servants on whom the ministers had to depend for advice and for the administration of their ministries were almost all expatriate British officers. By deliberate policy Nyerere had placed the few experienced Africans in responsible positions in the field rather than in the central ministries. This quickly proved politically unacceptable. There was a general reaction within the party against a policy which meant that the civil service advisers of most ministers, including the prime minister himself, were expatriates. By December 1961 Nyerere recognized that he must yield to these party demands, and, abruptly, he asked for the resignation of Kim Meek, a senior British civil servant who was his own permanent secretary. Thereafter high priority was given to the appointment of African permanent secretaries in each of the ministries.

The problem was not thereby solved. Other suspicions and hostilities, different from those felt toward British officers but equally intractable, quickly marred relationships between the African politicians and the senior African civil servants. These civil servants had benefited personally from the achievement of independence. They had enjoyed vastly accelerated promotions as a result of that independence but they had not at all shared in the political struggle for it. Some politicians resented the influence these civil servants were able to exert because of their high office and knowledge. The civil servants on their part often displayed impatience with the less experienced and sometimes less well educated politicians.

This suspicion and hostility marred the operation of government in a number of important ways. The cabinet system, for example, was designed to assure that major policy decisions were taken by the political leaders after a full deliberation and on the advice of their civil servants. The system also sought to assure that these decisions were not undermined or reversed by individual ministerial actions.

One important feature of the procedural rules relating to the cabinet was the opportunity they provided for the senior civil service to exert influence. The preparation of cabinet papers relating to items on the agenda of the cabinet, treasury comments upon the financial implications of proposals being made to the cabinet, and even the mere fact that prior notice was required of items to be raised at cabinet meetings gave the civil service the opportunity to submit ministerial ideas to close scrutiny. The hostility felt by some ministers to their senior civil servants made these procedures hard to work. Some ministers did not like to have to defend their ideas before their senior civil servants, which they needed to do if they were to be helped by those officials to draft an effective cabinet paper. Ministers sometimes resented being told by a civil servant in the Office of the President that a draft cabinet paper was inadequate or that it had first to be sent to the Treasury or to another ministry for comments.

These are specific illustrations of a general reluctance on the part of some of the political leaders to accept that the political power they had won with independence had now to be exercised through procedures and institutions which greatly limited arbitrary action on their own individual part. Inevitably the restraints of the system which were hardest for ministers to accept were those which were enforced by members of the civil service. A revealing illustration of this was the difficulties the principal secretaries had as the accounting officers of their ministries. As an accounting officer, a principal secretary was legally responsible for the expenditure of his ministerial votes. He was obliged, therefore, to disallow any expenditure if there was in fact no budget provision for it or if the relevant vote in the ministerial estimates had been exhausted.

The attempt to exercise this responsibility against spending which had been approved by his minister caused much friction between some permanent secretaries and a few of the ministers. Although the points under dispute were often minor, they were of a sort which irritate personal relationships: Mr. Kambona, as minister of External Affairs, approved the appointment of a number of assistant protocol officers whom he himself had chosen but for whom there was no budget provision; the same minister approved the purchase of an Austin Princess limousine for the Tanganyikan high commissioner in London although the budget provision was inadequate for such a car; a minister refused to repay overseas allowance which he had drawn for the whole of a ninety-one-day overseas trip, even though he was the guest of a foreign government during that period; a parliamentary secretary rented a Jaguar in London over an Easter weekend holiday and sought to have it paid for from public funds.

Theoretically, at least, Nyerere could have done much to overcome these various difficulties between some of his ministers and the senior administrators in their ministries. For example, he might have been expected unambiguously to back principal secretaries when they ran into trouble with their ministers over financial matters. He might also have been expected to discipline those of his colleagues who refused to accept that they must operate within the established procedures. It is important to recognize that Nyerere was very reluctant to take this sort of disciplinary action against his political colleagues. Time and again in the period between 1962 and 1965, he acquiesced in minor abuses of office by his ministers. The minister of External Affairs, for example, got his assistant protocol officers; the Tanzanian high commissioner of London got his Austin Princess; and the traveling minister did not have to repay the 6,000 shillings overseas allowance he had received. Nyerere also allowed Kambona to push Dr. V. Kyaruzi out of the civil service altogether, even though he was one of the most experienced civil servants in Tanganyika.

This failure of Nyerere in these early years to back the administrators against ministers when the latter were clearly in the wrong illustrates the importance he attached to the continued accommodation of these ministers within the movement. Inevitably, however, it further increased the tension between some ministers and civil servants and therefore further complicated the operation of the cabinet.

The fourth factor that adversely affected the working of the cabinet was the comparative weakness of the Office of the President. The scarcity of senior staff in the Office of the President made it easy for cabinet procedures to be bypassed by ministers wishing to do so. The office has not had the senior administrators who could intervene in jurisdictional disputes between ministries. These disputes, in consequence, tended to develop into major clashes between ministers which, having taken on a personal aspect, became vastly more difficult to resolve. A stronger president's office could also have been responsible for important interministerial committees. These committees, thus having the authority of the Office of the President behind them, might have achieved closer and more effective interministerial cooperation. Without this sort of effective staff work, interministry difficulties tended to come before the president or were exposed at cabinet meetings in a raw form which further exacerbated relations among cabinet colleagues.

These four factors, the style of decision making to which the ministers were accustomed, the range of opinion within the cabinet, the unsettling tensions between some ministers and their senior civil servants, and the weakness of the Office of the President, all complicated the work of the cabinet and made it less efficient. Each of these factors, however, could reasonably be expected in time to be of declining importance.[20] Had there

20 In particular, the suspicions and lack of cooperation between the ministers and the senior civil servants were very largely overcome. As ministers became more confident and as civil servants identified themselves more firmly with TANU, these difficulties lessened appreciably.

been no other relevant developments, one might have expected that the cabinet would be likely to be of increasing importance within the political system of Tanganyika and that it would operate with increasing efficiency. That hypothesis cannot, however, be offered.

THE DECLINE IN THE IMPORTANCE OF THE CABINET

By 1966 the cabinet in Tanzania no longer occupied as central a position within the governmental system of Tanzania as it had occupied in the period 1960 to 1962. Two major developments account for this: the decline in the political importance of many cabinet ministers and the president's increasing tendency to take policy decisions without reference to the cabinet. These two developments will now be separately analyzed.

Most of the ministers in 1962 were men who were of political importance in their own right. Some of these ministers, such as Kahama, Bomani, and Kawawa, had had leading positions in the cooperative movement or in the trade union movement; some, such as Fundikira and Eliofoo, were accepted leaders of an important tribe; others such as Kambona had proven rhetorical skills which made them a power before the party's Annual Conference. The cabinet was a collection of political leaders whom it was of real political value to keep loyal and united. Cabinet discussions, therefore, served an important political purpose. Whatever the constitutional provisions about the powers of the president, it made very good political sense to regard the cabinet as the central policy-making body.

This political factor gradually became less significant. The members of the cabinet were much less important in 1965 than in 1960. Ministers who had had a strong institutional base to their political influence found that it was of declining importance. Organizations in which they had been dominant figures had gradually been brought under closer government control. Their own influence within these organizations diminished as they became fully absorbed in their government responsibilities. Other ministers who had had an unquestioned authority within a district or among a tribe had tended to center their life too fully in Dar es Salaam and to become so absorbed in the affairs of their ministries that they too were less important political figures than they had been.

Moreover, after independence was achieved politics as such began to appear less important to many cabinet ministers. No political opposition threatened TANU. There was, therefore, no pressing need for cabinet ministers to exert themselves greatly in political activity. Even the 1965 election did not thrust cabinet ministers into any national prominence. Each minister campaigned in his own constituency. The regulations relating to the election were designed to discourage factional politics. They did not permit ministers to make any political speeches during the election campaign in any other constituency than their own.

In this situation many members of the cabinet could increasingly be viewed as belonging to one of the two major "tendencies." These two groupings cannot properly be labeled "factions." They were not always sharply identified, and they have had a somewhat shifting membership. But progressively they became more clearly recognizable and they have exerted quite different and largely contradictory influences on government policies.[21] The members of the first group were the "administrator-ministers." These were the ministers who engaged themselves primarily in the detailed work of their ministry and who were, at the level of cabinet discussions, primarily concerned with the efficient operation of government, the improvement of social services, and the economic development of the country. The administrator-ministers inevitably lost much of their political importance because of their full involvement in government matters. Administratively, they became more valuable to the president, but they became less important politically.

The second controversial group were the "political ministers," those whom Nyerere once labeled the "talkers." [22] These ministers, of whom Kambona was the most prominent, sometimes had ideological pretensions which separated them from the main direction of government policy. However, the essential distinction was not ideological. The talkers were those activists from the earlier struggle for independence who had proven unable to exchange their earlier declamatory and oppositional style of politics for hard, sustained work. These ministers were disinclined to remain wholeheartedly involved in the stern, continuing efforts to promote development. They were prone instead to throw their main energies into the exploitation of the purely political issues which from time to time have disturbed the political scene in Tanzania. Whenever there were occasions which made Tanganyika particularly responsive to racist or to strident anti-Western sentiments, such as the Stanleyville parachute drop in 1964, the forged but momentarily effective documents which suggested an American plan to overthrow Nyerere, or the inadequate British response to the unilateral Declaration of Independence by Rhodesia, the talkers flourished politically and were a major force in Tanganyikan politics.

[21] It is not easy to attach descriptive labels to these two groups; "left" and "right" is not too helpful, for the distinction is more a matter of capacity and of inclination than of conviction. One shrewd Dar es Salaam friend once used the labels "the doers" and "the wreckers," labels which were apt enough in the particular context but which involve an underestimation of the positive value of skills that are purely political. Others might wish to use the terms "neocolonial" and "radical." These, however, would be inaccurate and misleading in this instance.

[22] In an interview with the author, June 1968.

When, however, the preoccupations of the government were primarily developmental, their interest flagged and they played a much less important role.

A further important aspect to this decline in the political importance of cabinet ministers was the fact that most of the ministers were not active within the deliberative organs of the party. Indeed, because the practice did not develop for ministers to seek election to regional conferences of the party and hence to the National Executive Committee of the party, a great majority of the ministers were members of neither the National Executive Committee nor, until 1965 of the Annual Conference, of the party. In 1965 amendments to the party's constitution made all members of parliament, and hence all ministers, members of the National Conference.[23] To this day, however, very few ministers, save the several who are officeholders within the party, are members of its National Executive Committee. This failure to integrate the political leadership of the government with the political leadership of the party inevitably lessened the political influence of the individual cabinet ministers.

The rise to prominence of the regional commissioners has also affected the political position of the ministers. In 1962 the country was divided into ten regions, and the president appointed a regional commissioner as the political head of each of these regions. The number of regions has gradually increased and there are now seventeen regional commissioners. Although the regional commissioners are the senior government officers within their regions and are responsible for the coordination and the effective promotion of government policies, their main work has tended to be political. As a group they parallel if not rival the cabinet as the senior advisers to the president. Their perspective on many problems is likely to be quite different to that of the ministers and may often be a helpful corrective to it. It is they rather than the ministers who are in a position to be well informed about political sentiment within the country. Moreover, they have been ex-officio members of the National Executive Committee as well as the Annual Conference and have been active in both.

These various developments inevitably lessened the political influence of the ministers and in particular of the administrator-ministers. One minister, however, Oscar Kambona, was in a position to use his ministerial and party offices to secure a strong base for his own personal political power. Throughout the whole period from independence until his fall from political grace in 1967, he was secretary-general of the party. In

[23] These amendments included changing the name of the Annual Conference to National Conference. The party constitution was included in the 1965 Interim Constitution of Tanzania Act. No. 43 of 1965.

addition, for long periods he held particularly sensitive ministries. He was, for example, minister of Regional Administration and Local Government from October 1965 until his resignation. This gave him a major influence over the regional and area commissioners. Before that, he had been minister for Home Affairs, from January 1962 until March 1963, when he became minister of External Affairs and Defence. He lost Defence in April 1964, but remained with External Affairs until October 1965. He had thus been in a position, had he had organizational skills, to build up a powerful body of men in the party, the regional administration, the police, and the army who would have owed a particular loyalty to him. To a certain extent, Kambona did indulge in nepotism more than other ministers. But it was much more at the level of a self-gratifying exercise in favoritism than a deliberate effort to build up a personal political machine. What Kambona clearly enjoyed and was good at was the public denunciation of imperialism. The ministry which he above all preferred was External Affairs. Although Defence or Regional Administration would have provided him with vastly greater influence within Tanganyika, External Affairs permitted him to play a role in Pan-African politics and to give frequent and vigorous expression to strongly worded anti-Western sentiments.

One other senior politician continued to be extremely important politically. Rashidi Kawawa was Nyerere's choice as prime minister when he resigned himself from the prime ministership in January 1962. In December 1962, when Nyerere returned to head the government as president, Kawawa became vice-president. In 1964, following the union with Zanzibar, Kawawa agreed to become second vice-president so that Karume, who was giving up a presidency of an independent country, might become First Vice-President of the new United Republic of Tanganyika and Zanzibar. While Kambona was a troublesome and difficult colleague toward whom Nyerere felt a strong loyalty as an old comrade, Kawawa was a close and trusted colleague whose influence and authority in that capacity have become very great.

Although the diminishing individual political status of most ministers contributed to the overall decline in the importance of the newly formed cabinet, the political authority of Kambona and Kawawa did not act to reinforce the cabinet. Kawawa's power within the government was due to his special relationship with the president. He did not particularly ignore the cabinet, but neither did he need to make it the main channel through which he exerted his influence on government policies. Kambona's contribution to the cabinet was more clearly negative. He rarely sought to exert an influence through the medium of the cabinet. He tended, rather, to ignore the cabinet and its committees. He acted unilaterally or after direct discussions with the president. He behaved as if he were free of any necessity to consult with his ministerial colleagues. He was, for example, a member of the presidential advisory commission on the one-party state. As secretary-general of the party he might have been expected to play a particularly prominent part in its deliberations. In fact, however, he attended very few of its meetings, made no contribution to its proceedings after its first meeting, and did not sign the report. Similarly, he attended very few meetings of the Economic Commission of the cabinet which prepared the First Five Year Plan. Kambona felt little loyalty either to cabinet decisions or to the procedures relating to it. He failed, for example, to submit to the Directorate of Planning any estimates of the requirements of his ministry when the Five Year Plan was being prepared and he felt himself in no way bound or even inhibited by its provisions when he later sought additional capital expenditures. By ignoring the cabinet and by operating largely outside of it, Kambona further weakened it.

For these various reasons, the cabinet gradually lost much of the political importance which earlier it had had. Parallel to that general development there has been an increasing tendency for Nyerere to take decisions outside of the context of the cabinet and without reference to the procedures which he himself had laid down. In the early years these were largely on matters of secondary importance and could be attributed to his desire to cut through bureaucratic regulations in order to permit a bright project to move forward more rapidly or to correct an obvious anomaly or error. However, by the end of the period under review, President Nyerere had begun to take major policy decisions without any consultation with the cabinet. These, I believe, have included: the announcement in January 1964 that discrimination against non-African citizens within the civil service would cease forthwith; the decision to seek a union with Zanzibar in April 1964; the decision to introduce a one-party state; the refusal in August 1964 actively to support the charge that there was an American conspiracy to overthrow his government; and the decision to break off diplomatic relations with Britain in December 1965. More recently, the Arusha Declaration, which announced a major revitalization of Tanzania's dedication to socialism, had not been preceded by any cabinet discussion. His two major policy statements soon after this declaration, the first on Socialism and Rural Development and the second on Education for Self-Reliance, were each made without any prior discussion even with the ministers most directly concerned, let alone with the cabinet as a whole.

These major presidential initiatives were, of course, in no way unconstitutional. Nevertheless, they constituted a major development in the pattern of decision making in Tanzania. This tendency for the president to take major decisions without consulting his cabinet can in part be explained by some of the characteristics of that cabinet which have already been noted. Because the cabinet embraced a wide range of political opinion, there were a number of important issues on which no amount of discussion would produce any satisfactory compromise within the cabinet. When such an issue arose the president, rather than force the issue to a point where it might severely strain relationships within the cabinet, chose instead to avoid cabinet discussion of the issue altogether, and to take what initiatives he wished without any reference to the cabinet. This is believed to have happened, for example, when the cabinet failed to agree in 1964 on whether to divide the economy into sectors which would be reserved for the cooperatives, for government enterprises, and for private firms. The cabinet was also unable to decide upon a national wage policy, and on this issue too Nyerere took his own initiative. He also anticipated a similar deadlock in 1966 when he drew back from the establishment of a commission on Tanzanian socialism, despite the fact that in the previous year he had announced that it would be established. He recognized that the range of views which would have to be represented on such a commission made it unlikely that a consensus would emerge. In consequence, he initiated, and dominated, the National Executive Committee discussions in Arusha in January 1967, which led to the Arusha Declaration.

The declining political importance of many cabinet ministers was a second reason for major presidential initiatives independent of the cabinet. A full cabinet discussion was often no longer the appropriate way for the president to seek an effective compromise on a complex and potentially divisive issue. The effective promotion of government policies and the maintenance of national unity became increasingly the direct responsibility of the president. He had to choose from issue to issue how best to assure the cooperation of those whose participation would be essential to the success of the particular policies being considered. When the policy under discussion was one whose success depended upon the commitment to it of the party leaders throughout the country, Nyerere tended to bring his proposals first to the National Executive Committee and the National Conference of the party rather than to the cabinet. In such cases it was more important that the regional commissioners and the TANU regional chairman should be involved in the discussion of these policies than that the cabinet should be. Thus, to give a recent illustration, Nyerere sought National Conference endorsement in October 1967 for making the promotion of cooperative villages (*Vijiji Vya Ujamaa*) a major aspect of the government's rural development effort.

He chose these means to launch this policy rather than invite the ministers of the relevant departments to prepare a cabinet paper on the question, because he wanted to keep a firm hold himself on the definition of the new policy. He chose the conference rather than the cabinet and parliament as the assembly to receive this major policy initiative, because the people who had to be won over to the policy if it was to succeed were more easily reached through the party conference than through the National Assembly.

The various presidential policy initiatives cannot entirely be explained in terms of the factors so far mentioned; they were more than a presidential reaction to changing features of the cabinet. In addition to these factors, and more important than them, is the fact that Nyerere was becoming surer of the policies that were required of his government. By 1962 he had already formulated and expounded his basic political values. At their heart was a deep commitment to racial equality, to political democracy, and to communal socialism. At that date, however, he had not yet perceived in detail the policies he felt these basic values would demand in the particular context of modern Tanzania. During the period 1963 to 1967 his ideology became more clearly defined and its policy implications emerged more sharply. In consequence, the pragmatism which had often marked his policies in the four years from 1960 to 1964 was partially replaced by a much more focused purposefulness. Nyerere knew more clearly what he wanted and therefore took a more prominent lead in setting the policies of his government.

By this time Nyerere was also seized with a special sense of urgency. He had come to the view that the tropical African countries were at a particularly crucial stage in their development. Traditional institutions were being undermined at such a rapid pace that their value systems were extraordinarily plastic. This meant that those exercising political authority during this period had a correspondingly greater responsibility.

The change which is taking place in Africa now is so fundamental that the society itself is being transformed. . . . Choices which involve clashes of principle must thereefore be answered in the light of the kind of society we want to create, for our priorities now will affect the attitudes and institutions of the future.[24]

Because Nyerere vastly preferred an egalitarian society in which acquisitive individualism would be comparatively undeveloped and communal cooperation would be natural and widespread, he was increasingly concerned that government policies should not contribute to the growth of class divisions and of a selfish and materialist individualism. Nyerere was thus opposed to the encouragement of an indigenous capitalism in Tanzania. Such a policy would stimulate and further entrench values and

[24] Nyerere, *Freedom and Unity*, pp. 6–7.

attitudes which were antipathetic to him. In direct contrast to such a policy, Nyerere urged:

We should deliberately fight the intensification of that attitude which would eventually nullify our social need for human dignity and equality. We have to work towards a position where each individual realizes that his rights in society—above the basic needs of every human being—must come second to the overriding need of human dignity for all; and we have to establish the kind of social organization which reduces personal temptations above that level to a minimum.[25]

By 1966 Nyerere had become a modern equivalent to Rousseau's legislator. For a brief period society's values and attitudes were malleable and in flux. Nyerere hoped, as Rousseau had hoped for his legislator, that, by example, by leadership, and by teaching, but without coercion, he could lead his people to adopt institutions which would then bolster and reinforce rather than undermine and corrupt the social values that featured in his vision of a just society. As Nyerere came to see his role in terms such as these, he sought to exercise a much more direct leadership within his government and his party. From then on, presidential leadership played a more prominent role and the genuinely collegiate element became less in the operations of both the cabinet and of the National Executive Committee.

Tordoff, on the basis of interviews with several senior civil servants who had been principal secretaries to the president, summarized the style and manner of proceedings within the cabinet in these terms: "In 1963, the President normally took the chair at meetings of the Cabinet. Mr. Nyerere was an effective chairman: he did not impose his own views on ministers but usually spoke last. . . . An attempt was made to secure unanimity and a vote was rarely taken." [26] Few participants deny that since 1966 the president plays a much more prominent role in regard to many issues raised in cabinet and that, in addition, he takes important initiatives and final decisions on many other matters without any reference at all to the cabinet.

CONCLUDING OBSERVATIONS

By 1965 the cabinet was no longer, to the same extent, the institution through which the president exercised his policy initiatives. We have argued that the comparative decline in the importance of the cabinet has been due in lesser part to the difficulties which affected its operation. The

[25] See R. C. Pratt, "Tanzania Finds Its Own Way," *The Round Table* (Oct. 1968), p. 386.
[26] William Tordoff, *Government and Politics in Tanzania*, p. 74.

major causes of this decline, however, have been that the cabinet has become less important politically and the president has tended to break with the practice of the politics of accommodation in order to promote major policies of his own design.

The style of government and the choice of the administrative and political devices to promote presidential policies have become more pragmatic as the objectives of policy have become more purposeful. To achieve a new constitution, he appointed a handpicked commission of civil servants and political leaders, whom he quietly advised and who in turn produced a report on a democratic one-party state that closely reflected his own values. To correct the administrative chaos of the party in 1966, he transferred a senior, and nonpolitical, civil servant to the party to be its de facto secretary-general. On many matters the line between party members and civil servants is blurred, with ad hoc committees containing both working on problems of special interest to the president. Occasionally, brand-new institutions are created, such as the Village Resettlement Agency in 1963 or the National Development Corporation in 1964 in order that favorite ideas of the president could be promoted without the encumbrance of regular bureaucratic controls. Increasingly a presidential decision based on tactical considerations rather than clearly defined procedures determines whether a major question is referred to the cabinet, discussed with the regional commissioners, raised at a National Executive Committee meeting, or handled by direct presidential initiative after whatever discussion he judges necessary.

The net result is certainly not the cabinet system of 1961. It is a presidential system in which the president plays a major initiating role but not yet through a fully articulated political or governmental system which has been designed for such a major role. It is a system, moreover, which leaves the second vice-president a good deal of near-autonomous authority over a number of very important matters which are not in the forefront of the president's mind. It is a system in which other ministers as well have a surprising degree of autonomy for as long as the president does not turn his attention to matters covered by their portfolios.

In the political system that is emerging, a powerful and assertive president, a single party, a cabinet of political ministers, and a civil service of high professional standards are combined together in quite workable if somewhat unique relationships. If the result is not immediately identifiable as a near copy of an existing system, it nevertheless does have features which have helped it to avoid easily identifiable failings. For example, as long as it continues with its present balance, Tanzania is unlikely to be dominated by a self-seeking political and administrative oligarchy: this is rendered unlikely by the reality of the democratic participation provided for in the 1965 constitution, by the continued vitality of the representative institutions of the party, and by the president's own commitment that the regime must remain responsive to popular needs. Other features of the system have helped Tanzania to avoid decisions that are ideologically motivated or emotionally conceived and that are also ill-considered and unworkable. The close relationship between ministers and senior civil servants achieved within the ministerial system and the importance still of the cabinet have meant that the experience and professional advice of the senior civil service is taken into account when most major policy decisions are made. Finally, TANU remains an open party which, at least until recently, has always sought mass membership, and has permitted a wide range of political opinion within the ranks of its leadership. Moreover, the democratic participation provided for in the 1965 constitution is genuine and meaningful. In consequence, Tanzania has largely avoided the authoritarianism and the doctrinaire determination of policies which are the likely consequences of rule by an ideologically committed elite.

The political system in 1966 was not yet a stable and established system whose components had settled into a fruitful set of relationships. It was still in a state of some flux and could be upset by any one of at least three possible developments:

1. The "politics of accommodation" could be totally abandoned and an attempt could be made to convert the party into an ideologically committed elite.

2. TANU could aspire to a much more prominent, indeed to a dominant, role in the initiation and consideration of policy. Such a development would seriously upset the present interrelationships of the party, the political ministers, the legislature, and the president. The result would be a different and quite probably less efficient political system, in which the cabinet as it is now known would play a much diminished role.

3. The president could seek to exercise much more fully than he has in the past his constitutional right to initiate policies. If Nyerere were to do this and to reconstruct the party and perhaps the civil service in order more effectively to promote the realization of his own vision of a new Tanzania, the result again would be a quite different political system.

Each of these three developments is quite conceivable in present-day Tanzania. Indeed, it can be argued that tendencies in each of these three directions have appeared in the period 1967–1969. However, Tanzania has experienced several years of a system in which presidential initiatives, genuine democratic participation, a cabinet of political ministers, a self-confident civil service, and a robust and representative party have each played a major positive role. Many in Tanzania are likely to recognize that the balance which has emerged between these major participants, far from being a barrier to effective government, may indeed be a key feature of Tanzania's political system which should be safeguarded and perfected rather than overturned.[27]

[27] The author wishes to thank the Canada Council for a generous Killam Award which made possible a period of concentrated research and writing on Tanzania, of which this essay is one product. He wishes also to express his appreciation to the Ford Foundation for its earlier support for his research in Tanzania. Neither the council nor the foundation is, of course, responsible for the material or the opinions in this essay.

Chapter 6 A Local Perspective on Developmental Strategy in the Ivory Coast

Richard E. Stryker

The study of political institutions and processes in the new states has been tied, from the beginning, to a "developmental" perspective. In part this merely reflects current fashion, whereby, as Samuel Huntington has pointed out, "political development" is defined so broadly that it "loses its analytic content and acquires simply a geographic one. At the extreme, it becomes synonymous with the political history of Asia, Africa, and Latin America." [1] A more important consideration underlying this emphasis has been the widespread belief among social scientists that the processes of change initiated in the Third World by contact with the West are decisive and predictable. In spite of "setbacks" or "crises of development," the long-range direction of change is toward some variant of generic "modernity" in all spheres and aspects of social activity. The ultimate predictability of direction is based on assumptions of the relative fragility of "tradition," the relative thrust of "modernity" (reinforced by the syndromatic character of its components), and the mutual exclusivity or at least incompatibility of the basic elements in any given confrontation of these two types of social order. [2]

Several penetrating critiques of this position have recently been pub-

[1] Samuel P. Huntington, "Political Development and Political Decay," in Claude Welch, ed., *Political Modernization* (Belmont, Calif., 1967), pp. 211–212.
[2] Despite varying nuances and qualifications, this position remains the dominant perspective of contemporary scholarship on social change. Perhaps no major scholar represents a perfect "fit," though Parsons, Levy, Pye, and Apter are certainly good examples. A partial listing can be found in C. S. Whitaker, Jr., "A Dysrhythmic Process of Political Change," *World Politics*, XIX, 2 (Jan. 1967), 190–217.

lished; there is little need therefore to reiterate their major points here.[3] For analytic purposes, however, we reject the traditional-modern dichotomy and particularly reject the idea that one can identify concrete actors within the new states with either the forces of tradition or of modernity. The structure, behavior, and values existing at given centers (regimes) or at particular localities is a question to be determined empirically, not definitionally. It is an empirical fact that wealth and power and the symbols and appurtenances of modernity are concentrated at the centers almost everywhere in the new states. It is an altogether different matter to ascribe (or assume) an identification of concrete centers with any sort of historical justice, in the Marxian sense of inevitability, or with generic motivations. Almost any policy can be preferred in the name of modernization or development, but credulity no more behooves the social analyst than does cynicism. (The "healthy skepticism" recommended by Aristide Zolberg seems perhaps most apt.) [4] Ascertaining motivations is, at best, a hazardous enterprise; assuming them as given is incognizant subjectivism. It is possible, on the other hand, to analyze regime policies in the light of their ideological and strategic coherence and in terms of their empirical consequences. That, in any case, is the solution adopted here.

We can use the term "development" in two senses. Loosely speaking, it refers simply to the goals of the regime under study; as Edward Shils says of modernity, it is espoused by the leadership of almost every state.[5] The concept of development can also be an external measure of particular types of change. In this case, various spheres of life, each with at least partially autonomous dynamics and alternative directions of change, must be distinguished. Most obviously, political and economic change cannot be reduced to a single process; each possesses partial autonomy.

Within each sphere of life, change may lead not only to development or to decay, but also to partial development. Extending an economic analogy, this latter can be labeled "growth." Economic growth means more output, and economic development refers to changes in the structure and distribution of inputs and outputs as well as to more output.[6] A similar distinction can be applied to political change. Political growth can refer to increased control over the affairs of a polity by its center: more effective coordination of decision making over a wider scope of affairs. Political

[3] See especially Whitaker, "A Dysrhythmic Process," and also Reinhard Bendix, *Nation-Building and Citizenship* (New York, 1964); J. R. Gusfield, "Tradition and Modernity: Misplaced Polarities in the Study of Social Change," *American Journal of Sociology*, vol. 72, 4 (Jan, 1967), 351–362; and Huntington, "Political Development," in Welch, pp. 211–212.

[4] Aristide Zolberg, "Military Intervention in the New States of Tropical Africa," in H. Bienen, ed., *The Military Intervenes* (New York, 1968), p. 76.

[5] Edward Shils, *Political Development in the New States* (The Hague, 1968), p. 7.

[6] See, e.g., Charles Kindleberger, *Economic Development* (New York, 1965), p. 3.

development, on the other hand, means a wider distribution of effective participation by the members of a polity as well as more effective coordination by the center. Political growth is partial political development, just as economic growth is partial economic development. Political decay is assimilable to Huntington's characterization of praetorianism (the intrusion of unregulated participation), or to sheer atrophy of an identifiable polity.[7]

We will be concerned in this paper with the goals and strategies of the Ivory Coast regime for directing internal political and economic change. We will briefly delineate the ideology of the regime, several of its major policy commitments and their consequences, and some of the resulting dilemmas facing the regime.

The goals of the Ivory Coast regime, as constantly reiterated by President Houphouet-Boigny and his aides, appear quite uncontroversial and ideologically unencumbered: to improve the well-being of the Ivorian people and to make the Ivory Coast a modern, model state. This regime bears no responsibility for ideological novelties; its most prized self-image is pragmatic. In the words of the president, "lacking flashy and sterile ideologies, we have chosen the humble path of success and happiness." The new planning minister aptly summarizes the regime perspective: "ideological choices matter little, what is essential is the development of the country." [8]

The Ivorian leadership is not unique, of course, in confining "ideology" to its pejorative connotations, usually with reference to the left. However, unless pragmatism is to be regarded as merely a synonym for muddling through, which it assuredly is not in the Ivory Coast, then a more operational definition of ideology is required for analysis. For our purposes, the definition of T. W. Adorno and his associates is adequate: ideology is simply "an organization of opinions, attitudes, and values—a way of thinking about man and society." [9]

In these terms, every political regime, indeed every individual, has an ideology, though there are certainly great variations in degrees of elaboration, internal consistency, and rhetorical stylization. In the case of the Ivory Coast, there is no regime theoretician, but Houphouet-Boigny is indisputably the ultimate authority, for whom a handful of other leaders are recognized spokesmen. Unlike many other such figures in the new states, Houphouet has not been overly concerned to provide a regular or

[7] See Huntington, *Political Order in Changing Societies* (New Haven, 1968), pp. 80, 192–263.

[8] Houphouet-Boigny, "Discours du Chef de l'Etat," *Fraternité-Matin* (Nov. 1965); Mohamed Diawara, "Interview," *Jeune Afrique* (April 1968).

[9] T. W. Adorno, et al., *The Authoritarian Personality* (New York, 1950), p. 2.

comprehensive rationale to justify the Ivorian regime's options. He has written no book nor even had his speeches collected for publication! Nevertheless, his expressed views and the policy priorities of his leadership over the past two and one-half decades reveal a remarkably consistent ideology.[10]

At the core of Houphouet's ideology is the belief that man must be understood primarily as *homo economicus*, not exclusively, but irreducibly. *Homo economicus*, in the Ivory Coast, is supremely embodied in the wise practical peasant. He is the referent of Houphouet's prosaic appeal to ignore Nkrumah's utopian "political kingdom" and to seek instead a more earthly kingdom based on coffee and cocoa production: "They will fetch you a good price and you will become rich." [11] The self-interest of the Ivorian must be enlightened, of course, even effaced. He must place his career in the context of service to his country and eschew personal ambitions. His political role is to encourage support for a wise leadership which knows how to maximize the use of expertise to promote well-being.

By contrast, *homo politicus* represents an unnatural character type, distorted by excessive pride, who places personal ambition above all else. For the Ivorian regime, such immoderation has a special name: *ascencionnisme*, the attempt to gain public recognition, not through patience and merit, but "by some miraculous pole vault." Its spread is regarded by the regime as the greatest ill that could befall a country.[12]

Men do have needs which can only be satisfied by their involvement in public life, but these are clearly of a secondary order. Their gratification can be more easily postponed, or satisfied through public rituals and other symbolic outputs.[13] Well-being, on the other hand, demands more immediate gratification, although even minimal Ivorian standards of living are high by African standards. This need is defined in such a manner as to induce expectations that there are not necessarily any upper limits. Well-being is not merely freedom from hunger, disease, and ignorance, or dignified poverty above the subsistence level; it is the veritable panoply of goods and services present in the most developed countries. When leaders of the

[10] We will be concerned here only with selected aspects of this ideology. The characterization is intended to be suggestive rather than definitive, but such an effort seems useful in light of the pervasive interest in the highly stylized ideologies of leaders like Nkrumah or Touré, and the rather naive belief that leaders like Houphouet are merely "pragmatic."

[11] Cited in Zolberg, *One-Party Government in the Ivory Coast* (Princeton, 1969), p. 151.

[12] The term *ascencionnisme* was coined publicly for the first time by former Party Secretary-General Auguste Denise at the 1965 PDCI congress. His speech is cited in a provocative study by Lyman Drake, *The Anxious Generation* (Ph.D. dissertation, M.I.T., 1968), pp. 381–385.

[13] See Murray Edelman, *The Symbolic Uses of Politics* (Evanston, 1964).

regime proclaim that their goal is to make Ivorians the equals of the most advanced (*évolués*) peoples of the earth, their reference is less to psychological abstractions than to concrete socioeconomic benefits: public health services and education for all, a modern house for every family, a high income, and the provision of every imaginable consumer satisfaction. In a preview of the regime's plan for the 1971–1975 period, the goals set for Ivorian society have been recently and clearly reiterated: "Now, it is not necessary to conceal that our developmental efforts lead toward . . . the consumer society [as it is known in the West]." [14]

If other African regimes opt for a different set of goals, this is because, as in Ghana under Nkrumah, a *homo politicus*, with his distorted priorities, had gained control of the state. Or, it may be, as in Mali under Modibo Keita, that the country's resources are too meager to envision serious progress toward a consumer society. In 1965, during one of the periodic dressing downs which Houphouet administers to young Ivorians dissatisfied with regime policies, the president insisted that Modibo Keita, whose "socialist option" was widely admired among the educated youth, had told him (Houphouet) that "If I were at the head of a country like the Ivory Coast, with its [economic] realities, my policies would be the same [as yours]. . . ." [15]

Houphouet's interpretation of Ivorian interests, reinforced by ideological affinity and cultural familiarity, have led him to seek close cooperation with the West as the key to a strategy for development. This is a tactical policy, but there is no conflict with long-range goals, as Houphouet would ideally develop the Ivory Coast "as an extension of the West." [16] Solidarity with the Third World is to be rejected, because these other new states "cannot, given the present state of affairs, offer us anything other than the sharing of their own poverty." [17] In other words, Ivorian development is not only geared to significant Western assistance; it is also oriented to the West as a model for this development.

The West is, of course, a highly ambiguous and multifaceted model, but those aspects selectively perceived for emulation by Houphouet's regime are the West as foremost consumer society, as *homo economicus* writ large. Western politics of democratic competition and pluralistic conflict is disconcerting, even frightening, to the Ivorian leadership; but this is regarded as a peculiarity of Western development, unnecessary and undesirable for African development.[18] Lyman Drake found that many educated Ivorian

---

[14] M. Diawara, "Le Second Plan," *Fraternité* (2 Aug. 1968).
[15] "Les Six Heures d'Exposé du Président," *Fraternité* (15 Jan. 1965).
[16] "Le Voyage Américain du President," *Fraternité* (20 Nov. 1959). No wavering of this conviction is apparent over the past decade.
[17] "Délirant Accueil A Man," *Fraternité* (5 Feb. 1960).

youth shared the regime's view that " 'unity' and 'unanimity' are virtually the same": they are conceived as an imperative condition of national survival in a multiethnic society.[19] Unity, and therefore the "postponement" of politics, is also conceived by the regime as a *sine qua non* for development.

To Ivorian leaders, development is almost solely a socioeconomic term, and it is invariably interpreted in terms of certain "indices." From this perspective, there can be little doubt that the Ivory Coast *is* developing and at an impressive rate. The growth since independence of such indices as gross domestic product, industrial and agricultural production, per capita income, investments, and balance of payments surpluses has led many observers to speak of the "Ivorian miracle," especially in comparison with other new states. Statistics equally demonstrate the great expansion of the country's economic infrastructure (ports, roads, hydroelectric power, etc.) and of its social services (health, education, government welfare). Perhaps the most dramatic testimony to the reality of these indices for well-being in the Ivory Coast has been the massive immigration of Africans into the country from neighboring states, especially Upper Volta, Mali, Guinea, and even from relatively prosperous Ghana. Fully one-fourth of the total Ivory Coast population of four million (in 1967) is composed of foreign Africans. The number of Europeans and Lebanese in the country has also increased, severalfold since independence, to reach some 40,000.[20]

Not surprisingly, the Ivorian miracle is not universally regarded as such. Given the magnitude of the problems facing the new African states, no program could be without serious deficiencies in some respect. Yet the common theme in almost every critique of Ivorian policies is one of challenge to the basic priorities of the regime: its emphasis on external infusion rather than internal mobilization. The regime's infusion-orientation has three distinct strands: reliance on European capital, both foreign and local, for industrial expansion and agricultural diversification; reliance on expatriate European cadres for top-level staffing in both the private and the public sectors; and reliance on expatriate African labor, especially seasonal mi-

[18] The fact that Western democratic ideals were utilized by Ivorian leaders in their struggle against French colonialism is less an argument for the universal relevance of these ideals than an example of the peculiarity of the colonial situation, the unique political elements of which were removed by independence.

[19] Drake, *The Anxious Generation*, p. 211 and passim. Also see Zolberg, *Creating Political Order: the Party-States of West Africa* (Chicago, 1966), chap. 2.

[20] Recent Ivorian socioeconomic indices are available from a number of sources: Ivory Coast Planning Ministry, *Perspectives Décennales De Développement Economique, Social et Culturel, 1960–1970* (Monaco, 1967); Ivory Coast Planning Ministry, *Les Comptes de la Nation, 1960–1965* (Monaco, n.d.); Ivory Coast Economic and Social Council, *Rapport Sur l'Evolution Economique et Sociale de la Côte d'Ivoire, 1960–1964* (Abidjan, 1965); and Samir Amin, *Le Développement du Capitalisme en Côte d'Ivoire* (Paris, 1967).

grants from Upper Volta, for the production of cash crops. Each of these strands of infusion involves complex issues which permit divergent interpretations as to the responsibility or wisdom of regime policy. But the thrust of this strategy has been to give priority to considerations of rapid economic growth over considerations of structural change or independence.[21]

The obverse of the emphasis on infusion is the regime's seeming aversion to internal mobilization. While these two strategies are not, theoretically, mutually exclusive, they are seldom associated in practice in the new states. Given the interpretation of regime ideology which I sketched above, the commitment to infusion rather than mobilization does reflect a certain consistency in the case of the Ivory Coast. The dynamics of mass mobilization for development can pose unpredictable problems for regime control. Mobilization can take many forms, but it must at least involve large-scale organization and an effort to politically educate people for collective participation in developmental tasks. The mere existence of an enthusiastic mass organization might greatly increase local conflicts between ethnic and generational rivals. As will be seen below, such conflicts have long plagued the Ivorian scene and are ever near the surface. In addition, political mobilization could provide a weapon for those hostile to the regime's heavy reliance on expatriate European cadres and who would like to institute much more rapid, if not sweeping, Africanization. Such a policy change could, in turn, seriously threaten the flow of European capital into the country. This capital is very sensitive to the political climate, and European capital is closely tied to the European presence, as top-level staff and advisers, in the Ivory Coast.

The tactical incompatibility between infusion and mobilization for development and the priority given to considerations of economic growth over other competing demands and problems have shaped patterns of change peculiar to the Ivory Coast. They have also created several distinctive dilemmas for the Ivorian regime. As used here, the term "dilemma" will be restricted to issues in which the policy alternatives, as recognized and formulated by the regime, are (more or less) equally undesirable.[22]

In these terms the problem of Africanization or continued heavy reliance on expatriate cadres is not a real dilemma for the Ivorian regime. In the first place, the alternatives, as formulated by the regime, are not equally undesirable. To maintain the rate of Africanization at a slow pace, while it offends the sensibilities of the younger elite, does not appear to provoke sustained or organized opposition to the regime. The recurrent crises be-

---

[21] The most comprehensive critique of Ivorian economic strategy is the recent book by Samir Amin, Le Développement du Capitalisme.

[22] For an insightful study of Senegalese developmental dilemmas, see the paper by Jonathan Barker in this volume.

tween the leadership and Ivorian students provide a partial exception to this generalization; but the students have few resources with which to pose a serious political challenge, and their hostility to the regime tends to dissolve when their status changes from student to prospective cadre.[23] The "plots" of 1963, on the other hand, did apparently constitute a serious challenge to the regime, but the actual events remain far too obscure to permit a confident assessment of the motivating issues. While Houphouet is sympathetic to the demands for more rapid Africanization and is making an increasing number of gestures in this direction, the issue remains for him one of recruitment on the basis of absolute achievement criteria, with minimal concessions to nationalist sensitivities: "Pas d'africanisation au rabais!" ("No cut-rate Africanization!") The alternative, threatening the confidence of European capital, is utterly unacceptable.

In the second place, the problem as stated, and as it usually is stated by critics, Africanization *or* expatriate cadres, is a false dilemma from the perspective of the Ivorian regime. The question of high-level manpower recruitment is not a "zero-sum game" in an economy expanding as rapidly as that of the Ivory Coast. Positions are not lacking for trained Ivorian personnel: high-level jobs (managerial, professional, technical) will nearly double in number between 1960 and 1970, and the number of Ivorians professionally qualified for these jobs will be far from sufficient to fill all of them, much less to also replace existing expatriate cadres. According to Elliot Berg, "the manpower deficit—the gap between needs and potential supplies of indigenous high-level manpower—is so vast as to be unbridgeable for two decades." More, not fewer, skilled expatriates will be needed, in addition to maximizing the output of trained Ivorians, in order to staff the country's growing economy.[24]

opment can be viewed as nation building in the hinterland, the process of extending the political, economic, social, and psychological attributes of

If Africanization does not provide a real dilemma for the Ivorian regime, several aspects of local development do.[25] As an area of policy goals, local development encompasses a large part of regime concerns in any new state: the integration or linkage of diverse localities with the center. Local devel-

---

[23] The ambiguity in the attitudes of educated youth toward the Ivorian regime is treated at length in Drake, *The Anxious Generation.*

[24] Elliot Berg, "Education and Manpower in Senegal, Guinea and the Ivory Coast," in F. Harbison and C. A. Myers, eds., *Manpower and Education* (New York, 1965), pp. 254 and passim, 247–255.

[25] For a more detailed analysis of local development in the Ivory Coast, see the author's *Center and Locality: Linkage and Political Change in the Ivory Coast* (Ph.D. dissertation, UCLA, 1970). Other studies of Ivorian local development are also currently in progress, by Leonard Jeffries at Columbia University and Martin Staniland at Sussex University, England.

citizenship within the new national boundaries. Douglas Ashford uses the phrase "local reform" with much the same reference: "the continuing process in every new nation of seeking a way to bring the activities of government closer to the citizen"; indeed, "to make the nation a meaningful frame of reference for millions of subjects, who are citizens in only the most elementary and formal sense." [26]

The major variables distinguishing local development strategies in new states are the spheres selected for regime emphasis, the regional distribution of investment allocation, and the institution(s) utilized for linking policy and locality. We will examine each of these in turn, though the discussion inevitably involves some overlap.

Few, if any, regimes in the new states possess the capability of pursuing local development in every sphere of activity, so that, no matter what priorities are established, there remains a "residual political space which is filled by other structures." [27] Ivorian priorities have eventuated in an emphasis on technical projects designed to increase and diversify agricultural production. There has also been an expansion of primary and, to a lesser extent, secondary educational facilities; the enactment of legal codes, especially in the realms of personal status and land tenure, designed to replace the multiplicity of existing customs with a uniform, modern system of law; and the creation of new, more localized administrative units so as to deconcentrate the authority and services of government.[28] These are conceived as technical-administrative outputs of the regime, and any political-participatory content is heavily circumscribed if not absent altogether. The longer-term strategy behind these programs is to create an "Ivorian identity" for a multiethnic population "as a result of predominantly nonpolitical factors." Nation building is to be achieved almost as a byproduct of the processes of socioeconomic modernization: through "transactional integration" as opposed to integration through participation in affective solidarities.[29]

Generalizing about the economic programs for local development is

[26] Douglas Ashford, *National Development and Local Reform* (Princeton, 1967), pp. 7, 10.

[27] Zolberg, *Creating Political Order*, p. 133.

[28] We will not be concerned in this paper with the educational and legal programs, though they partially fall under the rubric of local development. On the new Ivorian civil code, see two recent papers read at African Studies Association meetings: D. Vallenga, "Attempts to Change Family Law in Ghana and Ivory Coast" (1967), and J. Salacuse, "Modernization of Law in French-Speaking Africa: Revolution or Fantasy?" (1968). Educational problems in Ivory Coast have been the subject of several works: Remi Clignet and Philip Foster, *The Fortunate Few* (Chicago, 1966); Efrem Sigel, "Ivory Coast Education: Brake or Spur?" in *Africa Report* (Jan. 1967); and the works cited by Drake and Berg.

[29] Zolberg, "Patterns of National Integration," *Journal of Modern African Studies*, V, 4 (1967), 464.

hazardous due to the sheer quantity of ongoing projects at any time and the regular announcement of new undertakings. The ambitions and resources at the disposal of the Ivorian regime are markedly greater than in most of West Africa, and at least part of the Ivory Coast does seem, as Houphouet often says, with understandable pride, "a vast construction site." Yet, given the omnipresent risk that observations today will be obsolete tomorrow, the Ivorian strategy for local development appears to contain several unavoidable dilemmas, which I shall attempt to outline under two broad rubrics.

The first might be phrased in the following manner: the regime must modify its present growth priorities and reorient many current programs based essentially on the rationale of attracting external capital for continued growth of "the indices" *or* further exacerbate the already serious regional and social disequilibria engendered by this growth. The latter alternative, namely, a continuation of present policies, does not necessarily imply any threat to regime stability, at least in the short run. But the problems arising from these disequilibria are increasingly cumulative, and the capability of the regime to deal with them will be correspondingly challenged. Furthermore, the increasing conspicuousness of the differences in *relative* well-being in the Ivory Coast poses a credibility gap for the regime with respect to its avowedly nonpolitical developmental goals.

As in much of West Africa, the various components of socioeconomic modernization have progressed at highly uneven rates in the two major regions, north and south, of the Ivory Coast. The northern or savanna region covers roughly one-half of the territory of the present Ivory Coast and, at the turn of this century, possessed about one-half of the estimated population.[30] During the eighteenth and nineteenth centuries, the Mandé of the northern Ivory Coast had developed more sophisticated administrative, economic, and military structures than had their forest neighbors. To the extent that there was contact between the two regions, it was the north which dominated.[31] French colonial rule decisively reversed the traditional advantages of the savanna peoples in favor of those in the forest zone, especially in the southeastern area. This shift was due to longer and more intensive colonization in the south, to a far greater effort of mission and government education, to the introduction of cash crops suited to the forest zone, and to the development of transport and communications be-

[30] Derived from the administrative census of 1901, in F. J. Clozel and Roger Villamur, *Les Coutumes Indigènes de la Côte d'Ivoire* (Paris, 1902), pp. 1–5.

[31] On precolonial political and economic relations between the savanna and forest of contemporary Ivory Coast, see Claude Meillassoux, *Anthropologie Economique des Gouro* (Paris, 1964), chap. 11; Jean Tricart, "Les Echanges Entre la Zone Forestière de Côte d'Ivoire et les Savannes Soudaniennes," *Cahiers d'Outre-Mer*, 35 (July–Sept. 1956), pp. 209–238.

tween the plantation areas of the forest and the coast, whence the cash crops were exported.[32]

By the early 1950s, the terminal colonial period, the inequalities between north and south had been greatly intensified by the cumulative impact of differential rates of socioeconomic change. The north's share of the total Ivorian population had declined to about one-third, chiefly due to the emigration southward. The participation of the savanna zone in the modern sector of the economy was reflected in its mere 7–8 percent contribution to the country's total commercialized production. Per capita monetary income in the north averaged 1,100 CFA francs, compared to 7,100 in the south generally and more than twice that in the plantation areas. And primary school attendance was less than 10 percent in the north, compared to some 50 percent in much of the south.

Over the past fifteen years, when Ivorians have become responsible for national decision making, the disparities between north and south have continued to increase due to the momentum of colonial-induced changes and to the priorities of the Houphouet regime favoring the type of growth already begun. By 1965 the population of the north had continued its relative decline, to slightly over one-fourth of the country's total, and its proportion of commercialized production dropped to 6 percent. Per capita monetary income rose to 2,400 CFA francs, though it still averaged only 1,300 francs outside a project area for cereals among the Senoufo. This compared to 14,000 francs in the south generally and, again, nearly twice that in the plantation areas. Primary school attendance in the north increased slightly to a range of 9–16 percent, compared to a 60–90 percent range in various southern areas.[33]

The French colonial regime had little concern for the fostering of economic integration, either at the level of its West African Federation or within individual territories. According to Elliot Berg, these new states became independent with hardly a semblance of national economies. "The productive coastal regions have been tied to the world market rather than to their own hinterlands or to each other." [34] The new African regimes in these states are all desirous of creating economies that are more national in character, but the economic limitations of most offer few opportunities for exploitations other than those begun under colonial rule. The Ivory

[32] See Zolberg, *One-Party Government*, chap. 1.

[33] These statistics are derived from Amin, *Le Développement du Capitalisme*, pp. 81–82, 290–293; Ivory Coast Ministry of Finance, Economic Affairs, and Planning, *Inventaire Economique et Social de la Côte d'Ivoire, 1947–1958* (Abidjan, 1960), p. 48; and *Ivory Coast Year V; Education* (Paris, 1965), p. 4. Monetary figures reflect only "rural" income averages. If urban and expatriate incomes are added, the "national" Ivorian per capita income exceeds $200 presently.

[34] Berg, "The Economic Basis of Political Choice in French West Africa," *American Political Science Review*, 54, 2 (June 1960), 400.

Coast, however, is considered to have excellent opportunities in almost every sector of the economy. The country is widely regarded as the surest "development prospect" in tropical Africa.[35]

There can be little question of the Ivorian regime's desire to diversify the economy and to integrate the poorer northern areas into a more truly national economy, hitherto dominated by the coffee- and cocoa-producing southern zones. Houphouet has staked the justice of his option on the improved well-being of *all* Ivorians. His reliance on the processes of socio-economic modernization and the spread of prosperity to dissolve particularist loyalties and create "Ivorians" can only succeed if all social and regional groups have access to the possible effects of transactional integration.

Regime recognition of the need to manifest concern for regional inequalities was first symbolized by the creation of new district and regional administrative units (discussed below), and by the decision to hold successive independence day celebrations in the major towns of the interior, with Abidjan as the seat only every five years. Thus far, Bouaké and Korhogo in the savanna region have been so honored, as well as Daloa and Man, which are located on the northern fringe of the forest, Gagnoa in the western forest, and Abengourou in the southeast. The independence celebration becomes the occasion for focusing on the problems of the various areas of the interior.

From 1965 the regime began to devote a good deal of rhetoric to the necessity for development of the north, and to "the unity and especially the equality of all Ivorians, north, south, east and west." Houphouet made a tour of the north, promising that "the savanna will have its revenge . . . [and that] each peasant . . . will attain equality with his southern brothers within five years." [36] A series of foreign journalists "discovered" the Ivory Coast at about this time, and they were all cited in the party weekly, *Fraternité*, with such comments as: "In ten years the southern forest region will envy the north. . . ." "The inhabitants of the forest will immigrate into the savanna zones, which will become the richest regions of the country." [37]

More recently, the public rhetoric of regional equality has been muted (as, indeed, have forecasts of imminent 100 percent primary school attendance and of "no more huts or slums" by 1970 or 1975) in favor of more modest and long-term predictions. There are several reasons why development of the north must remain a fairly low priority within the present

[35] See, e.g., William Hance, "Development Limitations and Opportunities in Tropical Africa," *Africa Report* (Jan. 1967).

[36] "Le Chef de l'Etat à Korhogo," *Fraternité* (14 May 1965).

[37] *Fraternité* (19 Dec. 1964; 1 Jan. 1965; 10 Sept. 1965).

Ivorian developmental strategy. The rapid rise of output indices has been, and probably could only have been, based on large-scale investment in "critical sectors" of the economy—those already most developed, and therefore most likely to return a sure and quick profit to the investor. A number of eminent economists, such as Albert O. Hirschman and W. Arthur Lewis, fully endorse the critical sectors approach. Lewis believes that redistribution of developmental efforts to benefit the poorer areas within the new states would "nip development in the bud." [38] Houphouet is certainly not predisposed to discourage those investors, whom he has striven so successfully to attract, by establishing priorities seriously at odds with their own, and perhaps also at odds with continued rapid growth. He does, however, occasionally upbraid the resident French "patronat" for their conservatism in investing almost exclusively in the established sectors and most developed areas.

A second reason for assigning low priority to development of the north is, as noted earlier, that European capital is closely tied to the European presence in the Ivory Coast; and that presence is heavily concentrated in Abidjan and several secondary towns in the south. There are Europeans throughout the country, but these are mainly "technical assistance" personnel, especially young teachers and rural extension agents. Abidjan alone contains 69 percent of all commercial and industrial establishments in the Ivory Coast and 85 percent of all salaried employees. Needless to say, these figures approach 100 percent if only the largest businesses and the top-level personnel are considered.[39] European investments, then, continue to be concentrated in Abidjan and its rather immediate hinterland, because, among other things, European personnel involved in managing and staffing investment projects prefer to reside in or very near the capital with its comforts and European social life, rather than in the bush—and the northern region offers very little except bush.

A third reason behind the low priority for northern development is that the probable requirements for a successful strategy in this region may be incompatible with the general Ivorian strategy based on infusion. If foreign capital cannot be attracted easily to the north, and if there is very little indigenous momentum (both of which are true), then the alternative lies in some form of mobilization to promote development from below, as it were. Poor countries call for very different strategies than do relatively rich ones, and the Ivory Coast is really composed of both types. However,

[38] W. A. Lewis, "Random Reflections on Local Development in Africa," in Foreign Service Institute, *Local Development in Africa* (Washington, D.C., July 1967), pp. 34–35.
[39] Victor DuBois, "Social Aspects of the Urbanization Process in Abidjan," *American Universities Field Service Reports*, X, 1 (Nov. 1967), 6.

the regime is overwhelmingly southern-born and/or southern-oriented, so that a distinctive northern strategy has never been evolved. Indeed, a strategy which called for mobilization in the north, but not in the south, could involve a certain political risk for such a regime.

It should be reemphasised that I am discussing relative priorities, because there has been some socioeconomic progress in the north. One has only to compare the Malian or Upper Voltan side of this same general region to realize how wealthy the Ivory Coast is by African standards. Capital and cadres have been injected into the north to improve its infrastructure and to expand its monetary economy. A major hydroelectric project, the Kossou Dam in the south-central part of the savanna zone, is scheduled for completion in 1972, which should certainly offer new productive opportunities for cereal crops, at least among the Baoulé and Senoufo of the region.

Nevertheless, these programs taken together remain extremely modest by the standards of continuing socioeconomic advances in the southern Ivory Coast, where vast infusions of capital and cadres are working to diversify and expand the Ivorian economy. A recent report of the Planning Ministry admitted that "all [of the major new economic projects] are located in the southern part of the country. We run the risk, therefore, of further accentuating the disequilibrium which already exists between the north and the south, if we are not careful." [40] The role of the north in a continuing strategy of growth through infusion is the marginal one of reducing the need for Ivorian food imports through cereal production, thereby releasing some foreign exchange to finance increasing capital-goods imports. The economic benefits to the north are very slight in monetary terms and limited to select areas along the railroad that runs from Abidjan into Upper Volta.[41]

The Planning Law for 1967–1970 points out very clearly the danger of greater regional inequalities, and especially the disequilibrium between Abidjan and the hinterland. The population of the capital tripled between 1957 and 1967; it rose to 500,000 in 1970 and will attain 1,000,000 shortly after 1980. The eighty towns next in size in the Ivory Coast have a combined population inferior to that of Abidjan currently. Per capita income in the capital is equally beyond common measure with the hinterland: thirty-seven times the northern average and sixty times the rural northern average. There is thus, understandably, a heavy exodus of youth from the rural north to the southern towns, especially to Abidjan. Even by 1975 it is estimated that Ivorian growth will provide jobs in the urban centers for only 9 percent of the active population, adding urban sprawl and spiraling unemployment in the south to rural stagnation in the north. In the words of

[40] Ivory Coast Planning Ministry, *Perspectives Décennales*, p. 111.
[41] *Perspectives Décennales*, p. 111.

the regime planners, "it is unthinkable to allow such a process to develop without reacting." [42]

The manner in which the regime will react to the dilemma of regional disequilibrium has not been detailed as yet. Apparently the problem has not been accepted, at least by Houphouet and his closest advisers, as a dilemma in the terms in which I have formulated it, but, as in the case of Africanization, as a "non-zero-sum game." In other words, the regime intends to maintain and intensify its strategy of growth through infusion, while expanding programs for the development of the "traditional rural world," that is, the non-cash-crop areas, primarily the north. These programs will demand a certain decentralization of investments, mostly from public sources, and participatory efforts at the local level so as to involve a greater number of Ivorians "in the productive effort and in the benefits of growth." [43]

Although these added efforts on behalf of the disadvantaged areas will probably enhance the well-being of northerners and subsistence farmers generally, continued growth, with its own cumulative effects, will likely relegate the consequences to little more than a peripheral modification of present trends. Due to the momentum toward ever greater inequalities between regions (and between various social strata, a subject beyond the scope of this paper), the dilemma inevitably takes on some of the characteristics of a zero-sum game. It is difficult to see how such a dilemma can be resolved through the priorities of liberal, expansionist policies. The regime is, of course, counting on economic progress to sufficiently ameliorate absolute well-being that the dilemma will be superseded, or at least prevented from becoming a dangerous political issue.

At present, the regime is faced with a second local development dilemma, which is, in effect, an extension of the first dilemma, but which also reflects a new flexibility in Ivorian ideology. The pursuit of continued growth and the amelioration of the disequilibria engendered by this growth increasingly require, it is now believed, "the participation of the people." Even economic growth can no longer be assured, apparently, by infusion alone. Regime spokesmen have begun to distinguish, publicly, economic growth and development in the terms presented at the outset of this paper. In the words of Planning Minister Diawara, participation is necessary "in order for growth to become development." [44]

This statement apparently presages an attempt, at the policy-planning

---

[42] "Loi portant loi-plan de développement économique, social et culturel pour 1967–1970," *Journal Officiel de la République de Côte d'Ivoire, 1967,* no. 37; pp. 1083, 1086, 1106; and *Perspectives Décennales,* p. 90.

[43] See M. Diawara, "Le Second Plan"; *Perspectives Décennales,* p. 28; and "Loi-Plan, 1967–1970," pp. 1104, 1106.

[44] M. Diawara, "Le Second Plan."

stage, to reconcile the hitherto empirically exclusive strategies of infusion and mobilization. Yet a strategy of mobilization, however its relationship to a continued reliance on infusion is conceived, presents certain political risks for the regime, which it has shown no indication of being willing to accept. Political risks are, perhaps, inherent in mobilization of the population in underdeveloped countries, as Huntington has argued.[45] The potential for conflict in the Ivory Coast is certainly very great, particularly along ethnic and generational lines. Conflict may well erupt, of course, in the absence or outside the framework of structures designed for mobilization, as it frequently has in the Ivory Coast. Yet such conflict is more easily isolated and suppressed by the regime than were it to occur within an arena that provided access to modern organizational resources.

I will broach only selected aspects of this second dilemma here, because, although the Ivorian regime has committed itself to somehow engaging the participation of the people, its methods and organizational vehicles for carrying out this task are not clearly revealed as yet.

Thus far, local development has been primarily a series of technical projects, for which the prototypes are those undertaken by publicly chartered *Sociétés d'Etat* to diversify the economy by organizing the production of new crops: rubber, fruits, palm oil, rice, etc. The *Sociétés* are assisted by research organs, by professional agencies for the training of local cadres, and by the technical field agents of the Ivorian ministries. Their goal is to augment, improve, and diversify production. The operation of these projects is heavily dominated by Europeans, and they are not integrated into any general Ivorian program for "animation rurale" or cooperatives.[46]

The function of a mobilization strategy must be to develop participatory structures which can link the technical projects to supportive organizations among the populace. Among the structures at least potentially available for this task are the party, local government councils, and cooperatives; ideally, all three would be complementary. Activation or reform of these structures, however, has been consistently deferred by the regime. This dilatory policy is, in part, a result of fear that existing social cleavages might be crystallized in struggles for control of local offices endowed with decision-making authority; but it is also due to regime reluctance to decentralize controls.[47]

[45] See Huntington, "Political Development and Political Decay," in Welch.
[46] A study in progress by L. Jeffries examines the role of the *Sociétés d'Etat* in the development of southeastern Ivory Coast.
[47] Cooperatives are little developed in the Ivory Coast and will not be treated here. For a history of the failures of cooperatives in Ivory Coast, see *Fraternité* (18 Feb. 1966). I have analyzed the role of party and administrative structures for linking policy and locality more extensively in "Political and Administrative Linkage in the Ivory

The rise of African political organization following World War II ushered in a period of intense rivalry in the Ivory Coast. Although even the dominant Parti Démocratique de Côte d'Ivoire (PDCI) was never a mass-based organization, there was widespread political mobilization and activity during the party's apogee, 1948–1951.[48] Some Ivorians look back on this period almost nostalgically as a time of excitement, of glorious deeds, of "politics." They remember it as a clear-cut and historic struggle against colonial and native enemies.[49] Yet, for many Ivorians (and almost all express some ambiguity), "the experience of militancy revealed the dangers of separatism . . . by reviving the centrifugal tendencies stemming from the sharp cultural differentiations that exist in the country. . . . The memory of conflicts during this period instilled . . . a fear of the consequences of political competition and mass mobilization for action."[50]

In both urban and rural areas throughout the country, party recruitment and election campaigns crystallized local cleavages between immigrant "strangers" and settlers, between Muslims and animists, between youth and elders, and among ethnic groups. Political competition sparked latent *racisme* among Ivorians and often led to violent conflicts, over which party leaders had very little control.[51] Organized political competition came to an end in 1957 with the establishment of the PDCI as the de facto single Ivorian party. Since that time, overt local conflict has been muted or forcibly and quickly suppressed by the regime; but many of the old (and some new) tensions remain exceedingly close to the surface. During the past three years Abidjan, particularly, has witnessed demonstrations and violent clashes based on ethnic, labor, and student grievances.[52] These events cause great anxiety among Ivorian leaders, to the extent that stability has become synonymous with quiescence and "unity is perceived as the alternative to chaos."[53]

In order to achieve stability, if not unity, the regime has attempted to concretize its authority and expand central controls through the imposition

---

Coast," in Philip Foster and Aristide Zolberg, eds., *Patterns of Modernization: Ghana and the Ivory Coast* (forthcoming).

[48] See Zolberg, *One-Party Government*, chap. IV; and his *Creating Political Order*, chap. I.

[49] Based on personal interviews. Also see Zolberg, *One-Party Government*, p. 132n.

[50] Zolberg, *One-Party Government*, pp. 144–145.

[51] On local political conflicts, see Zolberg, *One-Party Government*, pp. 131–134, 202–205; Ruth Schacter Morgenthau, *Political Parties in French-Speaking West Africa* (Oxford, 1964), pp. 206–209; Henri Raulin, *Mission d'Etude des Groupements Immigrés en Côte d'Ivoire* (Paris, 1957), pp. 88–9, 120–130; and my *Center and Locality: Linkage and Political Change in the Ivory Coast*.

[52] Such incidents are frequently unreported in Ivorian newspapers, but regular accounts can be found in *Le Monde* and *Le Mois en Afrique*.

[53] Drake, *The Anxious Generation*, p. 211.

of a common institutional grid on the country. Labor and youth organizations have been purged, dissolved, and then re-created under the control of central party leadership. The PDCI organization has been extended throughout the villages of the hinterland, dissident leaders have been purged, and the president and his most loyal aides have regained control over the party apparatus (which they had lost partially from 1959 to 1963).

Finally, the governmental bureaucracy has been greatly centralized and the number of its agents multiplied throughout the country. The territorial administrative apparatus is an integrated prefectoral system based on the deconcentration of central authority from the Ministry of Interior to twenty-four prefects. Hierarchically subordinate to the prefects are more than a hundred subprefects, who administer district units called subprefectures. Other ministries have their own field agents (agriculture, health, etc.), whose activities are coordinated at the prefectoral level. This administrative "deconcentration is only another form of centralization" and must not be confused with any devolution of central authority to autonomous local bodies.[54] As Zolberg notes, "there is little doubt that this downward penetration represents a substantial increase in the center's potential for control over the localities." [55]

This political growth by the center has not been matched by any significant structural reforms to permit effective participation by the people. Following the time of politics noted above and the ensuing repression by the French colonial administration, the PDCI seriously declined as an organizational reality in the Ivory Coast. Articulation between the national leadership and the local sections became intermittent, at best, and intraparty democracy never developed at any level. Since independence, there have been periodic attempts to revive the party organization, but the persistence of ethnic and generational conflicts have frustrated most efforts at reform. Then the "plots" of 1963 called into question the very reliability of a more active PDCI from the perspective of the regime. A measured and deliberate effort to reimpose central control over the party apparatus has been in evidence since the crises, and the regime felt there had been sufficient progress by 1965 to hold the first PDCI congress since independence. Although the congress was more a display of the new sense of confidence among the Ivorian leadership than of intraparty democracy, there have

[54] The quotation is from R. G. Lavallé, *Le Manuel du Sous-Préfet* (Abidjan, 1965), p. 5. On Ivorian local administration, see M. J. Campbell, et al., *The Structure of Local Government in West Africa* (The Hague, 1965) pp. 160–177; Martin Staniland, "Local Administration in Ivory Coast," *West Africa*, 2649 (9 March 1968), and 2650 (16 March 1968); and Lavallée, *Le Manuel du Sous-Préfet*. On "integrated prefectoral systems" in general, see R. C. Fried, *The Italian Prefects* (New Haven, 1963), pp. 306–310.
[55] Zolberg, *Creating Political Order*, p. 115.

been, for perhaps the first time, contested elections in many of the local party sections over the past four years. The PDCI would appear to have stemmed, if not reversed, "the trend . . . toward inanition," which Wallerstein detected generally in West Africa.[56]

Yet the party does not have a privileged, nor even an observably discrete, role in Ivory Coast development. In spite of occasional rhetoric about its "explanatory and persuasive" role in local development, the party is not a focus for either educational or organizational tasks. Ivorian plans, even the more recent and comprehensive documents cited in this paper, omit any reference to the PDCI. There is little evidence that regime efforts to obtain the participation of the people in local development will entail significant reliance on the party organization.

Apart from the party, the most symbolically important participant structures in the Ivory Coast have been the municipal councils in the larger towns. Nine Ivorian towns had been granted varying degrees of municipal autonomy by the mid-1950s, following years of colonial vacillation on the subject. Although the functions of these councils are rigidly circumscribed (as in France, it is the mayor and other administrative officials who "run" the municipal communes), their institution represented the most significant devolution of decision-making authority to any locally elected body. Consequently, the muncipal elections of 1956 were the occasion for intense rivalry to obtain seats in the multiethnic Ivorian towns. "In Bouaké, for example, though only 31 municipal councillors were elected, in November 1956 fully a thousand candidates sought the nomination. Inevitably the competition took an ethnic form." [57] In Bouaké, as in Man, Gagnoa, and probably other towns, the elections crystallized ethnic tensions and led to violence, particularly between "strangers" and settlers.[58] There have been no subsequent municipal elections.

Furthermore, despite legislative proposals to promote a number of new towns to communal status, no new communes have been created; and, among existing communes, one has lost its municipal status and another has seen its council dissolved by decree. In a recent paper by an Ivorian state prosecutor, which appears to reflect regime policy, the role of municipal communes in the Ivory Coast is called into question. There are indi-

[56] I. Wallerstein, "Decline of the Party in Single-Party African States," in J. LaPalombara and M. Weiner, eds., *Political Parties and Political Development* (Princeton, 1966), p. 208. On regime efforts to revitalize the PDCI, see Zolberg, *Creating Political Order*, pp. 99–101. The 1970 PDCI Congress appears to have been a replay of the 1965 Congress, and no significant personnel or policy changes occurred.
[57] Morgenthau, p. 216.
[58] On the violence in Bouaké and Gagnoa, see Zolberg, *One-Party Government*, pp. 202–203; information on Man is from personal interviews.

cations that they may be phased out altogether in favor of less autonomous local units, defined by the territorial administrative structure.[59]

At independence, two extant models were available to the Ivorian regime for organizing some sort of local participation in rural areas. One of these structures was that of the old *conseils de notables*. These had been notoriously ineffective since their inception at the end of World War I. They had been reformed to some extent during the terminal colonial period to enhance their representatives and their influence. Their reformation may have been no more than a belated effort by the colonial administration to counter the influence of the PDCI in rural areas, but the councils as reformed clearly represented a structure for more significant local participation in development activities than any previous conciliar organs. The other potential participatory structure, more explicit in its "democratic" conception, was that of the *collectivités rurales* proposed in the Loi-Cadre reforms of 1957. These were to possess elective councils and considerable financial autonomy, and to be consultative rather than merely advisory.[60]

The Ivorian regime opposed the project for *collectivités rurales* from the beginning, allegedly because Houphouet insisted that "the people are not mature enough politically." [61] The more limited reforms in the *conseils de notables* were also circumscribed at independence with the elimination of their only significant financial resources; and they were formally dissolved in 1967. In place of these councils, the regime recently instituted new local organs called *conseils de sous-préfecture*, based on the territorial administrative units. The new councils are composed primarily of ex officio members—the field agents of the ministries resident within the subprefecture—plus a dozen members appointed by the subprefect. The council must be consulted on the use of certain, extremely limited, taxes collected locally; but it meets only twice yearly, and the agenda is controlled entirely by its president, the subprefect.[62]

At the next-higher administrative level, the regional *départements*, the regime has begun to institute councils called *commissions de développement régional*. Their composition and apparent procedures are parallel to the district *conseils de sous-préfecture*. Eventually the regional commissions may replace the elective, but dormant, *conseils généraux*, created a decade ago but never operative.[63]

[59] See Camille Hoguie, "Structure et Organisation Communales en Côte d'Ivoire," *Revue Juridique et Politique*, XXII, 2 (April–June 1968), 371–378.

[60] See Montagnat, "Les Collectivités Rurales," *Revue Juridique et Politique*, XII, 2 (April–June 1958), 331–336.

[61] Information supplied by a central administrative official who prefers to remain anonymous.

[62] See *Journal Officiel* (1967), no. 27, special issue.

[63] See "Loi-Plan, 1967–1970," pp. 1106–1107; and *Fraternité* (21 March 1969).

Quite clearly, these proposals are designed to maximize control by agents of the central administration over local participatory organs and to minimize local autonomy. The territorial administrative organization and the councils attached at its several levels increasingly appear to be the privileged institutional grid for linking central policy and the localities in the Ivory Coast. In the words of the judicial official cited earlier, "Given the [present] state of the social and economic situation of the country, it is on the basis of this administrative structure that we must envision the future of Ivorian communes." [64]

Whether or not participation in any meaningful sense can emerge within this structure remains to be seen. The political risks of mobilization still outweigh the potential contributions of participation to local development from the perspective of the regime. However, if Minister Diawara and the planners are correct in viewing widespread and effective participation as a requisite of local development; and if Ashford is correct in assuming that "very little developmental activity can begin at the local level until some decentralization takes place," then the regime may find this dilemma to be its most critical challenge in the near future.[65]

This outline of major developmental dilemmas facing the Ivorian regime should not be construed as a broadside condemnation of the regime and its policies, in spite of my critical perspective. The dilemmas discussed, after all, are relatively sophisticated and noncatastrophic by the standards of the new states: neither institutional breakdown nor even the certain limits of spreading well-being can be foreseen in the immediate future. Ivorian economic change may or may not be growth without development; [66] but Ivorians are a relatively privileged people within the Third World. On the other hand, *political* change in the Ivory Coast *would* appear to be a case of growth without development thus far. Ivorians are not yet on the road to becoming a citizenry.

[64] Hoguie, pp. 377-378.
[65] Ashford, *National Development and Local Reform*, p. 10.
[66] See Amin, *Le Développement du Capitalisme*; and R. H. Green, "Ghana and the Ivory Coast, 1957-67" (paper presented to African Studies Association meeting, 1967); both of whom argue that the Ivory Coast is a case of economic growth without development. For a vigorous contrary view, see Elliot Berg, "Structural Transformation vs. Gradualism: Economic Development in Ghana and the Ivory Coast," in Foster and Zolberg, eds., *Patterns of Modernization: Ghana and the Ivory Coast* (forthcoming).

Chapter 7 Agricultural Policy in Uganda: Capability and Choice

M. Crawford Young

INTRODUCTION

Cotton and coffee are the lumbering oxen that draw Uganda's chariot of development.* Steel mill and oil derrick may symbolize more dramatic propelling mechanisms for the developmental process, but these lie beyond the pale of possibility for Uganda and many other African states. Economic environment, political scale, and geological endowment impose the parameters of choice; the resources for development must be generated in the cash agricultural sector. The problem is given succinct summary by Uganda's planners:

Agriculture is at present by far the most important sector of the Ugandan economy. It accounts for more than half of gross domestic produce and for 80–90% of overseas export earnings. Perhaps even more important is the fact that as much as 90 per cent of the population are dependent in this sector for their income.

For the next generation and longer, even with the maximum possible diversification of the economy, agriculture will remain the most important source of domestic income, foreign exchange and employment . . . .

Thus, if Uganda is to develop rapidly and if the mass of the population are going to benefit from this development, agriculture must play its role as a major spearhead of development.[1]

A related, and central, postulate unanimously shared by political elites,

*This chapter was completed before the coup of early 1971 which overthrew the Obote government.

[1] *Work for Progress: Uganda's Second Five Year Plan, 1966–1971* (Entebbe, 1966), p. 55.

planners, and advisers is that the state must organize and direct the developmental effort. Agricultural growth will not come from the occult workings of an invisible hand, but through the guidance and stimulation of the political and administrative structures. This, then, poses an important set of questions, which are asked all too infrequently: What are the capabilities of the polity in fulfilling these tasks? What boundaries upon policy choice are placed upon the policy makers by the limitations in system capability?

More frequently, these issues are translated into more technical questions of seed strain and marketing mechanism, and handed over to the agronomists and economists for solution. In the process political variables tend to disappear. Political scientists, on the other hand, have ascribed to themselves the field of "political development," where topics such as national integration and nation building, political elites and parties, socialization and recruitment are contemplated. In these analyses the role of economic factors is small indeed, and their absence is defended in terms of the "primacy of politics." But the central issues of Uganda's development cannot be addressed by the political scientist without integrating into his analysis the concerns and contributions of the economist and the agricultural scientist. James S. Coleman has lucidly delineated the requirements of the situation: "The time has come to recognize the professional respectability as well as the practical essentiality of the ancient and honorable hybrid discipline of 'political economy.' . . . The interdependence of political, administrative and economic aspects of modern statecraft must be matched by an interdisciplinary perspective among those scholars essaying to comprehend, analyze and provide policy guidance for national development." [2]

The authors of the best extant discussion of system capabilities note that "Empirical study of what political systems actually do in their social and international environments represents something of an innovation in political theory." [3] It is suggested that capabilities may be analyzed in terms of extractive, regulative, distributive, symbolic, and responsive categories. In relating these to the specific context of agricultural development in Uganda, we will be particularly concerned with the capacity of the government and political elite to effectuate measurable change in the agricultural sector. At stake is the ability to reorganize the structure of agriculture, to reorient production toward maximum economic return to both state and producer, to diffuse new technology to rural smallholders, and to enhance the productivity of the peasant. The Almond and Powell model lies too far from Coleman's new frontier of political economy to provide

---

[2] James S. Coleman, "The Resurrection of Political Economy," *Mawazo* (June 1967), p. 31.
[3] Gabriel Almond and Bingham Powell, Jr., *Comparative Politics* (Boston, 1966), p. 190.

a fully serviceable conceptual infrastructure, but their categories are very suggestive and partly usable.

The range of inputs in agricultural policy choice is very substantial. An agricultural program is a composite of seeds, fertilizer, pesticides, energy sources (human, animal, medicine), marketing, processing, price manipulation, credit, taxation, land tenure, conservation practices, credit facilities, extension services, cooperative organization, farmer education, and research and experimentation.[4] In this discussion we are primarily concerned (as is the Uganda government) with the export crops which have made the major contribution to Ugandan development both now and in the past: cotton and coffee. We will summarize the central aspects of postindependence agricultural policy, consider the political environment within which it has occurred, analyze the structural resources of the Uganda government in policy implementation, and finally suggest possible relationships between system capabilities and policy choice. The very nature of the exercise compels us to trespass into the domain of those technically trained in the agricultural field; we do not pretend to a full grasp of the technology of agricultural development, but the effort rests upon the conviction that a dialog between agricultural technocrat and social scientist is indispensable to the emergence of a policy-relevant science of development.

AGRICULTURAL POLICY CHOICES

The theme that runs through Ugandan agricultural policy is the drive to increase the productivity of farmers producing cotton and coffee. The methods have varied since World War I, when agricultural policy became directed wholly toward African producers, but the central thrust has been the same. The main trends in cotton and coffee development, however, were toward enlarged production through increased acreage, rather than higher productivity. The record cotton crop of 1938 was not surpassed until 1965. During the period in between, the most significant development was the shift out of cotton into robusta coffee in Buganda, and a compensatory spread of cotton cultivation among previously subsistence farmers in the northern region.[5]

Independence brought in its wake an enhanced sense of urgency in accelerating agricultural development, but it also brought a stubborn set of problems. Cotton productivity had, according to official calculations,

[4] See the more comprehensive list mounted by an interdisciplinary team at M.I.T. in Max Millikan and David Hapgood, *No Easy Harvest* (Boston, 1967), p. 15.

[5] For the most useful surveys of Uganda's economic history, see C. C. Wrigley, "Crops and Wealth in Uganda," in *East African Studies*, no. 12 (Kampala, 1959), and Cyril Ehrlich, "The Uganda Economy, 1903–1945," in Vincent Harlow, et al., *History of East Africa*, vol. II (Oxford, 1965), pp. 395–475.

remained nearly static at the low level of 450 pounds of seed cotton per acre.[6] Agricultural specialists believe that yields of 1,000 pounds per acre are within the reach of smallholders if optimum procedures are followed. On the coffee front, the establishment of the International Coffee Agreement set an export quota closely related to the existing crop size. Therefore, policy had to be directed to improving the quality of the existing crop, so that a higher return could be achieved on the basis of the same or only a slowly rising total output. A panoply of policies was defined to enlarge the pool of resources being generated by cotton and coffee; centrally directed initiative, for several reasons, tended to focus upon the cotton sector.

In the management of cotton production, the role of the state in supervising peasant cultivation has been substantial, although not as pervasive and coercive as in the neighboring Congo. Only improved seed strains distributed by the state were permitted to be sown. Explicit rules on spacing of crops, weeding, and planting dates were adopted under administrative pressure as district bylaws, and enforced by the customary judicial system. The principal pest control measure was the uprooting and burning of the harvested plants, which required active enforcement measures by the local government.

The major innovation since independence has been the effort to generalize the use of DDT spray for pest control. The Agriculture Department promised farmers who used the spray properly yield increases of 50–70 percent,[7] although it was conceded that the average increase for spray users had been only 174 pounds per acre rather than the 400 promised.[8] In 1963, the first year that spray application was general policy, spray was distributed free; the following year a charge of Sh10 per tin was levied (the recommended spraying program required four tins per acre during the growing season). In the following years it was planned to charge only five shillings, or 25 percent of cost.

Fertilizers have made possible major yield increases elsewhere; for example, the spectacular growth in cotton production since 1960 in northern Nigeria has been largely through higher yields achieved by fertilizer inputs. In Uganda, however, the Agriculture Department has long been skeptical of the feasibility of a major fertilizer campaign, and uncertain as to the

[6] The preliminary results of the agricultural census carried out by the FAO and Uganda Government, 1962–1966, suggest that the real cotton acreage may have been only 60% of the previous estimates on which yields were calculated. Thus real yields may be significantly higher than previously believed, although still low—in comparison with the UAR, Gezira, northern Nigeria, or the U.S.

[7] Uganda Government, *Agricultural Production Programme—1964* (Entebbe, 1964), p. 16.

[8] *Work for Progress: Uganda's Second Five Year Plan*, p. 64.

proper variety. The result has been delay in implementation of a fertilizer program. The Second Five Year Plan pledged action on this front, and suggested that a yield increase of 200 pounds per acre could be achieved.[9] Nothing, however, can be done until the agricultural service mobilizes its full resources behind the introduction of fertilizer. The smallholder is dependent upon the Agriculture Department for initial access to a major innovation, such as fertilizer use.

The commitment to accelerated development since independence has led to a major allocation of resources to related policies such as group farms and mechanization. The group farm policy was initially inspired by the Israeli *moshav*. It was introduced by former Agriculture Minister Matthias Ngobi [10] after a visit to Israel; the Ugandan adaptation combined aspects of the *moshav ovdim* (with plots allocated to individual farmers) and the *moshav shitoufi* (with work tasks being performed in collective teams). A group of farmers, usually between a hundred and three hundred, organized into a cooperative, is situated on unused land to which title can be cleared by the local government land board. The government provides extensive supervisory personnel, including an expatriate technician, and an ample endowment in tractors to clear and plow the land. The first three group farms were established in 1963; forty were in existence by 1966, and at least a hundred new ones were pledged for the Second Five Year Plan period. The pivotal cash crop for most group farms so far established has been cotton. Coffee areas are not suitable for mechanization. Also, the Buganda government until its dissolution in 1966 controlled its own agricultural policy, and was resolutely opposed to group farms as a potential threat to the *mailo* land tenure system in effect in the kingdom. In the other major coffee-producing area, Bugisu, a high population density has long since brought into coffee cultivation virtually all suitable land on Mount Elgon.[11]

The heavy investment in group farms is closely related to the conviction that mechanization of agriculture is crucial to development. Of the 876 tractors which Uganda had purchased in the first five years of independence, approximately two-thirds were assigned to group farms, with the remainder placed in tractor-hire stations.[12] On repeated occasions, Uganda's leaders have proclaimed their pledge to mechanization to hasten the

---

[9] *Work for Progress*, p. 64.

[10] Ngobi was minister of Agriculture and Co-operatives from 1962 to 1966; he was one of five ministers arrested in February 1966 on charges of conspiracy to overthrow the Obote government, and has been in confinement since that time.

[11] On group farms, see Aaron Segal, "The Politics of Land in East Africa," *Africa Report*, XII, 4 (April 1967), pp. 46–50; Simon Charsley, "Group Farming in Bunyoro (Uganda)," East African Institute of Social Research Conference Paper, 1966.

[12] *Uganda Argus* (15 Feb. 1968).

pace of agricultural expansion; tractors are a veritable symbol of urgency. Typical is the assertion in the Second Five Year Plan that "It is important that mechanization methods of cultivation be made available to as many farmers as possible so that they become involved in modern farming techniques." [13] The projected development expenditure for 1966–1971 shows £5,790,000 allocated for group farms and tractors, or more than one-fourth of the total planned investment in agriculture of £19,640,000.[14] The degree of stress that mechanization has received has come under attack both by the opposition and by agricultural economists. Democratic party parliamentary leader Alex Latim has claimed that "tractors were distributed to farmers on political grounds." [15] Economists have challenged the high cost involved in both mechanized group farms and tractor-hire schemes. The fee charged for tractor use is Sh45 per acre; this fee is deemed too low to cover the costs of the tractor-hire service, and unless yields are sharply increased the rental is too high for a peasant farmer to afford (at 450 pounds per acre the cash return on cotton was only Sh270 per acre even with the exceptionally favorable prices in 1965–66).

Credit is believed to be another major bottleneck, and has received priority attention since independence. Superficially, the problem is obvious; peasant farmers by definition do not have the cash liquidity to make any investment in improved agricultural techniques. The tax collector and school treasurer are waiting at harvest time, and little is on hand by the next planting season. Indeed, a striking aspect of Ugandan (and most African) agriculture is the near-total absence of private credit mechanisms, and the attendant problem of rural indebtedness. Thus, if farmers are going to be induced to utilize pesticides or fertilizers for which a charge is made, or to hire tractors, a functioning credit system must be available. For some years various approaches have been essayed and problems of enforcing appropriate utilization of loans and eliminating high default rates have been a chronic obstacle. In 1961 J. C. Ryan of the Reserve Bank of India proposed a credit plan based upon an Indian scheme, by which loans were made in the form of goods or services (spray, tractor hire) through cooperative societies; repayment was assured through the requirement that crops be marketed through the cooperative, with the loan repayment simply deducted.[16] In 1962–63, 7,000 loans were made, and in the following year over 17,000. On this pilot basis, a very good repayment record of over 90 percent was maintained. The impact on production, however, was

[13] *Work for Progress*, p. 59.
[14] *Work for Progress*, p. 75.
[15] *Uganda Argus* (21 June 1966).
[16] Some observers have expressed doubt about the Ryan Scheme's success in India; see Daniel Thorner, *Agricultural Co-operatives in India: A Field Report* (Bombay, 1964); Kusim Mair, *Blossoms in the Dust* (New York, 1961).

very small; the loans themselves were for petty amounts, ranging from Sh30 to Sh1,000. The Second Five Year Plan proposed expanding the scheme to offer loans to 150,000 farmers (of a total of 1,170,921 land-holders).[17]

A growing emphasis in agricultural policy is on diversification of crops. Approximately 70 percent of total export earnings, and roughly 90 percent of agricultural exports, are accounted for by cotton and coffee. Histori-cally, the agricultural extension services were primarily geared to the promotion of these two crops; the processing and marketing infrastructure is even more exclusively bound to them. The International Coffee Agree-ment precludes any significant expansion of coffee production, while cot-ton prospects on the world market are only fair. The additional crops that will receive major emphasis are tea, tobacco, and sugar. Also, planners hope to expand both beef and dairy cattle production.

These, then, are the major policy goals as reformulated by Uganda since independence. Before examining the policy instruments available to the polity in implementing these choices, we need to give brief examination to the political environment within which agricultural policy is formulated and executed. Important in this regard are the political resources and dif-ficulties of the Obote government, the web of partisan identification in rural Uganda, demand inputs from the peasant sector, and regional varia-tions in both agriculture and politics.[18]

THE POLITICAL ENVIRONMENT

Terminal colonial nationalism did not generate the same degree of radi-cal populism which characterized many African states, and was deflected from its normal course of development by the peculiarities of the Buganda question. Uganda protest movements originated in Buganda after World War II. The massive confrontation with the colonial administration came in 1953–1955 on the issue of the deportation of the Kabaka. Subsequently, rural restlessness in Buganda tended to focus upon questions of the rela-tionship of Buganda and its monarchy to the rest of the country. The political movement which was to achieve postindependence leadership, the Uganda People's Congress (UPC), took shape in 1960 as a rejection of Ganda hegemony at the national level; its peak strength was found in

[17] *Work for Progress*, p. 61. On the credit scheme, see D. Hunt, "A Preliminary Note on Research into Agricultural Credit Schemes in Uganda," Makerere University College, 1966.

[18] For postindependence Uganda politics, see Donald Rothchild and Michael Rogin, "Uganda," in Gwendolen Carter, ed., *National Unity and Regionalism in Eight African States* (Ithaca, 1966); Cherry Gertzel, "Report from Kampala" and "How Kabaka Yekka Came to Be," in *Africa Report*, IX, 9 (Oct. 1964), 1–13; M. Crawford Young, "The Obote Revolution," *Africa Report*, XI, 6 (June 1966), 8–15.

the north and west of the country. A third dimension was supplied by the Democratic Party (DP), founded in 1956, and drawing much of its strength from a sentiment on the part of Catholics that Protestants enjoyed preferential access to opportunities for social promotion.[19]

Two bitterly contested national elections occurred in 1961 and 1962 to determine the allocation of power in the postindependence state. The net result was the emergence of Kabaka Yekka (KY), a neotraditionalist populist movement in Buganda, and the politization of religious cleavage between Catholics on the one hand and Protestants and Muslims on the other elsewhere in the country. The independence government was formed by an uneasy coalition between the UPC and KY. The politizing impact of the national elections was enhanced by a series of district council electoral contests both immediately before and after independence, which intensified the degree of partisan cleavage in the countryside.

Until the 1966 transformation of the parameters of politics by Obote, the government had a somewhat precarious hold on power. From 1962 to 1964 Obote led an uneasy coalition with KY. Although regime strength was enhanced by the steady defection of opposition members to the government benches, beginning in 1965 an anti-Obote group within the party and cabinet developed. The independence constitution specified elections for 1967, and the UPC had been torn by a bitter fight over the secretary-general post in 1964, then by the "Bantu-Nilotic" controversy in 1965–66.

The triumph of Obote in the 1966 crisis led to a sweeping redefinition of the political arena. New constitutions in 1966 and 1967 sharply centralized power; the exile of the Kabaka and dissolution of Buganda into four districts under central rule eliminated the institutional focus for Ganda autonomy and challenge to the power of the Obote regime. The postponement of elections for at least five years eliminated the perspective of an imminent opportunity to dispute the authority of the incumbent government. At the same time, Kampala asserted a substantially greater degree of supervisory control over local administrations in other districts, which also significantly enhanced the concentration of political power at the center. The changing nature of power relationships at different phases of Uganda's recent history transformed the arena within which agricultural policy formulation occurred.

Despite the sharpness of conflict, the political elite faced the dawn of independence confident of their ability to accelerate the pace of change, and pledged to their rural constituency to succeed. In specific terms, the

[19] The survey was carried out as a 5% sample of selected parishes, drawn from the taxpayer registers, in Buganda, Busoga, Bugisu, Teso, Acholi, Bunyoro, and Kigezi. We gratefully acknowledge the support of the Rockefeller Foundation and the research program in political science of the Makerere Institute of Social Research in the conduct of the study.

array of promises included improved prices for cotton and robusta coffee (which are fixed by the government), elimination of Asian buyers and processors, offering of loans, and mechanization. The price issue in particular was explosive in a politicized atmosphere. When former Governor Sir Andrew Cohen embarked on a decolonization course in 1952, one of the measures taken was to permit cash prices for cotton and coffee to move up to the level set by the extraordinary Korean War boom in primary commodities. The world market then sagged badly, and the temptation was strong to soften the blow to smallholders by running down the enormous surpluses which had built up in the coffee and cotton stabilization funds immediately after World War II. Thus the independence government was mortgaged to high price pledges but inherited largely depleted funds with which to underwrite trading losses; by 1965 the funds were gone. Illustrative of the importance of price fixing to maintenance of active rural support was the cotton price increase from 50 to 60 cents in 1965–66, at the moment when elections were being seriously contemplated. This price involved a £4,000,000 loss for the Lint Marketing Board.[20] The following year, with an indefinite moratorium on elections in effect, the government sharply cut back on the cotton price to 40 cents.

A crucial moot point is the precise nature of demand input in the rural environment. A fascinating recent study in Uganda suggests that the "revolution of rising expectations" cliche is considerably overstated; the author concludes that most peasant cultivators have a fairly realistic assessment of their prospects of obtaining the goods and services which virtually all desire in the abstract.[21] His data, however, is cross-sectional. One may speculate that there is an accordion effect to rural demands and expectations. Moments of intense cultivation of latent aspirations may increase the level of demands substantially. The perspective of imminent satisfaction automatically dilates demand; the dimming of prospects would tend to shrink demand back toward its previous level. The prospect of a competitive election, with mutual escalation of promises, clearly generates a temporary increase in demand input. Rural depolitization, the de facto policy since 1966, probably has at least the short-run effect of diminishing demand.

Another way of stating the same problem is to suggest that a difficult choice exists for governments whose resources fall far short of possible responsiveness to all latent demands. Implicitly or explicitly, some strategy for screening demands must be found which reduces the load to some ap-

[20] Uganda Government, *Background to the Budget, 1965–66* (Entebbe, 1965), p. 61.
[21] Anthony Oberschall, "Media Exposure, Information Level, and Aspirations in Rural Uganda," mimeographed, 1967. See also the sensitive and penetrating study of local politics and development in Acholi by Colin Leys, *Politicians and Politics* (Nairobi, 1967).

proximate balance with the level of responsive output supportable from available resources. A political, participation-oriented response requires screening of demand at the highest echelons of the political system, and presumably requires a securely legitimated process of authoritative allocation at the center. An alternative policy is to restrict the flow of demands at the source, by constricting the input channels. This choice, too, has its costs, in probably diminishing system supports, and favoring withdrawal and apathy.

The issue of mechanization and group farms provides a useful illustration of the elastic character of demand. The evidence strongly suggests that most smallholders were very skeptical of vague promises of tractor plowing. When group farms were launched as a vehicle for mechanization, peasants were initially suspicious, and fears were expressed that the scheme was a trick, like earlier land tenure proposals, and concealed government machinations to despoil them of their land. However, when politicians portrayed group farms as schemes by which land was cleared free, and initial experience confirmed this picture, a vigorous clamor for participation arose. We may suggest that the average small farmer considered a tractor beyond his means. Confronted, however, with an example whereby the government apparently was offering free plowing services, his demand would be strong. If, as appears likely, the group farm scheme is eventually terminated, or shorn of its mechanized superstructure, the peasant demand for mechanization in the area would likely again become quiescent.

There have been some crucial demands which the system has been able to largely satisfy since independence; perhaps the sharpest of these was for displacement of immigrant (especially Asian) buyers and processors of peasant crops. This sentiment has been so visible and articulate to the most casual observer that no corroboration is really necessary, but our survey responses were eloquent on this score.[22]

TABLE 1

Do you feel that the private Asian traders carry out their business honestly?	
all of the time	3%
most of the time	1%
only some of the time	18%
never	70%
don't know	8%

[22] Part of the animus apparently is directed against petty traders in general, and is not just racial. A similar query about African traders produced the following response:

all of the time	4%
most of the time	7%
only some of the time	25%
never	45%
don't know	19%

The nationalization of cotton buying and ginning through the cooperative movement is now complete, and the government has announced plans to accelerate a similar process for robusta coffee, where the role of private traders, African, Asian, and European, has remained substantial. Otherwise, demand is most sharply felt on issues of immediate material benefit, where experience has established concrete expectations. Availability of small loans, where credit schemes have become known, is one such demand; some 10 percent of those surveyed had received loans, and their popularity was evident from many of the open-ended responses. Another such issue is payment of a bonus by the cooperatives. Many farmers do not sharply distinguish between the cooperative movement and the government (46% on the survey indicated that cooperatives were a part of the government, as against 41% who perceived them as separate agencies), and thus performance of cooperatives in keeping the pledges made in membership solicitation has direct repercussions on the attitudes toward government.

A fundamental political fact affecting all aspects of government policy is the curious paradox of weak political parties and intense partisan identification. Neither the ruling UPC nor the DP are well organized in the countryside. Until it was removed from the scene in 1966, KY probably had the most effective rural structure in the country. However, the hard-fought elections of 1961 and 1962, grafted onto the legacy of thorough and highly competitive evangelization by the Church of Uganda (Protestant) and Roman Catholic orders, left in its wake an extraordinarily intense sense of party identification. Many rural Ugandans identify themselves as UPC or DP. The identity appears sharpest in districts such as Ankole, Kigezi, and Acholi where the religious competition was the most intense, and the rate of conversion to Christianity the highest. In this context it is extraordinarily difficult for any government representative or agricultural body, such as a cooperative, to preserve its appearance of neutrality. Peasant farmers are quick to identify a new extension worker as a Catholic or a Protestant and presumptively as DP or UPC. This perception establishes a set of behavioral expectations and a cognitive screen for interpreting observed performance. Similarly, it compels the government to preach administrative apoliticism, in sharp contrast to neighboring Tanzania. To bind the fortunes of administration and ruling party would be to foreclose access to significant segments of the population. In like manner, "politics" in the cooperative movement is excoriated as divisive and dangerous.

The regional contours of Uganda have had a marked impact on the patterns of political development. There is an intriguing interaction between differentials in type of agricultural development and political characteristics, which is another important dimension of the environment of agricultural policy implementation. Politically speaking, the ruling UPC initially derived its strongest support in the western and northern regions of Uganda; support in the eastern region was at first spotty. The party made little headway in Buganda, at bottom because it was founded as a reaction to Ganda domination of earlier political formations. The 1965–66 crisis found important factions of the UPC elite in the west siding with the anti-Obote faction. The key lieutenants of Obote have tended to come from the north.

Agriculturally, the land best endowed both in soil and favorable rainfall is on the shores of Lake Victoria, especially Buganda. Although cotton was the first cash crop in Buganda, after World War II the majority of Buganda farmers switched to robusta coffee; this crop is heavily concentrated in Buganda. The volcanic soils and relief rainfall of Mount Elgon provided ideal conditions for the cultivation of arabica coffee, which is primarily produced in the Bugisu and Sebei districts. Bugisu has played little part in national politics. It has been the home, however, of the turbulent and powerful Bugisu Cooperative Union. Eastern and northern Uganda are the centers of cotton production. The western region has the lowest development of cash agriculture, especially Toro and Kigezi.

Thus policies aimed at cotton development affect mainly the east and north, while robusta coffee is almost exclusively a Buganda problem. In 1965–66, there was clearly a differential price policy pursued, with cotton price fixed at an exceptionally high level, while the minimum robusta price was set at 40 cents a pound, the lowest price to growers since World War II.[23] In addition, until 1966, the Buganda government operated its own agricultural service and pursued somewhat different policies. The constraints of the world coffee market led inexorably to a policy disadvantageous to Buganda but advantageous to the country as a whole. Because production could not be increased, a higher return from coffee could be achieved only by obtaining a higher return from the existing export quota. The Second Five Year Plan states the choice clearly: "Uganda arabica coffee fetches at least £90 more per ton on the world market than does Uganda robusta. Thus, as the quantity of coffee that Uganda can export is limited by international agreement, the production of arabica must be increased rapidly so as to increase the total value of the coffee crop." [24] Arabica requires an elevation over 4,000 feet in Uganda, which rules out all but a small part of Buganda; the opportunities for expansion lie in the Kigezi, Toro, and West Nile districts. And the growth

---

[23] There is a difference in the two policies: the cotton price is a fixed price, which must be paid for each pound of seed cotton of specified standard of quality. The coffee price is a minimum price; however, as it was calculated on the world market, there was no market force likely to push it above the minimum.

[24] *Work for Progress*, p. 65.

of arabica acreage necessarily requires removing (Buganda) robusta acreage from production. Civil servants in the Ministry of Agriculture indignantly refute the implication that regional considerations have shaped policy choices. Equally strong is the pervasive conviction among Buganda farmers that "Obote's government" refuses to assist them.

POLICY IMPLEMENTS

The capabilities of the government to implement its policy goals are defined by its array of policy instruments. In terms of formal structures, these include the extension service, local governments, the cooperative movement, and the party. Each of these merits brief consideration. The most obvious, and presumably the most important, is the agricultural extension service.

The extension service consists of agricultural officers for each district, plus one or two assistant agricultural officers. The district agricultural officer (DAO) posts have been Africanized since shortly after independence; in all cases the posts are manned by university-trained agricultural specialists. In addition, specialist officers, usually expatriates, are found in many districts charged with the development of particular crops, such as tea, cocoa, or coffee. Below the district level, there is a cadre of agricultural assistants and field assistants who have substantially lower qualifications and training. Many of the field assistants have only a primary school background. In 1966 there was only one extension worker per 2,000 farmers; during the course of the present five year plan, the aim is to sharply upgrade the service, to assure one extension worker per 1,000–1,500 farmers, with as many as possible having three years of specialized agricultural training beyond the Cambridge School Certificate.

In theory the wide range of innovative measures developed on the excellent research stations maintained by the Ministry of Agriculture is simply diffused to the farmers through the extension service once the new findings are transformed into a package of standardized instructions. In practice only the most naive observer could expect this to occur as stated. A number of structural impediments exist within the extension service. Talent flows to the top; the ablest of the Ugandan staff serve in the headquarters at Entebbe. At the district level, there has been since Africanization great instability of assignment. At the time of our field investigation in 1965–66, district annual reports revealed that very few DAO's had remained at a given post as long as a year. This is a problem of transition, as the swift pace of Africanization continually creates vacancies at Entebbe; each promotion sets in train a chain reaction of transfers. District agricultural officers have to exercise political caution; few if any have political ambitions, but the partisan climate at the local level, plus the automatic confusion of religious affiliation with partisan identification, renders the energetic officer subject to attack by local politicians.

District agricultural officers, by and large, have direct contact with relatively few farmers. The reporting requirements are substantial, and a significant fraction of working time is spent at headquarters on paper work. Major projects, such as group farms, take first priority. For example, the DAO or his representative is expected to attend monthly meetings at each of the group farms in the district. These generally last a full day, plus travel time. In addition, the multiple organizational problems of the group farms compel attention. The handful of large, relatively successful farmers recognize the value of the free counsel, and of the surprisingly wide range of subsidized government services available for those who know how to take advantage of them. These farmers command an important part of the DAO's time. Whatever is left over is devoted to supervising the field staff.

Face-to-face contact with most farmers is maintained by the weakest element of the extension service, the field assistants. In many cases they do not understand the instructions they are conveying, and do not follow Agriculture Department doctrine on their own farms. This imposes severe constraints on the extension service, and the type of information it can transmit. Advice must be standardized over wide areas; one cannot rely on the field assistant to make appropriate adjustments to take into account the specific priorities of a given holding. To maintain its credibility, the extension service cannot afford to risk diffusing instructions which may fail in many areas; accordingly, established doctrine tends to evolve more slowly than research findings accumulate.

Some indication of the extent of penetration by the extension service is given by the survey responses. Of 480 who responded, 43 percent could recall a visit by an agricultural assistant; 63 percent could name the local agricultural assistant. Some 19 percent reported having been visited several times within the past year, 13 percent twice, 14 percent once, and 53 percent not at all. These aggregate figures conceal substantial variation between districts and parishes. In one Bunyoro parish only 5 percent could name the agricultural assistant, while in Bugisu the extent of visitation was particularly high. We might add that the figures are probably somewhat skewed on the high side, because sample areas were selected from cotton- or coffee-producing zones, where the extension effort has tended to be concentrated. On the whole, the capacity of the extension structure to relate to cash crop producers is substantial, in purely quantitative terms; nothing is demonstrated in these figures about the qualitative impact of the relationship.

On policies for which a maximum effort is made, such as cotton insecticides, the penetration capability of the extension service is impressive. Our survey data indicated that, in cotton zones, virtually all farmers knew about the pesticide "dudumaki," and had either tried it or considered the possibility of doing so. However, mere transmission is not sufficient. The rural smallholder is not simply an inert vessel into which new technology can be poured. Nor is simple "traditionalist" resistance to change the explanation for the frequent skepticism about government instructions. Extension is a sufficient part of rural experience, so that peasants have learned that government advice is by no means infallible; it must be carefully assessed in the light of the farmer's own knowledge. Consider, for example, the following findings in a study of extension service in the Lango district:

With regard to dates of planting, the optimum planting periods have been established on research stations for some major crops. The field study has revealed that the farmers hold different views on these recommendations. For instance, while the Agricultural Department advises planting in May, farmers in the drier areas of the District regarded April as the optimum planting date. In the wetter areas some farmers . . . gave guarded support for the recommendation as planting in May would require several weedings, and the cotton opened early in the season while the second rain was still falling which stained the cotton.
   As regards optimum spacing of cotton at 26" by 6" some farmers argued that the spacing was too close to allow air circulation; others having seen the spacing at the District Farm Institute argued that closely spaced cotton carried fewer bolls than widely spaced ones. In the wetter areas some farmers wondered whether or not the labour requirement would not be great particularly for the seed bed preparation for the spacing.
   When spraying was introduced for the first time some farmers suspected that the chemical would damage the soil fertility and the following staple food crop, millet, would not yield well. . . .[25]

A Kenya study confirms the paradoxical conclusion that the average farmer is better informed than the average field assistant.[26]

The insecticide chronicle is an excellent example of the vagaries of introducing innovation. Experimentation at the main cotton research station at Serere extends back many years. By 1957, in Lango, field tests on farmer plots were completed, and appeared to demonstrate conclusively that correct use of dudumaki would virtually double yields. In 1958 promotion of dudumaki was Agriculture Department policy. Two one-week demonstration courses were organized for all field assistants, to teach them how

[25] Matthew Okai, "Field Administration and Agricultural Development," mimeographed, Mekerere University College, 1966.
[26] E. R. Watts, "A Study of Agricultural Extension in Embu District of Kenya," mimeographed, Makerere University College, 1966.

to use the pumps, spray, and maintain the equipment. Each field assistant was then instructed to organize spraying demonstrations in his area. The spray was then sold at cost (Sh20 per tin, good for one spraying of an acre), and the pump for dispensing it was marketed for Sh27.50. Efforts were made to sell pumps and spray through the extension service, then through the cooperatives, but with little success. In 1960 a partial subsidy was introduced for the spray, then in 1963 it was distributed free. In 1964 a 50 percent charge was imposed, which was cut back to 25 percent in 1966. But the pumps proved difficult to use and were subject to unanticipated malfunctions. The FAO agricultural census revealed that few farmers carried out the full four sprayings recommended; the average figure was somewhat less than two applications. Also, the average farmer had only a vague idea of what an acre was, and tended to dilute the spray and use it over a wider area. Many used papyrus or banana fronds to dispense the spray rather than use the unwieldy pumps.[27] Thus a decade of intensive effort has produced nearly universal awareness of insecticide, but highly selective application of the instructions.

A careful case study of the introduction of arabica coffee in one parish of the Kigezi district adds further insight into the capabilities and limitations of the extension service. The key change agent in the parish was a retired chief, who had acquired a substantial tract of land and had an estimated income of nearly Sh5,000 from his coffee stand. The chief had direct access to the highly qualified advice of the district agricultural officer for Kigezi; he would not dream of asking a field assistant for information. Not only did he receive a very high income by local standards, but he enjoyed substantial status gratification; his visitor's book bore the signature of a former governor of Uganda, and he proudly displayed a letter from a coffee research specialist stating, "I can say without fear of contradiction that no finer planting of arabica coffee can be seen in Uganda." The DAO had provided him with a special coffee hulling machine, which produced both parchment coffee and prestige. There is little doubt that the former chief is the most important single source of innovation in the parish.

Coffee had first been introduced into the parish in 1936, but quickly became disease-ridden; in 1938 the agricultural service ordered all the coffee bushes uprooted. Renewed planting began in the early 1950s; then, in 1958, arabica coffee promotion in Kigezi again became doctrine. At this stage, the first farmers to reestablish coffee plantations were relatively high income individuals, many of whom had already had a commercial apprenticeship in petty trade. A considerable lag occurred before purely subsistence

---

[27] This farmer-generated innovation is an interesting case in itself. The Agriculture Department strongly discouraged the practice, but this substitute for the unpopular pump was a widespread and, after its fashion, standardized reaction of smallholders.

farmers began planting. The district coffee specialist and his staff played a measurable part, through distribution of seedlings and dispatch of spraying teams to combat antestia. Government commitment to the expensive spraying scheme reflects the changed political environment; in 1960, when disease again threatened, the instinctive reaction was once more to order the uprooting of coffee bushes. Rural politization had begun in 1960, unlike 1938, and local political leaders generated pressure sufficient to force government to abandon the uprooting order. Some farmers have now bought their own spray pumps, and complaints begin to emerge of poor quality spraying or political discrimination in spray distribution—sure signs that pesticide is now an established part of the technological landscape.[28]

Apt summation of the role of agricultural extension in transmitting change has been offered by a Ugandan student of rural development:

The introduction of coffee culture in Nyakishenyi cannot, in my opinion, be explained in terms of any one single factor per se. It would be gross simplification to assume that government efforts alone have brought about this change. . . .

Many of the present coffee farmers testify to having worked in Buganda, particularly in the coffee producing region of Mityana. At the same time not every coffee farmer in Nyakishenyi has worked in Buganda. Conversely, not every Nyakishenyi farmer who has been in Buganda grows coffee. . . . Moreover, there is a widely held belief that most of the coffee farmers in Nyakishenyi have emulated the example of one man—Tomasu Rwomushana. . . . All these influences have to be taken into account in the name of objectivity, whose price may be the impossibility of assessing the contribution of any one factor precisely.[29]

The Agriculture Department also operates a string of District Farm Institutes, of which there will shortly be one per district. The institutes organize a series of short residential courses, aimed at conveying basic information on a range of farm innovations possible within the district. The target audience of the DFI is small; attendance at the weekly courses is 20-30. Thus, for example, the Kigezi District Farm Institute can serve rather less than 1,500 farmers per year. Participants are invariably the more successful farmers; even though the numbers are small, the quality of the program and information transmitted is high. The following table, based on a sample of high- and low-income farmers in a Kigezi parish, clearly shows the audience affected by the institute, as well as the extension service and cooperative society.

[28] The Kigezi data is drawn from an excellent senior honors thesis by James Katorobo, "Agricultural Modernization: Kahoho Parish—Kigezi District," Makerere University College, 1968.

[29] James Katorobo, "Agricultural Extension in Nyahashenyi," typescript, Makerere University College, 1966.

To assess the impact of the institute, a qualitative weight would need to be added for the vastly superior information available through attendance at a course.[30]

Other instruments for improving agriculture available to the government, in theory, include the local government infrastructure and the co-operative movement. Historically, agricultural change was first imposed upon the country through the apparatus of local chiefs built up in execution of the ideology of indirect rule, flavored in Uganda by the Kiganda model. Cotton was introduced in the first decade of the century in Buganda

TABLE 2

CONTACT WITH INFORMATION CHANNELS

(Based on yes or no response)*

type of channel	high income (n = 12)	low income (n = 12)
extension service	75%	50%
cooperative society	83%	25%
district farm institute	50%	0%

*James Katorobo, "Agricultural Modernization: Kahoho Parish—Kigezi District," Makerere University College, 1968, p. 30.

simply by fiat; the administrative support of the chiefs was highly efficacious, and coercion was only briefly required. Major alterations such as the terracing of the Kigezi hillsides were also achieved in the comfortably authoritarian days of pre-Cohen Uganda, by administrative decree enforced by the chiefs. Also, many prescribed agricultural practices, such as uprooting and burning the harvested cotton plants, bunding and mulching coffee fields, were passed as bylaws by compliant district councils, at the nudging of the colonizer, and enforced by fines by the customary local tribunals.

The role of local government underwent a radical change in the terminal colonial period. Beginning in 1955, elected district councils were established; these acquired control over appointments of chiefs. Local politicians acquired a resource base and offered an alternative authority channel. Political notables and those who felt aggrieved by chiefly actions interacted. Criticism of chiefs was openly voiced, and incumbents had to carefully trim their sails to the new political winds, on pain of displacement. Prosecutions of farmers for violations of agricultural bylaws became, after independence, extremely infrequent. The local government as a coercive

[30] Jon Moris makes an interesting and impressive case for training rather than extension as a key strategy in James Sheffield, ed., *Education, Employment and Rural Development* (Nairobi, 1967), pp. 322–365.

resource for imposing agricultural innovation was no longer available. Persuasion and the simple capacity to communicate new information and make adaptation possible are now the keys to success in policies involving major adjustments of customary practices. At the same time, there is apparently some continuing belief that sanctions which chiefs and agricultural officers reported to be no longer enforceable were still in effect. Some 85 percent of those surveyed claimed that there were agricultural bylaws they were compelled to obey in farming, 84 percent maintained that fines and imprisonment were still imposed for disregard of these rules, and 56 percent affirmed that they knew personally recent cases where such sanctions had been used. The most salient single rule was the requirement that harvested cotton plants be uprooted and burned, to prevent insect breeding; belief that this rule was being actively enforced was well-nigh universal in cotton-growing zones, despite the simultaneous belief of those whose task it would be to prosecute violators that such rules were unenforceable. Neither we nor the agricultural service have precise figures on the percentage of actual compliance with such rules. We suspect that most farmers do in fact uproot dead cotton plants, in part because the utility of this exercise is understood and partly because of a lingering belief that non-compliance may be punished. However, reliance on coercive machinery to impose an entirely new practice would be a very different matter.[31]

Even without the coercive dimension, the chiefly microbureaucracy constitutes a major communication resource. The subcounty of Nakishenyi, for example, had two extension field assistants but thirteen chiefs (1 subcounty, 6 parishes, 6 subparishes). Even with diminished authority, the local chiefs are in intimate contact with the population and can, if they choose, assure the diffusion of information. In fact, the field assistants make considerable use of the chiefs, in distributing coffee seedlings or summoning meetings of farmers.[32]

Cooperatives have received major support from the government. They are the chosen instrument for a wide range of policy goals, ranging from displacement of immigrant and expatriate groups from the processing and marketing sectors to management of the credit scheme. Cooperative development was swift in the terminal colonial period, and has redoubled since. By the end of 1964, there were 400,000 members, or nearly one-third of the potential participation. Cooperatives have been awarded an almost complete monopoly of cotton ginning, and process a substantial portion of

[31] Even in the terminal colonial period, coercive introduction of major changes was likely to encounter serious difficulty. See, for example, Roland Young and Henry Fosbrooke, *Smoke in the Hills* (Evanston, 1960), pp. 141–167, for an interesting Tanzania case.

[32] Katorobo suggests that the religious hierarchies are in even closer contact with the populace, but are not exploited as a communications channel.

the coffee. The cooperative structures, however, are not nearly as strong as mere numbers would suggest. Several of the largest cooperative unions, including the Uganda Growers Co-operative Union, the Bugisu Co-operative Union, and the Busoga Growers Co-operative Union have required government intervention between 1965 and 1968.[33] At the local level, the primary societies do not appear to have the capacity at the moment to function as a major communication resource. However, the government now plans to integrate extension, credit, and cooperative development by focusing a large part of the extension effort into assisting members of primary societies that qualify for participation through the Ryan credit scheme.

Although there is an appealing logic to this proposal, it is doubtful whether in practice the cooperative mechanism will be capable of playing the ambitious role envisaged for it. Again, the range of variation between districts is substantial. The strongest cooperative union in Uganda in the 1965-1967 period probably was the Bunyoro Co-operative Union. In this instance the capability of the cooperative structure was very high. The survey indicated a high degree of participation through the local structure of the cooperative, and a very favorable attitude toward the union. The Bugisu Co-operative Union also had very effective structures, but was locked in combat with the central government on several issues, and in late 1966 was taken over by the government. Elsewhere among the districts surveyed, skepticism on the part of farmers toward cooperatives and their effectiveness was high.[34]

Other potential instruments for diffusion and implementation of policy deserve brief mention. Political parties have not been a significant asset to the government, although they do, through local influentials identified with them, offer an important channel for protest and grievance articulation. The UPC is simply too weak structurally to perform functions other than demand input. Mass media as well seem destined for a very modest role, despite ambitious claims advanced by some students of mass communications.[35] The vernacular press in Buganda does have a large readership, but very little agricultural information. The rest of the country is served by the national English-language press, restricted to the top elite, and a few local vernacular papers with a very limited audience. The

[33] See the devastating *Report of the Commission of Inquiry Into the Affairs of the Busoga Growers Co-operative Union Limited* (Entebbe, 1966). For further details on the cooperative movement, see Crawford Young, "Cooperatives, Politics and Development," in E. A. Brett, ed., *Agricultural Development in East Africa* (forthcoming).

[34] On Bunyoro, the survey findings coincide with those of Joel Barkan in "Bunyoro, Sectional Rivalry or Religious Pluralism?" in E. Bundy and Michael Davis, eds., *District Administration and Politics in Uganda* (forthcoming).

[35] Wilbur Schramm, *Mass Media and National Development* (Stanford, 1964).

transistor revolution has brought the radio within the reach of more prosperous farmers, but program content is determined by the Ministry of Information and little weight is given to farmer education. The Nakishenyi
survey did show that the majority of high-income farmers used the radio
to learn about prices but not innovation. And the great majority of
Uganda's 5,000 television sets, in 1966, were owned by immigrants and expatriates.

SYSTEM CAPABILITY AND POLICY CHOICE

To conclude, we must return to our point of departure, the relationship
between system capability and policy choice. The exercise of reviewing
major policy directions and the mechanisms by which they are carried out
suggests that a somewhat amended set of analytical capability categories
may better direct investigation to the critical factors. Communication,
regulation, adaptation, exhortation, and resources appear to incorporate
most relevant dimensions.

1. Communicative capability defines the ability of the political system,
through the various structures available to its leaders, to convey information. Major innovation opportunity, in an age of permanent technological
revolution, is almost certain to enter the system from the top, often from
the international environment. The process of diffusion is far more complex than it would first appear; messages must be converted into a form
wherein they are congruent with the accumulated stock of knowledge and
practical wisdom of the rural smallholder, as well as his accessible fund of
land, labor, and capital resources. In the words of a particularly astute student of rural development, Jon Morris, "The least capable members of the
communication chain . . . determine the message-transmitting capacity of
the entire system." [36] A severe constraint on the communicative capability
of the primary instrument of communication, the extension service, is the
critical gap between skilled experts at the top of the agricultural service
and the mass of potential information consumers at the bottom.

2. Regulative capability is retained from the Almond-Powell list; it
refers to "the political system's exercise of control over the behavior of individuals and groups. . . . In characterizing regulative performance one
must consider what individuals and groups are being subjected to regulation, what areas of individual and collective life are affected, and what fre-
quency or intensity of intervention is exercised." [37] In the colonial period,
agricultural development involved extensive reliance upon the high regulative capabilities of the protectorate. Politization of the countryside, vulner-

[36] Sheffield, *Education, Employment and Rural Development*, p. 333.
[37] Almond and Powell, *Comparative Politics*, p. 196.

ability of chiefs to attacks by local politicians, and a relaxation of bureaucratic controls resulting from the rapid turnover of personnel in the immediate postindependence period have significantly diminished the coercive capacity of government. Further, both political and civil service elites are committed to development by consent; the proposition that change should be imposed by force on a recalcitrant peasantry is intellectually offensive, although a practical temptation. Regulative capability remains important in certain policy areas; for example, the survival of the credit scheme, and cooperative development depend heavily upon thorough government supervision. But coercion is unlikely to play a significant role in the diffusion of new technology to smallholders.

3. Adaptive capability describes the ability of the polity to secure measurable change in agricultural procedures by its peasant members. Recent empirical studies suggest that invaluable contributions to our understanding of the developmental process can be made by attempting to measure along this dimension. Because the number of instructions transmitted is limited, and policy history can be readily reconstructed, a reasonably precise estimate of the relationship between governmental input and actual adoption of changed methods can be made. The issue is, of course, complicated by the multidimensionality of the change process. Government is by no means the sole mechanism by which innovation is diffused. The example of successful farmers and traders, and commercial apprenticeship or migration are all contributory vectors. Although the formal institutions of the political system may have been the ultimate source of the new knowledge, the role of secondary agencies of adaptation is more important than is generally recognized. Thus a range of factors which affect the ability of the smallholders to learn and absorb innovation need to be considered. These include the level of education, accumulated experience with cash agriculture which heightens awareness of opportunities for income improvement, travel in and contacts with surrounding regions to learn of their practices, and possibly a sense of efficacy and optimism regarding prospects for an improved position in the future.

4. Hortatory capability suggests the capacity of the political system to inspire, stimulate, or motivate rural smallholders. Available evidence suggests that the role of exhortation is very modest. Some effort is deployed through the "barazas" held by itinerant district officers, demonstration sessions by extension officers, and, more rarely, mobile film units or rural progresses (ceremonial tours) by leading political figures. Unlike Tunisia and Tanzania, where the dominant party plays a significant hortatory role, in Uganda the dominant party lacks the capacity to offer much assistance. Although the concrete evidence at our disposal does not lend strong support for the proposition, we remain disposed to believe that the capacity

to induce a generally favorable attitude toward the policy efforts of the government is important in legitimizing its advice. To the extent that regulation must be downgraded as a policy mechanism, communicative and hortatory capabilities assume greater importance in the postindependence environment. It would appear that both communication and exhortation are most effective with the larger farmers, who are best situated to make use of government aid and advice.

5. Resource capability refers to the array of limitations imposed by the obvious scarcity of both money and human skills. This category is closely related to the "extractive" capability suggested by Almond and Powell; however, we would focus more directly on the cost-benefit calculations that must underlie rational policy choice at the central level. The key human resource, in the agricultural field, is the pool of people who have a command over agricultural technology. The political system makes a heavy investment in their training, and the question may be raised whether full exploration has been made of the opportunity costs in present deployment of the highly skilled and talented Ugandans who are primarily concentrated in the ministry. Another, and paradoxical, aspect of the human resources problem is the ambitious training program now underway. A vastly increased number of diploma-holding agricultural specialists, with three post-Cambridge School Certificate years of training, will be entering the ranks of the Agriculture Department. This will mean a sharp rise in personnel costs, and should mean close attention to utilization of costly personnel. It is a sobering thought that the annual budget of Uganda is significantly less than that of the University of Wisconsin. It is in this connection as well that a careful assessment of policies such as group farms and mechanization must be made, weighing the impact of a concentrated investment on a restricted number of farmers against a more diffuse commitment of resources through extension, research, and possibly subsidized introduction of key innovations such as pesticides and fertilizers.

Microanalysis of the processes of social and economic change, combined with macroanalysis of system capabilities, should offer a useful framework for policy choice. Our own inquiries suggest important limitations to system capabilities within all five of the categories suggested. At the same time, it is easy to lose sight of the extremely important changes that are occurring at the local level. In Buganda, for example, farmers are actively seeking alternatives to robusta coffee; this will be the third major shift in farming patterns (subsistence to cotton, 1900–1910; cotton to coffee, 1945–1955). Insecticide has been made part of the farming pattern in cotton areas, even though the precise instructions of the Agriculture Department are not generally observed. Over a period of time, fertilizer can be introduced.

The wastage of scarce resources is most likely to occur when policies outstrip capabilities. Many observers would cite group farms as an example. They are by no means a total failure; a certain number have enjoyed a modest success. However, if the full toll they have taken on available capabilities were calculated, it is difficult to see how they could be justified against alternative resource uses. Mechanization as well gives the illusion of transformation at great cost. In 1963, the year of highest efficiency, the service incurred a loss of Sh13/63 per tractor hour. At the 1967 level of tractor commitment, a loss of £1,000,000 could be projected. When one considers that the tractor and group-farm losses are concentrated on a small number of farmers, the opportunity cost to the mass of smallholders and the country as a whole is clear.[38]

Agriculture is not a dramatic engine of transformation. At times the pace of change seems barely perceptible. But more closely examined, the process of change is occurring. Transformation is too much to ask; continuous and significant change is within grasp.

[38] Malcolm Hall, "A Review of the Experience with Mechanization in East African Agriculture: Some Implications for Planning," mimeographed, Makerere University College, 1967.

Chapter 8 Ranching and Scheming: A Case Study of the Ankole Ranching Scheme

Martin R. Doornbos and Michael F. Lofchie

The exact value of case studies has long been a matter of discussion among social scientists. One of the most common generalizations is that case studies seem to furnish tentative hypotheses which may then be tested—and validated or disproven—with reference to other comparable cases. A similar view holds that by accumulating and examining a number of cases, the social scientist may discover common patterns and, in this way, go on to establish a set of empirically valid propositions about human interaction. In both these views, case studies are justified as the essential building blocks of a true social science. Actual instances of the hypotheses derived from one such study being tested in a series of subsequent studies, however, are fairly rare. This fact, together with the generally turbulent state of theories of the development process, should probably caution individuals engaged in case study research to cast their claims in more modest terms.

Case studies of development planning are sometimes justified on somewhat different grounds. It is said that they can be of practical use to development administrators in improving and sharpening their techniques. The notion of policy relevance has increasingly been raised with respect to research in developing countries, and this imperative has been an additional inducement for scholars to take up case study research.

At the opposite extreme is the view that case studies have very little academic value. One viewpoint suggests that at this stage of research on developing areas, case studies at best provide background information on a particular country or region and, like newspaper clippings and documentation, are essentially raw materials for scholarly analysis.

Without prejudice to any of these positions, the possible value of the following case study may be stated in somewhat different terms. While there is growing awareness of the complexity of factors that intervene at various stages of the planning process, only in relatively few instances have any of these been adequately documented. As a result, discussions of these problems tend to be conducted at a nonempirical, "general" level, leaving room for a considerable amount of speculative thought. In the present study, the authors have traced some of the major conditions and considerations which were operative in a concrete case, that is, the planning process of a single development project. Actions at different levels of policy making have been analyzed as to their effect on some of the most critical organizational aspects of the project. It was found that several of the recurrent problems encountered in development planning were strikingly exemplified in this case:

1. the difficulty of carrying out effective government planning in situations where central government authority is weakened by the presence of countervailing local elites;

2. the possibility that development strategies, conceived of and initiated as forces of egalitarian social change and overall modernization, may, in the process of being implemented, lead to exactly opposite consequences;

3. the highly political nature of "administrative" decision making in developing areas, minimizing the role and effect of technical criteria in these processes; and

4. the operation of certain guiding norms of foreign policy, in this case American, in opposition to one another, which makes it possible that the principle of noninterference in the domestic affairs of another country may nullify the principle that aid ought to serve progressive social and political objectives as well as the objective of economic growth.

The Ankole Ranching Scheme [1] is a project assisted by the United States Agency for International Development (USAID) and undertaken by the government of Uganda to promote commercial cattle ranching in southwestern Uganda. The declared objective of the scheme is to construct more than one hundred cattle ranches, of several thousand acres each, and to place them in the hands of competent ranchers who will be able to undertake large-scale beef production on an economically viable

---

[1] Officially the scheme is known as the "Ankole/Masaka Ranching Scheme" as it is projected to extend over a large area of open plain which overlaps both the District of Ankole (until the 1967 constitution known as the Kingdom of Ankole) and the Masaka District of the former Kingdom of Buganda. Since most work to date has been concentrated in the Ankole area, however, the scheme is commonly referred to as the "Ankole Ranching Scheme."

basis. The highly complex scheme has involved a wide range of activities such as tsetse fly eradication projects, the construction of roads, bridges, and valley tanks, perimeter fencing, pasture research, and the creation of an experimental cattle breeding station adjacent to the ranch area proper. As such the ranching scheme has gone through several phases—from initial planning to the selection of ranchers—and has involved a host of governmental decisions about a wide range of economic, technical, and, due to United States financial involvement, foreign policy matters. As of 1968, the scheme had not yet been completed, and only forty of an anticipated 125 ranches were allocated.

The ranching scheme may be expected to have a dramatic effect on the economic development of Ankole. It also has a great potential for exacerbating or modifying social tensions that exist there. Exactly how the scheme's impact will be felt depends very much upon the structural arrangements that determine the distribution of social benefits. This case study is primarily concerned with the most important of these arrangements, the criteria for the recruitment of ranchers. These criteria, more than any other administrative feature of the project, determine which individuals and strata will benefit from the vast outlay of funds, from the long period of government planning, and from a considerable investment of expertise.

The selection of ranchers is also one of the most important economic aspects of the ranching scheme, for the success of the entire project depends upon the capability, commitment, and responsiveness to modern methods of the individual ranchers. Since the basic concept of the scheme is that each ranch will have to be large enough to achieve a high degree of productivity, individuals selected as ranchers will almost automatically be thrust into a position of major economic prominence in the society. If the first group of ranchers is unable to meet exacting standards of performance, their failure will not only compromise the expenditure of over $4,000,000 but will have serious repercussions for Uganda's economic development.

The determination of criteria for the selection of ranchers became a matter of intense controversy both within Uganda and between the government of Uganda and USAID. Underlying this controversy was the possibility that highly placed politicians and administrators or other political influentials, attracted by the material benefits of ranch ownership, would use their position to gain possession of the ranches. This possibility, it was feared, could jeopardize the economic goals of the scheme and lead to serious political consequences. For it would be in direct contradiction to the original concept of the scheme, namely, that ranches were to be awarded only to resident owners on the basis of proven ranching ability in order that the project might serve as a model of social change. Though rarely articulated directly, fear of political exploitation precipitated a lengthy and heated dialog over whether ranchers would be expected to reside on their ranches or whether the principle of absentee ownership would be accommodated in the scheme. The final outcome of the controversy was that residence would not be required and that individuals who were selected as ranchers would be allowed to place managers in charge of their ranches. As a result, of the first forty ranches allocated, it became possible for approximately fifteen to be awarded, on an absentee basis, to members of a political elite.

The distinctive and possibly unique feature of the political elite that has been able to exploit the Ankole Ranching Scheme is its local character. It is not an uncommon phenomenon in developing countries for government projects, especially those that involve a heavy investment of foreign capital, to fall into the hands of influential politicians. Usually, however, the individuals who are able to benefit in these situations exercise power and influence at the national level. Often, regardless of the ethnic composition of areas where such projects are located, those who profit represent different ethnic groups, ones which are nationally dominant. This is not so in the case of the Ankole scheme. While the political elite that gained control of the majority of the ranches allocated on an absentee basis included two cabinet ministers and several members of the Uganda parliament and central government administrators, it is predominantly composed of individuals whose basis of political status is within the Ankole area. Even those who occupied formal positions at the national level are members of Ankole society and have risen to national prominence by virtue of their ability to exercise influence within the Ankole community.

The vast majority of the members of the Ankole political elite who have been given ranches and who manage them as absentee owners are members of an ethnically differentiated elite stratum within Ankole society known as Bahima. In addition, all but a few of the remaining twenty-five ranches have been acquired by other prominent Bahima. The district of Ankole has historically been composed of two ethnic groups, the Bahima and the Bairu. The former, who today constitute about 5 percent of the population (of about 800,000), were traditionally the dominant political element. The Bahima have always been engaged in cattle herding and, until the early part of this century, had exclusive ownership of all cattle. This formed an important buttress to their political authority. The Bairu, the overwhelming majority of the population, have primarily been cultivators and were, in the past, the subordinate element in the society.

Although the Bahima were the traditional cattle keepers of Ankole, Bahima identity is not presumptive evidence of superior cattle-keeping ability. Despite the fact that the Bairu have been permitted to acquire cattle only since 1907, they now possess more than the Bahima. As early as 1938 an official government report observed that "the Bairu seem to have certain advantages over Abahima as stock-keepers." [2] In recent decades the Bairu have been gradually absorbed into the political elite of Ankole. In spite of Bairu upward mobility, the Bahima for long retained a disproportionate amount of political influence and until today remain an important element of the Ankole political elite. Because of past discrimination, many Bairu still have a sense of resentment against the Bahima. Indeed, one of the most conspicuous features of recent Ankole politics has been a continuing tension between these two groups. Bahima preponderance in the present distribution of ranches has added to the Bairu sense of unequal treatment and thus accentuated the tension between the two groups. Consequently, the pattern of rancher selection has not only threatened the economic viability of the ranching scheme, but also has made it a source of political irritation in Ankole.

The objective of this case study is to explore the conditions that permitted a locally based elite to take advantage of a largely foreign financed project whose implementation was the responsibility of the central government of Uganda. Broadly speaking, four separate conditions can be distinguished. These are: (1) the special political climate of Uganda which, in the early postindependence period, was characterized by a generally tolerant attitude toward local elites and considerable flexibility in accommodating their interests; (2) an ineffectual planning apparatus at the national level which was unable to govern the specifics of plan implementation; (3) the particular problems and attitudes of American foreign policy in central and eastern Africa; and (4) the ability of the Ankole elite to exercise influence at the national level together with an absence of effective opposition within Ankole. Although the politics of the Ankole Ranching Scheme should not be construed as being necessarily typical of the pattern of decision making in Uganda (or of the United States Department of State), this case study may help illuminate a set of factors which can be expected to influence decision making in a wider context.

The Ankole Ranching Scheme had its origin in the long-standing efforts of the Uganda government to eradicate the tsetse fly (*Glossina morsitans*) from southwestern Uganda. As early as 1908, the fly had begun to cross the Kagera River, part of the boundary between Uganda and Tanganyika, and moved steadily northward into an area of Ankole where cattle raising was the traditional occupation of a significant sector of the local population. Throughout the early decades of the century, there was a substantial

2 W. L. S. Mackintosh, *Some Notes on the Abahima and the Cattle Industry in Ankole* (Entebbe, 1938), p. 26.

migration of cattle raisers out of the infected areas. Large numbers of Bahima moved into other parts of Ankole but many migrated into Buganda and some Ankole cattle herders went as far as Lango and Teso districts in central and eastern Uganda. The problem of tsetse infestation became especially acute during the 1940s and '50s, when further encroachments of the fly led to an increasing incidence of trypanosomiasis (sleeping sickness) among the remaining cattle of Nyabushozi county of Ankole. By the end of this period, an area of nearly 2,000 square miles of open grassland, otherwise ideal for beef production, had become affected.

Danger that the entire cattle industry of the area would be wiped out necessitated emergency eradication measures by the Uganda government. In 1959, after other approaches had proven ineffective, the government decided to evacuate all the remaining cattle, by coercion if necessary, and also to kill off the game species in the area in order to remove the carriers of tsetse. These measures, combined with large-scale bush clearance to destroy the habitat of the fly, finally proved successful in halting and even pushing back the tsetse infestation. Effective tsetse control proved so costly, however, that it posed a difficult dilemma for the Uganda government. To abandon or even cut back on fly eradication would leave the cleared area open for reinfestation, invalidating all previous efforts, and would place an additional 400 square miles in jeopardy.[3] To continue the tsetse elimination program while allowing a reoccupation of the area by traditional Bahima cattle herders would pose a crippling financial burden and would, in the long run, be grossly ineffectual. For traditional Bahima pastoral practices, largely rooted in the attitude that cattle were a factor of social status, were wasteful of grazing land and did not make a contribution to the economy of the country. Moreover, these practices were such as to invite renewed spread of the fly over the entire area.

A third approach to the problem, favored by veterinary officers of the Uganda government and supported by the visiting World Bank Mission to Uganda of 1961,[4] was to create a settled commercial cattle-ranching operation in the area. This would not only justify the economic costs of continued eradication programs but could be organized in such a way that it would, in itself, constitute an impediment to the movement of the fly. An additional advantage of stabilized commercial ranching lay in its potential as a model of modern practices and a stimulus of cultural and social transformation. If the largely seminomadic Bahima cattle herders of Ankole could be induced to abandon their traditional attitudes of self-sufficiency

[3] *The Ankole/Masaka Ranching Scheme*; Loan Application to USAID by the Government of Uganda, Appendix 9, "A Brief Background on Tsetse Eradication in Ankole/Masaka" May 1964).

[4] *The Economic Development of Uganda*, International Bank for Reconstruction and Development (Entebbe, 1961).

and to adopt more up-to-date methods of animal husbandry, they would become more fully integrated into the developing sector of the Ugandan economy and would be encouraged to take advantage of educational and other opportunities for social advancement.

In order to explore the feasibility of stable ranching, a Land Use Investigational Unit was set up in Nyabushozi county in 1957. This unit, which occupied 30 square miles, created approximately half a dozen small ranches in order to conduct experiments on such problems as pasture improvement, land rehabilitation, and optimum cattle density per acre. These ranches were the prototypes of the present Ankole ranches and were eventually incorporated into the scheme.

A major boost to the creation of commercial cattle ranching in Ankole came in the early 1960s, when USAID, which had been giving support to the bush-clearing operations, became interested in the broader idea of large-scale ranching and beef production in southwestern Uganda. In order to assess the prospects of such an industry, AID sponsored an American research team which spent several months, during early 1963, conducting an intensive on-the-spot investigation of the ecological, economic, and social conditions in the plains area of Ankole. Ths team produced a comprehensive analysis, commonly referred to as the "Gregory Report," [5] which strongly endorsed the principle that cattle ranching could become a major source of wealth for Uganda and an important vehicle of social change in the Ankole area. The technical recommendations contained in the Gregory Report have, in large measure, become the basis of the Ankole Ranching Scheme.

Among the various factors enumerated by the Gregory Report as preconditions for the success of commercial cattle ranching, the form of ranch tenure was singled out as being of central importance. In a lengthy analysis, the report stressed the necessity of adopting some type of individual tenure which would ensure that the owner-operator actually reside on his ranch. The basic argument was that in order to provide the maximum incentive for efficiency and productivity, the economic rewards of ranch operation must accrue to the person having responsibility for day-to-day management. In opposing any form of absentee ownership, the report commented that "the family which must rely solely upon a ranch for its existence and financial progress is much more apt to bend every effort towards its successful operation than if their interests are divided between the operation of the ranch and other activities." [6] A second reason for compelling the

---

[5] The official title of this document is "The USAID Livestock Survey Team Report." Dr. Keith E. Gregory, of the University of Nebraska, was Team Leader (USAID mimeo, 1963).

[6] Gregory Report, p. 4.

ranchers to reside on the ranch was that this would assure effective communication between veterinary experts attached to the project and the ranchers. Such communication was essential if improved techniques of animal husbandry emanating from the adjoining experimental breeding station were to be put into practice on the ranches. Only if this were accomplished would the broader educational purposes of the scheme be facilitated. Effective diffusion of modern cattle-raising methods throughout the Ankole area required that the Ankole Ranching Scheme itself function as a conspicuous model of successful innovation and adaptation.

While the Gregory Report tended to place primary stress on the economic and educational factors as grounds for advocating individual tenure and on-the-site residence, a final and perhaps most persuasive argument lay in the historically known social consequences of the institution of absentee landlordism, namely, the tendency toward a growing economic cleavage between different strata in the society. The Gregory Report warned that:

caution needs to be exercised . . . by both central and District Governments in order to prevent the concentration of land ownership in the hands of a small number of owners. *Concentration of ownership, particularly in the hands of absentee owners, too often has resulted in a peasant type agriculture in which land owners have little interest in anything except 'mining' both human and land resources* (authors' emphasis). In the interests of a strong and viable economy in Uganda, every effort should be made to avoid development in this direction.[7]

Thus absentee ownership or control would not only present a major obstacle to accomplishing the communication and educational purposes of the plan, thereby preventing it from functioning as a model of social change, but would inevitably intensify the social and economic cleavages in Ankole society.

An important theme in the Gregory Report was that a successful commercial ranching scheme, of the type envisaged, could only come about as the result of a slow, balanced development in a number of areas such as breeding experimentation and rancher training. The Gregory team had recognized that there was not a sufficient number of adequately trained people to man the ranches. They argued that, since the first group of ranchers would have to play a crucial role if fundamental social transformation of the area was to be achieved, it was essential not to rush the scheme ahead until a competent cadre of ranchers had been formed. The team's report also recommended that a substantial enlargment of the experimental cattle breeding farm should precede any major construction

[7] Gregory Report, p. 127.

work on the ranches. Following these suggestions, AID agreed to finance the expansion of the breeding farm and thus became further involved in livestock development in the Ankole area.

There was a discernible contrast between the viewpoint of the Gregory team—that the establishment of cattle ranching should be a gradual matter —and the keen expressions of interest in more rapid progress which emerged from certain local quarters. The most conspicuous of these local persons were officials of the Ankole kingdom government, veterinary officers working in the field of livestock development in Ankole, and high-ranking administrators in the Ministry of Animal Industry, Game and Fisheries. The Gregory team indicated some concern at the desire of local leaders in Ankole to move rapidly ahead with the project and warned that such an attitude was not compatible with effective, long-range development.[8] Implicit in their caution was an anxiety that if Ankole notables, who perceived the scheme merely as an opportunity for immediate economic gain, were to obtain control, the opportunity for using the ranches as a vehicle for recruiting and training individuals who could function as a nucleus of modernization, would be lost. Indeed, as a means of ensuring adequate rancher responsiveness to the broader modernizing objectives of the project, the Gregory team went so far as to spell out an elaborate set of special requirements for operators, which placed particular emphasis on an appropriate attitude and commitment, a sufficient level of education, and demonstrable management potential. To be able to delay the scheme long enough to develop a modernizing cadre would have required a central government sufficiently strong to resist local elite pressure.

Local and ministerial pressure for quick action on the ranching scheme also presented a contrast with the more routine approach taken by government planning officials. The Ministry of Animal Industry, in which the Ankole elite had strong representation, had forwarded first drafts of an application for USAID assistance for the project to the Ministry of Economic Affairs (which then performed the function of plan evaluation) toward the middle of 1963. Officials in Animal Industry expressed the urgent hope that the Uganda government would take action quickly enough so that Washington could approve the loan as early as July of that same year. The planning machinery was simply not equipped, however, to act on such short notice. Serious consideration of the loan request was not begun until early 1964.

At this time it became quite clear that there was a marked discrepancy between the manner in which the Ministry of Animal Industry conceived of the ranching scheme and certain of the original ideas contained in the

[8] Gregory Report, p. 10.

Gregory Report. In particular, there was basic divergence over the question of land tenure. In a draft of the loan application prepared by the Ministry of Animal Industry in December 1963, the anticipated mode of ranch tenure was described as follows: "The ranches would . . . be offered on lease to farmers selected as candidates of sufficient capacity, business acumen, educational background and integrity or some satisfactory combination of these requirements, *or, to individual Co-operatives or similar bodies who would undertake to put in a Manager of the same calibre*" (authors' emphasis). Another difference between the loan application and the Gregory Report was that the loan request did not include provision for a marketing cooperative for the ranchers. This indicates that among the Ugandans concerned to promote the ranching scheme, absentee ownership had become an accepted principle rather than an exception. For cooperative arrangements are feasible only when those on the spot have authority to make important decisions about the day-to-day economics of ranch operation.

Even in the daily routine of plan reviewing, these departures from the original formulation of the ranching scheme caused raised eyebrows among members of the government's planning staff, who felt that the innovations were sufficiently questionable to refer the loan application back to the Ministry of Animal Industry for specific explanation. However, when a rewritten version of the loan application, with no significant changes in the approach to ranch tenure was submitted again to planning officials, it was accepted without further ado. On the basis of the new version, the Uganda Planning Commission (a select cabinet committee with special representation from parastatal bodies), which has supreme statutory authority over all governmental development programs, agreed to make a formal request to USAID for financial assistance. The official loan application of the government of Uganda (dated May 1964), which included a request for $1,830,000 out of a total projected scheme cost of over $4,000,-000, was thus quite explicit in accepting the principle of absentee ownership. In a section entitled "Economic and Technical Soundness Analysis," paragraph 48 read: "Most ranches will be run by resident owner-managers, though some may be run by managers on behalf of co-operatives, companies, or individual absentee-owners."

The inclusion of the principle of absentee ownership in the official loan application was a concrete demonstration of the relative weakness of the planning staff in the Uganda government. Despite the fact that the departures from the Gregory Report might lessen the appeal of the project to AID, the Ministry of Animal Industry and its Veterinary Department had been successful in pressing for their version of the scheme against the better judgment of the planning officials. The Ministry of Planning and

Community Development, which had succeeded the Ministry of Economic Affairs in carrying out project evaluation, was unable to make any significant impact on these aspects of the loan request.

The Ministry of Planning was weakened by the fact that it did not possess final authority to approve or disapprove foreign aid requests. This power rested solely with the Uganda Planning Commission which, as essentially a cabinet committee and, therefore, a political rather than a technical body, did not necessarily base its decisions on purely economic considerations (which could have been the case had the commission been composed of politically neutral technical experts). The ineffectuality of the Ministry of Planning was also a result of a combination of other factors, the most important of which was that it did not possess administrative mechanisms of its own, such as budgetary powers, for exercising effective control over other governmental ministries. In addition, it was weakened by shortage of staff, lack of independent access to critical information, and chronic organizational changes.

Exactly why officers of the Veterinary Department in charge of implementing the scheme should have been so anxious to press for quick acceptance of their particular version of the project is a complex question. One possible factor was a belief that unless some rapid results could be shown, the Uganda government might lose interest in supporting livestock development in the Ankole area. There was also a fear that the cattle herders who had migrated due to the incursion of tsetse fly would attempt to move back into the cleared area and resume their traditional method of grazing with its attendant dangers of reinfestation and economic stagnation. Only if ranches were established, it was felt, could the gains made through eradication programs be preserved. A third factor was that the scheme had long since begun to arouse considerable interest among part of the local population and there was already some pressure to adopt a format which would leave the matter of ranch tenure flexible and open to alternative arrangements. The local veterinary officers had begun to identify with Ankole, possessed close social contacts with leaders of the community, and were highly responsive to these leaders' sentiments and interests. Moreover, their intimate association with the early development of the idea of a ranching scheme had created a sense of personal stake in its successful fulfillment and this may also, to some extent, have led to a willingness to accommodate local preferences in order to be able to produce visible results.

The tendency for field officers to become personally absorbed in such a syndrome of local conditions is a widely observed phenomenon of administrative behavior. The critical difference in the case of the Ankole Ranching Scheme was that there was during this period no countervailing pressure on the local officials from the central office of the ministry to adhere closely to a predetermined set of rules. Indeed, perhaps partly because some key officials in the ministry were themselves an integral part of the local interest group, one of the unique features of the ranching scheme was the extent of the discretion and autonomy left to the field staff in the entire development of the project. This could never have occurred in a country where the political process did not exhibit a high degree of regional pluralism. In Uganda there has been a marked tradition of pragmatic adaptation by the central government to local demands and pressures.

After several months of cooperation with the Uganda government in ironing out various technical and statistical details, AID/Kampala forwarded the loan application to AID/Washington for its decision in August 1964. Included with the loan request were some of the remarks of Dr. A. J. Howarth, one of the members of the Gregory team, who had been asked by AID/Kampala to comment on the Uganda government's proposals. Dr. Howarth called attention to the fact that the loan application did not give serious consideration to the question of who, in the last analysis, would be helped most by the project:

In discussing the benefits to be derived from this ranching scheme very little is said regarding its most far-reaching benefit. This is the educational and demonstrational aspects of a stabilized ranching project as compared to traditional nomadic raising. When the project is successful, it will be an example to Africans in Uganda and elsewhere in Africa. The final impact of this ranching scheme would not be measured on the benefits to 700 square miles of land in Ankole/Masaka but to untold thousands of square miles in Africa.[9]

The specific paragraphs of the loan application criticized by Dr. Howarth (nos. 43 and 165) referred to the creation of a cadre of experienced ranchers and to the impact of the scheme on the general standard of living of the people of the area. The brunt of his argument was that, as judged by its written proposals, the Uganda government was giving only token consideration to these matters. Concern over the human factor, first articulated by Dr. Howarth, became the heart of the entire controversy over the ranching scheme between the United States and Uganda.

As of fall 1964, AID/Washington had not acted on the ranching scheme. There was evidence that it had become reluctant to proceed with the project until several questions, especially that of social benefits, were satisfactorily clarified. AID officials had become acutely sensitive to criticism of projects that served to entrench local elites. Persistent requests were made that Uganda "describe procedures and criteria in selection of ranch-

[9]The authors wish to express their gratitude to USAID/Kampala for generously making available their files on the Ankole/Masaka Ranching Scheme.

ers and allocation of ranches to successful applicants." The tone of AID's position indicated a growing suspicion that the issue of rancher selection was more than an abstract consideration and that there was an active lobby in Ankole eager to capitalize on any flexibility in the criteria of eligibility for rancher ownership. Washington's tendency to take a critical position, in turn, aroused the sensitivity of officials in the Ministry of Animal Industry, who became impatient at what they viewed as "America's dilatory tactics." Official contacts between the two countries were accompanied by mounting tension as the problem was treated in a more and more unequivocal manner.

Toward the end of 1964, the issue of ranch tenure became the all-absorbing focus of attention in the negotiations between AID and the government of Uganda over the ranching scheme. From being, at an earlier point, one among a host of administrative, technical, and economic details which seemed to require last-minute tidying up, it now loomed as a major political issue which forced all other considerations into the background. The growing estrangement of the two governments over this matter generated strong expressions of indignation among Uganda officials. They claimed that the United States' desire to have a voice in the policy of ranch allocation was an unwarranted interference in the exclusive right of the Uganda government to implement its development programs as it saw fit, and amounted to nothing less than an accusation of bad faith on Uganda's part. There was a noticeable closing of ranks among the government branches connected with the scheme and the view that the country's integrity was involved became readily accepted. A few radical politicians even found this issue a convenient one for expounding anti-American views. Sentiments of righteous indignation, whether genuine or contrived, had become so much a feature of the political climate that the officials concerned could afford nothing less than complete triumph. By the end of November 1964, some went so far as to declare that if Uganda's stature as a sovereign nation were to be properly upheld, it must either insist on complete acceptance of its terms or withdraw its application from AID. This suited the narrow interests of the Ankole elite more than those of the society as a whole since this elite was basically indifferent to the ranching scheme unless its members were to obtain ranches.

A tactical error by AID enabled this group to turn the confrontation to their own advantage. The director of AID/Kampala, prophetically aware that political interests were ready to exploit the ranching scheme, became impatient at the interminable haggling in the abstract. On 2 December 1964 he addressed an outspoken letter to the permanent secretary of the Ministry of Animal Industry, in which he sought to make it clear once and for all that AID viewed the principle of absentee ownership as a thinly veiled subterfuge by which a pressure group of political influentials wanted to acquire ranches. The critical passage of his letter read:

We wish to reiterate our reservation and deep concern over the procedures for the selection of ranchers for the Ankole Ranching Scheme and the problem of absentee-landlords. I think that it is unlikely that the United States A.I.D. would be able to participate in a project that allows people of political influence in your government to secure any of the ranches in the Ankole Ranching Scheme which the U.S. is asked to help finance. We believe in the original concepts of the project in which the U.S. was requested assistance [*sic*] specifically for cattle producers in Uganda. . . . The second problem of absentee landlords is also of concern to U.S.A.I.D. since this would tend to subvert the real purpose of the scheme wherein bona fide cattle producers would be the benefactors [*sic*] of this project and who would eventually spearhead the development of the livestock industry in Uganda.

The author of this letter was determined to prevent the U.S. government/ USAID from being drawn into supporting the economic enrichment of an established political elite. The tragic irony was that precisely because of his overzealous attempt to elicit a more egalitarian approach on the part of the Uganda government, the director of AID/Kampala inadvertently supplied fuel to the charges that the United States was interfering with the internal affairs of a developing country. His letter furnished Uganda spokesmen with the ideal opportunity to present their government as the offended party.

The nature of the reaction among government circles to the AID letter was quite significant. Instead of denying that the principle of absentee ownership would lead to political influentials gaining ranches, the Ministry of Animal Industry made the observation that participation by the local influentials would enhance the prospects of the ranching scheme. In a statement remarkable for its candor and insight into the elite pattern of Ankole society, one high official observed that "it is quite impracticable to exclude people with some standing in Ankole, as so many of them are closely connected or related to someone or other wielding good influence." The same spokesman, offering a sort of "opinion leader" theory, took the position that "if local leaders, political or otherwise, are excluded, other local farmers may become suspicious of the Scheme as they may not understand the reason for their leaders not taking part in it." He further asserted that "experience elsewhere has shown that absentee landlords may be very suitable ranchers, provided that they have a suitable manager."

None of these views, however, took into account the argument at the basis of the Gregory recommendations—that unless the owners resided on their ranches, the educational and modernizing objectives of the scheme could not be achieved. For the scheme would not produce any visible or dramatic changes in the lives of ranchers whose basic involvement was other occupational pursuits. This is the basic reason to doubt the validity of an opinion leader theory based on popular allegiance to established traditional leadership as a justification of absentee ownership. The purpose of the scheme was not simply to gain local acceptance in a traditional context, but to employ a modernizing cadre of ranchers as opinion leaders to induce a fundamental transformation in the socioeconomic culture of the Ankole area.

At the next scheduled meeting of the Uganda Planning Commission, in December 1964, the Ministry of Animal Industry recommended that the government of Uganda withdraw its loan application from AID. It offered three principal reasons for urging this course of action. Most importantly, it considered AID's position to constitute interference in Uganda's internal affairs and took the view that "it is vital that internal operations be unfettered by unreasonable terms and conditions imposed by donor countries." Secondly, the ministry argued, AID's charge that the Uganda government had departed from the original concept of the ranching scheme was ill-founded since the "original" loan application, submitted in May 1964, had explicitly provided for the possibility of absentee ownership. This argument was somewhat paradoxical since the original formulation of the scheme had, in fact, been contained in the Gregory Report and not in the loan request which, precisely because of its innovations, was being questioned by AID. Lastly, ministry officials felt that it was unlikely that AID would change its position and they concluded that it was therefore pointless to continue negotiations. The Uganda Planning Commission accepted these views. It decided to withdraw the application from AID and to go ahead with the project on the basis of Uganda's own financial resources, meanwhile seeking alternative sources of foreign assistance. On 17 December 1964 the Uganda government officially informed AID that the application had been withdrawn.

Shortly after the withdrawal had been effected, Uganda took the position that the wording of the AID letter of 2 December was so offensive that it constituted more than simply an unacceptable condition of economic assistance and was a major breach of diplomatic etiquette. It was decided that the minister of state for Foreign Affairs should raise the issue with the American embassy. This was done, and in response the U.S. ambassador to Uganda sent an official apology for the incident on 9 January 1965.

In his apology he stated that the letter signed by the director of AID/Kampala did not reflect the policy of the American government. He also took pains to point out that any innuendoes contained in the letter were made without the knowledge or authority of American officials either in

Washington or the embassy. The American apology was followed by a series of ad hoc meetings between the U.S. ambassador and his chargé d'affaires and representatives of the Uganda government, particularly the ministers of Foreign Affairs and Animal Industry and the prime minister of Uganda. The purpose of these meetings, which were held during the remainder of January and in early February, was to explore whether the Ugandans could be persuaded to reconsider their decision to withdraw the loan application. Some Uganda officials left these meetings with a clear impression that if they should decide to resubmit the loan request, there would be no need for further negotiation and that the application would be given immediate favorable attention on the terms proposed by the Uganda government. As one of them put it, "the only final procedure will be the signing for the loan by the Uganda Government and offering the money in the normal channels."

The U.S. embassy's effort to persuade the Ugandans to proceed with the project revealed a significant difference in approach between the State Department and AID. Whereas AID had viewed the ranching scheme in developmental terms as a stimulus of economic growth and social change, and was largely concerned with organizational safeguards, the State Department was primarily motivated by diplomatic considerations and saw the scheme as an aspect of American-Ugandan relations. Once the issue had been raised to the diplomatic level, the State Department placed strong pressure on AID to relax its restrictions on ranch ownership in the interest of broader international objectives.

The American State Department generally is anxious to gain the friendship of developing countries and this is a strong incentive for its diplomatic personnel to strive for cordial relations. This concern alone would probably have been sufficient reason for the American ambassador to Uganda to seek to smooth over the Ankole Ranching Scheme crisis. Ordinarily, since the reputation and career of high-ranking diplomats often depend heavily upon their ability to maintain an untroubled atmosphere, American ambassadors are frequently motivated to reduce friction by considerations other than the merits of a situation. In early 1965 the American ambassador to Uganda was under increased pressure, for American relations with Uganda had already begun to suffer considerably due to the Congo crisis and to United States support for the Tshombe regime. It had been reported that the Tshombe forces, using American aircraft, had bombed two Uganda villages in February of that year and this had aroused considerable anti-American feeling as well as suspicion of America's objectives in central and eastern Africa. This situation coincided exactly with the critical moment in the controversy over the ranching scheme. Consequently, the State Department was especially determined to prove the goodwill of the

American government and to show that the United States had no desire to interfere in Uganda's internal affairs.

The intention of the American authorities to conciliate the Uganda government and to have the loan application reactivated was also the product of several additional factors. AID had already become deeply involved in paving the way for the ranching scheme, for example in supporting bush-clearing and tsetse-eradication projects as well as the experimental cattle-breeding station, and there was a natural desire to show results after several years of effort and expenditure. Budgetary considerations were equally important. United States officials in Kampala had already persuaded Washington to set aside funds for the ranching scheme and feared that if these funds were unused, subsequent requests for appropriations might not be granted. This became such a compelling consideration that at one point in the discussion over resumption of the loan, the acting director of AID/Kampala [10] offered Uganda an outright capital assistance grant, to be spent on any project of Uganda's own choosing, which was equivalent to the sum budgeted for the ranching scheme. Moreover, several previous offers of American assistance, including aid for police housing and Peace Corps projects, had been declined by the Uganda government and ultimately this proved to be an incentive on both sides to reconsider the ranching scheme loan. Underlying this entire controversy was the legacy of America's failure to finance the Aswan Dam and the fact that this had helped to strengthen the ties between Egypt and the Soviet Union. AID and the Department of State were both anxious to help finance the ranching scheme if only to prevent this sort of situation from arising.

One noteworthy feature of the American government's response to the ranching scheme controversy was its ability to present a single policy to the Uganda government. This could in large measure be attributed to the fact that, when the crisis occurred, the State Department was able to assert its exclusive authority to represent American policy. This enabled it to submerge AID's position and, thereby, to conceal any differences between the diplomatic and technical assistance perspectives toward the scheme. Thus, a facade of unity was created which gave the impression that America was willing to accommodate Uganda's political sensitivities especially regarding ranch tenure.

The appearance of unity on the part of the American government was in stark contrast to the disarray of the Uganda side during the first few months of 1965. Each sector of the Uganda government involved with the scheme took a different position. Lack of experience in handling this sort of situation resulted in confusion over exactly who had authority to decide

[10] This official had succeeded the writer of the controversial letter.

whether and on what basis aid negotiations with the United States should be resumed. There was also a failure of communication within the Uganda administration; the various branches of the government were essentially uninformed as to each other's viewpoints and activities with respect to the loan application. The Ministry of Foreign Affairs, viewing the conflict in diplomatic terms, felt that its discussions with the American ambassador had cleared the ground for a resumption of negotiations and asked the Ministry of Animal Industry to reopen discussions with AID. The Ministry of Animal Industry took the view that the American government had already agreed to finance the project on Uganda's terms and that therefore further discussions were not called for. The Uganda Planning Commission took the position that it had decided to withdraw the loan application from AID and that there was no need to reconsider this decision. It stated that it would be prepared to allow the Americans to finance another project but not the Ankole scheme.

Once these positions had been taken, each government branch developed a vested interest in its own viewpoint. The Ministry of Foreign Affairs, for example, believed that it had undertaken a diplomatic commitment to the American embassy and argued that it would be "diplomatically bad" not to resume negotiations. To this, the Ministry of Animal Industry responded that further negotiations would result in little more than "delaying tactics" by the American government and now asserted that it would be preferable to finance the scheme from Uganda's own resources. The prime minister of Uganda, Milton Obote, whose view corresponded roughly with that of the Ministry of Foreign Affairs, had meanwhile acted on his own authority and agreed with the U.S. ambassador to allow AID to finance the scheme. Finally, the Uganda Planning Commission, which had been unaware of the discussions with the American embassy, was forced to seek clarification of its position as the sole body empowered to approve development loans and, in early April, asked the prime minister whether it was expected to reconsider its previous decision.

The prime minister decided, at that point, to use his influence to resolve the deadlock. He was concerned that the ranching scheme should move more rapidly toward implementation since it had already been announced several times in parliament and had received considerable press coverage. In his opinion the preliminary work done by AID entitled it to some consideration and the Uganda government should not be precipitate in dismissing the contribution American assistance had already made to the development of the Ankole scheme. Moreover, he noted, the Uganda Planning Commission's decision to withdraw the loan application was prompted less by a sense of offense at the AID letter than by reluctance to accept the restrictions AID was imposing on ranch tenure. Since the American government had apologized for the letter, the Uganda government should, in his view, take the wider political and diplomatic repercussions of its decision into account and resume discussions with AID.

Obote's perspective on this issue was strongly influenced by evidence he had received confirming the AID allegation that absentee ownership would lead to political influentials acquiring ranches. An official Rancher Selection Board, appointed by the Ministry of Animal Industry (which was proceeding with the ranching scheme on its own), had held its second meeting on 1 April 1965, and had allocated the first twenty-eight Ankole ranches. A substantial number of these ranches had been awarded to people of high political status. Concerned with the fact that this was damaging Uganda's image, the prime minister called a special meeting of Uganda officials to settle the ranching scheme controversy. At this meeting, which was held on 3 May 1965, it was decided that subsequent allocation of ranches should be handled by a subcommittee of the Uganda Planning Commission and that the loan application should be resubmitted to AID. Significantly, the Uganda Planning Commission was not asked to confirm this decision. On 18 May USAID/Kampala was informed that the Uganda government wished its loan application to be revived.

This was by no means the end of a confused situation as regarded the status of the loan application. Somewhat belatedly the Uganda government had also begun to make internal adjustments in its personnel and transferred several of the officials who had been most deeply involved in the conflict. The new officials, however, did not immediately become familiar with the background of the project or the details of the controversy and this led them to make some bizarre assumptions about the previous contact between AID and the Uganda government. A member of the Ministry of Foreign Affairs, for example, stated that AID had wished to interfere unduly in the details of how the money was to be spent and to participate directly in the selection of ranchers. And a Ministry of Planning spokesman asserted that the original breakdown was caused by AID's desire to influence the appointment of the director of the ranching scheme. The basic cause of confusion, however, was that most of the Uganda officials were unclear as to exactly what concrete changes the American embassy had brought about in AID's policy toward the ranching scheme.

The essential misunderstanding, from May until August 1965, was that the Ministries of Animal Industry and Planning believed that the loan application would be approved immediately, whereas AID/Kampala felt that the entire situation had merely reverted to what it was before the 2 December letter. When AID asked to be informed about the composition of the Rancher Selection Board, the Ministry of Planning responded that the American embassy had already agreed to regard this as a matter of

Uganda's internal affairs and to approve the loan without delays for information of this kind. There was also a rather minor misunderstanding over whether Uganda would be allowed to apply for funds to finance the entire ranching scheme or whether the project would have to be financed in separate stages.

These misunderstandings were, in fact, highly anticlimactic. By the fall of 1965, it was clear that AID had no alternative but to accept absentee ownership. Once the American embassy had intervened in the principal dispute, it became diplomatically impossible for AID either to take a strong position on the question of ranch tenure or to refuse to finance the ranching scheme. The diplomatic factor constituted an enormous and visible pressure on AID to proceed with the scheme on terms acceptable to Uganda. Moreover, it was necessary to rationalize the distribution of the first twenty-eight ranches, many of which were already awarded on an absentee basis. Indeed, the pressure on AID was so great that it led to a curiously harmonious working relationship between American experts and Uganda government personnel. The Ugandans, probably recognizing that a victory on ranch tenure was imminent, agreed to supply technical and organizational information, to frame procedures for the Rancher Selection Board which met with AID approval, and to cooperate with AID in preparing an acceptable version of the loan application. During the final stages of discussion, the two groups of officials worked closely together to formulate the detailed regulations governing ranch tenure. Thus, paradoxically, AID was placed in the position of having to assist Uganda to draft precisely the sort of ranch tenure arrangement to which AID had previously raised such strong objections.

AID's efforts to help the Ugandans prepare an acceptable formula for ranch tenure led to a rather ironic exchange of correspondence. In a letter to the acting secretary of Planning, dated 30 August 1965, the acting director of AID/Kampala forwarded a paper entitled "Rancher Selection" which, he said, "was prepared by Uganda Government technical personnel with some assistance from USAID technicians." Suggesting that this document would satisfy Washington's requirements, the acting director of AID/Kampala wrote that "this paper, if transmitted to us officially, would provide the information required" on "procedures and criteria for selection of ranchers." The critical passage in the paper read:

In general terms the ranches will be offered on conditional lease for two years to individuals selected on the basis of business acument [sic], educational background, integrity, experience and financial capacity or some satisfactory combination of these criterion [sic], or to individuals, cooperative societies or companies who would employ a Manager of similar calibre.

The following day, the acting secretary of Planning responded that:

As regards the procedures and criteria for selection of ranchers, the proposals contained in your paper headed "Rancher Selection" have been *approved* (authors' emphasis) by the Minister of Animal Industry Game and Fisheries, and as such, are acceptable to the Government subject of course to correction being made of two words contained in the first paragraph, i.e., "acumen" in place of "acument" and "criteria" instead of "criterion". . . .

Agreement on this formulation of ranch tenure removed the major obstacle to completing the actual loan agreement.

The last remaining snag concerned those of the twenty-eight ranches already allocated which had been given to political influentials. AID/Washington was extremely reluctant for American funds to be used to finance "men of top political influence" and wanted assurance that this would not occur. After consultations with Uganda officials, AID/Kampala cabled Washington, in early October, that the Uganda government had offered "full assurance that AID funds will not be used to finance ranches for any politically important people." This assurance was impossible to fulfill. The Uganda government was in a position to take steps to minimize the amount of benefit enjoyed by political influentials, for example, by denying certain specified ranchers such facilities as credit arrangements. Since, however, the bulk of the expenditure was being used for the simultaneous physical preparation of the ranches, it would be quite impossible to distinguish the funds spent on one ranch from those spent on another. The inescapable conclusion is that Uganda's assurances and AID/Kampala's confirmation of these assurances were largely for Washington consumption. Thus, against the background of existing absentee ownership and the striking prominence of high-ranking politicians as ranchers, the critical wording of the official Loan Agreement, signed April 1966, had a sardonic quality:

Selection of Ranchers. Borrower warrants that during the life of this Agreement with respect to any ranches approved hereunder, it will maintain a system of rancher selection satisfactory to AID.[11]

The final irony of the conclusion of the ranching scheme controversy was that the decision to allow manager-operated ranches came at precisely a moment when important voices in Uganda had begun to echo AID's early fear that political influentials would exploit any flexibility in the criteria for eligibility of ranchers. After the prime minister of Uganda had

[11] *Loan Agreement,* 2 April 1966, sect. 6.2. Against this background, the assertion in a recent paper on the scheme that "the Ranching Selection Board has been particularly careful and unbiased, and has refused applications, even from prominent persons, if it has not thought them suitable" is most surprising. The statement is made in G. D. Sacker, "The Ankole-Masaka Ranching Scheme, Uganda," Conference Paper, International Seminar on Change in Agriculture, Reading, England, 1968, p. 3j: 3.

voiced his dismay over the allocation of the first twenty-eight ranches, as early as May 1965, several other political leaders in the country started to take up his viewpoint. The director of the Uganda Planning Commission, for example, stated that the "common man" had been neglected and should be given top priority. On 6 September the minister of Animal Industry went so far as to direct that "in future, applications made only by Co-oper-tive societies or similar associations will be allocated ranches." None of these concerns made any immediate impact on subsequent allocations of ranches. For adequate mechanisms whereby the central government could exercise effective control over its local personnel and ensure their full compliance with its directives had, at that time, not yet been established in Uganda. Moreover, by the fall of 1965, the Uganda political system was in the shadow of an impending crisis and political leaders became more preoccupied with basic problems of stability and survival than with the details of development projects.

Resentment within Ankole over ranch allocation has also been too late and ineffective to alter the distribution of ranches up to this time. Popular expressions of grievance had only begun to emerge after the announcement of the first allocation of ranches. Until that time, there had been very little effort to inform the people of Ankole about the ranching scheme and especially about such fundamental matters as eligibility, and how and when to apply. Moreover, there had been practically no attempt to bring about an awareness of the potentially widespread social benefits which might accrue from the scheme.

Several distinctive structural features of Ankole politics also made it extremely difficult for local resentment to the ranching scheme to gain effective national political expression. Of the six Ankole members of par-liament, four received ranches. Three of these were influential members of the Bahima elite and two were ministers in the Uganda government. These individuals were evidently unprepared to scrutinize the social equity of the scheme as it developed, or to act as spokesmen of discontent after the first allocation of ranches had been made. The two remaining Ankole M.P.s were not particularly influential figures and were, at the time, rather dependent upon the others. Indeed, it is remarkable that of the national political leaders who spoke out in favor of a more equitable distribution of ranches, none came from Ankole. Nor did the Ankole district council become a voice for the dissension which had emerged, largely because the most influential leaders in Ankole were personally interested in the ranch-ing scheme.

Perhaps the most important reason why local resentment of the scheme did not find adequate expression was that leaders of both national political parties had an interest in the project. This meant that an issue which otherwise might have become an ideal subject of partisan conflict, remained outside the scope of party politics. It is, indeed, indicative of the absence of channels for the articulation of popular discontent, that the only group which organized an opposition to the inequities in the scheme were the Ankole students at Makerere University College. Discontent remained and the scheme has persisted as a political irritant.

Part III The Political Context of Future Development

Preface to Part III

The political context of future African development is likely to be one of chronic institutional weakness. There is substantial agreement among the authors in this section that African nations do not currently possess and are unlikely for the time being to attain adequate institutional capacity to carry out the developmental objectives they have set for themselves. The following three essays, concerned respectively with the nature of African political parties, the political role of the African military, and the prospects for democracy in African nations, state this basic argument in different ways.

In his essay on "Political Parties and Political Machines in Africa," Henry Bienen deals primarily with those African nations which had come to be identified as "mobilizational" or "revolutionary-centralizing" in their approach to development. Such nations had come to be widely regarded as possessing extremely powerful party organizations characterized by an effective organizational hierarchy, ideological cohesion, strategic and tactical flexibility, and, as a consequence of these qualities, a high level of capacity to mobilize the human resources of their societies for development programs. Bienen's essay calls into question one assumption which, though rarely stated openly, occupied considerable importance as an unspoken premise in studies of such societies: namely, that in countries weak or lacking in economic and financial resources and where prospects of an infusion of external capital are small a monolithic political party, espousing socialist objectives, could compensate for lack of material resources by its ability to mobilize popular participation for developmental purposes.

Bienen's criticism of this assumption does not take the form of calling into question this premise. More importantly, he argues that in none of these countries where such "revolutionary-centralizing" regimes have been said to exist has this, in fact, been the case. Rather, in his view, there has been an unfortunate tendency among observers to treat rhetorical descriptions of politics as if they were accurate characterizations of reality. Politics have, despite rhetoric to the contrary, taken highly pluralistic forms quite similar to the political processes of countries long identified with a high degree of political pluralism. The argument that interpretations of African political systems which focus on the capacity for mobilization of a revolutionary disciplined mass party have been more inclined to deal in appearances than reality has great importance. It means, for example, that there is very little prospect of African nations actually testing the theory of development based on human mobilization, less because of the accuracy or inaccuracy of that theory than because the organizational capacity requisite for such mobilization does not in fact exist.

The model of politics proposed by Bienen is that of the political machine. Machine politics are characterized, in his view, by considerable give and take between the party core and its outlying branches. Regional, district, and local compliance with the edicts and instructions of the party center depend upon an intraorganizational process of bargaining and compromise. Local party machinery is often more under the control of local leadership than it is of the party center and this leadership uses its power and influence to extract a range of concessions from the party core. These concessions may be material ones including patronage and high positions, but they may also include the modification of policy directives and development plans about which the periphery does not agree with central party leadership. Such politics may be perfectly viable in a relatively affluent or well-to-do nation where the political process is mostly concerned with the distribution of political and economic resources, but there is every reason to doubt that a machine system is adequate to the task of resource creation implicit in the mobilizational concept of development.

Claude E. Welch deals with the role of the military in African development. The question is, what sort of a contribution may the military be expected to make to the developmental process? On this point, Welch is not encouraging. Military leadership in Africa often assumes control under an extremely adverse set of political conditions. These may include corruption, political breakdown, parliamentary and cabinet immobilism, violence among claimant groups in the society whether economic or ethnic, and a widespread loss of faith in existing leaders and institutions. Welch's principal argument is that armies, upon assuming power, may be able to resolve the most dramatic of these problems but their capacity to engineer long-term developmental change is unlikely to be greater than that of the civil regimes that preceded them.

Initially, African armies create an impression of organizational hierarchy and discipline not strikingly dissimilar from that often ascribed to mobilizational or revolutionary-centralizing political parties. On this basis, there is at least superficial hope that armies might undertake the sort of social and economic reordering observers had anticipated from the monolithic party model of development. The major problem arises from the fact that the military out of power can remain essentially nonpolitical. The military in power is unable to do so and military governments in Africa have often been susceptible to the same fissiparous and fragmentary political forces as the civil regimes that preceded them. Indeed, one of the strongest incentives for the military to surrender control back to civilian leadership is precisely to preserve its unitary character as a military organization. This point bears directly on the prospects of a military withdrawal from politics. The conclusion is inescapable that the single most determinative condition as to whether the military will agree to surrender power back to civilian leadership is its own willingness to do so. The desire to avoid internal politization is a strong incentive but there are equally powerful if not more powerful disincentives including the material rewards of power and the fact that civilian authority, once having crumbled, cannot easily be expected to acquire even its former degree of legitimacy.

Military regimes may achieve dramatic success in eliminating the grosser forms of corruption and in subduing patterns of violence and disorder but their developmental capability is problematic. As Welch observes, "the organizational characteristics of the armed services—their centralization, hierarchy, discipline, communication, and esprit de corps—may work against effective governance in certain respects. Military governments may simply not be prepared to cope with the bargaining, compromise, ethnic arithmetic, and host of ancillary skills that politicians—but not necessarily soldiers—develop as a matter of course." The one unavoidable feature of development is that it is a political process in which the skills of bargaining and persuasion are critically necessary. For this reason, the military may be able to sustain political order, but it is unlikely to be able to achieve far-reaching developmental progress.

Whether African nations may be expected to develop under democratic conditions is equally problematic. Rupert Emerson argues that virtually none of the conditions frequently associated with the emergence and perpetuity of democratic government are to be found in most African nations. While democracy may, even under adverse conditions, emerge in one or another state from time to time, the prospects of this form of government becoming a regular feature of the political landscape of the African continent are limited. Few African nations, for example, have developed an overarching sense of national unity sufficient to enable democratic institutions to sustain themselves during periods of travail.

Of equal importance is the lack of an adequate socioeconomic basis for democracy. A certain minimal level of national wealth has been associated with a variety of factors conducive to democratic rule. These include a level of education and literacy sufficient to permit a substantial proportion of the citizenry to be politically informed and sufficient leisure time for large numbers of people to participate in the political process. The level of wealth of a society is also related to the growth of a middle class which can anchor a political system because its grievances are not so great that it would be inclined to topple an entire order for the sake of their amelioration and whose presence as an intermediary class diminishes the possibility of intense conflict between have and have-not elements in the society. Growing national wealth may also be associated with the proliferation of an array of professional, occupational, and functional groups which can cut across ethnic lines, create patterns of overlapping cleavages, and thus produce a politics of bargaining and restraint. One additional aspect of national wealth conducive to democratic politics is that it makes horizontal mobility in and out of politics possible. A change of power between ins and outs is realistically only possible if those who hold power do not feel that the loss of it will entail a great sacrifice in material and social status. There must, in other words, be an opportunity for political ins to move "out" into roughly comparable socioeconomic levels of the society. If a society is not sufficiently affluent for this pattern of horizontal mobility to occur, there will be a strong incentive for the ins to want to remain in at all costs.

Few African nations conform to this pattern of conditions. The sense of overarching national solidarity is incipient but weak in most cases. It is an old generalization but a vital one that the national boundaries laid down by colonial powers had little to do with emergent African patterns of association either on ethnic or regional-economic lines and that the colonial experience did little to rectify this situation until very shortly before independence. Nor is there generally to be found that degree of national wealth which would modify the intensity of demands being made by groups that experience their position in society as a disadvantaged one and want this situation quickly rectified. To the extent that certain kinds of modernization associated with democracy elsewhere occur in Africa, they are often counterproductive. For example, the emergence of new social classes and professional strata does not, in many cases, represent the growth of cross-cutting political solidarities, but rather these tend to follow ethnic lines in large part, thus producing aggravating economic inequalities between elements of the society which are already regionally and culturally differentiated. Emerson's conclusion is the likelihood of some variant of authoritarian rule. This will take different forms under different conditions and may include a number of benevolent and enlightened, if dictatorial, situations, but until such time as more of the basic conditions for democracy have been created, such values as freedom and opposition are likely to be held in abeyance.

Michael F. Lofchie

Chapter 9 Political Parties and Political Machines in Africa

Henry Bienen

I have suggested previously that our thinking about one-party systems in Africa could benefit from analyses of American party machines and especially those that have existed in one-party states.[1] My argument was not that American political machines constitute a model for African one-party systems. Rather, I said simply that politics as described in accounts of American party machines bears many more resemblances to politics in Africa than do descriptions of African one-party systems made within frameworks which single out ideology, formal party structure, and charismatic leadership as crucial variables. These frameworks or typologies which have proliferated in the study of new states, and African ones in particular, have meant to distinguish between parties which are concerned with national integration and far-reaching social change on the one hand and those which are status quo and based on a narrow class or ethnic grouping on the other. They are meant to distinguish between elite and mass political organizations; revolutionary and evolutionary ones; ideological and pragmatic ones.[2] While parties have been the defining political organizations for the typological characterizations, military and/or civil service regimes could be, in principle, similarly differentiated.

One reason that descriptions of American machine politics which emphasize secular leadership, patronage, struggle of groups within the party

[1] Henry Bienen, "One Party System in Africa," in C. H. Moore and Samuel Huntington, eds., *One Party System* (New York, Basic Books, 1970).
[2] I am not going to once again criticize these typologies here. For such criticism see Bienen, "The Ruling Party in the African One-Party State: TANU in Tanzania," *Journal of Commonwealth Political Studies*, vol. V (Nov. 1967), pp. 214-230.

and within society, self-interest, and localized politics may sound familiar to students of African parties once they are studied on the ground is that politics shows these features when political organizations are examined at a certain level of analysis. With this in mind, the concept of political machines as it defines parties which rely characteristically upon the attraction of material rewards rather than enthusiasm for political principles [3] is a very limited one. To say this is not to say that there is any excuse for describing politics, whether it be the politics of "totalitarian systems" or African one-party states, or military regimes, as if patronage and struggle of self-interested groups did not exist. Soviet studies, for example, have long suffered from a relative neglect of these aspects of politics, in part because many of the characterizations of the system by its rulers were accepted, in part because it was not possible to have the close access to politics through firsthand research which would reveal otherwise. Above all, the idea was influential that a particular political elite in a totalitarian system was powerful enough to abolish personal and group struggle over parochial interests, through the wielding of organizational weapons and by terror, propaganda, and agitation. Recent studies have begun to disabuse us of this idea and in the process to make us refine, perhaps abandon, our past understandings and definitions of totalitarian systems.[4]

Students of African one-party systems have rarely claimed that the parties they were looking at were so powerful that they could abrogate interest group politics; nor did they argue that the ruling parties were internally centralized because the inner party cores were so powerful that they could brook no dissension. Nonetheless, typologies were elaborated which did pose organizational weapons, mobilizational parties, and mass movement regimes which were engaged in a process of directed social change made possible by certain structural characteristics of the party; that is, centralized, hierarchical arrangements institutionalized leaderships. Perhaps most important of all, the parties that defined the systems as mobilizational or revolutionary-centralizing were said to monopolize legitimacy, and within the party a single leader was seen to concentrate legitimacy in his own hands. This concern that analysts had for legitimacy

[3] Edward C. Banfield, *Political Influence* (Glencoe, 1961), p. 237.

[4] Even before recent revisionist literature on the Soviet Union, some authors had insisted that factions had persisted in Soviet politics even after Stalin's ascendancy. See especially, Franz Borkenau, "Getting at the Facts Behind the Soviet Facade," *Commentary*, vol. 17, no. 4 (April 1954), pp. 393–400, where Borkenau describes a political patronage system or *sheftsvo*. Boris Nicolaevsky was another analyst who stressed that Soviet elite politics was a continuous struggle. In the 1960s, a "conflict" school has developed in the study of Soviet politics as analysts now describe not only struggles at the top of the hierarchy but the clash of interest groups. Cf. Robert C. Tucker, "The Conflict Model," *Problems of Communism*, vol. XII, no. 6. (Nov.–Dec. 1963), pp. 49–51; Sidney Ploss, *Conflict and Decision Making in Soviet Russia* (Princeton, 1965); Carl A. Linden, *Khrushchev and the Soviet Leadership, 1957–1964* (Baltimore, 1966).

is not surprising given that the states were newly independent, often not thought to be nations, that is, socially and ethnically unintegrated and with an elite that had emerged in a very short time-span and assumed power.

The focus on legitimacy led to seeing the ideology of parties and leaders as a distinguishing variable of systems. And the ideologies elaborated by leaders postulated a harmony of interest, an absence of class struggle in the social realm. While African leaders could not say that the nation was ethnically or tribally homogeneous, some denied that heterogeneity of their countries had, or should have, political import. The political community could remain monolithic as the single party gathered all under its wing. Opposition was seen in highly personal terms as, for example, when Sékou Touré asked his opponents to surmount their "self-love, complexes, rancor, selfishness and jealousy." [5] The individualism of Nyerere was the collective individualism of a certain strain of Rousseau and the French Revolution where individuals ought not to disagree about the essentials *of* a good society *in* a good society. Thus the diversity of individuals that Nyerere accepted could have no organized political expression. Not only an antiparty ethic exists in Nyerere's writings but an antipolitical ethic as well. His *Democracy and Party System* expresses a desire to abolish politics from society insofar as politics means conflict.[6]

Observers of the African scene did not jump to the conclusion that there was no conflict, anymore than the leaders who postulated conflict-free societies were unaware of dissension and disagreement, although both observers and leaders were engaged in a certain amount of wishful thinking and incantation. They hoped by invoking unity to create it. My point here is that the attention of students of African one-party states was on the formula for unity, ideology, and one-party structure rather than on political conflict. Where this conflict was overt, and particularly violent and ethnic, it was indeed considered. In fact, the tendency in such cases was to ignore party structures and ideology and presume they were not important, in, for example, Congo or Rwanda.[7] Conflict was seen as being tribal or regional and the more mundane struggles centering around internal party competition, electoral battles for office, and group economic self-interest

---

[5] Sékou Touré, *Expérience Guinéenne et Unité Africaine* (Paris, 1962), p. 32.

[6] I have discussed Nyerere's ideology in *Tanzania: Party Transformation and Economic Development* (Princeton, 1967), pp. 203–257.

[7] It was not that students of the Congo ignored ideology and party structure, as Crawford Young's *Politics in the Congo* (Princeton, 1965) and Herbert Weiss's *Political Protest in the Congo* (Princeton, 1967) and René Lemarchand's *Political Awakening in the Congo: The Politics of Fragmentation* (Berkeley, 1964), show. But the Congo was rarely fitted into schemes which distinguished African parties along mass-elite lines or pragmatic/pluralistic versus revolutionary-centralizing. Aristide Zolberg in 1966 said "Although the Congo crisis has attracted much attention as an issue in international politics, it has little impact on the academic study of new states," in "A View From the Congo," *World Politics*, vol. XIX, (Oct. 1966), pp. 137–149.

were neglected. But where public order did not break down, there was an assumed connection between one-party rule and the maintenance of that order.

Similarly, it was believed that military coups tended not to displace the single mass-party authoritarian regimes.[8] However, as Samuel Finer has pointed out, between 1960 and 1966 in Africa (including Africa north of the Sahara) military interventions took place in eight of fifteen multiparty states and nine of twenty single-party states. Six single-party states had their governments overturned by violence between 1960 and 1967.[9] There were, of course, plots and civil disturbances that occurred while states were in a single-party condition. The problem is that insofar as "single mass-party authoritarian regime" implied a monolithic party whose control extended out into all areas of the countryside enabling it to mobilize political and economic resources from a central core, such regimes did not exist.[10]

It has been said elsewhere that we might have known this deductively—that is, by inferring political consequences from economic or, more broadly, ecological conditions.[11] But the reasons these deductions were not made are of some interest, the more so because the failure to carry out certain kinds of research in the rural areas is related to this failure of deduction.

The salient political structures were national ones in independent Africa. The shift from observing colonial ruling institutions was natural enough. Furthermore, individual national leaders often personified their countries to observers. The parties which led the national independence struggle were perceived and heard, literally, through discussions with leaders. The impact of the parties was felt through the parties' presence in the capital cities and major towns and through the forcefulness of leaders. And there seemed to be few competing institutions or groups at the national level. The exception was the civil service as a potential counterweight to parties. But civil services were still not completely Africanized immediately after independence; civil servants were indispensable but they were in the shadows. It was party leaders who dominated independence celebrations, made speeches, and published articles establishing the party's ideology.

[8] Morris Janowitz, *The Military in the Political Development of New Nations* (Chicago, 1964), p. 29.

[9] Samuel Finer, "The One-Party Regime in Africa: Reconsiderations," *Government and Opposition*, vol. II (July–Oct. 1967), pp. 505–506.

[10] For a critique of this view with specific reference to military takeovers see "Introduction," in Henry Bienen, ed., *The Military Intervenes: Case Studies in Political Change* (New York, 1968). For analysis of the weaknesses in mass-party regimes see Aristide Zolberg, *Creating Political Order* (Chicago, 1966).

[11] Zolberg, op. cit., Bienen, "What Does Political Development Mean in Africa," *World Politics*, vol. XX (Oct. 1967), pp. 127–141.

Militaries were small, had little firepower, and usually remained officered by expatriates for some years after independence. Perhaps most importantly, at the national level indigenous economic interest groups were not manifest. Industry was in the hands of government or expatriates or minority "Asian" groups. The African interest groups that existed were not those of big business men or merchants or organized artisan associations but rather trade unions and cooperatives. And these were seen as being linked to parties—transmission belts for them or integral parts of the party.

This was not entirely wrong, but neither was it very accurate. The few histories of trade unions and cooperative movements showed a sometimes uneasy relationship between them and parties or national movements prior to independence and it might have been expected that when independence was won, the new governments would be exacerbating relations through demands on economic organizations linked to the ruling party. Some countries did, indeed, have important farming groups. The cotton and coffee farmers of Uganda and the cocoa farmers of Ghana and Nigeria had played a role in the independence struggle. But insofar as these groups became visible to political scientists it was often through their identification with a particular tribe, Baganda, Ashanti, Yoruba. It was not that political scientists were unaware that tribal and economic grievances might reinforce each other, and thus that a particular ruling party could be very unpopular in Ashanti or Buganda. But the tendency was to see the national impact of unhappy cash crop farmers in tribal terms, because at this level immediate threats were posed to national unity through tribal separatism. Where cash crop farming was not being done by one or two major tribes, the questions were less frequently asked concerning the operation of the ruling party in these areas. Where there were subsistence farmers whom government was not reaching through tax mechanisms, government's popularity or unpopularity could not be posed in the same terms. But precisely how the party operated in these areas was never an irrelevant question either.

I am suggesting that the focus was on national structures or tribal/regional separatism rather than on bread and butter local issues of economic self-interest and patronage for groups and individuals, because analysts were concerned with national integration and for obvious reasons the national institutions were more visible.[12] It also happened that research

[12] Richard Sklar criticizes the view that tribalism is supposed to be the most formidable barrier to national unity in Africa when he says that "It is less frequently recognized that tribal movements may be created and instigated to action by the new men of power in furtherance of their own special interests which are, time and again, the constitutive interests of emerging social classes. Tribalism then becomes a mask for class privilege." See his "Political Science and National Integration—A Radical Approach," *The Journal of Modern African Studies*, vol. V, no. 1 (1967), p. 6. Whereas

was easier to do in the capitals and that neither political scientists nor economists usually had the skills to work in the countryside in one or two places for long periods of time. Hence a mutually reinforcing pattern of lack of empirical work, poor deductions, and a failure to perceive the need for different kinds of empirical research. This pattern had now been broken. Political scientists, economists, and sociologists are concerned with "micropolitics," and with rural change.[13] As more historical work is done on the preindependence period, awareness is heightened of the role of farmers and of protest against enforced agricultural change.[14] As more research is done in the localities, the importance of "parochial" but non-tribal factors and issues becomes increasingly evident.[15] We are being brought into greater contact with politics in an everyday sense of the word. But as emphasis shifts from the macro to the micro, it becomes incumbent to make sense of the larger pattern—hopefully in a more realistic way. This requires that academicians from the various disciplines make their results known in terms of an explicit set of problems examined and couched in a shared language.[16] It requires above all the refining of new concepts which take account of the work now going on.

I think the notion of the political machine is worth exploring as an organizing concept, but not because the idea of a political machine constitutes a full-blown typology into which African political systems can be put. Moreover, in looking at the idea of political machines as described in the literature on American politics, it seems to me that the concept has not been an entirely successful one. That is, it remains a limited concept which is both too broad and too narrow at the same time. Perhaps the study of

---

Sklar prefers to stress class formation and class interests, I am referring to a clash of interests which may or may not be class or tribal but which do not have to be either. As Sklar himself points out, competition between groups for economic and political goods can be thought of within frameworks other than those of class struggle or ethnic heterogeneity. There are the conflict model theorists who owe a great deal to Simmel and the theorists of pluralist competition who are so much in evidence in treatments of American politics and democratic theory.

[13] Witness the new publication at Michigan State University, *Rural Africana*, panels on micropolitics at African Studies Association meetings, conferences on local development in Africa held at the Foreign Service Institute, Washington, 18–19 July 1967, and on African local institutions and rural transformation at Lincoln University, 20–21 April 1967.

[14] See, for example, Lionel Cliffe, "Nationalism and the Reaction to Agricultural Improvement in Tanganyika During the Colonial Period," East African Institute of Social Research Paper, Kampala, 1964; John Kesby, "Warangi Reaction to Agricultural Change," EAISR, Kampala, 1964.

[15] See, for example, Martin Kilson's political history, *Political Change in a West African State* (Cambridge, 1966); Colin Leys's *Politicians and Policies: An Essay on Politics in Acholi* (Nairobi, 1967); Lionel Cliffe's electoral study, *One Party Democracy: The 1965 Tanzania General Elections* (Nairobi, 1967).

[16] See Henry Bienen, "Political Factors in Agricultural Change," *Rural Africa*, vol. 3 (fall, 1967), pp. 13–14.

African politics can lead us to refine the concept so that it becomes more useful for the study of politics in general.

The concept of the political machine is too broad in that the characterization of parties that are concerned with material rewards, that is, with the perquisites of office, direct economic benefits, would apply to most parties for at least part of their history. No simple distinction can be made between parties that are concerned with rewards rather than political principle. Aside from the problems that arise in defining "political principle," and even the seemingly less vague term "issues," in the real world, parties are concerned with both. Ideological parties too are concerned with taking office and distributing offices even if they want to change the system after achieving power or during the process of so doing. Parties that have no interest in attaining office but simply exist to affect values or policies in society are rare birds; in any case, such parties are by definition not ruling parties. True, some parties appear more concerned with issues, change, and principles than others. Lenin did not forge the Bolshevik Party to create jobs for the boys. Quite the contrary, he looked forward to the breaking up of the administrative machine which was a major provider of these jobs. Nonetheless, the Communist Party of the Soviet Union did in fact put its personnel into jobs in government, factories, and farms; it abolished the distinction between governmental and nongovernmental jobs over wide functional areas in the economy and administration. Furthermore, the Communist Party itself became a major employer in the system, creating its own security apparatus and supervisory posts. The appeals of the Communist Party of the Soviet Union to the community at large were not and are not in patronage terms. Rarely do parties appeal exclusively in such terms, at least when the relevant political community is large and heterogeneous and there is competition electorally. In this sense, parties, as V. O. Key points out, are different from pressure groups. "Yet in one respect the inner core of the party—the machine or party organization—may be considered in the same category as a pressure group." [17]

Here Key is distinguishing between the party organization, that is, the permanent bureaucracy, and the party members at large, as did Robert Michels before him. Michels called attention to what he called the "echeloned aspect" of party.[18] African leaders have distinguished between party militants and those who were not militants but to be a militant one did not have to be a permanent paid official. Rather militancy is a state of mind and is expressed through nation-building activities. For Michels and Key the echeloned aspect is expressed organizationally and in terms of benefits received from membership. Michels says that the German practice was to pay for all services to the party:

[17] V. O. Key, *Politics, Parties and Pressure Groups* (New York, 1958), p. 381.
[18] Robert Michels, *Political Parties* (New York, 1959), p. 52.

Whilst this deprives the party to a large extent of the spirit of heroism and enthusiasm, and of work done by voluntary and spontaneous collaboration, it gives to the organization a remarkable cohesion, and an authority over the personnel which, though doubtless detracting from its elasticity and its spirit of initiative, and in essence, tending to impair the very socialist mentality, constitutes nonetheless one of the most important and indispensable bases of the party life.[19]

We can compare parties to see what kinds of recompense they give to members for services rendered and we can see what kind of inner cores various parties have in terms of size of paid officials. In other words, we can measure for "party militants" along other axes than those of attitude and ideological commitment. If all parties have inner cores, that is, machines, as Michels asserts, some might be called "party machines" as compared to others that met established criteria such as size of cadres as percent of total membership and types of payment for various services. The great problem with focusing on commitment to political principle as opposed to concern with material reward is in determining who is committed to what principles and especially in finding which principles various levels of and groups within parties hold. In studies of African parties the tendency has been to treat the views of one man as if they were the belief system of an entire party. Without asking how an ideology elaborated at the top might be communicated, even disseminated throughout the party (not to say the society as a whole), it has been assumed that TANU or the PDG or the Union Soudanaise held certain ideologies. This is not to deny that large segments of a given party's membership may be concerned with certain issues that have nothing to do with their economic self-interest, or their advancement, or their power and status. It is crucial to differentiate the kinds of issues, for example, foreign/domestic, ethnic/economic, and the various combinations thereof that parties and elements of parties concern themselves with and it is crucial to distinguish between styles of rule and commitments to policies. But in so doing we must be aware of the possibility of varying commitments of the different layers of party officials, of the distinctions between elected and appointed officials, and between officials and members at large.[20] Such distinctions are made all the time in analysis of American parties but they are much more rarely made in studies of African parties.

Concern with interparty relationships must be related to significant variables that distinguish polities. Obvious variables to be considered are size, heterogeneity, communication systems, levels and structure of economy, and nature of colonial administration. These variables can be related

[19] Ibid., pp. 115–116.
[20] See Bienen, *Tanzania*.

to propositions about party machines. For example, I have just asserted that parties rarely appeal in patronage terms to a large and heterogeneous political community. But where they are appealing to a particular ethnic group, and striving for either local power or a place in the national arena on the basis of being the spokesman for a given tribe or clan or religious group, then "ethnic" appeals are usually mixed with patronage ones. Where groups are fearful of their relative status and economic well-being, they are keen on having their own spokesman fill critical offices. Moreover, upward mobility for the group as a whole may be perceived, symbolically, in having one member rise high. Ethnically based spoils systems exist in both one-party or multiparty systems in Africa. There is nothing new about this and since spoils systems are as old as human government and since the spoils of power are used to gain support for individuals and groups of all regimes, the simple identification of a spoils system with a party machine does not tell us enough. In other words, spoils system as part of the concept of party machine is not discriminating enough and its inclusion as a basic feature of a machine-type party is another example of the broadness of the concept of machines.

But we can raise questions about the functions of a spoils system and ask questions about structure too. On the functional side, spoils are means in the aid of financing party activities. The entire spoils system works to maintain discipline within a political organization, or, as Key notes, more precisely within segments of it.[21] Banfield, Wilson, and Merton have stressed the function of the boss in the American machines to overcome a constitutional dispersion of authority typical of the separation of powers [22] and to organize, centralize, and maintain in good working condition the scattered fragments of power in American political organization.[23] The personalizing and humanizing of assistance and power has been noted.[24] Those who seek "irregular" assistance are not only the poor who do not know the rules of the legal game or don't want to play by them and those groups who come new to a given system, immigrants, migrants, upwardly mobile social groups, but also the large economic interests who want to have greater economic security and privacy.[25] The machine provides goods and services, albeit sometimes illicit ones.

In Africa machines function not to overcome a constitutional dispersion of power but to overcome a low level of political capacity at the center. Because the resources in the hands of central elites are few, elites have a

21 Key, op. cit., p. 402.
22 Edward Banfield and James Q. Wilson, *City Politics* (Chicago, 1963), p. 237.
23 Robert Merton, "The Function of the Political Machine," in Charles G. Mayo and Beryl L. Crowed, eds., *American Political Parties* (New York, 1967), pp. 425–427.
24 Ibid., p. 428.
25 Ibid., pp. 430–432; Key, op. cit., p. 404.

hard time centralizing authority over their own local party organizations.[26] Since the economic pie is small and usually not rapidly growing, it is difficult to distribute patronage as a means of centralizing authority. It is no accident that one of the most effective party machines has been the Parti Démocratique de Côte d'Ivoire operating in a country which has had one of the highest growth rates in Africa. But even where the economy is not expanding, the leverage even small amounts of patronage give may be great. In Africa, where large business interests are often foreign ones, the protection of privacy and the granting of ease of access involve foreign policy decisions. Some ethnic groups may be more concerned with defending their positions than advancing them. Martin Kilson has suggested that in African politics people are more often concerned with conserving rather than advancing interests because, given the general conditions of backwardness, people are less capable of regrouping political losses through alternate outlets.[27]

In other words, machines may be fulfilling functions comparable to those performed in America but not precisely the same ones or not performing functions in the same way. Moreover, the relative importance of the functions, as well as the dysfunctional spoils activities, would have to be spelled out.[28] A number of analysts in developing countries have pointed to the obligations of extended families and loyalty to tribe or clan as generating pressures on bureaucrats to bring them to personal considerations instead of public duties. Social and economic gaps between high and low level civil servants, as well as high and low level party officials, also may increase propensities for corruption. Civil service as well as party organizations may be geared more to integrative functions than economic performance and thus nepotism and other irregularities appear.[29] To get at the functions of a party machine involves asking questions about the entire society so that activities of the party organs become explicable. But at the same time, structural questions must be addressed, not only in terms of the specific arrangements of party, but also by relating party organizations to constituencies.

A rather old-fashioned concern for the uses (and misuses) of patronage may lead further than elaborations about "aggregating interest" activities

[26] Bienen, "What Does Political Development Mean in Africa," p. 140.
[27] Kilson, op. cit., and Bienen, op. cit.
[28] See the attempts of J. S. Nye, "Corruption and Political Development: A Cost Benefit Analysis," *American Political Science Review*, vol. LXI (June 1967), pp. 417–427; Colin Leys, "What is the Problem About Corruption," *The Journal of Modern African Studies*, vol. III, no. 2 (1965), pp. 215–230.
[29] See in particular, Bert F. Hoselitz, "Levels of Economic Performance and Bureaucratic Structures," in Joseph LaPalombara, ed., *Bureaucracy and Political Development* (Princeton, 1963), pp. 168–198, and Fred Riggs, *Administration in Developing Countries: The Theory of Prismatic Society* (Boston, 1964).

of parties, particularly where organized interest groups, apart from organs within the ruling party itself, may not be evident. For the party itself, we can ask, who become brokers rather than organizers or managers within the party. That is, who is in charge of distributing spoils; how centralized are decisions about patronage; how specialized are the party institutions for dealing with these matters? Do brokers and expediters appear from any special group in society? [30] More generally, we want to know how institutionalized are the roles for handling complaints within the party and in society, and are disputes settled largely by recourse to distribution of goods and services, coercion, or appeals on the basis of personality, and/or moral rectitude? Machines have been very much associated with the carrot and the stick rather than appeals to principles. This is only another way of saying that machines try to persuade with appeals to material rather than ideal interests; at least, this has been our definition of them in the past. Would examination of African parties lead us to revise this notion of machinelike characteristics since party organizations exist below the normative appeals that individual leaders make in Tanzania and Guinea, and in the past, in Ghana and Mali?

If a spoils system, manipulated by a party machine, exists underneath and even alongside a leadership at least rhetorically committed to social change and constantly making normative appeals to the party and society as a whole, how are we to understand it? It is possible to argue that the elite simply appropriates power and wealth to itself and sloganizes to justify its activities. Frantz Fanon has accused African elites of doing just this and Odinga has seen the Kenya African National Union's politicians clinging to position and abandoning principles because they have developed an appetite for power and property.[31] It could be said that normative injunctions are simply a style of rule. Whereas it may be acceptable to say that "someone is stealing in Beaumont, Texas today" in America, in Africa a moral reprobation attaches to regarding private interest as primary and thus "honest graft," theft, spoils, and patronage must be obscured by rhetorical appeals. No fundamental revision of an understanding of party machines is required here because the African machine would differ only in style rather than substance from the generic organization. This would not be the most fruitful approach, I think, and it can be traced to a con-

---

[30] Myron Weiner has described the Congress Party's creating a class of expediters within Congress who serve as a link between administration and citizens. Yet expediting was an old function in India and expediters *joined* Congress after it took power. Weiner points to traditional patterns of social life that may be important determinants of the kind of party organization which develops and its capacity to be effectual. See his *Party Building In A New Nation* (Chicago, 1967), pp. 459–481, and especially pp. 465–467.

[31] Frantz Fanon, *The Wretched of the Earth* (New York, 1963); Oginga Odinga, *Not Yet Uhuru* (New York, 1967).

ception of machines which is too narrow rather than too broad. Whereas a characterization of machines as parties concerned with material rewards rather than principles applies to most parties at least some of the time, an emphasis on spoils may obscure some important relationships between ruler and ruled even when the "latent functions" of machine operations are taken into account.

Oginga Odinga has said that "Political intrigue, caucus decisions and ambitions for office cannot thrive side by side with a vigorous popularly based party machine, or democratic decision-making of any kind." [32] Pluralist theorists of democracy would disagree. It is interesting, however, that Odinga associates the term party machine with "popularly based" in opposition to political intrigue and caucus decisions. The political machine is not undemocratic per se for Odinga, because he envisions an inner core of the party which animates the party as a whole and is connected to the people, leading them as it at the same time identifies with them. His understanding of the party machine is of an organizing, vanguard machine. In pre-Soviet Russia, Lenin's treatment of the vanguard was of a revolutionary inner core. After the seizure of power, his emphasis was on an organizing, controlling inner core.[33] The function of the party changed obviously although the leading role of the party did not. The tasks of the party were to undergo further changes as Stalin stressed the extractive roles and managerial roles of the CPSU. In the Leninist tradition "party machine" refers not to spoils but to organizing capabilities. In Africa a number of ruling single parties have adopted Leninist organizational forms, often a Leninist rhetoric which stipulates leading roles, discipline, and militancy, although they have usually dispensed with the class struggle in favor of a more populistic mode. At the same time, African ruling single parties share many characteristics of decentralized political machines in that the organization is held together in good part by the perquisites of and desire for office, and internal cleavages within the parties are often not over policy issues.

My characterization of African parties as machines in the American sense which refers to spoils, bossism, and local autonomy would be readily accepted by most observers insofar as it was applied to the Parti Progressiste du Tchad or the Uganda People's Congress, at least prior to 1965, and to the host of parties that have been dubbed patron parties or parties of notables. And use of "party machine" in the Leninist sense would be accepted for the so-called mass mobilization parties, the PDG in Guinea,

---

[32] Ibid., p. 286.

[33] Compare Lenin's *What Is To Be Done?* (1902) and his *"Left Wing" Communism: An Infantile Disorder* (1920). Both documents are "Leninist" in that they stress discipline and vanguard relation of party to mass. It was the tasks of the party that had changed between 1902 and 1920.

the Union Soudanaise in Mali, TANU in Tanzania, and the Convention People's Party at an earlier time in Ghana. Yet the mass parties are machines in the American sense also and in the Leninist sense rather by aspiration of some of their leaders than reality of organizational strength. Moreover, some leaders who use the language of social revolution in a spurious and cynical way and who have no desire to encompass the entire population within their party or to be mass leaders may nonetheless want a tight and tough political machine around them, even if they rule by tolerating pluralism in the country as a whole—and making alliances with traditional groups.

At this point, I want to address myself to those situations where elites would like to construct parties that reach out for all members of the body politic and bring them under party control. Some party elites have aspired to forge an organizational weapon and to change the normative and social structure of their societies. Yet they have operated in an environment where it has not been possible to forge such an instrument and thus to accomplish these changes through central political direction. This same environment, and here I refer to that complex of features—low levels of economic development, poor communication systems, lack of urbanization, etc.—that we call underdevelopment, has thrown parties back on playing integrative and distributive roles and periodically coercive ones rather than extractive and systematically organized ones. In other words, the parties have tended to do what they could do. However, the process of economic development has required the ruling single parties to transform themselves into organizations different from what they were in the national movement phase and the early independence period. But the circle has tended to be a vicious one for them; they could not expropriate the human and material resources necessary to rapidly build an organization that could extract economic resources and implement economic decisions. Thus the Leninist rhetoric and organizational forms have appeared ironic given the actuality of machine performance of distributive and integrative roles. Elites have appeared to the Fanons as parasites living off the people: a new bourgeoisie. Visions of the end to group struggles and group interests are seen as being self-serving. Appeals to nonpolitical motivations made at the top are posed against the activities of party leaders in the villages, districts, and regions not to say those operating at the centers. At issue is not necessarily the matter of corruption versus honesty but politics versus antipolitical ethics. Leaders who do not like the politics of politics appear as either knaves or fools in the light of both their own actions and those in their organizations who behave as politicians.[34] Their

---

[34] For a discussion of the antipolitical ethos of leaders of new states and a defense of politics, see Bernard Crick, *In Defense of Politics* (London, 1963), and James

desire for rapid economic development leads them to organizational models and "administrative concepts" instead of "political concepts" based on a vision of interests in conflict, and awareness of the problem of reconciling diverse interests, as James Heaphy puts it.[35] But the conditions they operate within make them dependent on political machines, not organizational weapons.

Thus within the remaining "mass" ruling parties of tropical Africa two conceptions of political participation coexist with each other and in uneasy relationship with yet another type of political participation which has not been surrounded by any public conception at all but which exists in the world. The Leninist political machine mode calls for a widening of political participation, because, from an administrative point of view and from the viewpoint of increasing the scope of control, the more people that are brought into political action through participation the better. But this is an envisioned participation in which all move toward the same goals in the same way. The American political machine mode, which is a reality in Africa but which has no rhetoric attached to it,[36] comprehends a different notion of political participation in which interests of various forms and types associate, conflict, and change alliances.[37] But there is, of course, yet another public conception of political participation in Africa in which decision making is meant to be direct, centered in "the people."

Neither Leninist nor plebiscitary conceptions of political participation have been institutionalized in operating political structures. But because the aspirations of elites in African parties have been more than mere wishes, that is, elites have had political influence within their parties, African ruling single parties have been mixtures of different types of political participation, different styles or political modes, and different kinds of political functioning. At the center, decisions may well be made in accordance with democratic centralism, that is, in a highly centralized way. But decisions are rarely implemented throughout the country by commands flowing smoothly down through the hierarchy and radiating out to all branches without deflection and distortion. Moreover, while total political capacity may be very low at the center so that government and party seem ineffective when we raise questions about central control and efficiency in the economic and administrative realms, in certain political spheres the center may be effective. For example, top party elites may be able to veto party

---

Heaphey, "The Organization of Egypt: Inadequacies of a Nonpolitical Model for Nation-Building," *World Politics*, vol. XVIII (Jan. 1966), pp. 177–193.

[35] Heaphy, op. cit., p. 177.

[36] This is not to say that politicians in Africa have no conception of the kind of politics they are in fact engaged in. Private expressions are not the same thing, however, as publicly articulated conceptions.

[37] I have taken some of Heaphey's ideas on political participation and used them here for purposes different from his own.

candidates down the line and appoint men they want. Furthermore, party leaders so far have monopolized ideology formulation. While we cannot conclude that the party elites are all-powerful, these constitute important powers which affect decision making in national plan formulation, foreign policy, and recruitment of party and governmental personnel.

Still, the discrepancies are real between the aspirations of elites in African one-party states and the possibilities for centralizing and extending political power. I have argued elsewhere with specific reference to Tanzania that the structure of the economy (agricultural/industrial balance, subsistence/monetary sector proportions), the level of resources (physical output in gross domestic product and per capita income), and productivity (of labor, capital/output ratios) have worked against the formation of a disciplined and centralized party, and have precluded the possibility of a totalitarian or "revolutionary-centralizing" system.[38]

If mobilizing mass parties are not extant in tropical Africa and are not going to come about in the foreseeable future, there are numerous other alternatives possible: military takeover, the persistence of ruling single parties that do not mobilize resources, machine politics American-style, competitive party situations, rule by administrative elites, breakdown of central rule, and various combinations of all these alternatives, some more likely than others. Here I do not want to discuss what may be the best institutional source for political development nor try to come to grips with the meaning of political development in Africa.[39] I take it for granted that whether or not the only organization in Africa that can become a source of authority and can be effectively institutionalized is the political party,[40] political parties are not exempt from tendencies toward obsolescence and that they may lose the loyalty of important constituents. Moreover, as Carey McWilliams has pointed out, an institutional system presumes that certain patterns of organization and behavior become so deeply identified with goals and values as to acquire a moral value themselves and that institutionalized ends require a history of successful action before identification is achieved.[41] Precisely how success may be defined and by whom are important questions.

[38] Bienen, *Tanzania*, op. cit., p. 261.
[39] I have tried to do this in "What Does Political Development Mean in Africa," op. cit.
[40] For arguments about the efficacy of political parties as the best possible source for political development in new states, see Samuel P. Huntington, "Political Development and Political Decay," *World Politics*, vol. XVII (April, 1965), pp. 386–430, and Manfred Halpern, *The Politics of Social Change in the Middle East and North Africa* (Princeton, 1963), pp. 281–317.
[41] Carey McWilliams, "Political Development and Foreign Policy," forthcoming as a University of Kentucky Press collection of papers on Foreign Policy and National Development, a seminar held in August 1967 at the Patterson School of Diplomacy, Lexington, Kentucky.

The discrepancy between postulated styles of rule, organizational forms, ideological symbols, modes of political participation all on the one hand, and the operation of political machines working as patronage and spoils systems in decentralized fashion on the other, may be suggestive for looking into a number of problems. Specifically, internal party tensions between various levels of elites and political competition between party elites and other elites—civil service, military—ought to be related to this situation. Similarly, elite/nonelite relationships and rural and urban protest ought to be viewed with these discrepancies in mind.

It may be no accident that Robert Michels, in analyzing the deradicalization of European Marxist parties in the late nineteenth and twentieth centuries, treated the patronage and spoils process in these parties, in the German Social Democratic Party (SPD) in particular. Michels, as is well known, also examined the process of rule by oligarchies in parties. More recently, Robert C. Tucker, treating both the SPD and the Communist Party of the Soviet Union, has written: "Not the end of ideology but rather the growth of a stable discrepancy between ideological symbols and political deeds is the true mark of deradicalizing change in once-radical movements." [42] For Tucker, it appears to be the fate of radical movements that survive and flourish for long *without* remaking the world that they undergo eventually a process of deradicalization. This process Tucker describes as having to do with the action pattern of the movement, its relation to its ideological goals, the development of its strategy and tactics, and, finally, its inner conflicts. The movement settles down and becomes reformist, although not necessarily conservative, that is, opposed to social change; rather it accepts the system it officially desires to overthrow and transform and becomes absorbed in everyday party work.[43] The SPD that Tucker deals with remained an out-of-power party undergoing deradicalization. But the Communist Party of the Soviet Union had a worldly success by taking power and Tucker is able to point to changes in party composition and adjustment to new realities at home and abroad in arguing his thesis. Although Tucker examined movements that existed over at least four decades, I find his analysis suggestive for studying African ruling parties once it is attached to a concern with explaining political machines.

We have been aware that elites who promised much before independence and when they took power have been vulnerable to attacks from counterelites as well as from mass protest once they confronted the stark realities of their environments. Arguments to the effect that Africa faces

[42] Robert C. Tucker, "The Deradicalization of Marxist Movements," *The American Political Science Review*, vol. LXI, no. 2 (June 1967), p. 358.
[43] Ibid., pp. 348–349.

endemic instability are based on a postulation of intractable problems and rising expectation, a combination which presumably leads to frustration.[44] I am suggesting a narrower focus on the disparity between conceptions and realities of political participation and kinds of party organization. What we may be witnessing in Africa is a speeded up, highly telescoped process of deradicalization. The process is accelerated in Africa because of the perception on the part of elites at all levels in society of the difficulties involved in bringing about social transformation and economic growth. One possible reaction to these difficulties is to give up on trying to get economic growth and to try for national integration and a place in the sun for one's country by reiterating ideological commitments and stressing racial or ethnic solidarity where possible (that is, where a dominant ethnic core may exist as in Mali). But this reaction, be it conscious or unconscious, is fraught with danger for rulers. Party leaders become highly vulnerable to ostensibly efficiency-oriented elites—the military, police, and civil service. Thus the very perception of difficulties has required from ruling parties a new emphasis on governmental efficiency, on everyday work in economic affairs. While the connection can be made between the need to strengthen the party's organization and achieving economic development by arguing that the party will bring about development through its activities, party work more and more comes to mean collecting economic statistics, planning and supervising local agricultural projects hand-in-hand with technical specialists (where they are available), and having party members and officials themselves act as "economic" men.[45]

In his examination of communist and social democratic movements and parties, Tucker saw an inverse relation between a radical movement's organizational strength and the preservation of its radicalism.[46] This proposition seems well substantiated also in the histories of millennial movements. In Africa, while worldly success has come to nationalist movements, and they have acquired a bigger organizational structure along with a ruling place in society, these nationalist movements become ruling parties are still organizationally weak in terms of the tasks of rule and development. But organizational weakness does not seem to have fed the fires of radicalism in the sense of refusing to accept the established system and its institutionalized procedures as the framework for further efforts in the direction of social change. Rather, the rulers' perception of their organizational weakness seems to have accentuated movement toward accommodation with a number of former targets: colonial powers, traditional groups,

[44] For only one example among very many, see James O'Connell, "The Inevitability of Instability," *Journal of Modern African Studies*, vol. 5, no. 2 (1967), pp. 181–192.

[45] See Bienen, *Tanzania*, pp. 307–360.

[46] Tucker, op. cit., p. 348.

civil service personnel, private economic interest groups. Tanzania is an important exception. The Arusha Declaration and subsequent formulations and policies in the course of 1967 to 1969 do reassert Tanzania's independence and insist on government's hostility to the development of private economic interest groups. The Arusha formulations, however, return in many of their specifics to policies of the colonial period, albeit in a vastly different political and social context. The Arusha Declaration is both a reaction to and a recognition of the TANU government's inability to control change in Tanzania through central direction.[47]

Perhaps the explanation of the tendency toward accommodation and deradicalization lies in the fact that staying in power is of overriding importance and while African ruling parties are not becoming stronger in the sense of becoming organizational juggernauts, they nonetheless are ruling groups and thus have a stake in the maintenance of stability.[48] It matters whether a party is a weak organization out of power or a weak organization in power: deradicalization is probable in the latter case.

As for stability of the political system, the process of deradicalization does not guarantee it. Africa has already shown us cases of limited instability, as well as major instability associated with violence, for example, Nigeria and the Congo. There has been the military coup sequence which has changed the form of government but does not seem to have worked profound changes between rulers and ruled. This has occurred in a country ruled by a party which was Leninist in aspiration although it had American machine characteristics—Ghana and the CPP. It has occurred also, of course, in other one-party states.

It is not clear at this point whether or not stability can be maintained either by deradicalized party machines or by the military. The outcome will be influenced by factors involved in rural and urban protest that I have not dealt with here. There are factors internal to the parties which will be of importance too. For example, the place of the electoral process in both one-party states and multiparty systems remains in doubt. Yet the presence or absence of elections alters the nature of alliances and bargaining in machine politics. If political machines must settle disputes without recourse to an open electoral process, they may have to develop their own mechanisms of coercion and control or manipulate state agencies that are specialists in coercion and control. This has been true of the American political machine as well as ones in a Leninist mold. In Africa, where it is not possible to exert systematic coercion throughout entire societies, free

---

[47] For a discussion of the Arusha Declaration, see Henry Bienen, "An Ideology for Africa," *Foreign Affairs* (April 1969), pp. 545–559. Also see Henry Bienen, *Tanzania* (expanded edition), chapter on "The Arusha Formulations."

[48] I am not saying that stability is per se a valued thing.

elections may be a necessity for maintaining machine rule. Tanzania suggests that competition within a ruling single party for party and parliamentary offices does work to lessen dependence on coercion in a one-party state. And Tanzania is a case where the present leadership self-consciously seeks to strike ground between oligarchic authoritarianism and a fragmenting of the party which it is feared would multiply competing political organizations.

The development of oligarchic authoritarianism at the top of political parties while centrifugal forces are growing at other levels of the party and in society is a possible outcome in Africa. Ghana already gives us such a case. We should examine non-African party systems to come to grips with prospective outcomes. Thinking about political machines, be they the Congress Party in India, the SPD in pre-World War I Germany, the Communist Party of the Soviet Union, or state parties in America, will help us to clarify the problems of party development in Africa.[49]

[49] This paper was written under the auspices of the Center of International Studies, Princeton University.

Chapter 10 Cincinnatus in Africa: The Possibility of Military Withdrawal from Politics

Claude E. Welch, Jr.

Generations of classics teachers have enlightened their pupils with the semimythical story of Cincinnatus. Cincinnatus entered the annals of history nearly 2,500 years ago, when conflicts between patricians and plebeians had weakened Rome, and the invading Aequian army was nearing victory. Only a man of unquestionable virtue, military know-how, and political acumen could save the city. A delegation was dispatched to implore Cincinnatus to accept complete control. They found him at his plow, persuaded him successfully, and watched Cincinnatus achieve victory. Rather than stay in control, however, he returned to his farm, not demanding further recognition. Thus runs the legend. Cincinnatus was a model of willingness to perform civic duty and defend the home country. He carried out his tasks, quickly and effectively. He scorned the palms of office, having fulfilled his civic obligation.

What is the likelihood that the new military rulers of tropical Africa will return to their barracks after a brief period of control? The thesis of this chapter is relatively simple. Officers are acquiring pivotal positions in African political life, from which they are unlikely to be displaced—either voluntarily or involuntarily—except under special conditions. I base this prognostication upon two propositions:

1. The desire for speedy withdrawal expressed by the military will be undercut both by the inevitable complexities of righting the real or alleged shortcomings that led to military intervention, and by the difficulty of reestablishing effective civilian control following a coup d'etat.

2. The source of legitimate authority in African states remains open to question. This uncertainty opens the way for further military intervention in politics. The coup d'etat may serve in effect as a political institution, as a major mechanism for change.[1]

On the other hand, specific examination of Dahomey, Ghana, and Sierra Leone indicates that strong pressures may operate upon ruling juntas to bring about a return to the barracks.

1. The exercise of political power may so weaken and divide ruling officers that, for the good of the armed forces, they prefer to divest themselves rapidly of their political responsibilities.

2. Mounting pressure from civilians may hasten withdrawal. Such pressure is likely to result both from insistence that the military make good its promises for "temporary" rule and from the inability of controlling juntas to resolve certain basic conflicts.

To carry out this assessment, I shall analyze the context within which military intervention occurred, the various ways in which withdrawal might occur, and the series of difficulties the military confront.

No one can doubt that army officers now control many African states. Discovering *why* the military increasingly has intervened in political life has become the scholarly fashion of the moment, just as charismatic leadership and single-party mobilization systems dominated analysis of African politics a few years back. In focusing upon the causes of intervention, however, we risk ignoring far more subtle factors that may ease the return to civilian rule. This return may occur without the immediate drama of a coup d'etat. One military-dominated African government, that of the Sudan, was toppled and replaced by civilians, then replaced once again by an army-based regime. Three other states—Dahomey, Ghana, and Sierra Leone—witnessed the voluntary withdrawal of ruling juntas by the end of 1969. In Congo-Kinshasa, Central African Republic, and Nigeria, continued domestic instability paradoxically may have further entrenched military control, since a group that intervened purportedly to correct internal difficulties will not willingly withdraw if these problems remain unresolved. In Burundi, Congo-Brazzaville, Mali, Togo, and Upper Volta, spasmodic discussions of a return to the barracks remain without impact. The political intentions of the military governments of Libya and Somalia cannot be clearly discerned at this point.

Military withdrawal from intervention in politics may occur as the result of four factors:

[1] Aristide R. Zolberg, "The Structure of Political Conflict in the New States of Tropical Africa," *American Political Science Review*, LXII, 1 (March 1968), 77–81. Zolberg also argues that political revolutions in Africa are unlikely to succeed through force.

1. voluntary withdrawal, due to division within the military and/or pressure from civilians;

2. disappearance or diminution of the conditions that initially brought about intervention;

3. conscious civilianization of the military government, making it indistinguishable, in the long run, from a government with more "ordinary" origins.

4. overthrow of the military-dominated regime, leading directly to a civilian-controlled government.

VOLUNTARY WITHDRAWAL

Three West African states—Dahomey, Ghana, and Sierra Leone—have restored civilian rule after an interlude of military rule. Apart from their geographic propinquity, the three countries share few common characteristics. French-speaking Dahomey was—and is still—afflicted with chronic regionalism, manifested (prior to intervention by Colonel Christophe Soglo) in a tripartite division of political power among north (Maga), center (Ahomadegbe), and south (Apithy). English-speaking Sierra Leone suffered from complex divisions between the Mende (best represented in the Sierra Leone People's Party of Milton and Albert Margai) and other ethnic groups, notably the Temne. A flourishing two-party system in Sierra Leone contrasted with the three-party division of Dahomey and the enforced single-party system of Nkrumah's Ghana. While Ghana achieved one of the highest standards of living in tropical Africa, largely through cocoa, Sierra Leone experienced far more modest development through its exports of diamonds and iron ore and Dahomey suffered chronic economic stagnation. Although all three states suffered major international trade and payments deficits, such deficits were the rule rather than the exception in postindependence tropical Africa.

The manner in which military intervention occurred showed marked variations. In Dahomey economic vicissitudes, trade union unrest, and inability of the three major politicians to work together effectively led to a brief intervention late in 1963; Colonel Soglo handed over control after general elections in January 1964. In late 1965 two further interventions occurred, the first transferring power from Ahomadegbe to the speaker of the National Assembly, the second resulting in full military control under Soglo. The economic crisis continued unresolved, and on 16 December 1967 Soglo was himself ousted, the new group of young officers promising to hold general elections within six months. Unmitigated regionalism, political rivalries, and a seemingly insoluble economic crisis thus brought military rule.

Ghana under President Nkrumah obviously suffered grave economic difficulties, but these resulted more from the absence of any policies of fiscal restraint than from inherent economic liabilities and limitations. Inflation, blatant corruption, and shortages of both domestic and imported goods undermined popular support for the Nkrumah regime. Political rights were denied leading opponents, many of whom were incarcerated under the Preventive Detention Act. Elections were rigged, or ignored; a 1964 constitutional amendment established the Convention Peoples Party as the sole political party. No outlet or safety valve existed, in the form of opposition parties, that could assuage the frustrations arising from the power situation and the discrepancy between actual and expected returns without fundamentally challenging the one-party system.[2] In addition to these economic and political grievances, Nkrumah incurred the enmity of army and police officers by a series of heavy-handed efforts at control—a fact that probably was most significant in bringing about the coup d'etat of 24 February 1966. The President's Own Guard Regiment (POGR), whose head reported directly to the president rather than the general officer commanding, was established and in the view of army officers lavishly equipped, seemingly at the expense of "regular" forces. Officers whose advice ran contrary to Nkrumah's desires were sacked, including expatriate General H. T. Alexander in September 1961, ex-Ghanaian Chief of Defence Staff S. I. A. Otu and Army Chief J. A. Ankrah in August 1965. Institutional grievances were thus coupled in the Ghanaian coup with the government's arbitrary rule, repression, corruption, and economic ineptitude.[3]

The first coup in Sierra Leone resulted from the inability to transfer control peacefully. In a bitterly contested election in March 1967, the opposition African People's Congress apparently ousted the ruling Sierra Leone People's Party. Shortly after the leader of the APC had been sworn in as prime minister, however, Brigadier David Lansana intervened and suspended the new government; in turn, he was supplanted within two days by a National Reformation Council (NRC), composed of young officers drawn from all ethnic groups. Andrew Juxon-Smith was named head of the NRC, which immediately launched austerity programs to correct Sierra Leone's parlous economic conditions.

Intervention in these three countries, as in many other African states, was prompted by a variety of factors. In related publications I have suggested the following eight factors:[4]

[2] Jack Goody, "Consensus and Dissensus in Ghana," *Political Science Quarterly*, LXXXIII, 3 (Sept. 1968), 341.

[3] Jon Kraus, "Arms and Politics in Ghana," in Claude E. Welch Jr., ed., *Soldier and State in Africa: A Comparative Analysis of Military Intervention and Political Change* (Evanston, 1970), pp. 154–221.

[4] Claude E. Welch, Jr., "Soldier and State in Africa," *Journal of Modern African Studies*, V, 3 (1967), 313.

1. Declining prestige of the major political party exemplified by (a) an increased reliance upon force to achieve compliance, (b) a stress upon unanimity in the face of centrifugal forces, and (c) a consequent denial of effective political choice.

2. Schism among prominent politicians, weakening the broadly based nationalist movement that had hastened the departure of the former colonial power.

3. The lessened likelihood of external intervention in the event of military uprising.

4. "Contagion" from seizures of control by the military in other African countries.

5. Domestic social antagonisms, most obviously manifested in countries where a minority group exercised control (e.g., the Arabs in Zanzibar, the Watusi in Burundi).

6. Economic malaise, leading to "austerity" policies, which most affected articulate, urbanized sectors of the population (members of trade unions, civil servants).

7. Corruption and inefficiency among governmental and party officials, a corruption especially noticeable under conditions of economic decline.

8. A heightened awareness within the army of its power to influence or displace political leaders.

Obviously, the combination of factors was unique in each state afflicted by military takeover. However, a general impression of institutional weakness emerges—a basic debilitation of the political system that helped prompt intervention.

If military regimes set themselves up as doctors of the body politic, they risk being infected by the ills from which the previous civilian governments suffered—or, should the patient fail to improve, the physician may be discharged. There is thus a dual danger. On the one hand, military regimes may fall prey to corruption, unwarranted use of force, electoral or ethnic manipulation, or the denial of political rights—all weaknesses that helped justify (or, at least, rationalize) the toppling of the civilian government. To avoid such "infection," the army may prefer withdrawal. On the other hand, the popular welcome that accompanied the military takeover may soon be exhausted. The medicine prescribed for the cure may well prove unpalatable. Accordingly, to avoid forcible eviction and to retain some public support, the armed forces may wish to stage a graceful retreat.

The restoration of civilian rule in Dahomey exemplifies these two tendencies. The young officers who intervened in 1967 complained that Soglo had failed to achieve his basic objectives: "to put a stop to absurd quarrels between rivals by appeasing the people and restoring respect for the sense of duty which many Dahomean citizens were beginning to ignore, to

remedy the economic and financial ills from which the country was suffering, and to reconcile the children of Dahomey and enable them to
reassume control of the management of their country's affairs in order,
harmony and newly restored fraternity." [5] These hopes had not been fulfilled. "The very people who we had promised to defend and protect now
hate and despise us." As Radio Cotonou broadcast,

This is why we, the young cadres of the army, aware that the role of the whole
army was in question; considering that our seniors in the army had disappointed
the people and betrayed the national army; aware that it is the duty of us, the
young army cadres, to restore the situation as well as the authority and dignity
of the nation; decided in the higher interests of the nation to dissolve the government of General Soglo and the military committees of vigilance, to create
a revolutionary military committee, to form within 24 hours a provisional government responsible for day-to-day state affairs, and to create a constitutional
committee.[6]

Colonel Alley, the senior officer of the new regime, declared that elections would be held within six months, "no matter what the consequences."
It seemed as though the consequences of elections would be favorable.
Skurnik has noted that restoration of civilian rule provided the military
regime "with the only solid and widespread popular approval which it
enjoyed." [7] Given the six-month deadline set by Alley, speed was essential.
The president of the Supreme Court was named to head a civilian constitutional committee, whose proposals included a centralized presidential
system, an amalgamated "Parti Dahoméen Unifié" to diminish the regional
and personal strife of the past, a legislative assembly whose members
would receive only modest recompense, a politically independent supreme
court, and opportunities for citizens to appeal directly to the supreme court
for rulings on legislative or executive decisions. On 31 March 1968 an
astonishing 82 percent of registered voters trooped to the polls, approving
the draft by better than an 11:1 margin. Buoyed by this victory, members
of the Military Revolutionary Committee faced the difficult decision about
candidates for the presidency. The "Big Three"—Justin Ahomadegbe,
Sourou Migan Apithy, and Hubert Maga, who had dominated post-World
War II Dahomean politics—were barred from running, a contrary ruling
of the supreme court notwithstanding, on the ground their candidacy
"would consecrate the atmosphere of hatred, of division, of distrust which
surrounds us. . . ." [8] Apithy and Maga called for a boycott of the presi-

[5] *Africa Research Bulletin*, IV, 12 (Jan. 1968), 927E.
[6] *Africa Research Bulletin*, IV, 12 (Jan. 1968), 927E.
[7] W. A. E. Skurnik, "The Military and Politics: Dahomey and Upper Volta," in
Welch, *Soldier and State in Africa*, p. 110.
[8] *Le Moniteur Africain du Commerce et de l'Industrie*, no. 341 (11 April 1968),
quoted in Skurnik, p. 111.

dential elections, in which five relatively obscure candidates stood. Just over a quarter of the registered electorate balloted, largely in districts supporting Ahomadegbe. Stung by this rebuke, and deeply divided about the appropriate means of withdrawing, the young protagonists of the December 1967 coup replaced half the cabinet with paratroop officers, then ousted Alley after he unsuccessfully attempted to patch up a Big Three coalition and to stage a putsch on his own. Military unity evaporated further every day; trade union restiveness increased markedly. With the Big Three unable to reconcile their differences, the only suitable course appeared to be formation of a civilian government, sanitized of party divisions, and headed by a civilian of impeccable credentials. In selecting Emile Derlin Zinsou, the officers chose well.[9]

He was appointed president for a five-year term, taking office 17 July 1968, and received a plebiscitary majority in a referendum 28 July.[10] "We can now go back to our barracks, convinced that we have precisely laid down the framework in which the new President and Premier will develop following the objectives which we fixed on December 17, 1967," Captain Mathieu Kerekou, head of the Military Revolutionary Committee, announced.[11]

These intensions lasted barely eighteen months. Zinsou was summarily dismissed and briefly imprisoned 10 December 1969 by the Chief of Staff, Lt.-Col. Maurice Kouandete. A three-member military directorate took over all ministerial portfolios. Once again, how might civilian rule be restored? The directorate announced that politicians should set aside their differences and nominate a single candidate for president—a nomination it proved impossible to obtain.

As previously noted, intense regionalism makes political agreement in Dahomey difficult to obtain. All the "big three" (Ahomadegbe, Apithy, and Maga announced their candidacies for the presidency; the directorate bowed to the inevitable, and permitted all to run. Presidential and parliamentary elections were to be carried on between 9 and 31 March 1970. Three days before its formal conclusion, balloting was abruptly suspended, following widespread violence in the north. (Despite Apithy's substantial lead in the south, it appeared that the solid support for Maga in the north

[9] Zinsou, a graduate of the prestigious Ponty school, served in the Assembly of the French Union 1948–1953, and the Senate of the Fourth Republic 1955–1959. His concern for federal unity helped make him political vice-president of the executive bureau of the Parti de la Fédération Africaine. Following independence, he served as foreign minister and ambassador to France under the Maga government, then again as foreign minister under Soglo in 1966. His 1967 refusal to serve under the Military Revolutionary Committee helps explain why he did not run in the abortive 3 May 1968 presidential election.

[10] 72.61% of the voters participated with a 73.6% yes vote. *Africa Research Bulletin*, V, 8, col. 1149A.

[11] *Africa Research Bulletin*, V, 7, col. 1119A.

would bring him victory.) Lt.-Col. Emile de Souza terminated the election for fear of "the imminence of civil war owing to the aggravation of the irregularities and violence." Obviously, only a truce among the leading politicians could allay the growing tensions. On 1 May 1970, the directorate (which, according to de Souza, had "never stopped expressing our determination to lead the country to a constitutional regime") handed over control to a three-member Presidential Commission, composed of Ahomadegbe, Apithy, and Maga. (Zinsou declined an invitation to serve.) Maga was selected to fill the presidency until 1972, when the position would pass to Ahomadegbe. Thus, Dahomey lurched through yet another crisis in civil-military relations, with a denouement that underscored, yet again, the continued impact of regionalism and the weakness of the country's political institutions.

To "restore the country to an even keel politically, socially, and economically," the Ghanaian National Liberation Council administered a stiff dose of financial austerity, political retrenchment, and civic reeducation. The installation—or, rather, the reinstatement—of civilian government occurred 1 October 1969. Progress toward this goal was hardly smooth or continuous. Conflicts internal to the NLC and between the NLC and various influential groups brought, as in Dahomey, spasmodic steps in preparing a new constitution and holding elections.

Within the NLC, the strongest calls for a return to the barracks came from Major A. A. Afrifa, Sandhurst-trained follower of Colonel E. K. Kotoka, prime mover of the 24 February 1966 coup. Like other members of the NLC, Afrifa felt that the pace of military withdrawal should depend upon purging elements that remained of the CPP and reeducating the Ghanaian population to their civic duties.[12] The NLC initially basked in popular acclaim following the overthrow of Nkrumah and revelations about his followers' excesses. However, popular support started to shrink, as economic austerity measures were implemented and as a variety of groups whose claims had been stilled by the Nkrumah regime raised their demands, at first timidly, then with greater confidence. The return of prominent ex-politicians from voluntary evile (K. A. Busia, K. A. Gbedemah) or from imprisonment (Joe Appiah, M. K. Apaloo) further stirred the political cauldron. As Goody pointed out, relaxing the general pressure toward "enforced consensus" brought not only ideological uncertainty and restlessness about discipline, but also an atmosphere more tolerant of protest and dissent.[13] Traditional rulers, students, trade unionists, market mam-

---

[12] For example, Afrifa commented in March 1967: "It may be necessary to let the people get used to their newly won freedom and to familiarize themselves with the qualities that they require from potential leaders before they are called upon to go to the polls." Quoted in *West Africa* (1 April 1967), p. 446.
[13] Goody, "Consensus and Dissensus," p. 345.

mies, and other groups joined the intelligentsia in demanding a reordering of the political system. The shifting pressures of these groups, coupled with the NLC's own uncertainties about the most appropriate method and speed of restoring civilian rule, accounted for the intermittent steps.

Four months after the ouster of Nkrumah, a 23-member "Political Committee" with limited advisory powers was established. A Constitutional Committee was formed in November 1966. There appeared to be little sense of urgency about increasing civilian participation, given the magnitude of the task of revamping the Ghanaian political system. However, the Ghanaian army showed it was not immune to plots within its own ranks. Alleging that promotions for junior officers were not being granted rapidly enough, 25-year-old Lieutenant Samuel Arthur and his reconnaissance squadron nearly toppled the NLC 17 April 1967. Colonel Kotoka was slain and General Ankrah, who had been brought from retirement to head the NLC, barely escaped. The lessons were clear: countercoups would threaten the NLC unless it maintained a high degree of cohesion and morale; the meteoric rise of some officers aroused jealousies that undercut professional unity; professional ends might best be served by avoiding an undue prolongation of NLC rule. Accordingly, the NLC induced 14 prominent civilians, all but one of whom were former politicians, to accept ministerial portfolios and join the Executive Council in July 1967. Busia was asked to head a nonpartisan, government-supported Center for Civil Education—likely a factor in his 1969 electoral victory.

Contrasted with the frenetic pace and concealed nature of constitution drafting in Dahomey, the preparation and ratification of the constitution for the Second Republic of Ghana was spread over nearly three years. The Constitutional Committee (chaired, as in Dahomey, by the head of the supreme court) started its work in November 1966; its 18 members (11 of whom formerly belonged to parties that opposed the CPP) visited all regions, received 721 memoranda, and heard evidence from 567 individuals or organizational representatives.[14] The extensive proposals provided, *inter alia*, for a 140-member legislature whose members would receive only modest allowances, a prime minister, a president without executive powers, an independent judiciary, and a Council of State whose behind-the-scenes counseling, warning, encouraging, and arbitrating "do so much to smooth the rough edges of political conflicts and encourage compromise and moderation."[15]

Rather than submit this complex draft to an immediate referendum, the NLC continued to stall for time, the result of its own vacillation about the pace of civilianization. In May 1968, nearly five months after the submis-

[14] Kraus, "Arms and Politics in Ghana," p. 205.
[15] *Africa Research Bulletin*, V, 1, col. 953B.

sion of the constitutional proposals, the NLC announced that an elected—and nonparty—Constituent Assembly would meet one year later, deliberate for three months, then disband after ratification so that partisan elections could be held and a civilian government installed no later than 30 September 1969. In other words, parties would be permitted only a few weeks to organize, devise platforms, nominate candidates, and participate in the electoral campaign. This unrealistic timetable, which betrayed the NLC's lingering suspicion of political parties, was sharply criticized. Recognizing the strength of these concerns, the NLC revised its schedule. An indirectly selected Constituent Assembly started its deliberations in January 1969, while registration of voters and demarcation of constituencies were still in progress. The ban on parties was finally lifted 28 April 1969, after Afrifa had replaced Ankrah as NLC chairman.[16] With the Constituent Assembly in full swing and parties coalescing, the return to civilian rule could not readily be halted.

Five parties contested the 29 August 1969 election: the Progress Party of Kofi Busia; the National Alliance of Liberals of Gbedemah; the United Nationalist Party of Appiah; the All Peoples Republican Party of P. K. K. Quaidoo; and the Peoples Action Party of Ayarna Imoru. The PP's organization and strong support, especially in the center and south, was reflected in 59 percent of the votes and 105 of the 140 Assembly seats; the National Alliance of Liberals gained 14 of its 29 seats in the Volta region; and the other parties and independents shared the remaining six seats. The PP victory, Jon Kraus notes, may be attributed to three factors: the high visibility of the party, which was viewed as the NLC's successor and hence gained from a bandwagon effect; continued distaste for the CPP, with which NAL leader Gbedemah was identified; and distrust of possible Ewe dominance, which reinforced solidarity among Akan-speaking peoples against the NAL.[17] Thus, after an absence of three years, seven months, and seven days, civilian rule returned to Ghana.

One footnote must be added. The Busia-PP government assumed office without the presidency filled. Apparently uncertain of the most suitable candidate for the position after the resignation of Ankrah, the NLC asked the Constituent Assembly shortly before it disbanded to substitute a three-member Presidential Commission for an interim period. The Constituent Assembly agreed, with reluctance. The members of the Presidential Commission: NLC Chairman Afrifa, Vice-chairman J. W. K. Harlley, and

---

[16] Ankrah was removed by the NLC 2 April 1969, after disclosure that he had accepted a bribe from a polling firm. Determined to avoid any hint of corruption, the NLC apparently had no alternative but to replace its chairman who had, up to that point, seemed likely to run for the presidency.

[17] Kraus, "Arms and Politics in Ghana," pp. 218–220.

Chief of Defence Staff A. K. Ocran. Some—but not all—of the Ghanaian army returned to the barracks.

Publication of the Dove-Edwin report in December 1967 provided strong incentive for the Sierra Leone military to withdraw. This Commission of Inquiry criticized the many ways in which the SLPP had attempted to ensure a majority, such as having returning officers declare APC nomination papers invalid, and raising the required deposit by 150 percent. It declared that the APC won the election "on their own merit." [18] In its commentary on the report, the National Reformation Council announced the appointment of a Civilian Rule Committee, whose terms of reference were explicit:

(a) The National Reformation Council has decided to hand over the Government of Sierra Leone to a civilian government.
(b) The Civilian Rule Committee has been invited to deliberate and advise on the following:
(i) The necessity for a fresh General Election;
(ii) If (i) above is in the negative, the method of forming a National Government; if (i) above is in the affirmative, the stages in which the handover should be effected;
(iii) Any other action which the Civilian Rule Committee considers necessary to effect a peaceful handover.[19]

These prescriptions apparently had little effect. The Juxon-Smith government seemed primarily concerned with entrenching itself and enforcing fiscal austerity, far less with reducing ethnic tensions and encouraging a return to civilian rule. Insensitivity to civilian concerns was coupled with lack of attention to the armed forces. To the men in the ranks, the officers ignored pleas for pay raises, to compensate for sharp increases in the cost of living. In one of the most unusual seizures of control in recent African history, a group of warrant officers imprisoned all but two of the commissioned officers and cabinet members the night of 17–18 April 1968. Sergeant-Major Armada Rogers expressed these reasons:

It has (since 23 March 1967) become absolutely clear that most of the so-called National Reformation Council members only wanted to benefit their selfish ends; the rank and file of the Army and police have been ignored. All that was practised in both the army and the police were nepotism and blatant victimization.
Fellow Sierra Leoneans, we cannot continue any longer under such adverse conditions. The so-called National Reformation Council members have greatly mismanaged the nation's affairs. They have failed to fulfil their boastful promise to both civilians and members of the armed forces. And above all, they want to remain in office indefinitely. Soldiers and police have no business in the running

18 *Africa Research Bulletin*, IV, 12, col. 929C.
19 *Africa Research Bulletin*, IV, 12, col. 929C.

of this country. Our immediate aim is to return to civilian rule. . . . A new Council, replacing the former NRC, has now been formed, and it is named the Anti-Corruption Revolutionary Movement (ACRM).[20]

The evening of 18 April ACRM leaders announced that a National Interim Council had been formed to work out a peaceful return to civilian rule as rapidly as possible. Siaka Stevens returned from exile in Guinea 24 April, and two days later was sworn in as prime minister. No new constitution was necessary, nor new elections. The Anti-Corruption Revolutionary Movement had restored what David Lansana's earlier intervention had denied and Juxon-Smith's fumbling had precluded. Only an eruption within the ranks of the Sierra Leone army brought Stevens the honor he had earned electorally thirteen months earlier.

Four variables made military withdrawal from active political roles in Dahomey, Ghana, and Sierra Leone feasible.

First, the commanding officers were firm in their resolve to step aside—at least at some point. The Revolutionary Military Committee of Dahomey, the National Liberation Council, and the National Reformation Council did not envisage indefinite periods of rule, but a time for quick surgery of economic, social, and political problems, under military rule, and a time for convalescence, under civilian auspices. On the other hand, it often proved difficult, once in office, to step aside fully; this action required a decisive event, such as Alley's abortive putsch, Ankrah's dismissal, or the success of the Anti-Corruption Revolutionary Movement. Willingness to withdraw may result from many factors—but unless it exists, the prospects for displacement are negligible.

The second variable was a group of forceful, articulate civilians, who regularly reminded the ruling juntas of their rhetoric. In Dahomey, trade unionists and young intellectuals formed this group; in Ghana and Sierra Leone, opponents of the Convention Peoples Party and the SLPP, plus many members of the civil service and universities, did not look upon extended military rule with favor. The military's willingness to surrender control thus must be complemented by civilian desire to regain political power.

The third factor, far less significant and far more difficult to document than the preceding, was international political and economic pressure. The French government suspended financial aid to Dahomey following the ouster of Soglo—and with the country on the edge of bankruptcy, this action doubtless enhanced the desire to withdraw. Britain and the United States privately welcomed Nkrumah's downfall, but favored restoration of civilian rule. The actual impact of these moves cannot be accurately

---

[20] *Africa Research Bulletin*, V, 4, cols. 1035C–1036A.

assessed without more detailed information. That international pressures had some effect seems reasonable, but measurement of their extent lies beyond this paper.

Finally, voluntary withdrawal occurred when the military believed that the factors which impelled intervention no longer obtained. The accuracy of this belief was immaterial. Conditions may not have improved under army rule. However, if the ruling junta tires of its political duties and wishes to step aside, it may airily declare its objectives achieved and leave the political arena. It may do so to avoid deposition, to retain army unity, or simply to sidestep criticism. In other words, the effort to exercise power —and perhaps the feeling of powerlessness that comes from such exercise! —may persuade the officers in command to retire.

To put the matter in the bluntest terms, *the army will withdraw when and if it wishes, unless it is directly overthrown.* Without willingness to return to the barracks, officers may remain in control for an indefinite future—or at least until supplanted by the next junta.

Voluntary withdrawal appears unlikely as long as military leaders feel major issues remain unresolved. Only after the conclusion of the civil war could General Gowon speak of a transition to civilian rule by 1976. Brigadier Lamizana of Upper Volta confronts latent resentment between Mossi and Bobo, restiveness among supporters of former President Yameogo, and discontented trade unionists and unemployed young men in Ouagadougou. Under these conditions, he remained on as president after the revival of political parties and parliamentary elections 20 December 1970. In Togo, Colonel Etienne Eyadema has regularly cited ethnic and regional tensions, manifested in partisan feelings, as making a rapid restoration of civilian rule unlikely. Colonel Bokassa of the Central African Republic was forced to call upon French military assistance in November 1967 to prop up his regime; voluntary withdrawal appears unlikely, in light of this tension and (more important) the apparent desire of Bokassa to "civilianize" himself.

In Congo-Kinshasa, General Mobutu appears to be preparing for an extended period of strong personal rule. He heads the single legal political party, the MPR (Popular Movement of the Revolution), and was formally elected president in November 1970. Fragmentary evidence from Burundi suggests that, barring assassination or major domestic upheaval, Colonel Micombero will continue his astute balancing of Tutsi and Hutu interests for the foreseeable future. The evidence from Mali, Libya, Somalia, and Sudan is too sketchy to hazard any guesses at the time of writing. The nature of domestic crises makes voluntary withdrawal unlikely, unless the ranking officers decide that they cannot resolve the problems they have set themselves up to resolve, or unless they decide that professional interests would be better served by leaving the governmental arena. (To be certain, officers returning to the barracks may well set conditions, in order to protect their professional autonomy from future civilian governments.)

Voluntary withdrawal depends, accordingly, upon several unpredictable contingencies. The paramount contingency—and the one most difficult to analyze, save with the clarity of hindsight—appears to be the attitude of the ruling officers. Voluntary withdrawal depends primarily upon the officers' state of mind. Public avowals of eventual withdrawal, demands from aspirant politicians, and external pressures are far less significant than what a few top officers decide is the most appropriate course. Hence, until and unless the ranking junta decides to step aside, it would be unwarranted to expect a peaceful, smooth transition of control.

CHANGING CONDITIONS

A wide variety of factors impelled—or, perhaps more accurately, rationalized—military intervention in African politcs. It stands to reason that, were these conditions rectified, the return of civilian rule might occur without further ado.

S. E. Finer has provided an illuminating distinction between the "disposition to intervene" and the "opportunity to intervene." The disposition inherently precedes the opportunity. The strongest inhibition against the disposition to intervene is a belief in civilian supremacy—a belief whose strength varies from state to state, just as the degree of attachment to civilian political institutions varies from state to state. To quote Finer,

Where public attachment to civilian institutions is strong, military intervention in politics will be weak. . . . By the same token, where public attachment to civilian institutions is weak or non-existent, military intervention in politics will find wide scope—both in manner and in substance. . . . Where the parties or trade unions are feeble and few, where the procedure for the transfer of power is irregular or even non-existent, where the location of supreme authority is a matter of acute disagreement or else of unconcern and indifference: there the military's political scope will be very wide.[21]

In most tropical African states, one must agree that the opportunity for intervention is great indeed.

Development of a sense of civilian supremacy does not occur overnight. Such a sense is intimately linked with time and with respect due to governing institutions. It likely will be strongest in African states (1) in which the dominant party remains vigorous and able to mobilize the population,

[21] S. E. Finer, *The Man on Horseback: The Role of the Military in Politics* (New York, 1962), p. 21.

and (2) in which conscious efforts have been made to suborn the armed services to clear civilian direction. It is no accident that Guinea and Tanganyika (excluding the brief 1964 mutiny) have not yet experienced coups d'etat. The Parti Démocratique de Guinée (PDG) and TANU show a strength of organization and sense of purpose probably unmatched on the continent. In both states the armed services have been linked to the purposes and activities of the dominant party.[22] By enshrining the party and its leadership, and by maintaining party vitality despite economic vicissitudes, Presidents Touré and Nyerere have demonstrated a skill many of their deposed colleagues doubtless envy. On the other hand, as Senegal and the Ivory Coast appear to indicate, a relatively powerful leader (Senghor, Houphouet-Boigny) can help ensure military acquiescence in civilian control.

Once the aura that surrounds civilian supremacy is broken, its reconstitution within a short time is difficult—witness the 1960 intervention in Turkey or the 1967 seizure of power in Greece, states in which a successful transition to civilian rule purportedly had been made. If the "moral barrier" against military takeover is fragile to begin with, and then shattered by direct intervention, pious exhortations cannot restore it. All the king's horses and all the king's men cannot put civilian supremacy together again.

Of even greater difficulty is the establishment of legitimacy. The political transformation of tropical Africa came about swiftly, in terms of the formal shift from colonial rule to independence. However, the rapidity of this evolution was not matched, in most sub-Saharan states, by an equally striking implantation of a sense of national unity and by agreement on the political institutions necessary for peaceful transition. Social, economic, cultural, and political changes, though linked, did not vary at the same rate; distinctions among groups have become, or offer the potential of

---

[22] Victor DuBois, "The Role of the Army in Guinea," *Africa Report*, VIII, 1 (Jan. 1963), 3-5. More recently the Guinean armed forces have been further suborned to the PDG. In December 1968 the National Political Bureau announced it was examining ways of stimulating political commitment in the army; the army, the Bureau stated, served a social function, and its members should have recognized political rights—far removed from the French belief in *la grande muette*, an apolitical army standing on the sidelines. In March, Colonel Kaman Diaby, assistant chief of staff for the People's Army, and Defence Minister Keita Fodeba were arrested for alleged implication in a planned coup d'etat; they and 11 others were sentenced to death in May by a special revolutionary court. At the end of the trial, the National Revolutionary Council called for army restructuring, outlined in detail by President Touré in June. The would-be invasion of Guinea in November 1970 appears to have been supported, to a large extent, by former Guinean soldiers living outside their native state; the army was not involved in the insurrection. For TANU, see Ali A. Mazrui and Donald Rothchild, "The Soldier and the State in East Africa: Some Theoretical Conclusions on the Army Mutinies of 1964," *Western Political Quarterly*, XX, 1 (March 1967), 82-96, esp. p. 88.

becoming, sharply politicized. African societies illustrate low levels of integration.[23] These states thus appear to lack the three elements of a "high level of political culture" which might preclude direct military intervention: consensus on the legitimate locus of sovereignty; consensus on the procedures for establishing morally valid public decisions; and civilian organizations willing and capable of sustaining and defending the society's political institutions.[24]

To expect military rulers speedily to resolve problems of corruption and inefficiency that plagued previous civilian government seems unrealistic. Pious aspirations for moral rectitude and for efficient conduct of government rarely are fulfilled, even in highly developed societies. The organizational characteristics of the armed services—their centralization, hierarchy, discipline, communication, and esprit de corps—may work against effective governance in certain respects.[25] Military-dominated governments may simply not be prepared to cope with the bargaining, compromise, ethnic arithmetic, and host of ancillary skills that politicians—but not necessarily soldiers—develop as a matter of course.

Zolberg has defined the "most salient characteristic" of contemporary African politics as "that it constitutes an almost institutionless arena with conflict and disorder as its most prominent features." [26] Political institutions, as Huntington has noted, are not built overnight.[27] If we perceive military intervention in African political life as illustrating the weakness of political institutions and hence uncertainty about the legitimate source of authority, intervention can readily occur. No strong moral barrier precludes, or possibly even inhibits, the would-be *caudillo* from assuming control.

The conditions that helped prompt intervention, thus, will not disappear in the near future. The process of building legitimacy, valued political procedures and institutions, and a sense of civilian supremacy will encompass decades of conscious, dedicated effort. Accordingly, a change in the conditions that brought about military takeover is unlikely in the near future. Voluntary withdrawal, conscious civilianization, or overthrow would seem far more probable factors in altering the military's role in politics.

[23] Cf. Zolberg's remarks on syncretic societies in "The Structure of Political Conflict," p. 72.
[24] Finer, *The Man on Horseback*, p. 226.
[25] Welch, *Soldier and State in Africa*, pp. 36–50.
[26] Zolberg, "The Structure of Political Conflict," p. 70.
[27] Samuel P. Huntington, *Political Order in Changing Societies* (New Haven, 1968), p. 14.

CONSCIOUS CIVILIANIZATION

The extent of civilian participation in a military-dominated government admits of many degrees. The spectrum ranges from complete army control, in which all key governmental posts are occupied by officers, to behind-the-scenes manipulation, in which figurehead politicians carry out their activities under military surveillance. Most African states currently under military control fall near the center of this spectrum. Officers must make alliances with civilians to exercise and maintain control. When an army as miniscule as that of Sierra Leone or Nigeria (respectively 0.06% and 0.02% of the total population) [28] takes power, it can fill only a few top administrative posts with officers, without risking diluting energies or neglecting army command functions. The ruling junta must exercise its would-be power through civilians, whether civil servants, traditional chiefs, or some other group. Alliances are both natural and necessary.

Civil servants and officers may share an instrumental outlook, a belief that society can be altered by application of certain administrative techniques. The organizational structure of the civil service accords with the organizational structure of the armed forces: both are bureaucracies, or "rational-legal authorities" in Weber's phrase. Similarity of outlook thus makes alliance easy. A close working relationship with the civil service has the further advantage, for the officers, of bringing in a relatively uncorrupt group long overshadowed by politicians. Government employees threatened by party machinations have, in many African states, furnished strong support to newly installed juntas. What more suitable pact than that between groups that chafed under the inept control of venal politicians?

At a different level, the ruling officers may ally themselves with traditional chiefs, particularly in local governance. The chiefs represent a mixed blessing, for the support they command in rural areas must be weighed against the antipathy they arouse in some urban areas. However, for reasons that Edward Feit has examined,[29] military rulers may find it tactically appropriate to link themselves with the chiefs, and in the process reestablish the "administrative-traditional" framework that characterized the colonial period:

In Ghana and Nigeria the officers seem to have chosen the same alternative as was chosen by the British in their time: to abrogate all political activity, to rule

[28] As of January 1966 Sierra Leone counted an army of 1,360, while the estimated 1960 population was 2,250,000; the Nigerian army of 11,500 should be contrasted with the purported population of 56,000,000. For figures on the armed forces, see David Wood, "The Armed Forces of African States," *Adelphi Papers*, no. 27 (London, 1966), p. 28.

[29] Edward Feit, "Military Coups and Political Development: Some Lessons from Ghana and Nigeria," *World Politics*, XX, 2 (Jan. 1968), pp. 179–193.

by administrative fiat on the central level, and to reconstruct the alliance with the chiefs on the local level—in other words, to rebuild the administrative traditional system with the officers assuming the role of the British government.[30]

Members of the ruling military junta may simply divest themselves of their soldierly regalia and demeanor and become full-fledged civilians. They may endeavor to set themselves in the Kemalist model: military heroes who decide to immerse themselves fully in the civilian realm, renouncing all interest in the armed forces. Ataturk carried out such a change —his was a "determination to civilianize the Turkish Republic that cut wide and deep" [31]—but few of his would-be successors have proven successful. Probably the closest imitator is General Joseph Mobutu. Since seizing control in November 1965, Mobutu has engaged in a subtle effort to draw the nationalist, Lumumbist mantle to himself. He has announced his intention of leading a "revolutionary" mass political movement, the Popular Movement of the Revolution. A draft constitution approved in June 1967 stipulated parliamentary elections in 1968 and a Presidential election at the end of 1970. Several observers have pointed out that the timing of his election would allow Mobutu to reach the ripe age of 40— the minimum age for the president prescribed by the constitution. Mobutu thus appears to be attempting a personal transition from military hero to charismatic president—a tortuous transition that cannot, in and of itself, protect the Congo from dissension within the ranks, popular discontent, and the other difficulties officers face in confronting political responsibilities. However, his uncontested victory and the total parliamentary control won by his party in November 1970 seem to seal his desire to shift into the civilian political realm.

Brigadier Eyadema of Togo appears to vacillate between announced returns to civilian rule and actions apparently designed to maintain his personal control. Having assumed power 13 January 1967, four years after the assassination of former President Sylvanus Olympio, Eyadema confronted a regional dichotomy. Like the majority of the armed forces, Eyadema came from the relatively underdeveloped north; civil servants tended to come from the south, particularly from the Ewe, whose political awakening had provided the main issue in Togolese politics for many years.[32] Several announcements of voluntary withdrawal were later disavowed, often in response to pressures from the north lest the south reassert its political dominance. Late in 1969 Eyadema called for a single

---

[30] Feit, "Military Coups," p. 188.

[31] Daniel Lerner and Richard D. Robinson, "Swords and Ploughshares: The Turkish Army as a Modernizing Force," *World Politics*, XIII, 1 (Oct. 1960), 19.

[32] I have examined this development at length in *Dream of Unity: Pan-Africanism and Political Unification in West Africa* (Ithaca, 1966), pp. 37–147.

party "uniting all the sons of Togo in a vast regrouping." His rhetoric unabated, Eyadema called not for "party questing for power or a dominant party, but [for] a single movement which will form a really free platform from which all Togolese can take part in national reconstruction." [33] Did these moves portend an imminent civilianization of the regime? As *West Africa* subsequently commented, Eyadema appears to have had no serious intention of quitting, the result of northern concerns about southern domination, fear of reprisals from supporters of Olympio, and anxiety lest he, like Colonel Alley, be barred from the army and imprisoned following a return to civilian rule.[34] No advantages would seem to accrue to the military chiefs, either through voluntary withdrawal or through conscious civilianization.

The decision to civilianize, like the decision to withdraw voluntarily, is a lonely one. It depends fundamentally upon a leader willing to make the leap of faith that the new civilian government will not take reprisals against those who helped bring its return. Ataturk made a personal transition, for his unquestioned dominance and prestige made him the natural choice for the presidency of the new republic. Mobotu is trying the same transition. But can Eyadema? Lamizana? Bokassa? All have aroused antagonisms. Their personal security cannot be assured. Subordinates in the armed forces may not support their commanders who dabble overlong in "civilian" realms—witness the unceremonious sacking of Juxon-Smith and Alley. A basic dilemma and uncertainty thus exist. Having assumed political control, can military leaders gracefully step aside from the role that brought them to power? What guarantees can be developed for their safety? For their opportunities to exercise power when clad in mufti? The fundamental perplexities have been delineated by Finer:

Those armed forces that have tried to disengage from politics have had to hasten back as soon as their quondam political enemies came within sight of regaining power, while these that have elected to remain and rule have been rejected only by popular revolt, or by further military revolts of their own malcontents. In most cases the military that have intervened in politics are in a dilemma: whether their rule be indirect or whether it be direct, they cannot withdraw from rulership nor can they fully legitimize it. They can neither stay nor go.[35]

OVERTHROW OF MILITARY-DOMINATED GOVERNMENTS

The other side of the coin from voluntary withdrawal of ranking offi-

[33] *West Africa* (4 Oct. 1969), p. 1196.
[34] *West Africa* (18 Oct. 1969), p. 1233.
[35] Finer, *Man on Horseback*, p. 243.

cers and/or their civilianization is deposition. The two groups that most likely can overturn military-dominated governments are militant urban groups (particularly trade unionists and students) and junior officers. Recent African history furnishes several appropriate examples; I shall examine the fall of General Ibrahim Abboud, president of the Sudan for six complex years.

Tropical Africa's single major instance of military authority being ousted by civilians is furnished by the Sudan. In October 1964 students and trade unionists in Khartoum helped topple the government of General Abboud, who had taken control in November 1958. The Abboud government increasingly became involved with military repression in the south, whose significant ethnic, racial, cultural, and linguistic differences defied easy solution. (The readiness of the military to use force to achieve compliance obviously played a part here!) Military efforts to reduce dissidence led to civil war, with close to 100,000 Sudanese fleeing from the southern provinces into Uganda, Rwanda, and the Congo. Resentment grew against the conflict in 1964. Students at the University of Khartoum increasingly criticized the regime. These criticisms, in the government's view, were "unbecoming" and "violated the law." Despite a ban on further meetings, the students assembled on 10 and 21 October; their concerns about government policy in the south developed into an increasingly vociferous criticism of the military regime, then into a demonstration that brought police repression, including the death of one student. The university was closed, but demonstrations continued in Khartoum, and spread to Omdurman. Confronted with growing pressures, President Abboud dissolved the Supreme Council of the armed forces and the cabinet, and started "consultations with noble persons" to form a transitional regime. (It should be noted that the armed forces were not united behind Abboud, a not inconsequential factor in the collapse of the government.) As a general strike grew in effectiveness and the employees of the national radio and television stations halted transmissions, Abboud and officers close to him realized their position was untenable. On 29 October representatives of the armed forces and the "United National Front" agreed "in principle to liquidate the existing constitutional system and supersede it by a system based on the provisional constitution of 1956." A high-ranking civil servant, Sir al-Khatim al-Khalifa, was named prime minister. Within two weeks, all seven members of the dissolved Supreme Council of the armed forces were arrested, and Abboud stepped down as president of the Sudan.[36]

Tropical Africa's first military regime thus ran its course. Its effort to

---

[36] Information drawn from issues of *Africa Report* and Yusuf Fadl Hasan, "The Sudanese Revolution of October 1964," *Journal of Modern African Studies*, V, 4 (Dec. 1967), 491–509.

achieve greater civilian participation and backing, in the face of popular discontent and a distasteful conflict, brought disintegration. This breakdown points to the fact that military regimes are as subject to declining prestige and unity as their civilian predecessors. Disenchantment with a government that promises significant changes but fails to make them good can readily lead to frustration. Pent-up frustration, in turn, may explode in unfocused demonstrations, and bring, as in the Sudan, a return to civilian rule.

On the other hand, domestic disorders may prompt intervention and deposition of governing officers by ambitious subalterns. The toppling of General Soglo in December 1967 and of Colonel Juxon-Smith in April 1968 bear witness to this likelihood. The main danger rests in the episodic unleashing of violence. Coup begets countercoup. The meteoric rise of a junior officer to unchallenged military and political power does not pass unnoticed. Those who seize control risk arousing jealousies, thereby becoming victims of the whirlwind they unleashed.

To the outside observer, the armed forces of African states appear cohesive and monolithic. They are not. Forcible eviction of military-based governments more likely results from internal army splits than from pressures from students, trade unionists, unemployed youth, and the like. The reasons are obvious: members of the military have training in the use of force and the example of their colleagues to follow in overthrowing a government. As noted in the earlier discussion of Dahomey and Sierra Leone, the sudden rise of the Military Revolutionary Committee and the Anti-Corruption Revolutionary Movement testified to deep dissatisfaction with their leaders on the part of the armed forces. Many issues provide the nuclei around which grievances can cluster.[37] Regional, class, ethnic, personal, and professional differences can be inflated into countercoups. As a result, the interminable round of coup and countercoup familiar to students of Latin American and Middle Eastern history bids fair to repeat itself in Africa. Forcible eviction of military-based governments by segments of the armed forces seems the most likely immediate prospect in many African states, unless a restoration of civilian control (through a combination of voluntary withdrawal and civilianization) comes about. And, even in such instances, the specter of future intervention cannot be banished.

The contrasts drawn in this chapter must not be pushed unduly. No clear lines can be discerned between withdrawal to stave off a threatened

---

[37] Finer cites four grounds: defense of region, of class, of the army as an institution, and of personal status, *The Man on Horseback*, p. 40. Cf. J. M. Lee, *The African Military and Civil Order* (New York, 1969), p. 174.

countercoup and withdrawal to protect the autonomy and cohesion of the armed forces. Segments of the military may team up with civilians to topple an army-based regime. Civilianization may be accompanied by extensive behind-the-scenes pressure to obtain decisions favorable to the military—not an unknown tactic in more developed areas.

The fundamental factor remains the weakness of political institutions in Africa, including the armed forces. (A cohesive, "professional" army is, by definition, not subject to violent schism and countercoups.) African governments work within a relatively restricted range of policy options, a point convincingly demonstrated by Wallerstein's essay in this volume.[38] Given such constraints as he speaks of, does the allegedly civilian or military character of a particular African government have major relevance? As long as authority remains tenuous, a variety of groups will clamor over its exercise.

It is not rule by the military, but rule itself, on which political scientists concerned with contemporary Africa should focus. To speak of military withdrawal from politics in a context where the political community remains problematic risks focusing upon surface phenomena, upon short-term manifestations that may run contrary to a more complex, underlying pattern. Only as African governments acquire greater legitimacy and effectiveness—a question of time as well as expertise and resources—can civilian supremacy become entrenched. Positive support by the armed forces for the government of the day, or at least acquiescence in its policies, appears significant, but it is by no means the sole factor in precluding intervention.

The increased prominence of African armed forces and their willingness to intervene in political decision-making necessitate new patterns of civil–military relations. The size of African armies generally has been increased, although per capita military expenditure remains lowest of the major continents. Many politicians look on greater military appropriations as enhancing loyalty; the fate of Sylvanus Olympio warns those who would reduce those costs. Army shake-ups to reduce plotting have been common, as have appeals to "civic duty" (read: loyalty to the existing leader and party).[39] The question remains whether such exhortations, personnel changes, and expenditures can ensure civilian supremacy in a context marked by the relative absence of effective, national political institutions and by the consequent prevalence of conflict. Clearly, I do not believe that these are sufficient.

---

[38] See Immanuel Wallerstein, "The Range of Choice," pp. 19–33 here.

[39] Such methods, as Nkrumah's Ghana clearly illustrates, may have a countervailing effect in awakening officers to the dangers of "divide and rule" and its impact upon professional autonomy.

To return to the barracks, the African military must adopt the humility and priorities of Cincinnatus. Only when and if its members view their roles as *supporting* civilian authority, not supplanting it, will the African military shift away from its current political centrality. The long-range development of effective, national political institutions will determine the political roles the armed forces will play.

Chapter 11 The Prospects for Democracy in Africa

Rupert Emerson

This paper defends a proposition that can neither be proved nor disproved. The contemporary empirical evidence that can and will be mustered in its support is necessarily inconclusive because, no matter how overwhelming the evidence as to present trends may be, it is obvious that this cannot preclude future changes in direction. Similarly although I believe that the long-term perspective of history appears to support my contention, this again has no necessary bearing on a future which may choose a quite different path. Furthermore, it is arguable that even though the historical record in the large seems to be on my side, the more relevant considerations derive from the distinctive turn of events of more recent decades. These can be held to refute me, although I am not prepared, as will be seen, to accept the validity of the refutation. I have the gravest doubt that abstract theoretical argumentation has any significant bearing on either side of the controversy. The best that can be hoped is the discovery that a substantially greater body of proof can be laid on one side of the scale than on the other, but with full recognition that whoever undertakes prophecy is talking about matters beyond his possible knowledge or control, and with the inevitable prospect that history may play him false. I have somewhere come across the comment that historians are very convincing when it comes to hindsight of the past, but fall down badly when they undertake to foretell the future. I doubt that political scientists can lay claim to any greater prescience.

The proposition to be examined is the simple one that democracy—a term to which I will shortly give a reasonably precise meaning—is unlikely to establish itself as the generally prevailing form of government in Africa and will in fact appear only in relatively rare instances. More usually, even where it does appear, its life will be short and harassed. To undertake the descent from macro assertions such as these to their micro application to particular concrete situations is always a hazardous enterprise. Let me merely remark that I have no intention of saying that the emergence and flourishing of democratic institutions in this or that African country is ruled out, but only that this will be a rare event, standing in sharp contrast to the generality of nondemocratic polities whose norm will be authoritarian rule of one or another variety. Furthermore, I should add that although this paper concerns itself primarily with Africa, almost all of its general contentions apply equally to Asian and Latin American countries and peoples with only the reservation that in each instance there are differences in social makeup and historical experience which must obviously be taken into account.

I

With the end of colonialism it appears to have been the assumption on all sides that the alien colonial regimes would be replaced by democratic governments. The prestige of democracy stood very high and there were few who were prepared to dispute its preeminence. Those who ignored its substance were often pleased to draw upon the term and embellish their undemocratic systems with some of its trappings. Thus the Communists claimed to represent a higher form of democracy, embodying the true will of the people in the Communist party, as the operative instrument of the proletarian dictatorship. Even the Fascists and Nazis, although they were more likely to speak scornfully of democracy as one of the signs of bourgeois weakness and decay, put themselves forward as exemplifying a superior version of democracy, finding a Rousseauan general will immanent in Führer and Duce.

To put it in perhaps somewhat overemphatic terms, the most highly developed, most powerful, and most productive countries were democracies, and it was these countries, plus Japan in World War I and the USSR in World War II, which had won the great wars. Democracy appeared to be associated with wealth and power and advancement, leading to either or both of the assumptions that democracy opened the door to these desirable goods or that other countries would follow in the democratic path as they rapidly moved ahead in their new-found independence. Furthermore, the swing toward democracy fitted in with the rise, the social mobilization, of wider and wider segments of the populace at large. The building in each country of a single national culture and economy in which all would participate seemed clearly to involve a change in relationships of which the political expression was the elaboration of democratic institutions. If in the African circumstance this picture should be transferred to some broader Pan-African base, the basic propositions remained unchanged.

When the era of decolonization set in after World War II all the colonial powers save Spain and Portugal were democracies, unless the Soviet Union is also listed among the colonialists. The evidence indicates that these powers tended to see democracy as the only legitimate type of government for the successor regimes in their ex-colonial territories; and, indeed, it was one of the major justifications of colonialism that the peoples subjected to it were not yet able to manage democratic institutions on their own. Where the colonial powers departed on friendly and peaceful terms, as was generally the case in Africa, they sought to ensure that their former wards were endowed with democratic institutions which had imperial approval. To avoid confusion, I might remark immediately that these institutions were not necessarily good in themselves, well fitted to the needs of the peoples concerned, nor the free choice of those peoples; but they *were* democratic.

I believe that it may equally, and perhaps even more forcefully, be said that the politically relevant elements in the colonial populations also accepted democracy as the proper goal for their societies. Their most telling claim to power came from the fact that as nationalist leaders they were spokesmen for the nation, which is to say, for the people at large. The colonial rulers were alien intruders; the nationalists spoke with the democratic voice of the masses. They were wholly prepared to accept the at least implied challenge of the colonial authorities: they felt assured that they could manage democracy in their own countries far better than could any expatriate regime. As Edward Shils has put it:

There are no new states in Asia or Africa, whether monarchies or republics, in which the elites who just demanded independence did not, at the moment just prior to their success, believe that self-government and dmocratic government were identical . . . something like liberal democracy was generally thought to be prerequisite for the new order of things.[1]

It might be well to pause here to identify the sense in which the term "democracy" is being used in this paper—a sense which I believe is not significantly distinguishable from the conceptions of democracy held by the colonial powers and colonial peoples as they confronted the approach of independence. The two essential conditions of the "something like liberal democracy" which Shils mentions are that freedom of speech and organization be safeguarded and that the people at large, with a reasonable approximation of equality among them, be endowed with an operative opportunity to remove the existing regime and substitute another through peaceful and institutionalized means. The implications of such proposi-

[1] Edward Shils in John Hallowell, ed., *Development For What?* (Durham, N.C., 1964), pp. 104, 113.

tions are, of course, both extensive and complex. Among other things that must be included are not only the right to vote freely, but also the right to form political parties, to debate, to campaign, to meet, to publicize, and to stand for election. Perhaps the most subtle and difficult conception of all, which may be seen as the cornerstone of the system, is that of the loyal opposition, which implies restraints of vital importance both on those who would replace the government in power and also on that government in relation to individuals, minorities, and opposition groups who challenge, or are seen as challenging, the powers that be.

I am, of course, aware that this is only one of the various versions of democracy which are currently extant. Its polar opposite is presumably the version that rests essentially on unchecked majority rule. In this version the two or more parties that are assumed to be necessary ingredients of liberal democracy are replaced by a single party which is likely to be proclaimed indistinguishable from the nation itself, or by the no-party state in which, perhaps, the charismatic leader is the focal point for the wielding of all power. Opposition elements are granted no rights because they are obviously divisive, are suspected of being agents of alien neo-colonial forces, and impair the ability of the government to carry out the will of the people as a whole. From an electoral standpoint such a system is best maintained by a consultation of the people which consists of their being called upon to cast a plebiscitary vote for the single slate of names with which they are officially presented. In principle, if by no means always in practice, this majoritarian or plebiscitary democracy has the advantage of making possible a coalition of all available forces in the country for the realization of the common national ends. It also runs the risk, however, of losing touch with what the people actually want and basing policy on the assertion of the reigning authorities that they speak infallibly with the voice of the overwhelming majority.

I should like to make it clear that I set out from no presumption that any one of the variant forms of democracy is superior to another or that democracy in any guise is to be preferred to nondemocratic forms of government. I am here making no attempt either to impose or to arrive at value judgments, but only to indicate the existence of different political systems and to explore the likelihood that one or another, and particularly what I have called liberal democracy, will establish itself as the generally accepted form in Africa.

II

The widespread assumptions that democratic governments would take over on the demise of colonialism have proved to be gravely faulty, and the actual outcome has been a grievous disappointment to those who pinned their hopes on democracy. It is by now a commonplace that the democratic constitutions with which most of the new states started their life have been replaced in instance after instance by regimes which at the best have only some formal and verbal association with democracy. Often even where formally democratic institutions have been retained, the substance of political life has become authoritarian or dictatorial. It became apparent at a quite early stage, as for example in Ghana's political evolution, that the so-called Westminster system of parliamentary government could with exemplary ease be transformed into a one-party rule which in fact developed a cult of personality centered upon the leader. Given the unchallengeable majority of the ruling party, the complete solidarity of its parliamentary ranks, and the readiness to accept the lead given by Kwame Nkrumah, the stage was all set for what speedily became a travesty of the London model on which it was originally based. As far as the French model was concerned, de Gaulle had demonstrated that a charismatic figure might take command of the situation, and his African counterparts were often not slow to follow his example and improve upon it both in terms of silencing opposition elements and building up the authority of the premier or president, who also doubled as the head of the single or dominant party.

There is neither need nor time to go into detail over the familiar history of the last decade or two, except perhaps to indicate the general trend and to point out a few of the characteristic high spots. In the large, what is most striking is the constant repetition of similar swings away from established democratic constitutionalism. There are evident dangers in drawing upon Latin America as furnishing precedents for African or Asian peoples, and yet the instability and fragility of Latin American political systems, the repeated rise of dictators, and the prevalence of military takeovers seem closely to parallel the comparable developments in the countries that have come to independence since World War II. It is a matter for wide-open debate whether the Latin American experience may legitimately be called upon as foreshadowing the course of political developments elsewhere or whether it must be attributed primarily to special circumstances of that part of the world.

The constant drift in the Asian and African setting toward the substitution of authoritarian for liberal democratic government is surely one of the most striking phenomena of the political history of the present century. Leaving aside Japan as something of a special case, but certainly not a democratic one until MacArthur took it in hand, one can at least begin with Sun Yat-sen's conviction that it would be necessary to undertake a tutelage of the people before they could be trusted to manage their own affairs. Some decades later Sukarno contributed the useful term "guided democracy," although it might be difficult to establish that he gave much guidance that improved Indonesia's democratic prospects. The Middle East in its different fashions followed in the same path, with Ataturk as its most distinguished tutelary leader and one who took the transition to democracy seriously. The African countries have with a minimum waste of time turned to one-party and, in most instances, one-man regimes.

Nor, of course, has the matter stopped there. The "guided democracy" has in a number of cases been pushed aside, in good Latin American style, by military coups. In Africa the starting point is the overthrow of Farouk by the military in 1952, with Nasser coming to the fore in 1954. The year 1958 was one of military action as Pakistan, Burma, Iraq, and the Sudan were taken over by members of their respective officer corps. In sub-Saharan Africa the emergence of the military was somewhat delayed, in part, no doubt, because it took some time after the achievement of independence for the armed forces both to develop strength enough and to free themselves enough from the colonial control and tradition in which they had originated to be able to operate on their own. The dramatic intervention of the *Force Publique* in the affairs of the Congo immediately after independence was a warning of things to come. In 1963 President Olympio was killed, it seems almost inadvertently, by a handful of the Togo military. Since that time the military have played dominant and important political roles in a number of other African countries, such as Dahomey, Upper Volta, the Central African Republic, Congo-Kinshasa, Congo-Brazzaville, Algeria, and Sierra Leone. At least for the English-speaking world the most dramatic military takeovers were the overthrow of the civilian regimes in Ghana and Nigeria in early 1966. To the roster of African countries in which the military overtly seized power must be added others in which the military were very significant elements in the maintenance of existing civilian regimes, as in Senegal, or in the replacement of one civilian regime by another, as in the rise to power of Obote in Uganda. On the face of it, it seems more plausible than not to assume that the military will in the foreseeable future have a larger rather than a smaller share in Africa's political future, as it has had in Latin America and the Middle East.

In Africa, and in Asia as well, it is, indeed, markedly easier to run down the brief list of countries in which democracy has survived reasonably intact than to recite the far longer list of those which have taken the authoritarian path, whether under civilian or military auspices.

What are the major factors to which one must attribute the decline or disintegration of the democratic regimes which were the immediate heirs of colonialism? They have been analyzed and investigated by a number of journalists, scholars, and political spokesmen; and I fear that I can do little more than to recapitulate the arguments which have been frequently advanced by others, with some commentary of my own. In sum, they amount to the proposition that the conditions which make possible the survival and successful practice of democracy do not generally exist in Africa (or, for that matter, in Asia or Latin America), including the contention that the dangerous and critical times in which African states have come into being tend to make democratic institutions inapplicable.

A contrary view, tied to his insistent advocacy of the one-party system as best representing the nation as a whole, has been put forward by President Nyerere of Tanzania,[2] but it appears to rest on dubious foundations. Finding man a rational being and all men equal, he maintained that democracy, which he equated with government by discussion among equals, was the only defensible form of government. As he rejected the right of any one to govern another people without the latter's consent—"we are human: ergo, we *must* govern ourselves"—so he also rejected the notion that anywhere the conditions for democracy do not exist:

The only place of which it would be reasonable to say that the conditions for democracy did not exist would be an uninhabited island—or a lunatic asylum! For the "conditions" for democracy (or self-government, which is the same thing) exist wherever man exists as a rational human being.

While it is undoubtedly true that human communities have been able to govern themselves, as Nyerere remarks, regardless of poverty and lack of education, it is equally clear on the record that only in exceedingly rare circumstances have people, above the level of the face-to-face village community in fact governed themselves democratically, that is, by discussion among equals. Such negative evidence cannot justify the conclusion that peoples throughout history would not have been able so to govern themselves, but it is indisputable that in the overwhelming majority of cases they did not. It is not democratic government from within which has characterized the larger communities of mankind but autocratic government from above.

In searching for the causes of the abandonment and overthrow of democratic regimes, presumably the least interesting, but by no means necessarily the least significant, is original sin in the sense of a desire on the part of those concerned to hold on to or to capture power for personal gain, which may involve only the prestige and pomp of office but is likely also to bring pecuniary gain, perhaps magnified by illegitimate returns. We have no reason to think that Africans are worse sinners in this respect than the rest of mankind, but it may be that African circumstances offer greater temptation than exists in more advanced societies, because of the size of

[2] Julius Nyerere, *Democracy and the Party System*, mimeographed (Dar es Salaam, Jan. 1963).

the gap between the material rewards of office and the subsistence-level poverty of almost all the rest of the society. Here, no doubt, the colonial experience plays a role because of the level of the salary scale set for themselves by the expatriate colonial authorities, far out of line with the income of the people they governed, but inherited by their African successors. It is presumably also the case that in many instances African leaders can somewhat more easily get away with the manipulation of public office for private gain than can other leaders elsewhere, because of the lack of an informed, vigilant, and politically alert body of citizens. It would, however, be a mistake to lay too much emphasis on this aspect of the situation since it seems evident that in many countries the general populace or substantial segments thereof are both aware of and unhappy about what has been going on in the political management of their affairs. Among other things, one may cite in support of such a view the reports that military coups have been greeted with apparent glee by people who up to that moment were assumed to be devoted to the existing regime, the party, the charismatic leader.[3] Politics, it is not infrequently said, has come to be widely regarded in Africa as a dirty game of which people are glad to be relieved. Politicians are accused not only of taking special care of themselves but also of failing to produce the reordering and development of their societies to which independence was supposed to unlock the gates.[4]

What moral one can draw for the political future of African countries from this state of affairs, insofar as it in fact has any widespread existence, is not immediately evident. It might be interpreted as leading on toward a greater demand for effective democratic procedures as a means of checking on leaders who have lost or impaired the faith of their countrymen in them, or, alternatively, a readiness to accept a strong and self-contained regime, perhaps the military, which would throw the rascals out, do away with corruption and nepotism, and take charge of the society with firm new hands.

Leaving aside the question of personal greed for power and profit—which is, incidentally, often complicated by the concurrent belief of those in power or seizing it that they have a special ability and calling to run the country—a number of other factors have been suggested as sharing

[3] Allowance must be made for the fact that in many countries cheering crowds can be brought out into the street for almost any cause or person.

[4] Rita Hinden has effectively pointed out one part of the problem in noting the drastic change in the position of African nationalist leaders after independence: "Instead of being noble freedom-fighters, supported by the sympathy of all liberal minded people abroad, they had at once to become politicians and administrators, caught up in a new power struggle, which is an inevitable part of politics. And once they became politicians and administrators, they were open to all the seductions of power—intrigue, corruption, bribery, even thuggery." "Africa Without Tears," *Encounter* (May 1966), p. 56.

responsibility for the failure of democracy to take hold. There is no need to do more than mention the all too evident lack of what have frequently been singled out as elements which are regarded as either essential for the success of democracy or as highly conducive to it. Here I have in mind such matters as education and literacy, a standard of living sufficiently above a subsistence level to afford some leisure for social and political contemplation and activity, the existence of a strong middle class, and a degree of "social mobilization" providing some measure of acquaintance with the great world beyond. It is sometimes said that the illiterate peasant or villager is capable of as shrewd political assessments of persons and issues as the literate city dweller. It may be that he is, but the larger he bulks in the demographic makeup of his country, the less likely he is to have an opportunity to make political judgments, in the constitutional setting of a liberal democracy. For all practical purposes, I suggest, the existence of an informed, literate, politically participant citizenry is an indispensable foundation for the survival of democracy. Whether the existence of such a citizenry is a sufficient condition for democracy is another matter.

A different order of preconditions for the successful functioning of a democratic system is contained in the proposition that the society concerned must have a reasonably coherent and homogeneous population. Almost all commentators have set out from the assumption that explicit or implicit agreement on certain fundamental values is essential if the freedoms which are vital to democracy are to be made compatible with holding the society together. Such agreement embraces two main aspects: a pervading sense that the continued survival of the community is more important than the achievement of particular goals on which its people are divided, and acceptance of the basic rules of the political game, establishing indispensable restraints on both the uses of power and the activities of the opposition.

In contrast to these prescriptions for democracy it is notorious that the African societies are generally marked by gaps and fissures, both horizontal and vertical. It has been remarked that although its aspirations are to the broader unities of nationalism and Pan-Africanism, "the instincts of Africa are to fissiparity."[5] The last decade of African studies has seen much time, energy, and ingenuity devoted to the exploration of the fissures in African societies as a means for explaining, and perhaps justifying, the swing toward single parties and charismatic leaders, as well as the later rash of military coups.

The most immediately evident gap derives from the existence within

[5] John Day, "Democracy in Africa," *Parliamentary Affairs*, XVII, 2 (Spring 1964), 168.

almost every African state of several tribes speaking different languages and claiming distinctive lines of descent. Colonial authorities saw it as no part of their responsibility to create national solidarity, and where the principle of indirect rule was invoked it deliberately preserved the traditional communities as separate entities. Advance toward self-government tended to stir up tribal feelings since it directly posed the question as to who was going to rule whom, and the enfranchisement of the rural peasantry often enhanced the power of the traditional chiefs who were more closely and self-interestedly tied to the tribal scheme of things than were the city dwellers. For the aspirant political leader and manipulator, the tribal structure provided built-in constituencies which were close to the irresistible, even though the playing up of tribalism might threaten the society with disintegration. Ethnic arithmetic is a well-known political device around the world, but it can be peculiarly dangerous in the African setting where political unity within each of the states has so brief and inconclusive a history.

The other most grievous cleavage that exists in the African societies is that which divides the Western-trained évolué from those who have remained more closely attached to the traditional communities. The former is almost sure to be a city dweller while the latter either remains a villager or is a recent migrant to the urban slums. The two are likely, literally as well as figuratively, to speak different languages, the "mobilized" city dweller often conducting much of his business and perhaps much of his life in a European language while the villager lives in his native tongue. Increasingly, of course, gaps of this variety are being broken down and intermediaries between the two extremes are growing in number, but it will be long before they vanish; and those who constitute the new elite inevitably have a sense of superiority to their less developed countrymen.[6]

For political purposes these matters are made all the more serious not only because much of at least the upper levels of political and governmental life is usually conducted in a language alien to the mass, but also because the political and administrative institutions are so largely derived from Western models, often having been devised and imposed by the colonial power as the constitutional and governmental framework within which independence was conceded. Even those who are responsible for running such institutions have no extensive experience of them, and it

[6] James S. Coleman and Carl G. Rosberg, Jr., assert that the elitism of African leaders has "clearly furthered the one-party tendency, because it carries the implicit presumption that the governing group possesses a monopoly of wisdom and legitimacy. It follows, therefore, that in their view an opposition group recruited from the non-elite is incompetent and illegitimate and that one recruited from the same strata as the elite is either frivolous and irrelevant, or dangerously subservient because its members seek only power." *Political Parties and National Integration in Tropical Africa* (Berkeley and Los Angeles, 1964), p. 662.

must be extraordinarily difficult to make them meaningful to the populace at large. The political parties themselves, although they were built in the first instance by the indigenous nationalist movements and hence are closer to the soil than parliaments and bureaucracies, were still derived from a foreign model.

The African justifications of the single-party system are so familiar as to need no extensive recapitulation here. With supposedly biting sarcasm it is asked whether Africans, having achieved unity in a single nationalist party, must break it up to make Europe happy through the creation of one or more oppositions. Parties, it has been argued time and again, represent different classes, and where, as in Africa, societies are classless only one party is required. Again, it is an essential feature of an often recited African creed that it is an integral part of the African spirit and heritage, of *Negritude,* to be imbued with an all-embracing sense of community and communion which renders irrelevant and abhorrent the idea of an opposition.

To this external observer, the African claim to so profound a sense of community has a ring of falseness and unreality to it. A beautiful theoretical argument can be, and has been, created to establish that following African tradition and given the lack of classes, all can unite in a single party to pursue objectives which are essentially self-evident and agreed, any elements of discord being ironed out in free discussion which knows no majority or minority. This presents an ideal picture from which, unhappily, reality appears to diverge sharply. Albert Meister has recently protested, with special reference to East Africa, that what is involved is an idealization of a past golden age which ignores the less pleasant realities of the situation. Finding that the speeches of African leaders abound in references to lengthy discussions under the trees which result in decisions unanimously arrived at, he concludes that:

Le rappel à ce passé idéalisé est d'autant plus fréquent que les décisions actuelle^r sont prises par voie administrative.[7]

Perhaps somewhat to the embarrassment of those who too speedily and too warmly endorsed the turn which African political life took after independence, the one-party system has of late lost some of its luster and the glowing transcendent quality of charisma has been dimmed. The fragility and shallow roots of the parties and the dubious hold of some of the leaders were exposed by the ease with which the military took over in some countries, and in particular by the disappearance of Nkrumah from the Ghanaian scene and the vanishing of the CPP. The emperor has not been revealed

[7] Albert Meister, *L'Afrique, Peut-elle partir?* (Paris, 1966), note 6, pp. 326–327.

quite in full nakedness, but his clothes are both scantier and more thread-bare than had been supposed. No one has taken more pleasure in denouncing both single parties and charisma than Arthur Lewis who has asserted flatly that the single-party system meets none of Africa's basic requirements, and the allegedly charismatic leader he has dismissed with the comment that "Almost any charming rogue can get himself written up in the political journals of the Western world."[8] One hears much, he remarked, about the popularity of such leaders, but when they fall hardly anybody bothers to cross the street, even for a good man like Olympio. As for our political scientists, he added, "they fall all over themselves to demonstrate that democracy is suitable only for Europeans and North Americans, and in the sacred names of 'charisma,' 'modernization,' and 'national unity' call upon us to admire any demagogue who, aided by a loud voice and a bunch of hooligans, captures and suppresses his rivals."

Valid and penetrating as much of his criticism of African political systems and its commentators is, it is to be feared that his own proposals of coalition government as furnishing the answer to Africa's problems is not likely to prove acceptable. However much sympathy one may have for his basic proposition that in the true meaning of democracy all interests and groups affected by governmental decisions should have a right to participate in the making of them, coalitions are difficult instruments to operate under any circumstances and particularly so in the conditions that exist in Africa.

There is much to be said for the view that the paramount need of African states and peoples, confronted by all the crises associated with coming to independence, was strong government rather than adherence to the niceties of liberal democratic constitutionalism. Even when it is fully recognized that the costs of authoritarian single-party rule have often been heavy, among other things in terms of the silencing, exiling, or imprisonment of persons of stature and ability because of their disagreements with the ruling elements, it is still more plausible than not that an authoritarian system can make invaluable contributions at least in the early stages while nations are brought into being, development is just getting under way, and all the domestic and external adjustments to independence are being made. What Paul Appleby asserted in his report on public administration in India, although here in a democratic setting, has its applicability to Africa as well:

Not independence and popular self-government alone are the objectives, but such a government dedicated to achievement of mass welfare at a tempo never attained anywhere at this stage of what is being undertaken here.[9]

[8] W. Arthur Lewis, *Politics in West Africa* (London, 1965), p. 32. The following citation is found on pp. 89–90.
[9] Paul H. Appleby, *Public Administration in India* (Delhi, 1957), p. 1.

The basic issues are well illustrated in the contention of Ali A. Mazrui that the Congo can serve as an extreme case of incapacity for free institutions, needing not to be made capable of freedom but capable of authority.[10] Another aspect of substantially the same proposition was put forward by Aristide R. Zolberg who claimed that the insecurity and fears of Mali's rulers are reflected in the use of harsh repressive measures to put down what a well-established state would see as only minor disorders:

> Mali thus reveals most acutely the fundamental paradox of the African one-party state: namely, that while observers have been busy deploring authoritarian trends, the real problem is the weakness of their political structures.[11]

All countries in time of crisis—as witness the United States in wartime—move to a centralization and consolidation of power in order to assure their survival. The unavoidable tasks which independence laid on the doorsteps of the newly independent African states, setting off from the basic need to keep them alive as going concerns, are at least as challenging as any with which the advanced countries have had to deal. The adoption of authoritarian rule to speed the processes of nation building and development is wholly comprehensible—even though doubts may often linger as to whether the turn away from democracy was in fact motivated by such considerations or succeeded in making significant advance toward the desired goals.

III

If the analysis that has been undertaken up to this point is substantially valid, the inevitable conclusion is that the almost universal perversion or abandonment of democratic institutions in Africa in the last decade is to be attributed in large part to the circumstances and conditions within which they had to operate. Since these circumstances and conditions are not, as things stand now, likely to undergo any swift and radical change, one must presume that the chances that such institutions will be restored in any presently foreseeable future are slight, although Ghana's return to constitutional democracy in 1969 was encouraging. Development has in every sphere been a slower and spottier affair than many, perhaps most, people were prepared to assume as Africa surged forward into independence.

Independence has not brought with it the boons of development which it was hoped would follow in its train. There still remains an abiding confi-

[10] Ali A. Mazrui, "Consent, Colonialism and Sovereignty," *Political Studies*, X, 1 (Feb. 1963), 40–41.
[11] "The Political Revival of Mali," *The World Today* (April 1965), p. 155.

dence, however, that, in the fullness of time, the special conditions which have currently operated to make democracy in Africa unviable will be eliminated. If the UN Decade of Development has so far been an unhappy failure, widening rather than closing the gap between the rich and the poor countries, one may still hope that a Century of Development, or perhaps some less awesome period, will bring forth the transformation which the Third World has generally so far been denied.[12] If this comes to pass in the African setting, the earlier argument would suggest that a return to democracy would at least be made more possible, if not at all necessarily more inevitable, and would at the same time make less likely the overturn of democratic institutions by authoritarian forces, military or otherwise.

I am wholly prepared to concede that the chances for the emergence or survival of democracy are markedly better where, to substitute a single phrase for many, conditions of self-sustaining well-being have been achieved; but I continue to harbor serious doubts that democracy will in fact flourish in Africa.

A larger and far more hazardous argument than that which has so far been undertaken must be brought into play if one seeks to project conclusions of this variety into the further future, where my opening comments as to the dangers of prophecy become most pertinent. The heart of the controversy—obviously one which reaches far beyond the scope of this paper—is the contention that modernization in all its ramifications has either the certain consequence or the probable outcome of so structuring society as greatly to promote the trend toward democracy.

Assuming the impossibility of spelling this thesis out here, let me only suggest that the key phrases, drawn from the presently fashionable arsenal of social science terminology, are "social mobilization" and the "political culture of participation . . . the participation explosion."[13] In a few words, the basic rationale of this position is that it is the nature of a developed economy and all the elements of modernity that characteristically accompany it, such as transformed means of transport and communication and

---

[12] Reporting to the General Assembly on the second meeting of UNCTAD, over which he presided, Dinesh Singh, Indian Minister of Commerce, presented the lamentable estimate that after 45 sessions of ECOSOC and two sessions of UNCTAD, and despite the promises held out for the UN Development Decade, it would take the developing countries a century and a half to double the per capita income—and at the end of these 150 years, their income would be no more than fifty cents a day. *India News* (Washington, D.C., Nov. 1968), p. 4.

[13] See, for example, Karl W. Deutsch, "Social Mobilization and Political Development," *American Political Science Review* (Sept. 1961), pp. 493–514; and Gabriel A. Almond and Sidney Verba, *The Civic Culture* (Boston and Toronto, 1965), p. 2. Among the six crises which Lucian Pye sees as confronting the new states, he lists penetration, participation, and mobilization, all of which bear on the same theme. *Aspects of Political Development* (Boston, 1966), pp. 62–67.

universal education, to reach out into every layer and corner of the society. For the first time in history all people within each polity are in principle drawn into concerned association with each other and with the society as a whole on a differentiated and pluralistic basis.

Given this mobilization of modernizing mankind, it is further contended both that the governing elite recognizes that the people at large must be drawn into participation in the political management of the society and that the people demand that such participation be accorded them. This contention is buttressed by the presumption that the expanded role of government, impinging on more and more aspects of the life of every member of the society, makes the acquisition of some measure of popular control over government increasingly desirable and significant. Furthermore, the drive toward democratization itself, as well as the changed relationships deriving from the implementation of the principle of self-determination, have the effect of encouraging a sense of national participation in one's "own" government as contrasted with subservience to a government which is alien or at least remote and seen as rather an enemy than a friend.

In sum, it is persuasively argued on grounds such as these that democracy is the all but inevitable outcome of the processes of modernization, but I incline to the view that there is still ample room for a skeptical look at such a conclusion.

There would, I assume, be general agreement that new kinds of relationships between the mass of the people and the governing elites are a key feature of the contemporary scene in both the developing and the more advanced societies. Much greater controversy, however, attends any inquiry into the more precise nature of this new relationship in its various modes. I believe it is easily demonstrable that while democracy *may* be the political form taken by developed societies as they ultimately appear, this is by no means necessarily the outcome.

In the case of Africa the impact of colonialism itself has been a socially mobilizing force of great consequence whose dimensions depended on the extent and kind of political rule and economic exploitation which were undertaken. From another angle, one of the starting points of broad popular participation, deriving from the opposition to colonialism, is that the nationalist movements rested much of their claim to legitimacy on their representation of the people as against the alien rulers. The issue of participation was here immediately posed, but the conditions of African access to independence were generally such as not to put to any very effective test the question as to how widely and deeply the nationalist movements had penetrated among the people for whom they claimed to speak. Only in Algeria was there a war of liberation which forced the hardest choices to be made over an extended period of time. Elsewhere the occasional outbursts of violence which erupted within the colonial societies can scarcely be equated with the claims made for the subsequently much publicized struggle for independence. Of these presumably the most notable in recent decades was the Mau Mau movement but this was confined essentially to the Kikuyu, and the political leaders who presided over the transition to Kenyan independence had only an ambiguous relationship to it.

The much less demanding spheres of party membership and participation in elections and party activities produced relatively little trustworthy evidence as to the actual extent of involvement in national political affairs of the rural peasantry which made up the bulk of the population. Once independence was achieved—in almost every instance by peaceful and agreed means, at least in the concluding phases—even that degree of identification with the nation and the nationalist cause was subject to erosion, due, perhaps, both to a lapse of nationalist pressure and to the emergence of issues of internal controversy, whether ethnic or otherwise, deriving in part from differing rates of modernization and mobilization.

With full recognition that the African states differ significantly among themselves, it still appears to be justified to say, as has been indicated above, that with very rare exceptions the characteristic political style of Africa has come to be rule from above by the few; a plebiscitary democracy, if democracy at all, replaced in some cases by military rule. Dealing with the party-states of West Africa, Aristide Zolberg concluded that the inadequacies of the system and the setting of unrealistic goals which cannot be reached expose "the rulers to painful frustrations and in turn to a generalized loss of temper and a ritualization of authority which leads them to treat their countrymen as old-fashioned schoolteachers treat children." [14]

The most interesting exception to this state of affairs is Tanzania where President Nyerere, having earlier withdrawn from his high office as prime minister for the proclaimed purpose of making TANU in actuality a two-way road linking the center and the people of the hinterland, inaugurated the unique system of encouraging two candidates to stand for election in each single-member constituency, opposing each other but operating in a controlled fashion within the general framework of TANU. The defeat of several leading party and governmental figures bore witness to the free choice which was given the voters. (It is, no doubt, ungenerous to wonder whether, given such defeats, there will be the same readiness in succeeding elections for leading figures to put their heads on the electoral block.)

[14] Aristide Zolberg, *Creating Political Order* (Chicago, 1966), p. 159. Zolberg also developed a significant theme which is barely, if at all, touched on in this present paper: the distinction between the modern sector of the West African party-state and the residual sector in which entirely different norms prevail.

Elsewhere in Africa it has been the boast of the single parties, particularly in the more militant "mobilization" systems such as Ghana and
Guinea, that party and nation were one, with all the people sharing in the
party and hence in political control. Among other variants, the principle
of democratic centralism has been advanced as guaranteeing that the
people have freedom to speak and will be heard, but, not surprisingly,
centralism has usually outweighed democracy. To all outward appearance, in both party and government, it has in the ordinary course of events
been the few at the top who in fact exercise such power as generally
inefficient systems can bring to bear (to accuse African governments of
being totalitarian is surely to flatter them unduly); and when an extraordinary course of events turns up, these few at the top may find themselves replaced by another few, perhaps in uniform. The civilian few generally continue to rule under the symbols of democracy, however little of
the substance of democracy they may retain. The military abandon even
the symbols save in the sense that they usually pledge themselves to return
the country to a sounder democracy once they have rid it of the evils
brought on by the politicians.[15] No doubt they often mean it, and sometimes they may even do something about it, as in the case of Ghana.

We live, for the first time in history, in an age of mass society, and in
such a society the people must participate in a fashion in which they have
never participated before. Samuel Huntington has laid down the dictum
that "Mass participation goes hand-in-hand with authoritarian control."[16]
Mass society, as a product of modernization in general and industrialization in particular, cannot have taken very firm root in Africa yet, but
what there is of it tends to fit in with Huntington's version, which is
equally applicable in many other parts of the world, including some of
the advanced countries. For practical purposes what is sought is not the
positive collaboration of the people in choosing those who are to govern
them or in deciding policy issues but rather a "populist" regime in which
the people, guided and indoctrinated from above, support the existing
order by acclaim and play their assigned part in whatever programs the

---

[15] Although they have a certain ring of fantasy, there could not have been loftier
goals set than those of Lt. General Joseph A. Ankrah who held that, given the situation
left by Nkrumah, "there was no other recourse for the Ghana Armed Forces and the
Ghana Police Service but to destroy the tyranny of Kwame Nkrumah, to banish
privilege, overlordism, political opportunism, wasteful pompousness and incompetence,
and thereby to restore to the people of Ghana the blessings of liberty, justice, and
human dignity." "The Future of the Military in Ghana," *Africa Forum* (Summer
1966), p. 7.
[16] "Political Modernization: America Vs. Europe," *World Politics* (April 1966), p.
412. He adds, "Like the states of 17th century Europe, the non-Western countries can
have political modernization or they can have democratic pluralism, but they cannot
normally have both."

leaders of parties and governments may lay out for them. Bread and circuses, propaganda, rallies, plebiscites—these are the instruments of a politically participant society in which participation means control and tutelage from above and indoctrinated acquiescence from below.

Despite the catastrophe of the six-day war, President Nasser in a plebiscite on 2 May, 1968, which brought out 98.2 percent of the registered voters, won approval of his policies by a yes vote of 99.989 percent.[17] Such are the majestic workings of plebiscitary democracy.

Let me close with two points stated with summary brevity:

1. The evidence of history leaves us with no reason to think that the mass of mankind wants to run its own political affairs democratically. The emergence and survival of democracy has been a rare and limited event in other than small local communities. With a handful of exceptions working democracies have been confined in modern times to a few Western European countries and their overseas descendants, now joined by a few others, such as India, Israel, Lebanon, the Philippines, and Ceylon. These latter cases establish that democracy is not necessarily a peculiarly Western European form of government, but they do relatively little to establish the counterproposition that democracy is the desired and workable form of government for the rest of mankind. It is my own inclination to think that most people most of the time have no burning desire to assume political control of their destinies and are content to let someone else take charge of them. We may, of course, be sure that people will want to have some say in the distribution of governmental benefits and penalties, but I feel no confidence that this can be more effectively accomplished (or, perhaps more important, would be felt by the participants to be more effectively accomplished) by the routine working of democratic institutions in a mass society than by sporadic drives or upheavals. The sense of the submergence and insignificance of the individual in the mass is likely everywhere to tell increasingly against the flourishing of faith in the working of the democratic processes. The people will, to be sure, implicitly reserve to themselves the right to throw their rulers out on occasion. When they do throw them out, there may be an interlude of democracy, but the presumption must be that before long another superior authority will take over.

2. Such, surely, has been the general record of history. The continued validity of this record is challenged, however, by some who assert that for the present purpose we have come to the end of one chapter of history and must turn over to a new page. The basic assumption which has already been mentioned, is that the various characteristic processes of modernization, and notably industrialization, radically change the relationships of people within society in such fashion as to make the emergence of democ-

---

[17] *The New York Times* (4 May 1968).

racy both possible and probable. The demand for democratic political participation by the mass of the people, it is held, is likely to become irresistible, and the conditions for the flowering of democratic institutions are created. The major historical substantiation of this thesis is the growth of democracy in Western Europe in conjunction with the spread of enlightenment and the industrial revolution, carried to lands across the seas by migrants from Western Europe. An impressive body of evidence can be brought forward in its support; but an at least equally impressive body of evidence points in the other direction. I believe that it is correct to contend that the coming of modernization and industrialization has been associated more frequently with autocratic than with democratic regimes. The most striking examples which come immediately to mind are Germany, Japan, and the Soviet Union, and I am not persuaded of error by the fact that the first two, defeated in war, have so far maintained the political institutions installed by their democratic conquerers. These are the great countries which may be cited; a number of smaller ones have followed more or less in their footsteps, as, for example, in eastern and southeastern Europe. For such weight as it may add to my argument, I believe it to be the case that henceforward development is almost sure to be undertaken under authoritarian rather than democratic auspices, thus further strengthening the probability that the prospects for democracy in Africa within any time that one can now sensibly calculate are meager indeed.

Conclusion

Conclusion

Observations on Social and Institutional Change in Independent Africa

Michael F. Lofchie

The preceding contributions in this volume are linked by a common underlying attitude about the prospects for successful development in Africa. This attitude, which consists more of a diffuse mood than a precise estimate of development potential, is basically one of qualified pessimism. There is a sense of the enormity of the problems which African nations confront, of the overwhelmingly inhospitable environment both international and domestic in which they have come to independence, and of the extremely limited resources at their disposal with which to alter their social, economic, and institutional circumstances. It may be useful, as a conclusion, to sketch briefly some of the principal theoretical and empirical evidence which informs this attitude.

One of the most ancient tenets of political thought states that men, being rational, can devise and implement institutions suitable for their governance. In this view, political progress, or development, consists of the purposeful creation and refinement of institutions to meet changing conditions. The prescriptive dimension of this tradition is a broad principle calling attention to the need for any institutional framework to be designed both for its particular social setting and for the tasks which will be imposed upon it. Even by this general standard, African nations have been dealt with badly. African nationalist leaders were given very little voice, during the terminal colonial period, in determining what sort of institutional patterns their countries would carry forward to independence. It was widely assumed that progress toward independence meant progress toward the constitutional pattern present in the dominant colonial country. Thus nations under French domination became independent with constitutions patterned closely along Gaullist lines; those under British control became independent with fairly orthodox parliamentary systems.

The problems inherent in this sort of institution building are glaring. It uncritically assumes the transferabilty and relevance of institutions from one social and cultural setting to another with only minor modifications. More importantly, British and French institutions functioned in an economic milieu in which the entrepreneurial and developmental role of the state was far less pronounced than will necessarily be the case in postindependence African society. British and French institutions were designed, as it were, to perform a representative function and have been modified somewhat to administer a certain amount of welfare programming. Even where state administration of major sectors of the economy has occurred, this has taken place only after these economies were developed predominantly under private auspices. It is at best uncertain how well parliamentary institutions can perform in a context in which state structures are expected to play a major role in economic development and social reconstruction. There is little doubt that one of the major dilemmas of African nations has been how to perform a developmental role within institutional frameworks that historically were adapted for far different purposes.

Much of the political process analyzed in this volume may be best understood as a search for a new institutional formula. The uncertain utility of institutions patterned along British and French lines makes this search a critical necessity. It is rendered substantially more difficult, however, by the fact that the inherited institutions, whether or not they are adapted to the purpose, must be put into immediate use to confront the massive tasks of development and modernization. Thus African leaders are compelled to employ European frameworks they have fallen heir to in order to pursue entrepreneurial development programs at the same time that they are deeply involved in a search for more suitable institutional patterns.

Institutional innovation in Africa has been focused most centrally on political parties and has been most conspicuous in the radical states. As described in chapter 2 by Immanuel Wallerstein, these states have sought to lessen their dependence upon foreign and domestic capital investment by building socialist economies. The strategy of socialist development requires a capacity to mobilize and utilize human resources effectively for it depends upon an ability to substitute massive amounts of labor for capital in a wide array of development projects. States pursuing this pattern of development have generally sought to create a particular type of party organization, one which could be used to implement the strategy of human mobilization. The ideal type of party in these circumstances has been seen as possessing a hierarchical structure of authority, a high degree of internal discipline, and a nationwide organization of branches and committees accepting the norm of centralized command in decision making. Without an organization of this type, the capacity of government to organize and deploy the population is correspondingly reduced.

Radical African states have generally not succeeded in creating party organizations of this type. In chapter 9 Henry Bienen suggests that it is far more realistic to conceptualize African political parties in terms of a machine model with highly pluralistic patterns of authority, bargaining between center and periphery, and a very loose structure of command. The full implication of this view is that radical states simply do not possess the organizational instruments required to implement their social and economic intentions. It is possible to speculate that to some extent the difficult predicament of the socialist strategy of development thus far has less to do with the intrinsic merits of the strategy per se than with the inadequacy of available party systems to pursue it.

Postindependence Ghanaian politics provides a dramatic illustration of this generalization. In chapter 4 Barbara Callaway and Emily Card record the failure of CPP leadership in general and of Kwame Nkrumah in particular to maintain a unified and committed party organization in the midst of a socialist economic strategy which required one. Nkrumah's willingness to rely upon expatriate advisers rather than party leaders demoralized the party cadres as did his insistence upon an almost mystical reverence for himself. There emerged an atmosphere of cynicism and corruption in which politics became little more than a struggle for position and patronage. The internal organizational pattern of the CPP during the years preceding the military coup resembled an extreme caricature of the concept of party machine suggested by Bienen. Callaway and Card describe the party as follows:

After 1964, when the CPP became Ghana's only constitutional party and Nkrumah became the lifetime chairman of the party, the ambiguity (between ideal and reality in party organization) became more apparent. The "cult of personality" was encouraged, and the CPP became increasingly a political machine. The party's ideology continued to be directed at mobilizing the people for the tasks of national development, but in actuality the dynamics of the party were directed at vying for positions of influence and power within the party's various auxiliaries.

By the time the coup occurred, the CPP was little more than a loose assortment of competing factions and, as Callaway and Card make clear, this predicament was an integral aspect of the failure of the socialist development strategy.

A high degree of party unity and esprit may be a necessary but not suffi-cient condition for an effective socialist strategy. This is one of the argu-ments in R. Cranford Pratt's essay, chapter 5, on "Cabinet and Presidential Leadership in Tanzania." Pratt suggests that during the period from 1960 to 1966 TANU achieved considerably unity but at a sacrifice in the ration-ality of developmental decision making. Cabinet politics were character-ized by a number of features which Pratt feels were injurious to Tanzania's development as a socialist state. There was a high degree of tolerance for administrative individualism among cabinet members together with a re-luctance to impose collective discipline, a tendency to postpone vital but potentially divisive decisions or to pass them on to the president lest they inject political strain, and a tendency, on occasion, to alter or neglect the recommendations of economic planners and technical experts in the inter-est of political solidarity. TANU was a unified organization but only in the sense that it possessed a strong sense of collegiality and esprit, not in the sense of disciplined commitment to a common purpose. The overall result was that the cohesion of the nationalist period was sustained but at some cost in the capacity of the regime to carry its policies to their fullest potential.

The very looseness of the decision-making process, however, made pos-sible a high degree of representation. Varying interests throughout the society were effectively represented by their spokesmen at the cabinet level. Differing groups, classes, and regions could expect to have their claims articulated and, to some extent, responded to in the highest council of government; for cabinet politics were characterized by bargaining and give and take over major issues rather than the discipline of a transforma-tive political instrument. In general the internal pattern of TANU was far more that of a representative political party than that of an organization intent on social transformation. Since 1966, however, Tanzanian politics have been characterized by far greater unity of purpose. With the public declaration of a socialist policy of development and the announcement of concrete measures to achieve this objective, TANU politics have been changed substantially in the direction of a single focus of political action. The change from a politics of pluralistic accommodation to one of socialist discipline has given rise to a major political dilemma. Is the new discipline which now exists in high levels of the party organization compatible with the process of group representation which had gone on previously?

The dilemma of Tanzanian politics typifies one of the most general fea-tures of independent African political life in both radical and conservative states. There is a strong tension between the two principal commitments of government, first to a process of representation and second to a goal of social transformation. As a norm for the determination of public policy, representation generally involves using available resources to respond to popular demands for improved conditions of life. Expenditures on education, health, and other social services have a compelling justification in the extent to which they help alleviate some of the deprivations of life in an economically underdeveloped society; but the extent to which these alone represent fundamental changes in the social patterns inherited from the colonial period is limited. African governments are on the whole also motivated to implement policies designed to transform inherited patterns. Though such policies may have some consensual basis in society, they often place a government in a position of antagonism to powerful social forces. The "paradox of development," observed by Jonathan S. Barker in his analysis of Senegal in chapter 3, suggests that a government that intends to transform society runs the risk of losing some of its most essential popular support precisely when it is most in need of strength.

Tanzania has been uniquely successful in resolving the tension between representation and transformation. Within a decade of independence there have been great strides made in the creation of a democratic socialist state. The party enjoys overwhelming support throughout the society and its basis in consensual validation seems to include both the policies and the leadership of the regime. Through such institutional innovations as openly contested elections within a single party framework, TANU has made it possible for the policy values and personnel preferences of the Tanzanian people to make a significant impact on the outlook and composition of the political elite. In symbolic ways such as the lowering of officials' salaries and through nationalization of major sectors of the economy, Tanzanian leadership has committed itself to an equalitarian social structure. There is a strong determination to see that development does not occur in such a way as to foster deep economic cleavages between classes or regions and to infuse the development process with a libertarian content. These qualities have made Tanzania a model which other African nations increasingly seek to emulate; but whether they will be successful in doing so is an open question, for radical policies seem destined, in the normal course of things, to generate serious internal strains.

Transformatively inclined nations often seek to implement one or a combination of three different but mutually complementary policies: equalitarianism, capital formation, and state entrepreneurialism. Equality is one of the strongest and most operative values of this century. In many developing countries the prevailing conception of equality goes beyond equality of opportunity or equality of access to government to include substantive equality in social conditions. Virtually all African states include equality of opportunity or equality of access to government as an important developmental objective and initiate policies designed to remove the inequalities inherited from the colonial period. The determination to move in an equalitarian direction is sometimes based on the premise of full substantive equality. The political dangers inherent in such equalitarian policies should not be underestimated. Downwardly mobile groups which feel threatened by a narrowing gap between themselves and less advantaged classes in society have proven to be a volatile political force throughout human history. Since privileged groups are almost invariably in a powerful political position, their capacity to threaten a government with secession, counterrevolution, or obstruction is considerable. At the very least, a government inclined toward equalitarianism faces a prospective loss of support from some of the most influential elements in its society.

Nations motivated toward equalitarian transformation are often hostile toward foreign and private capital investment on the grounds that this builds inequalities into the development process. State capital formation and state entrepreneurship become the chosen alternative. Although it may be easier to control the pattern of income distribution in state-owned rather than privately owned enterprise, no state has yet succeeded in eliminating significant income differentials between managerial, technical, and working classes. Moreover, state entrepreneurialism seems to involve important political costs. In order to build up a reservoir of state capital it becomes necessary to impose austerity measures on some groups in society. Those most frequently chosen are the urban working class and rural peasantry. Since these groups are asked to accept a very real sacrifice in present living conditions on the prospect of greater long-term improvement, they can easily grow resentful of having to bear the brunt of economic sacrifice, particularly at a time when income differentials between themselves and managerial elements are both considerable and highly visible.

This problem can be seen with great clarity in the case of Ghana. Nkrumah's decision to have a period of mixed economic patterns, private and statist, before proceeding to full socialism resulted in a widening of class differentials in the society. Acceptance of a continuing private sector consisting largely of expatriate firms meant in practice that the state was constrained from interfering in the employment and wage policies of businesses comprising a large portion of the economy. The managerial and technical employees of these firms constituted a privileged and well-to-do social stratum. As Africanization occurred in the postindependence period, this stratum came to consist to a greater degree of Ghanaians whose terms of service, style of life, and position in society were comparable to the elite expatriate cadres of the colonial era. As a Ghanaian middle class, they had a deeply vested interest in preserving their position in the society and a determination to do so through political means.

Simultaneous with the preservation of a private economy with its attendant pattern of class differentiation, the Ghanaian state was initiating policies designed to facilitate local capital formation through the imposition of austerity upon subordinate strata in the society. Barbara Callaway and Emily Card have commented that for some segments of the Ghanaian urban working class, real wages in 1963 were lower than for 1939. Nkrumah's government found itself in an impossible predicament. Socialist measures threatened and undermined the confidence of the middle class but working class elements were alienated by the wide and expanding gap between themselves and elite sectors of the society. Working class discontent with the Nkrumah government was so strong that this group, although the designated beneficiary of Ghanaian socialism, offered practically no resistance to the military coup.

To the extent that capital formation is sought elsewhere in Africa through a policy of austerity imposed upon working class groups, the Ghanaian experience has general relevance. For African states do not, on the whole, exhibit the political conditions which make a policy of working class austerity a feasible political strategy over extended periods of time. In attempting to generate capital by this method, African states repeat a portion of Western industrial history. Therefore, a capsule comparison of the two is useful. There is little doubt that successful capital formation in Western society occurred to some extent through the imposition of sustained material deprivation on the lower classes. As this author has argued in chapter 1, this process was facilitated by two essential conditions. First, working classes were not enfranchised during the early industrial period and thus lacked structured opportunity for direct political participation. Second, the prevailing political ethic, whether laissez-faire or mercantilist, did not stress the legitimacy or necessity of state action to improve social conditions. Although working class discontent was considerable, the state was able to resist pressure for reform until the industrial revolution was significantly advanced.

Working class participation is an established fact of political life throughout independent Africa. Such participation was fostered during the nationalist period and is reinforced by a prevailing political culture which stresses the obligation of the state to redress harsh social conditions. It is further reinforced by the salient value of equality which makes social discrepancies appear illegitimate in the eyes of subordinate social classes. The full implication of this set of values is that any strategy of capital formation which depends upon the differential and unequal imposition of austerity or material sacrifice upon various strata in the society is likely to generate massive political discontent. Governments which rely upon this strategy will be increasingly confronted with strong popular pressures for political reform. Their choices will be a dilution of the strategy through acceptance of reformist demands or an attempt to maintain the inequality through coercion.

A comparable dilemma exists with respect to governmental entrepreneurialism. The one invariable aspect of government investment in industrial enterprise is that it involves subtracting funds from those which might be available for social services such as schools and dispensaries. Although state expenditure on projects such as hydroelectric installations, irrigation projects, and improved transportation can be plausibly justified on grounds of long-term economic growth and employment creation, the sacrifices involved in foregoing social services seem in the very nature of things to fall most heavily on the poorer elements in society simply because these groups pay a stiffer price in postponed access to educational and health facilities. The dilemma of inequality inherent in the use of resources to create commercial enterprise is further reinforced and exacerbated by the organizational pattern of modern enterprise itself. Large-scale corporations, whether state or privately owned, are steeply hierarchical in character and produce salient income differences between individuals of varying skills and levels of education. Indeed, a universal tension can be said to exist between the aspiration toward equality as an integral aspect of development and the fact that, due to their hierarchical quality, modernizing institutions such as corporations and bureaucracy add substantially to the amount of inequality in society.

The more radical African states thus confront two mutually reinforcing contradictions: one between representative and transformative commitments and a second between equalitarian aspirations and the hierarchical social implications of various modernizing structures. Political strains generated by these contradictions may be discerned in the more conservative states as well. Jonathan Barker's analysis of the development paradox in Senegal describes the dilemma of a government torn between the need to pursue a policy of representation in order to maintain its existing basis of support and its desire to pursue development policies involving substantial social change. The key issue for Senegal as for so many independent African nations is whether a fragile government can expect to maintain a viable basis of support within a society which its development programs are intended to transform.

The Senegalese government is heavily dependent upon the more privileged strata in the society including rural landowners and traders, commercial elements, and religious and chiefly notables. Whether it will be able to implement policies designed to benefit subordinate classes is indeterminate. Barker describes the dilemma as follows:

We conclude, then, that in principle, but only marginally as yet in practice, development policies threaten to undermine the support which the peanut region has accorded Senghor's party and government. The government appears to be caught between its need for support and its desire to implement its development policies, a circumstance that may explain the uncertainty surrounding the yet unimplemented policies.

The resolution thus far appears to be limited implementation of some development programs but only up to the point where such implementation does not threaten to undermine the existing social structure. This policy helps assure the present stability of Senghor's government, but if development programs continue to be abridged at a point short of offering concrete improvement to disadvantaged classes and regions, these may be expected to constitute an increasing source of pressure for major political and social reforms.

Although the extent to which a radical, or socialist, strategy of development can actually minimize social inequality is indeterminate, its major thrust lies in this direction. The value of equality is more salient than in conservative states and various specific programs are often judged on the basis of their contribution to this objective as well as their relevance to economic growth. The hierarchical nature of modern organization, the need to offer differential rewards for tasks requiring differing skills, and immediate pressures of political expediency may render equality such an elusive objective that the gap between goal and reality will remain quite considerable. But the explicitness of equalitarian values and their role as determinants of public policy create a strong potential for political change in this direction. At the very least, the logic of an equalitarian commitment is to respond to social discontent through concrete reform and to avoid development policies which have a clearly inequalitarian implication.

The conservative path strategy, on the other hand, has a vast potential for leading to expanding regional and class disparities. This is attributable in large measure to the nature of foreign capital investment. Besides gravitating toward areas where there are exploitable resources and a hospitable political climate, foreign firms in Africa tend to locate in cities where there are necessary infrastructural supports such as banking institutions, transportation facilities, and industrial services. The availability of a supply of experienced workers is also an important determinant of industrial location. All these factors mean that foreign financed industrial development generally takes place precisely where a certain amount of such development has previously occurred. Large cities that have already experienced an infusion of foreign capital tend to attract more. Smaller towns and more remote areas do not. The frequent result is an enormous disparity in the level and rate of growth between expanding urban centers, often national capitals, and the pace of change in rural communities.

An infusion of foreign capital also has great potential for creating a severe economic cleavage along class lines within the protoindustrial urban setting. Initially, the managerial element in foreign firms is almost always expatriate and the terms of service for this group reflect not only the level of affluence of a prosperous European middle class but a substantial increment often assumed necessary to attract skilled cadres to service in Africa. As Africanization of management occurs, the terms of service tend to be kept very nearly equal to those of the expatriate element both because Africans with technical and managerial training are often in short supply and because to do otherwise would be considered discriminatory. There gradually emerges a class of African managerial personnel whose level of income and style of life are those of an affluent bourgeoisie. By contrast, the wages of African workers do not compare at all favorably with those of their European counterparts. Indeed, the extremely low level of pay for industrial workers is one of the strongest incentives for investment in Africa. Not only are the material conditions of life of African workers considerably poorer than those in Europe, but the economic gap between the working and managerial classes is greater.

Nor is it likely that the African industrial worker will be able to improve his position vis-à-vis the management stratum. Africans in management are in a very strong bargaining position because of the scarcity of their skills. Indeed, there is evidence that in one or two African countries, the growth of industrial and commercial enterprise spurred by an influx of European capital is so great that vacancies requiring technical skills are being created more rapidly than increases in the supply of trained local personnel. The economic position of the African bourgeoisie in conservative states is further reinforced by a political unwillingness to interfere in wage and employment policy lest this be construed as the cutting edge of an effort to establish state control of the private sector.

Where the African manager-technician benefits by his scarcity, the African worker confronts a problem of massive urban unemployment. The reasons for this unemployment are complex and several factors contribute to it. When new industries are established in Africa, they are normally constructed on as advanced an automated model as possible. For despite the extremely low level of wages for African workers, automation nevertheless results in reduced costs of production. This means that a factory whose output represents a considerable increment in gross national product may have comparatively little significance in creating added employment. Examples of this phenomenon are numerous. One may suffice to illustrate the point. A new textile factory in Dar es Salaam, Tanzania, is able to produce sufficient piece goods for the entire country plus a surplus for export elsewhere in eastern Africa but will probably offer direct employment to less than 750 persons.

A second factor contributing to urban unemployment is an accelerated rate of rural-urban migration. Despite the fact that new industries may do little to create new jobs, the industrial cities take on an appearance of offering great opportunity. A resplendent scenario of new factories, office buildings, and construction sites creates a visual impression which greatly encourages rural-urban movement. The urban appearance of dynamism and growth is in sharp contrast to the slower pace of change in the agricultural economy, but it results in festering urban slums which contain growing masses of unemployed in materially abysmal conditions. The slums contrast cruelly with those sectors of the city which encouraged urban movement in the first place, but for a variety of reasons the outlets for this misery often remain nonpolitical. The high incidence of such phenomena as alcoholism, petty thievery, prostitution, and apathy reveal the human agony of slum life but indicate that the response to the situation has on the whole been a privatization of misery. The potential for long-range politization and for the emergence of radical discontent is enormous, but the more immediate significance of urban employment is that it places a fundamental constraint on the capacity of the African working class to bargain for improved conditions.

An African country which illustrates virtually the entire constellation of conditions associated with the conservative strategy of development is the Ivory Coast. As described by Richard E. Stryker in chapter 6, the Ivory Coast has three particularly significant characteristics: rapid economic growth, a grave developmental imbalance regionally between north and south, and growing urban unemployment. The Ivorian rate of economic growth has been prodigious and is so considerable that some observers are inclined to speak of an Ivorian "miracle." The rapidity of economic development is attributable largely to a heavy infusion of European capital. This has been encouraged not only by attractive investment opportunity but also by a highly receptive ideological climate which views development almost entirely in narrow economic terms.

The nation's capital city, Abidjan, has become the scene of a diversified and rapidly expanding commercial-industrial complex. The expansion of this sector of the Ivorian economy has been so rapid that Africanization is not a major political issue since the growth of vacancies for persons with managerial and technical skills is outstripping the availability of trained Ivorians. At the elite level, the Ivorian economy sustains a growing bourgeoisie composed of both expatriate and indigenous cadres and whose lifestyle reflects the affluence which an infusion of European wealth has made possible.

The politically portentous aspect of the Ivorian miracle is that it has been confined almost entirely to the southern portion of the country; that is, to the capital and its adjacent vicinity. This has meant a grave inequality in the level of wealth between northern and southern regions of the country. A disparity of some dimension had begun in colonial times when the south benefited disproportionately in the establishment of educational institutions, both government and mission sponsored, in the introduction of a commercial export agriculture, and in the development of a transportation and communications infrastructure. These inequalities have been increasingly exacerbated in recent times. By a range of standards including access to higher education, per capita income, and opportunity for participation in the elite levels of the commercial industrial complex, southern Ivorians enjoy substantial and growing advantages over northerners. To illustrate some of the dimensions of this inequality, Stryker points out that per capita income in the south in 1965 was over ten times that of the north, that southern primary school attendance, on a percentage basis, is approximately five to seven times greater, and that the city of Abidjan alone accounts for nearly nine-tenths of all the nation's salaried employees.

The growing disparity between north and south has been accompanied by the emergence of a second major cleavage in the society, that between employed and unemployed in the industrial areas. The population of the city of Abidjan is expected to double in the next decade from a current figure of approximately 500,000 to over 1,000,000. And even this staggering growth comes after a fifteen-year period during which the population had tripled. The stark fact of the matter is that there are simply not jobs available for more than a small fraction of this swelling population. Stryker portrays the combination of regional and urban inequality as follows:

Per capita income in the capital is equally beyond common measure within the hinterland: thirty-seven times the northern average and sixty times the rural northern average. There is thus, understandably, a heavy exodus of youth from the rural north to the southern towns, especially to Abidjan. Even by 1975 it is estimated that Ivorian growth will provide jobs in urban centers for only 9 per cent of the active population, adding urban sprawl and spiraling unemployment in the south to rural stagnation in the north.

Although the patterns of disparity are particularly pronounced in the Ivory Coast, this country is far from unique. Similar patterns of regional and urban disparity can be discerned in other African countries experiencing rapid industrialization.

The tendency for industrial development in Africa to generate such extreme inequality is of immense theoretical relevance. It casts serious doubt on a range of arguments which link industrial modernization with the conditions for democratic politics. The existence of a relationship between economic growth and democracy has been asserted in several ways. For example, growing access to education and increasing literacy reinforced by heightened participation in the modern media of communication have been viewed as the basis of a politically enlightened citizenry which would be unprepared to accept authoritarian appeals and anxious to participate in the political process in pursuit of individual and group interest. Similarly, economic growth is sometimes assumed to be conducive toward moderate forms of participation on the premise that a people who are experiencing improving material conditions are unlikely to support extremist political leaders or movements. In general, economic growth is often considered to be supportive of parliamentary and representative government because it links these institutions to improvements in social conditions and encourages the conviction that future progress can occur within these institutional frameworks.

Economic modernization is sometimes viewed as a stimulant to democratic politics in one additional respect: its capacity to reduce cleavage by producing a pattern of social pluralism corresponding to that often said to exist in Western society. In this view, economic growth fosters a wide array of occupational, functional, and professional associations. These cut across prior lines of cleavage and thereby produce multiple patterns of group membership for individuals throughout the society. Emergent affiliations with new functional and occupational groups intersect with those to regional and ethnic collectivities, creating an integrated network of group involvements. In Western pluralist thought, such cross-cutting ties have great theoretical importance as the primary source of democratic modes of political participation. Persons with memberships in multiple groups are ascribed an interest in the peaceful resolution of conflicts between them and a capacity to empathize more readily with the positions of other segments of society. In addition, overlapping group memberships are viewed as channels of communication for common political values, especially that of the need to bargain out political differences. The full implication of economic modernization in theories which link this process with democracy is a consensual politics of bargaining and compromise in an atmosphere of mutual restraint.

The pattern of industrialization in Africa does not sustain theoretical arguments linking economic growth with democracy. Rather, industrialization has its greatest impact in producing destabilizing inequalities. It is a universal attribute of industrial growth to divide societies into opposed classes: those who sell labor and those who control it. This division is especially severe in Africa due to the particularly wide gap in income between managerial and working classes. Moreover, far from producing cross-cutting group ties which mitigate social cleavage and integrate the society, economic divisions tend to parallel previous patterns of social difference.

One of the most common legacies of the colonial period was the tendency for educational opportunity and access to government employment to be unequally available to different ethnic groups within a society. Industrial growth almost invariably deepens and further entrenches this pattern of inequality, for the process of economic growth is quite similar to colonialism in its tendency to draw unequally from and to confer unequal benefits upon various regional, ethnic, and cultural segments of the society. As a result, industrialization in Africa tends not only to produce a widening gap between elite and mass but also to create an additional pattern of inequality, one in which the various strata of the society, especially the elites, are drawn disproportionately from various ethnic sources. For want of a better term, this situation may be called "proportional inequality."

Political tensions between ethnic groups in Africa are best understood as the consequence of proportional inequality rather than as the product of cultural factors. The fact that conflict takes place between culturally different groups does not mean that cultural differences were the cause of the conflict. Where such tensions emerge they almost always reflect significant inequalities of benefit from and access to economic modernization. The argument that cultural differences are of minor consequence as a source of political conflict has a powerful basis in logical social thought. No other position yields a plausible or intellectually satisfactory solution for the resolution of conflict. The view that ethnic or cultural factors are a source of political conflict carries with it the implicit prescription that the way to reduce political tension is to reduce or eliminate the cultural differences. There is an invidious and entirely questionable assumption that communities with differing cultural patterns cannot amicably coexist. On the other hand, the argument that economic inequality is the trigger mechanism for political conflict between groups of differing cultural identities carries the implicit suggestion that resolution of the conflict lies in reducing the extent of the inequality. There is no prescription for cultural homogenization and there is an assumption that pluralistic cultural communities can enjoy politically harmonious relationships.

Failure to identify the existence of proportional inequalities between cultural groups and to make them central to analysis has resulted in widespread misunderstanding and misrepresentation of political events in Africa. The essence of this misunderstanding is to view ethnicity or, in crude terms, tribalism as a source of political disunity. The analytical error in arguments that place ethnicity at the center of political conflict lies in their tendency to identify the form that a conflict assumes with the content and causes of the conflict. Patterns of political conflict in contemporary Uganda furnish an excellent illustration of this proposition. Uganda's principal political parties could easily be identified with differing ethnic communities. During its organizational lifetime, the Kabaka Yekka (KY) party was most heavily supported by the Buganda people in the south-central portion of the country. The Uganda People's Congress (UPC), though to a far greater extent a national party in terms of geographical distribution of support, had its principal popular basis in the north, particularly among the Lango and Acholi communities. The sheer visibility of differing ethnic bases for the parties has sometimes created an impression that the conflict between them could be understood in terms of ethnic tension.

Writing on agricultural policy in Uganda, in chapter 7, M. Crawford Young makes an important point of the fact that the basic differences between northern and southern Ugandans are essentially economic in nature. Uganda is quite comparable to the Ivory Coast in the extent to which the colonial period led to severe developmental imbalances on a regional basis. The northern areas of the country have benefited substantially less from economic and social change than the southern. Throughout the colonial period, northerners experienced far less development of cash farming for export, had far less opportunity for secondary education, and had far less access to government employment, especially at higher administrative levels, than southerners. Uganda's principal export crops—coffee, cotton, tea, and sugar—are grown almost exclusively in the south and, to a large extent, in the areas bordering Lake Victoria. Hydroelectric and industrial development have also been almost entirely southern in location and the south has, as well, been the center of administration and commerce. The primacy of Buganda in all of these spheres of development has been the most conspicuous feature of a regional economic dualism. Young's article makes it clear that political tensions between northern and southern Ugandans have sprung from this pattern of inequality. Much of the Obote government's development planning was based on the goal of reducing the historic economic discrepancies between north and south.

Since many of the most severe economic discrepancies in Africa occur on a regional basis and therefore coincide roughly with the boundaries between ethnically or culturally differentiated communities (as in Uganda and Ivory Coast), it is critically important to be conceptually precise about the role of culture and ethnicity in African politics. Culture is a vitally creative source of group identity. A community that possesses an articulated tradition of institutional practices defining such matters as religious belief, marriage, inheritance, and kinship naturally derives a profound source of group identity from that tradition. Ethnic heritage is thus a unifying ingredient which confers a sense of common membership upon members of a cultural collectivity. But there is no reason to assume that ethnic heritage is a source of conflict, nor is there any reason to assume that communities with different cultural practices will come into conflict with one another because their cultural practices vary. However, if proportional inequality exists between them, if cultural groups have experienced unequal access to the material advantages of development, there is every reason to assume that the ethnic communities will clash and that the clash will assume an ethnic form.

If proportional distribution of the benefits of development could be achieved, or, more precisely, if the income and occupational distribution patterns of various cultural communities in a society could be made roughly similar, this would do a great deal to eliminate political conflict between culturally differentiated elements in a society. Consistency of terminology warrants calling this set of corrective measures proportional equality. Such measures entail no more than that each ethnic or tribal group should be represented at various levels of the social structure roughly in proportion to its percentage of the population. The concept of proportional equality is less arcane than might initially appear. It is in direct contradiction to one of the most common ideas about the basis of political disunity in Africa, namely, the idea that disunity results from lack of a common identity. The notion of proportional equality suggests that common identity is far less essential to political integration than economic equality among groups that have different identities based on differing cultures and traditions.

The idea of proportional equality has had a considerable impact on development planning in Africa. Much planning exhibits an implicit premise that the correction of regional economic imbalances should be the primary focus of directed political change. This is true, for example, of both the Ivory Coast and Uganda. Development planning in each of these societies has the objective of reducing developmental imbalances between north and south. The political assumption underlying this planning is that the lowering of regional disparities will diminish the level of ethnic and, therefore, political tension in the society. It is uncertain whether this assumption will be fully tested in either of these societies or elsewhere, however, for the correction of regional imbalances has proven in practice to be an extremely elusive goal.

The extent of this elusiveness is perhaps best exemplified by the recent political experience of Uganda. Before the military coup of January 1971, the Uganda government appeared, in certain respects, to be well situated to alter regional economic patterns. The governing party, the Uganda People's Congress (UPC), had its principal basis of popular support within precisely those areas and strata of the society its development policies were intended to benefit, the relatively poor northern farming population. The core of the party's strength was in the districts of Acholi and Lango. Since the UPC was not tied to the more privileged farming classes in the relatively well-to-do southern areas of the country, it was considerably freer than many dominant parties in Africa to pursue policies with a redistributive, equalitarian implication. Indeed, since early 1966, President Obote had indicated a substantial willingness to alienate the south if this were the price of bringing economic growth to the northern regions.

Despite its popular strength in the north, the UPC had to confront several important constraints on its development policy. One stemmed from the intrinsic difficulty of improving conditions of life in agricultural communities at a time when world terms of trade are unfavorable to producers of primary agricultural products. Crawford Young's essay, "Agricultural Policy in Uganda" (chapter 7), illustrates the deeper complexity of this problem. In order to elicit the participation of northern farmers in schemes designed to boost their income, the government found it necessary to encourage heightened expectations. Otherwise, the incentive for mass participation in new agricultural programs might not be sufficient. The grave risk in such a policy was that if expectations outstripped real performance, a possibility which world market conditions made likely, the UPC would have succeeded only in alienating its northern supporters. Moreover, there was the added danger that as economic growth began to take place in the north, there would be intraregional developmental imbalances, either between districts or between groups. To the extent that the new military government has found popular support in the northern areas formerly loyal to the UPC, this factor seems to account for it.

The UPC had at all times to pursue a delicate and complex policy walking a sort of political tightrope between north and south. Its attempt to shift some agricultural production from south to north was constrained by a sense that if southern producers became completely alienated from the society, they might cease to cooperate altogether and their vital contribution to the national economy would be lost. If this should occur before northern commercial production was well underway, the society could be left without an economic base. At the same time, government efforts to involve northern farmers in the process of commercial production were limited by the danger that heightened expectations could easily lead to political resentment and frustration should these expectations be unmet.

Government policy depended at times upon the use of force. Buganda resistance to the policy of regional economic redistribution became so great that in early 1966 the government had to employ the army as an instrument of political pacification in that area. The Kabaka Yekka party (KY), identified with vested Buganda interests, was proscribed and a state of emergency was declared bringing all open political activity in Buganda to a halt. The government was also compelled to seek new institutional arrangements to reinforce redistributive development programming. In the spring of 1966, President Obote introduced a new constitution which deprived several southern kingdoms of certain autonomous governmental powers granted to them at independence and which considerably strengthened the legal authority of the president and the central government administration.

Neither military coercion nor constitutional centralization, however, endowed the Obote regime with an institutional capacity politically adequate for economic transformation. Throughout the independence period, effective implementation of regional development policy was hampered by institutional factors. One source of weakness was the bureaucracy. The Obote government, like that of Kwame Nkrumah, had to depend for the execution of its policies upon a bureaucracy which was profoundly hostile to them. The overwhelming majority of Uganda civil servants were from southern districts of the country, especially Buganda, and their political sympathies were predominantly with the south. This situation became especially severe after 1966 when, with the dismantling of the Buganda Kingdom Government, a large number of Buganda civil servants were absorbed into higher echelons of the central government civil service. Not only did numerous members of this group have close family ties with well-to-do southern coffee farmers, but many had also been particularlly embittered at the deprivation of southern constitutional autonomy and the severity of the army's occupation of Buganda Kingdom. Thus, among a great many government administrators, economic interest and ethnic identification converged to produce a deep antipathy to economic policies favorable to the north. Bureaucratic unwillingness to implement such policies became a major constraint on economic change.

A second source of institutional weakness was the fragmented and internally factionalized character of the governing party. The organizational politics of the UPC corresponded closely to Henry Bienen's model of a political machine. Since its inception as a coalition of two previously existing party organizations, the Uganda People's Union and one wing of the Uganda National Congress, UPC politics had reflected a series of regional and ideological splits. Even in the north where the party had its greatest popular support, the UPC was organizationally weak. In Lango district, for example, which was the heart of the party's strength and the home district of the president, the UPC numbered only about 2,000 dues-paying members out of a total population of over 300,000 in 1965. This pattern not only prevented the party from imposing effective discipline upon a recalcitrant bureaucracy, but also prevented it from acting on its own as an instrument of developmental change.

In a political context of bureaucratic antipathy and party fragmentation, President Obote was compelled to depend almost entirely upon the support of the army to sustain his authority. This dependence, however, placed the army in a position to extract major economic concessions. By 1968, Uganda's defense expenditures represented over 10 percent of the national budget as compared with less than 7 percent in Kenya and less than 4 percent in Tanzania. During that year, Uganda's total defense expenditures were nearly equal to those of Kenya and Tanzania combined. The political leverage of the Uganda army was also reflected in a pattern of extremely high salaries, especially at noncommissioned ranks. A Uganda private, for example, earned a base salary of approximately $685, in 1968, as compared with $310 in Kenya. At the rank of sergeant, the figures were $1,225 per year and $760 per year respectively. These figures are particularly significant in view of the fact that the average annual per capita income for Africans in Uganda at the time was substantially less then $50. At the level of commissioned officer, salaries corresponded closely to those for the highest ranks of the civil service. Such figures as these, combined with the fact that the army had also been able to extract a policy of rapid promotion and generous fringe benefits, lead to the inescapable conclusion that the Uganda army had come to occupy a highly privileged position within the society and constituted a kind of economic class.

The government's dependence upon the army was the cruel irony of Uganda politics for it confronted the political system with a unique form of the paradox of development. Despite the fact that the Obote regime had its mass base in the north where policies of economic redistribution were highly popular, the government was dependent for political support upon a military establishment with vested economic interests of its own. To the extent that President Obote sought to implement the radical socialist policies with which he had increasingly identified himself since late 1969, he clearly threatened the economic stake of the major effective buttress for his authority. It was by no means accidental that the military coup occurred within a year after Obote announced the first concrete steps toward nationalization of the economy.

Thus, the notion of a paradox of development provides a highly persuasive explanation for Uganda's military coup. The real basis of political authority in Uganda had lain not so much with the government's popular base in the north as in an uneasy accommodation with a privileged military class. The government's commitment to a policy of equalitarian redistribution threatened the interests of this class no less than it threatened those of the wealthy southern farmers. No other explanation can account for the unusual political alliance which has emerged since the coup occurred. This alliance unites an army officered and staffed almost entirely by northern Ugandans recruited initially from the lower strata of northern society with farming and administrative classes drawn overwhelmingly from the south.

The Ivorian regime also faces an extreme form of the development paradox. Regional and therefore ethnic inequalities are expanding rather than narrowing, for the rate of growth in the south is so high that it is doubtful whether even a dedicated commitment to administered development would enable the north to keep pace. Nothing less than a deliberate effort to arrest or slow down the southern boom and to redistribute economic resources regionally on a massive scale would be likely to correct the imbalance. Even if the political will for such a policy were present, the government would face major difficulties in implementing it, for this would certainly tend to undermine its basis of support.

The Houphouet-Boigny government has its principal popular base largely in the south and especially among well-to-do elements which are advantaged in the present social structure: businessmen, professionals, civil servants, and export farmers. This constituency would be strongly disinclined to accept policy changes which threaten its level of privilege and the ideological outlook of the current leadership does not indicate a willingness to alienate its major sources of strength. The government's reluctance to question the development strategy of continuing capital investment for the south has its obverse side in the generally lethargic character of administered development in the north.

The logic of the present situation is toward increasing instability and heightened pressure for radical change. For as regional and ethnic inequalities grow they become increasingly tantamount to class phenomena. At some point the extent of inequality is likely to become so great that the principal political issue for the society will cease to be a matter of equitable ethnic representation in an ongoing socioeconomic system and will become a matter of fundamental cleavage between privileged and subordinate strata in the society. There is growing potential for a radical coalition composed of northern peasant farmers and urban discontented groups. Tied as the present regime is to a base of support among commercial and bourgeois elements, and committed as it is to a perceived need to maintain a hospitable political climate for European capital, the present government seems unable even to conceptualize the direction of present trends, not to speak of its ineffectiveness in mounting a policy to halt the course of events.

The nature of political change in Ivory Coast suggests that it is important to assess the implications of the two forms of inequality which have emerged as important in many independent African nations, proportional inequality and class inequality. The concept of proportional equality, of course, addresses itself only to the first of these. The changes it implies are modest ones which do not involve fundamental alteration of the social structure. The implicit recommendation is simply that relatively disadvantaged ethnic communities be made the focus of planned efforts to equalize communal participation in the ongoing system. Nevertheless, proportional inequality is likely to remain an important source of political conflict in Africa, for current evidence does not on the whole indicate that efforts to achieve equal ethnic representation and participation in the structures of modernization have been successful. Proportional inequalities are also likely to be important in one additional respect. By their sheer saliency and visibility they tend to obscure the growing importance of class inequalities and thereby create a false impression that ethnic disunity is the principal issue in political development.

Even if proportional equality could be achieved, ongoing processes of economic modernization will tend to produce a growing pattern of social cleavage along class lines. Indeed, for reasons described in chapter 1, "Political Constraints on African Development," emergent class cleavages in Africa may be expected to be far more severe and to place far greater strain on emergent constitutional institutions than was the case at a corresponding point in the Western industrial revolution. Since the principal arguments for this position have been stated in that essay, they need only be briefly summarized here. First, industrialization under conditions of automation and technological complexity creates a far wider social fissure than gradual industrialization from labor intensive to mechanized processes of production. Automated production, for example, creates a major social break between the class of trained personnel with managerial and technical skills and the class of relatively unskilled laborers. In African countries the former are often remunerated at wage levels higher than those prevailing in Europe whereas the wages of African manual workers are only a small fraction of those in Western societies. In addition, automation creates the potential for mass urban unemployment. Not only can great increases in economic output be achieved with relatively little increase in employment opportunity, especially for unskilled or semiskilled workers, but the new industrial cities act as a magnet for considerable migration from the countryside to the city. The presence of unemployed rural migrants in the industrial cities is a basic constraint on the capacity of the workers to improve their conditions and, in this way, contributes to the persistence of a wide social gap between managerial and working classes.

Second, the industrial revolution in Africa is producing an immensely wider gap between the city and the countryside than was the case during the early phases of the industrial revolution in Western countries. To some extent, this phenomenon is also attributable to the intrinsic difficulty of having an industrial revolution at a time when industrial technology is already highly advanced. There is a strong tendency for industrial modernization to be concentrated in the urban context and for processes of production in the agricultural sector to be changed very little by comparison. This is in striking contrast to much Western experience where the industrial revolution has been as much a rural as an urban phenomenon with a clear thrust toward the application of new forms of machinery and labor-saving techniques to agricultural as well as industrial production. Indeed, mechanized harvesting was probably essential if the rural areas were to provide for the swelling industrially employed urban populations. Mechanization of agricultural production has been slow to occur in Africa and the result is a massive gap not only in income but also in overall life-style between urban and rural areas. As this gap increases, it is likely to focus rural resentment increasingly on the disparity in income distribution between the more affluent elements in the city and the relatively deprived character of the farming population.

Finally, there is every likelihood that subordinate strata in Africa will be far more assertive in their political expression of socioeconomic grievances than was the case in the West. Western working classes did not have the right to vote until relatively late in the industrial revolution and, for some time, confronted an antiwelfarist political climate which discouraged the articulation of economic demands. By the time that Western working classes were in a position to make ameliorative demands on the political system, through a gaining of the franchise, through a change of political climate, and through the creation of politically strong union organizations, the industrial process was sufficiently well advanced in terms of growing productivity for a number of the more material grievances to be met. Indeed, this fact may help explain the bread-and-butter orientation of many Western unions and their reluctance to challenge the pattern of income distribution as a whole. African workers are in a better position to be political participants from a very early point in the process of industrialization. Not only is suffrage universal in African countries, but also, due to the recent legacy of the nationalist experience, there is a strong sense of the legitimacy of mass participation and mass articulation of social grievances. Moreover, the prevailing political ethic throughout Africa is one which stresses the necessity of state action in the social sphere. As industrialization occurs, the intensity of equalitarian and redistributive demands upon the state is likely to grow correspondingly.

In a previous essay in this volume, chapter 10, Rupert Emerson raises the argument that the economic requisites of democracy, as they are most generally understood, are lacking in Africa due to the low level of economic transformation. The question being posed in this essay is parallel to that argument: given the vast historical differences between the character of the industrial revolution in Western society and that currently underway in African society, will economic growth produce a social basis for democratic politics or a social structure which, due to the profound cleavages in it, is inhospitable to democracy? The balance of evidence would appear to indicate a future of increasing class politics.

Bibliography

Bibliography

GENERAL WORKS

ABRAHAM, WILLIE E. *The Mind of Africa.* London and Chicago, 1962 and 1969.

ADU, AMISHADAI L. *The Civil Service in New African States.* New York, 1965.

ALMOND, GABRIEL A., and JAMES S. COLEMAN, eds. *The Politics of Developing Areas.* Princeton, 1960.

AMERICAN SOCIETY OF AFRICAN CULTURE. *Pan-Africanism Reconsidered.* Berkeley, 1962.

BALANDIER, GEORGES. *Sociologie Actuelle de l'Afrique Noire.* Paris, 1963.

BING, GEOFFREY. *Reap The Whirlwind.* London, 1968.

BOHANNAN, PAUL. *Africa and Africans.* New York, 1964.

BREZEZINSKI, ZBIGNIEW. *Africa and the Communist World.* Stanford, 1963.

BUCHMANN, JEAN. *L'Afrique Noire Independante.* Paris, 1962.

BUELL, RAYMOND L. *The Native Problem in Africa.* 2 vols. New York, 1928.

BURKE, FRED G. *Africa's Quest for Order.* Englewood Cliffs, 1965.

———. *Public Administration in Africa.* Syracuse, 1967.

BUSTIN, EDOUARD. *Guide des Partis Africains.* Brussels, 1962.

CARTER, GWENDOLYN. *Independence for Africa.* New York, 1960.

———, ed. *Five African States: Responses to Diversity.* Ithaca, 1963.

———, ed. *African One-Party States.* Ithaca, 1964.

———, ed. *National Unity and Regionalism in Eight African States.* Ithaca, 1966.

CARTER, GWENDOLYN, and WILLIAM O. BROWN. *Transition in Africa: Studies in Political Adaptation.* Boston, 1958.

COLEMAN, JAMES, ed. *Education and Political Development.* Princeton, 1967.

COLEMAN, JAMES S., and C. ROSBERG, eds. *Political Parties and National Integration in Tropical Africa.* Berkeley, 1966.

COWAN, L. GRAY. *The Dilemmas of African Independence.* New York, 1968.

COWAN, L. GRAY, JAMES O'CONNELL, and DAVID G. SCANLON, eds. *Education and Nation-Building in Africa.* New York, 1965.

DAVIDSON, BASIL. *Which Way Africa?* Baltimore, 1964.

DIA, MAMDOU. *The African Nations and World Solidarity.* New York, 1961.

DUBOIS, W. E. B. *The World and Africa.* New York, 1947.

DUMONT, RENE. *False Start in Africa.* London, 1966.

EMERSON, RUPERT. *From Empire to Nation.* Cambridge, Mass., 1962.

——. *Africa and United States Policy.* Englewood Cliffs, 1967.

EMERSON, RUPERT, and MARTIN KILSON, eds. *The Political Awakening of Africa.* Englewood Cliffs, 1965.

FANON, FRANTZ. *The Wretched of the Earth.* New York, 1963.

——. *Toward the African Revolution.* New York, 1967.

FORTES, MEYER, and E. E. EVANS-PRITCHARD, eds. *African Political Systems.* London, 1940.

FRIEDLAND, WILLIAM H., and CARL G. ROSBERG, eds. *African Socialism.* Stanford, 1964.

GANN, LEWIS, and PETER DUIGAN. *Burden of Empire: An Appraisal of Western Colonialism in Africa South of the Sahara.* New York, 1967.

HAILEY, LORD (William Malcolm Hailey). *An African Survey.* London, 1955.

HAMRELL, SVEN, and CARL G. WIDSTRAND, eds. *The Soviet Bloc, China, and Africa.* Uppsala, 1964.

HANNA, WILIAM JOHN, ed. *Independent Black Africa.* Chicago, 1964.

HODGKIN, THOMAS L. *Nationalism in Colonial Africa.* London and New York, 1957.

——. *African Political Parties.* Harmondsworth, 1962.

JAHN, JANHEINZ. *Muntu: An Outline of the New African Culture.* London and New York, 1961.

JULY, ROBERT W. *The Origins of Modern African Thought.* London, and New York, 1968.

KAMARCK, ANDREW M. *The Economics of African Development.* New York, 1967.

KIMBLE, GEORGE H. *Tropical Africa.* 2 vols. New York, 1961.

LaPALOMBARA, JOSEPH G., ed. *Bureaucracy and Political Development.* Princeton, 1967.

LaPALOMBARA, JOSEPH G., and MYRON WEINER, eds. *Political Parties and Political Development.* Princeton, 1967.

LEGUM, COLIN. *Africa, A Handbook to the Continent.* London, 1961.

——. *Pan-Africanism.* New York, 1965.

LEWIS, WILLIAM A. *Attitude to Africa.* Harmondsworth, 1951.

LEWIS, WILLIAM H., ed. *New Forces in Africa.* Washington, 1962.

LEYS, COLIN, ed. *Politics and Change in Developing Countries.* London, 1969.

McKAY, VERNON. *Africa in World Politics.* New York, 1963.

——. *African Diplomacy.* New York, 1966.

MAIR, LUCY. *The New Africa.* London, 1967.

MAZRUI, ALI A. *The Anglo-African Commonwealth: Political Friction and Cultural Fusion.* London and New York, 1967.

——. *Towards a Pax Africana.* London and Chicago, 1967.

——. *On Heroes and Uhuru-Worship.* London, 1967.

——. *Violence and Thought: Essays on Social Tensions in Africa.* New York, 1970.

MBOYA, TOM. *Freedom and After.* London and Boston, 1963.

MEZU, SEBASTIAN O., ed. *The Philosophy of Pan-Africanism.* Washington, 1965.

——. *Léopold Sédar Senghor et la Défense et Illustration de la Civilisation Noire.* Paris, 1968.

MIDDLETON, JOHN, and DAVID TAIT, eds. *Tribes Without Rulers.* London, 1958.

MILCENT, ERNEST, and MONIQUE SORDET. *Léopold Sédar Senghor et la Naissance de l'Afrique Moderne.* Paris, 1969.

NKRUMAH, KWAME. *I Speak of Freedom.* London, 1961.

———. *Africa Must Unite.* New York and London, 1963.

———. *Consciencism.* London, 1964.

———. *Neo-Colonialism: The Last Stage of Imperialism.* New York, 1966.

NYERERE, JULIUS K. *Freedom and Unity.* London and Nairobi, 1967.

OLIVER, ROLAND, and J. D. FAGE. *A Short History of Africa.* Harmondsworth, 1962.

PADELFORD, NORMAN J., and RUPERT EMERSON, eds. *Africa and International Organization.* Boston, 1962.

———. *Africa and World Order.* New York, 1963.

PADMORE, GEORGE. *Pan-Africanism or Communism.* London and New York, 1956.

PYE, LUCIAN W., ed. *Communications and Political Development.* Princeton, 1963.

PYE, LUCIAN W., and SIDNEY VERBA, eds. *Political Culture and Political Development.* Princeton, 1965.

QUAISON-SACKLEY, ALEX. *Africa Unbound: Reflections of an African Statesman.* London and New York, 1963.

QUIGG, PHILIP W., ed. *Africa—A Foreign Affairs Reader.* New York, 1964.

RIVKIN, ARNOLD. *Africa and the West.* New York, 1962.

ROTBERG, ROBERT I. *A Political History of Tropical Africa.* New York, 1964.

ROTHCHILD, DONALD. *Toward Unity in Africa.* Washington, 1960.

———, ed. *The Politics of Integration.* Nairobi, 1968.

SEGAL, RONALD. *African Profiles.* Baltimore and Harmondsworth, 1962.

SENGHOR, LEOPOLD SEDAR. *On African Socialism.* New York, 1964.

SHEPHERD, GEORGE W. *The Politics of African Nationalism.* New York, 1962.

SITHOLE, NDABANINGI. *African Nationalism.* London, 1959.

SPIRO, HERBERT J. *Politics in Africa.* Englewood Cliffs, 1962.

———, ed. *Africa The Primacy of Politics.* New York, 1966.

———. *Patterns of African Development.* Englewood Cliffs, 1967.

TEVOEDJRE, ALBERT. *L'Afrique revoltée.* Paris, 1958.

WALLERSTEIN, IMMANUEL M. *Africa: The Politics of Independence.* New York, 1961.

———, ed. *Social Change: The Colonial Situation.* New York, 1966.

———. *Africa: The Politics of Unity.* New York, 1967.

WAUTHIER, CLAUDE. *The Literature and Thought of Modern Africa.* New York, 1967.

WEINSTEIN, BRIAN. *African Schools of Public Administration.* Boston, 1965.

WELCH, CLAUDE. *Soldier and State in Africa.* Evanston, 1970.

WIDSTRAND, CARL G. *Development and Adult Education in Africa.* Uppsala, 1965.

———, ed. *African Boundary Problems.* Stockholm, 1969.

WOOD, DAVID, and W. F. GUTTERIDGE. *The Armed Forces of African States.* London, 1966.

YOUNGER, KENNETH. *Public Service in New States.* New York, 1960.
ZARTMAN, I. WILLIAM. *International Relations in the New Africa.* Englewood Cliffs, 1966.

REGIONAL AND COUNTRY STUDIES
AFRIFA, AKWASI. *The Ghana Coup.* London, 1967.
APTER, DAVID E. *The Political Kingdom in Uganda.* Princeton, 1961.
————. *Ghana in Transition.* New York, 1963.
AUSTIN, DENNIS. *West Africa and the Commonwealth.* London, 1957.
————. *Politics in Ghana, 1946–1960.* London, 1964.
AWA, EME O. *Federal Government in Nigeria.* Berkeley, 1964.
AWOLOWO, OBAFEMI. *Thoughts on the Nigerian Constitution.* Ibadan
and London, 1966.
————. *The People's Republic.* Ibadan, 1968.
BARBOUR, KENNETH M. *The Republic of the Sudan.* London, 1961.
BENNETT, GEORGE. *Kenya, A Political History.* London, 1963.
BENNETT, GEORGE, and GARL G. ROSBERG. *The Kenyatta Election—
Kenya 1960–61.* New York and London, 1961.
BIENEN, HENRY. *Tanzania: Party Transformation and Economic Develop-
ment.* Princeton, 1967.
BIRMINGHAM, WALTER, I. NEUSTADT, and E. N. OMABOE, eds. *A
Study of Contemporary Ghana.* Evanston, 1966.
BOURRET, F. M. *Ghana: The Road to Independence.* Stanford, 1960.
BRETTON, HENRY L. *Power and Stability in Nigeria.* New York, 1962.
————. *The Rise and Fall of Kwame Nkrumah.* New York, 1966.
BURKE, FRED G. *Local Government and Politics in Uganda.* Syracuse, 1964.
————. *Tanganyika: Preplanning.* Syracuse, 1965.
BUSTIN, EDOUARD. *La Décentralisation Administrative et l'Évolution des
Structures Politiques en Afrique Orientale Britannique; Éléments d'une
Étude Comparative.* Liege, 1958.
CASTAGNO, ALPHONSO A. *Somalia.* New York, 1959.
CLIFFE, LIONEL, ed. *One-Party Democracy.* Nairobi, 1967.
COLEMAN, JAMES S. *Togoland.* New York, 1956.
————. *Nigeria—Background to Nationalism.* Berkeley, 1960.
COWAN, L. GRAY. *Local Government in West Africa.* New York, 1959.
COX, RICHARD. *Pan-Africanism in Practice.* London and New York, 1964.
————. *Kenyatta's Country.* London, 1965.
CROWDER, MICHAEL. *Senegal—A Study in French Assimilation Policy.*
New York, 1967.
————. *West Africa Under Colonial Rule.* London, 1968.
DAVIDSON, BASIL, and ADENEKAN ADEMOLA, eds. *The New West
Africa.* London, 1953.
DIAMOND, STANLEY. *Nigeria: Model of a Colonial Failure.* New York,
1967.
DIAMOND, STANLEY, and FRED G. BURKE, eds. *The Transformation
of East Africa.* New York, 1967.
EZERA, KALU. *Constitutional Developments in Nigeria.* Cambridge, 1960.
FALLERS, LLOYD, and AUDREY RICHARDS, eds. *The King's Men—
Leadership and Status in Buganda on the Eve of Independence.* Lon-
don, 1964.

FITCH, BOB, and MARY OPPENHEIMER. *Ghana: The End of an Illusion.* New York, 1968.

FOLTZ, WILLIAM J. *From French West Africa to the Mali Federation.* New Haven, 1965.

GANN, LEWIS, and PETER DUIGNAN. *White Settlers in Tropical Africa.* Harmondsworth, 1962.

GARDINIER, DAVID. *Cameroon—United Nations Challenge to French Policy.* London and New York, 1963.

GENOUD, ROGER. *Nationalism and Economic Development in Ghana.* New York, 1969.

GHAI, DHARAM P. *Portrait of a Minority: Asians in East Africa.* Nairobi and London, 1965.

GRAY, RICHARD. *The Two Nations—The Rhodesias and Nyasaland.* London, 1965.

GREEN, REGINALD H., and K. G. V. KRISHNA. *Economic Cooperation in Africa Retrospect and Prospect.* Nairobi, 1967.

GREEN, REGINALD H., and ANN SEIDMAN. *Unity or Poverty?* Harmondsworth, 1968.

GREENFIELD, RICHARD. *Ethiopia—A New Political History.* New York and London, 1965.

HALL, RICHARD S. *Zambia.* London and New York, 1965 and 1967.

HENDERSON, K. D. D. *Sudan Republic.* London, 1965.

HESS, ROBERT L. *Italian Colonialism in Somalia.* Chicago, 1966.

HODGKIN, THOMAS. *Nigerian Perspectives.* London, 1960.

HODGKIN, THOMAS, and RUTH SCHACHTER. *French-Speaking West Africa in Transition.* New York, 1961.

HOLT, P. M. *A Modern History of Sudan.* New York and London, 1966.

HOSKYNS, CATHERINE. *The Congo Since Independence.* London and New York, 1965.

HUXLEY, ELSPETH, and MARGERY PERHAM. *Race and Politics in Kenya.* London, 1956.

INGHAM, Kenneth. *The Making of Modern Uganda.* London, 1958.

JAHN, JANHEINZ. *Through African Doors.* London, 1962.

JESMAN, CZESLAW. *The Russians in Ethiopia.* London, 1958.

———. *The Ethiopian Paradox.* London and New York, 1963.

JUNOD, VIOLAINE I., ed. *The Handbook of Africa.* New York, 1963.

KAUNDA, KENNETH. *Black Government.* Lusaka, 1960.

———. *Zambia Shall Be Free.* London, 1962.

———. *Zambia, Independence and Beyond. The Speeches of Kenneth Kaunda.* Ed. by Colin Legum. London, 1966.

KILSON, MARTIN L. *Political Change in a West African State.* Cambridge, Mass., 1966.

KIMBLE, DAVID. *A Political History of Ghana.* London, 1963.

KITCHEN, HELEN, ed. *Handbook of African Affairs.* New York, 1964.

LeFEVER, ERNEST W. *Crisis in The Congo.* Washington, 1965.

———. *Uncertain Mandate: Politics of the U.N. Congo Operation.* Baltimore, 1967.

LEGUM, COLIN. *Congo Disaster.* Baltimore and Harmondsworth, 1961.

LEMARCHAND, RENÉ. *Political Awakening in The Congo.* Berkeley and Los Angeles, 1964.

————. *Rwanda and Burundi*. New York, 1970.
LEVINE, DONALD. *Wax and Gold—Tradition and Innovation in Ethiopian Culture*. Chicago, 1965.
LEVINE, VICTOR T. *The Cameroons From Mandate to Independence*. Berkeley, 1964.
————. *Political Leadership in Africa*. Stanford, 1967.
LEWIS, I. M. *A Pastoral Democracy*. London, 1961.
————. *The Modern History of Somaliland*. London and New York, 1965.
LEWIS, WILLIAM A. *Politics in West Africa*. London and Toronto, 1965.
LEWIS, WILLIAM H., ed. *French-Speaking Africa*. New York, 1965.
LEYS, COLIN. *Politicians and Policies*. Nariobi, 1967.
LIEBENOW, J. G. *Liberia: The Evolution of Privilege*. Ithaca and London, 1969.
LISTOWEL, J. *The Making of Tanganyika*. New York and London, 1965.
LOFCHIE, MICHAEL. *Zanzibar: Background to Revolution*. Princeton, 1965.
MACKENZIE, W. J. M., and K. ROBINSON, eds. *Five African Elections*. London, 1960.
MACKINTOSH, JOHN P. *Nigerian Government and Politics*. London and Evanston, 1966.
MARKOVITZ, IRVING LEONARD. *Leopold Sedar Senghor and the Politics of Negritude*. New York, 1969.
MERRIAM, ALAN P. *Congo:Background of Conflict*. Evanston, 1961.
MILCENT, ERNEST. *L'A.O.F. Entre en Scène*. Paris, 1958.
————. *Au Carrefour des Options Africaines, Le Sénégal*. Paris, 1965.
MORGENTHAU, RUTH S. *Political Parties in French-Speaking West Africa*. London, 1964.
MULFORD, DAVID. *Zambia: The Politics of Independence*. London, 1967.
NERES, PHILIP. *French-Speaking West Africa*. New York and London, 1962.
NIELSEN, WALDEMAR A. *African Battleline*. New York, 1965.
NKRUMAH, KWAME. *Challenge of The Congo*. London and New York, 1967.
————. *Dark Days in Ghana*. New York, 1969.
NSARKOH, J. *Local Government in Ghana*. Accra, 1964.
NYE, JOSEPH S. *Pan-Africanism and East African Integration*. Cambridge, Mass., 1967.
O'BRIEN, CONOR CRUISE. *To Katanga and Back*. London and New York, 1962.
ODINGA, OGINGA. *Not Yet Uhuru*. London, 1967.
ODUHO, JOSEPH, and WILLIAM DENNY. *The Problems of the Southern Sudan*. London, 1963.
PADMORE, GEORGE. *The Gold Coast Revolution*. London, 1953.
PERHAM, MARGERY. *Native Administration in Nigeria*. New York and London, 1962.
POST, KENNETH. *The New States of West Africa*. Baltimore, 1964.
ROSBERG, CARL G., JR. *An East African Federation*. New York, 1963.
ROSBERG, CARL G., JR., and JOHN NOTTINGHAM. *The Myth of Mau Mau*. Stanford, 1966.
ROTBERG, ROBERT I. *The Rise of Nationalism in Central Africa*. Cambridge, Mass., 1965.
SAID, BESHIR MOHAMAD. *The Sudan: Crossroads of Africa*. London, 1965.

SCHWARZ, F. A. O. *Nigeria: The Tribes, the Nation, or the Race.* Cambridge, Mass., 1965.
SCHWARZ, WALTER. *Nigeria.* London and New York, 1968.
SEGAL, RONALD. *Political Africa.* London, 1961.
SHEPHERD, GEORGE W. *They Wait in Darkness.* New York, 1955.
SKINNER, ELLIOT. *The Mossi of Upper Volta.* Stanford, 1964.
SKLAR, RICHARD L. *Nigerian Political Parties.* Princeton, 1963.
SNYDER, FRANK. *One-Party Government in Mali.* New Haven, 1965.
SOUTHWOLD, MARTIN. *Bureaucracy and Chiefship in Buganda.* Kampala, 1960.
TAYLOR, JAMES C. *The Political Development of Tanganyika.* Stanford, 1963.
TEVOEDJRE, ALBERT. *Pan-Africanism in Action; An Account of the UAM in West Africa.* Cambridge, 1965.
THOMPSON, VIRGINIA, and RICHARD ADLOFF. *French West Africa.* Stanford, n.d.
——. *The Emerging States of French Equatorial Africa.* Stanford, 1960.
——. *The Malagasy Republic.* Stanford, 1965.
——. *Djibouti and the Horn of Africa.* Stanford, 1968.
TORDOFF, WILLIAM. *Ashanti Under the Prempehs, 1888–1935.* London, 1965.
——. *Government and Politics in Tanzania.* Nairobi, 1967.
TOUVAL, SAADIA. *Somali Nationalism.* Cambridge, Mass., 1963.
WALLERSTEIN, IMMANUEL M. *The Road to Independence; Ghana and Ivory Coast.* Paris, 1964.
WEINSTEIN, BRIAN. *Gabon: Nation-Building on the Ogooue.* Cambridge, Mass., 1966.
WEISS, HERBERT F. *Political Protest in The Congo.* Princeton, 1967.
WELCH, CLAUDE. *Dream of Unity.* Ithaca, 1966.
ZARTMAN, I. WILLIAM. *Destiny of Dynasty: The Search for Institutions in Morocco's Developing Society.* Columbia, 1964.
——. *Government and Politics in Northern Africa.* New York, 1966.
ZOLBERG, ARISTIDE. *Creating Political Order; The Party States of West Africa.* Chicago, 1967.
——. *One-Party Government in the Ivory Coast.* Princeton, 1969.

Index

Index

Index

Abbreviations in index

ACRM	Anti-Corruption Revolutionary Movement (Sierra Leone)
APC	African People's Congress (Sierra Leone)
BDS	Bloc Démocratique Sénégalais
CPP	Convention People's Party
CPSU	Communist Party of the Soviet Union
DP	Democratic Party (Uganda)
FAO	Food and Agricultural Organization of the United Nations
GNCC	Ghana National Construction Company
GNLC	Ghanaian National Liberation Council
GNTC	Ghana National Trading Company
KANU	Kenya African National Union
KY	Kabaka Yekka (Uganda)
MRP	Popular Movement of the Revolution (Congo-Kinshasa)
NADECO	National Development Corporation (Ghana)
NAL	National Alliance of Liberals (Ghana)
NASSO	National Association of Socialist Students Organizations (Ghana)
NCGW	National Council of Ghanaian Women
NLM	National Liberation Movement
PDCI	Parti Démocratique de Côte d'Ivoire
PDG	Parti Démocratique de Guinée
POGR	President's Own Guard Regiment (Ghana)
PP	Progress Party (Ghana)
PPT	Parti Progressiste du Tchad
SDP	Social Democratic Party (Germany)
SFIO	Section Française de l'Internationale Ouvrière
SIC	State Insurance Company (Ghana)
SLPP	Sierra Leone People's Party
TANU	Tanganyika African National Union
TUC	Trades Union Congress (Tanganyika)
UGCC	United Gold Coast Convention
UGFCC	United Ghana Farmers' Co-operative Council
UPC	Uganda People's Congress
UPS	Union Progressiste Sénégalais
US	Union Soudanaise
USAID	United States Agency for International Development

Index

Abboud, General Ibrahim, 234
Abengourou, 130
Abidjan, 44, 131, 271–272
Aborigenes' Rights Protection Society, 70n
Absentee ownership, 168, 174. *See also* Ranch tenure
Acholi, 151, 275
ACRM, 226, 235
Adaptive capability, 162
Administered development, 280
Administrator-ministers, 109–110
Africanization, 22, 29, 74, 76, 96, 125–126, 153, 266, 270–271
African nationalism, 10
African socialism, 14. *See also* Socialism
Afrifa, A. A., 89n, 222, 224–225
Agricultural transformation, 164
Ahomadegbe, Justin, 217, 221–222
AID. *See* USAID
Akan, 70, 224
Akasombo, 79
Alexander, General H. T., 218
Algeria, 27, 31–32, 244
Al-Khalifa, al-Khatim, 234
Alley, Colonel, 233
All People's Republican Party (Ghana), 224
American foreign policy, 169
Amin, Samir, 124n, 125n
Animation rurale, 134
Ankole, 45–46, 151; district council of, 186; kingdom government in, 173; politics in, 186
Ankrah, General, 223, 226
Apaloo, M. K., 222
APC, 218
Apithy, Sourou, Migan, 217, 220–222
Appiah, Joe, 222, 224
Apter, David, 49
Arthur, Lieutenant Samuel, 223
Arusha Declaration, 90, 212
Asantehene, 66
Ascencionnisme, 122
Ashanti, 68–70, 199
Ashford, Douglas, 127, 139
Aswan Dam, 181
Ataturk, Kemal, 233
Austerity policy, 31, 89–90, 219, 266
Authoritarianism, 40, 243, 250–251
Autocratic government, 245–257
Autonomous elites, 15, 18. *See also* Entrepreneurial class

Awolowo, Obafemi, 227
Ayeh-Kumi, E., 75–76

Baah, C. C. K., 76
Babu, A. M., 97
Baganda. *See* Buganda
Bahima, 45, 168–170
Baidoe-Ansah, W., 76
Bairu, 168–169
Balance of payments, 31, 85
Bantu-Nilotic controversy, 148
Baoulé, 132
Bargaining, 264, 273
Berg, Elliot, 126, 129
BDS, 51–52
Birkelane, 52–53
Black Star Line, 80
Boateng, Henry, 89
Bobo, 227
Bokassa, Colonel, 227, 233
Bolshevik party, 201
Bomani, Paul, 108
Botsio, Kojo, 71, 89
Bouaké, 130, 137
Bourgeoisie, 270–271
Breakdown. *See* Political breakdown
British Togoland, 69
Brong, 68, 70
Budgetary deficits, 6, 24–26 (chart), 27, 30–31, 84
Buganda, 30, 143, 147, 152, 170, 199, 278; government of, 145
Bugisu, 145, 152; Co-operative Union, 160
Bunyoro, 154; Co-operative Union, 160
Bureaucracy, 21–22, 41, 67, 86, 88, 94, 98, 136
Burma, 244
Burundi, 216
Busia, K. A., 69–70, 222, 224
Busoga Growers Co-operative Union, 160

Cabinet system, 94, 103, 105, 145, 153
Capabilities, 161–163
Capital: formation of, 84, 265, 267; for investment, 22, 65; outflow of, 75
Cash farming, 141–164 *passim*, 275. *See also* Cocoa; Coffee; Cotton
Catholics, 148
Central African Republic, 216, 227, 244
Ceylon, 256
Charismatic authority, 47, 49, 246
Chiefs, 22, 51–52, 68, 158–159, 231, 248
Child labor, 16
Church of Uganda, 151

Civil servants, 86, 105, 162, 198, 231
Clans, 59
Class. *See* Social classes; Social cleavages
Coalition government, 250
Cocoa, 69, 84, 122; farmers of, 69, 75, 199; Marketing Board, 69, 74, 78, 81; Purchasing Company, 86
Coffee, 122, 141–143, 152; farmers of, 199; arabica type, 152; robusta type, 143, 149, 152
Cohen, Sir Andrew, 149
Coleman, James S., 142
Collectivités rurales, 138
Colonial rule, 10, 20–21, 38, 60, 240, 246, 253; British practice of, 262; French practice of, 129, 136, 262; institutions of, 198
Commissions de développement régional, 138
Communal participation, 281
Communes, 137, 139
Communicative capability, 161
Communists, 240
Compromise, 273
Conflict, 197. *See also* Social cleavages
Congo-Brazzaville, 30–32, 216, 244
Congo-Kinshasa, 27, 33, 144, 197, 216, 227, 244, 251; crisis in, 180
Congress party (India), 213
Conseils de notables, 138
Conseils de sous-préfecture, 138
Consensual validation, 48, 265. *See also* Legitimacy
Conservative path, 6, 28–30, 37–39
Conservative states, 264–265. *See also* Conservative path
Conspicuous consumption, 90
Constitutionalism, 250
Constraints: defined, 4, 5, 18, 19
Consumer society, 123
Contagion effect, 219
Contractor financing, 85
Cooperatives, 53–54, 63, 71, 77, 134, 145, 151, 159–160, 174
Corporations. *See* International corporations
Corruption, 27, 72, 74, 86–87, 192, 246, 263; and military coups, 219
Cotton, 141–143, 149, 151
Coup d'etat, 216–237 *passim*
CPP, 41, 65–92 *passim*, 207, 218, 223, 224, 226, 249, 263; as political machine, 72–73; bureaucratization of, 91
CPSU, 201, 206, 210

Credit, 146
Critical sectors, 131
Cuba, 72
Cult of personality, 72, 90, 243
Cultural assimilation, 16

Dahomey, 30, 216–217, 244; Revolutionary Military Committee of, 226
Daloa, 130
Danquah, J. B., 70
Dar es Salaam, 104
Decade of Development, 252
Decay. *See* Political decay
Decolonization, 19–20, 91, 241–242
Deconcentration, 136
De Gaulle, Charles, 243
Demands. *See* Political demands
Democracy in Africa, 193–194; conditions for, 247–248
Democratic centralism, 208, 255
Democratic participation, 116–117
Départements, 138
Deradicalization, 210–212
De Souza, Lt. Col. Emile, 222
Development. *See* Political development
Development planning, 40, 43, 45, 142, 146–147, 152, 166, 169, 175
Diawara, Mohamed, 121, 123n, 139
Diourbel, 50
Disequilibrium, 132. *See also* Regional inequalities
District agricultural officers, 153–154
District councils, 158
District farm institutes, 157
Dove–Edwin report, 225
DP, 146, 148, 151
Drake, Lyman, 123
Dudumaki, 155
Dyarchy, 66

Eastern European countries, 32, 79
Economic closure, 39
Economic conservatism, 39. *See also* Conservative path; Conservative states.
Economic dependency, 83. *See also* Neocolonialism
Economic growth, 120, 272–273
Economic inequality, 274
Economic malaise, 219
Economic resources, 37
Education, 28, 81–82, 86, 127; and democracy, 193, 247
Education for Self-Reliance, 112
Edusei, Krobo, 71, 89

Egalitarianism, 11–12, 45, 114, 265, 269. *See also* Social equality
Eisenstadt, S. N., 4
Eliofoo, Solomon, 108
Elite-mass gap, 17, 37, 245–246, 248, 266, 269–270, 274
Elites, 58, 168–169, 196, 207, 209, 210, 271. *See also* Civil servants; Entrepreneurial class
Enfranchisement, 5, 13, 267
Entebbe, 153
Entrepreneurial class, 5, 14, 31, 33
Ethnicity, 274; as basis of cultural heritage, 275; as basis for political appeals, 203; as basis for representation, 280–281; political arithmetic of, 193, 248
European capital, 126, 131. *See also* Capital
Europeans, 124, 131. *See also* Expatriates
Ewe, 69, 232
Executive presidency, 96
Expatriate firms, 78, 266
Expatriate labor, 124–125
Expatriates, 105, 125–126, 270
Expenditures, 23, 24–26 (table)
Extractive capacity, 62
Eyadema, Etienne, 232–233

Factions, 60, 63, 108, 263. *See also* Pluralism
Fallers, Lloyd, 10, 12
Fanon, Frantz, 205
Fanti, 68
FAO, 156
Farouk, 244
Feit, Edward, 231
Female labor, 16
Fertilizers, 144
Field officers, 175
Financial constraints, 23. *See also* Budgetary deficits
Finer, Samuel, 198, 228, 233
Fisher, Carol, 104
Foltz, William, 59–60
Force publique, 244
Foreign aid, 27, 31
Foreign capital. *See* Foreign investment
Foreign domination, 85
Foreign exchange, 84
Foreign firms. *See* Expatriate firms
Foreign investment, 32, 42–44, 83, 85–86, 88, 99, 131, 269–270
Fragility of institutions. *See* Institutional weakness
French model, 243
French Revolution, 197

French Togoland, 69
Fria, 31
Friedrich, Carl, 61
Functionaries, 72, 87
Fundikira, Chief, 102

Ga, 68
Gagnoa, 137
Gbedemah, K. A., 75, 79, 222, 224
General will, 240
Ghana, 23, 31–32, 38, 123, 199, 205, 213, 231, 244, 251, 263; army of, 233; budget deficit in, 84–85; Commercial Bank of, 78, 80; Constitutional Committee of, 223; corruption in, 86–87; education in, 81–82; military coup in, 41, 216–218, 222–224, 226; Seven Year Development Plan of, 76
GNCC, 78, 81, 86
GNLC, 222–224
GNTC, 80–81, 86
Goody, Jack, 222
Government planning, 166. *See also* Development planning
Gowon, General Yabuku, 227
Greece, 229
Gregory Report, 171–174, 176
Group farms, 150
Growth rate, 83
Growth without development, 139
Gueye, Lamine, 51
Guided democracy, 244
Guinea, 30–32, 124, 205
Guinea Press, 76

Hirschman, Albert O., 131
Hortatory capability, 162
Houphouet-Boigny, Felix, 92, 119–139 *passim*, 229, 280–281
Howarth, Dr. A. J., 176
Huntington, Samuel, 4, 119, 230, 255
Hutu, 227

Ideology, 72, 121–123, 197; in political parties, 201
Immigration, 124
Imoru, Ayarra, 224
Imperialism, 77
Income distribution, 266
Independence, 251–252, 254
India, 256
Indices of growth, 124
Indirect rule, 158, 248
Industrial Development Corporation, 75

Industrialization, 5–6, 10, 12, 81, 255–257, 273
Industrial revolution, 5, 12, 17, 281
Infusion: defined, 124, 133
Inputs in agricultural policy, 143
Instability, 280
Institutional weakness, 6, 14, 21, 191, 219, 222
Intellectuals, 89
Interest groups, 199. *See also* Factions; Pluralism
International Coffee Agreement, 144, 147
International corporations, 84, 268
Intraregional imbalances, 277
Iraq, 244
Islam, 51, 56, 62
Israel, 256
Ivory Coast, 37, 44, 92, 229, 275, 280; economic miracle in, 124, 271; ideology of, 121–122, 133; local cleavages in, 135; national identity in, 127; planning law of, 132; policy of infusion, 124–125, 133; social inequalities in, 128–130, 133. *See also* PDCI

Jackson, Lord, 79
Jamal, Amir, 97
Judicial Service Commission, 93–94
Juxon-Smith, Andrew, 218, 225, 233, 235

Kabaka, 147
Kagera River, 169
Kahama, George, 108
Kaiser Aluminum, 80
Kambona, 104, 106, 110–111
Kampala, 148
KANU, 205
Karume, Abeid, 104
Kawawa, Rashidi, 108, 111
Keita, Modibo, 31, 123
Kemalist model, 232
Kenya, 279
Kerekou, Captain Mathieu, 221
Key, V. O., 210
Khartoum, 234
Kigezi district, 151, 156; farm institute of, 157
Kikuyu, 254
Korean War, 149
Korhogo, 130
Kossou Dam, 132
Kotokah, Colonel, 223
Kouandete, Lt. Col. Maurice, 221
KY, 148, 151, 275, 277–278

Kyaruzi, Dr. V., 107

Labor unions. *See* Trade unions
Labor unrest, 85
Labour government, 74
Laissez-faire, 5, 13–14, 267
Laministes, 51, 53
Lamizana, Brigadier, 227, 233
Land Use Investigational Unit, 171
Lango, 155, 170, 275
Lansana, David, 226
Latent functions, 206
Latim, Alex, 146
Lebanese, 53–54, 124
Lebanon, 256
Legitimacy, 14, 61, 66, 68, 100, 101, 196–197, 253
Lenin, V. I., 56, 201; concept of political party, 206, 208
Lewis, W. Arthur, 74, 131, 250
Liberalism, 14
Libya, 27, 227
Lint Marketing Board, 149
Loan Agreement, 185
Local cleavages, 135
Local councils, 54
Local development, 127
Local elites, 62, 166, 173
Local government, 97, 134
Loi-cadre, 52

Machine model. *See* Political machines
McWilliams, Carey, 209
Maga, Hubert, 217, 221–222
Mailo land, 145
Makerere University College, 187
Mali, 30–31, 32, 123–124, 205, 216, 227
Man (Ivory Coast), 130, 137
Managerial strata, 266
Marabouts, 51, 62
Margai, Albert, 217
Margai, Milton, 217
Marx, Karl, 55, 120
Mass participation, 282
Mass parties, 198, 208–209
Mass society, 255–256
Material rewards, 206
Mau Mau, 254
Mazrui, Ali, 251
Mechanisms of coercion, 212
Mechanization, 145–146, 150
Meek, Kim, 105
Meister, Albert, 249
Mende, 217

Mercantilism, 13–14, 33, 267
Michels, Roberto, 201, 210
Micombero, Colonel, 227
Middle class, 20, 23, 26, 28, 31, 33, 68, 70, 194, 266–267
Military: alliances by, 231; civilianization of, 236; coups by, 30, 32, 246, 263; regimes of, 192–193, 215
Mill, John Stuart, 49–50
Millennial movements, 211
Mixed economy, 266
Mobilization, 41, 43, 60, 71, 86, 124–125, 134, 240, 252–254, 262; as theory of development, 57, 191–192
Mobutu, Joseph, 227, 232
Modernity, 120
Modernization, 4, 128, 130, 166, 173, 252–257
Morgenthau, Ruth Schachter, 51, 52
Morris, Jon, 161
Moshav, 145
Moslem leaders, 71. See also Marabouts
Moslem Zongos, 68
Mossi, 227
MRP, 232
Mtemvu, Zuberi, 102
Municipal councils, 137

NADECO, 78
Nakishenyi, 159, 161
NAL, 224
Nasser, Abdul, 244, 256
NASSO, 73
National bourgeoisie, 75
National Congress of British West Africa, 70n
Nationalism, 95; leaders of, 261; movements of, 19–20, 198, 211
Nationalization, 151
National wealth, 194
NCGW, 73
Negritude, 249
Neocolonialism, 10–11, 50, 60, 74, 77, 87, 90
Nepotism, 247
Ngobi, Mathias, 145
Nigeria, 27, 30, 33, 199, 216, 231, 244
Nkrumah, Kwame, 31, 38, 41–42, 65–92 passim, 123, 217–218, 226, 249, 263
NLM, 69–70
No-party state, 242
Nyabushozi county, 170–171
Nyakishenyi, 157

Nyerere, Julius, 90, 93–118 passim, 229, 245

Obote, Milton, 46, 148, 182–183, 244, 277–279
Ocran, A. K., 89n, 225
Odinga, Oginga, 206
Oligarchic authoritarianism, 213
Olympio, Sylvanus, 232–233, 236, 250
Omdurman, 234
One-party states, 31–32, 49, 71–73, 95, 98, 101, 112, 195, 197–198, 249
Opinion leader theory, 178
Opportunity costs, 163
Opposition, 71, 242; parties in, 22, 31
Organizational weapon, 207
Otu, S. I. A., 218
Ouagadougou, 227

Pakistan, 244
Pan-African politics, 111
Paradox of development, 40, 265, 268, 279
Parliamentary immobilism, 192
Parochial interests, 196
Participation, 13, 133–134, 208, 273
Party militants, 202
Party-states, 254
Patronage, 62, 195–196, 203–205
PDCI, 135–137, 204
PDG, 202, 206–207, 229
Peace Corps, 181
Peanut trade, 53–54
Peasantry, 33, 45, 122, 151, 248, 266. See also Bairu
People's Action Party, 224
Perquisites of office, 201
Philippines, 256
Plebiscitary democracy, 242, 254, 256
Pluralism, 40, 56–60, 61, 63, 123, 192, 206, 247–248, 253, 263–264, 273–274; as condition of democracy, 194
POGR, 218
Political breakdown, 4, 9, 192
Political competition, 135
Political culture, 13, 15, 59
Political decay, 4, 120–121
Political demands, 16, 48–49, 150
Political development, 3–5, 119–121
Political influentials, 178, 185–186
Political machines, 57–63, 191–192; as model, 263; functions of, 203–206
"Political ministers," 109
Political Mobilization. See Mobilization
Political stability, 28

Politics of accommodation, 104, 106–107, 116–117
Populism, 255
PP, 224
PPT, 206
Praetorianism, 121
Preventive detention, 41, 71, 217
Privatization of misery, 271
Productivity, 82
Proportional equality, 276
Proportional inequality, 274, 276, 280–281
Protestants, 148
Pye, Lucian, 3

Quaidoo, P. K. K., 76, 224

Racisme, 135
Radical path: defined, 6; 30–32, 92. *See also* Radical states
Radical populism, 147
Radical states, 37–39, 262–265, 268–269
Radio Cotonou, 220
Rancher Selection Board, 183
Ranch tenure, 167–169, 171, 184, 186
Regional equality, 130
Regional House of Chiefs, 87n
Regional inequalities, 128–129, 132–133, 271–272, 275–276, 280–281
Regionalism, 199, 222
Regulative capability, 161–162
Report of the Presidential Commission on the Establishment of a Democratic One-Party State, 101
Representation, 264, 268
Resource capability, 163
Revolution, 58
Revolutionary-centralizing parties, 191
Reynolds Metal Company, 80
Rising expectations, 14, 45, 65, 82
Rogers, Sergeant-Major Armada, 225
Rousseau, Jean-Jacques, 115, 197
Rural depolitization, 149
Rural politization, 157
Rural-urban gap, 90
Rwanda, 197
Rwomushana, Tomasu, 157
Ryan, J. C., 146

Savanna zone, 129
Schism, 219
School attendance, 129–130
School leavers, 28–29, 30, 69
SDP, 210, 213
Sebei, 152

Secondary education, 275
Second Republic of Ghana, 223
Senegal, 40–41, 244, 268; Rural Animation Service of, 58, 63; Development Bank of, 53; rural development in, 56
Senghor, Leopold, 51, 55, 229, 269
Senoufo, 132
Serer, 51
SFIO, 51
Shils, Edward, 120, 241
SIC, 80–81
Sierra Leone, 30, 216, 218, 231, 244; military of, 226; Military Revolutionary Committee of, 221, 235; National Reformation Council of, 225–226
Sine-Saloum, 50
Single-party states. *See* One-party states
Sklar, Richard, 199n
SLPP, 217, 225–226
Social classes, 37, 39. *See also* Entrepreneurial class; Middle class; Working class
Social cleavages, 134, 219, 272, 273, 281. *See also* Elite-mass gap, Proportional inequality; Regional inequalities
Social egalitarianism. *See* Egalitarianism
Social disequilibria, 128
Social equality, 12, 39
Socialism, 42, 43, 53, 65–66, 70, 73, 90–92, 112, 114, 262–264, 269
Socialism and Rural Development, 112
Social mobilization. *See* Mobilization
Social transformation, 170
Social welfare: concept of, 15
Sociétés d'Etat, 134
Sociétés de prévoyance, 52
Socioeconomic transformation, 5, 73
Soglo, Christophe, 217, 226, 235
Somalia, 227
Soviet Union, 181
Spoils system, 203
Stability, 135–136, 212
Stalin, Joseph, 206
Stanleyville parachute drop, 109
State entrepreneurialism, 14–15, 265–266, 268
Stevens, Siaka, 226
Subprefectures, 136, 138
Substantive equality, 266
Sudan, 227, 244
Sukarno, 243
Suppliers' credits, 85
Swai, Nsilo, 97
System capabilities. *See* Capabilities

Tanganyika African Congress, 102
Tanganyika Legislative Council, 93
TANU, 93–118 *passim*, 202, 207, 254, 264;
  Annual Conference of, 99, 101; Central
  Committee of, 99; National Conference
  of, 100; National Executive Committee
  of, 95, 99–101, 110, 113, 115–116; Party
  Conference of, 100
Tanzania, 31, 42–43, 90, 162, 205, 254, 264,
  279; Council of Ministers of, 93;
  decision-making process in, 264; Directorate of Planning of, 97, 112; Economic
  Commission of, 103; Five Year Plan of,
  97, 103, 112; high commissioner of, 106–
  107; Ministry of Defence of, 97; Ministry of Foreign Affairs of, 97; National
  Assembly of, 114; Office of the President of, 96–97, 107; Police Service Com-
  mission of, 94; Presidential Advisory Commission
  on the One Party State of, 112; presi-
  dential system of, 116; Public Service
  Commission of, 93–94; Regional Admin-
  istration of, 97; Regional Commissioners
  of, 110; Republican Constitution of, 95;
  style of decision-making in, 103, 107;
  Treasury of, 96
Technical strata, 266
Technological unemployment, 17
Technology, 6, 15, 17–18, 282
Tema, 79, 81
Temne, 217
Teso, 170
Thies, 50
Third World, 66–67, 89, 119, 123, 252
Togo, 30, 69, 216, 227
Tordoff, William, 115
Toucouleur, 51
Touré, Sekou, 229
Trade unions, 27, 71, 89, 199
Tradition, 120
Traditional groups, 211–212
Traditional leaders, 87. *See also* Chiefs
Transferability of institutions, 262
Trans-Volta, 69
Tribalism, 29
Trypanosomiasis, 170
Tsetse fly, 166, 169
Tshombe regime, 180
TUC, 73
Tucker, Robert, 210–211
Tunisia, 162
Turkey, 229, 232
Tutsi, 227

Typologies of African parties, 195

Uganda, 44, 46, 165–197 *passim*, 199, 244,
  275; agricultural extension service of,
  153–154; Agriculture Department of,
  144, 154–155, 157, 164; military coup in,
  276–280; Ministry of Animal Industry
  of, 173–174, 177–179, 182–183; Ministry
  of Economic Affairs of, 173; Ministry
  of Foreign Affairs, 182–183; Ministry of
  Planning of, 174–175, 183; planning ap-
  paratus in, 169; Planning Commission
  of, 174–175, 179, 182–183, 186; Second
  Five Year Plan of, 145–147, 152; Veter-
  inary Department of, 174–175
Uganda Growers Co-operative Union, 160
Uganda National Congress, 278
Uganda People's Union, 278
UGCC, 69–70
UGFCC, 72–73, 81, 86n
Unemployment, 17, 30, 85, 271, 281
Unilateral Declaration of Independence,
  109–110
United Arab Republic, 31
United Ghana Farmers' Council, 78
United National Front, 234
United Nationalist Party, 224
United Republic of Tanganyika and Zan-
  zibar, 104n, 111
United States Department of State, 179–
  180; policy on aid, 177
Universal suffrage, 14, 282. *See also* En-
  franchisement
University of Khartoum, 234
UPC, 147–148, 151–152, 160, 206, 275–280
Upper Volta, 124, 216, 227, 244
UPS, 53
Urbanization, 5, 132–133
Urban-rural gap, 18, 282
US, 202, 207
USAID, 166, 171, 173–174, 176–178, 180–
  185

Valco, 31
Veterans, 52
Vijiji vya Ujamaa, 113
Village resettlement, 116
Volta River Project, 42, 79–81

Wage policy, 113
Weakness of state machinery. *See* Institu-
  tional weakness
Welfare socialism, 14
West: as model, 123, 248

West African Federation, 129
Western assistance, 123
Westminster model, 93–94, 243
Whitaker, C. S., 119n
Winneba, 76
Wolof, 51
Work for Progress, 141n
Working class, 13, 68, 266–277, 270–271, 282

World Bank, 170

Yameogo, President, 227
Yoruba, 199

Zambia, 23, 27
Zanzibar, 104, 112
Zinsou, Emile Derlin, 221
Zolberg, Aristide, 120, 251, 254